The White Man's Gonna Getcha:
The Colonial Challenge to the Crees in Quebec

In *The White Man's Gonna Getcha* Toby Morantz examines threats to the cultural and economic independence of the Crees in eastern James Bay. She argues that while their eighteenth- and nineteenth-century fur-trading relationship with the Hudson's Bay Company had been mutually beneficial, Canada's twentieth-century interest in administering its outlying isolated regions actually posed the greatest challenge to the Cree way of life.

Morantz shows that with the imposition of administration from the south the Crees had to confront a new set of foreigners whose ideas and plans were very different from those of the fur traders. In the 1930s and 1940s government intervention helped overcome the disastrous disappearance of the beaver through the creation of government-decreed preserves and a ban on beaver hunting, but beginning in the 1950s a revolving array of socio-economic programs instituted by the government brought the adverse effects of what Morantz calls bureaucratic colonialism.

Drawing heavily on oral testimonies recorded by anthropologists in addition to eye-witness and archival sources, Morantz incorporates the Crees' own views, interests, and responses. She shows how their strong ties to the land and their appreciation of the wisdom of their way of life, coupled with the ineptness and excessive frugality of the Canadian bureaucracy, allowed them to escape the worst effects of colonialism. Despite becoming increasingly politically and economically dominated by Canadian society, the Crees succeeded in staving off cultural subjugation. They were able to face the massive hydroelectric development of the 1970s with their language, practices, and values intact and succeeded in negotiating a modern treaty.

TOBY MORANTZ is an associate professor of anthropology at McGill University and the co-author of *Partners in Furs: A History of the Fur Trade in Eastern James Bay, 1600–1870.*

MCGILL-QUEEN'S NATIVE AND NORTHERN SERIES
BRUCE G. TRIGGER, EDITOR

1 When the Whalers Were Up North
Inuit Memories from the Eastern Arctic
Dorothy Harley Eber

2 The Challenge of Arctic Shipping
Science, Environmental Assessment, and Human Values
David L. VanderZwaag and Cynthia Lamson, Editors

3 Lost Harvests
Prairie Indian Reserve Farmers and Government Policy
Sarah Carter

4 Native Liberty, Crown Sovereignty
The Existing Aboriginal Right of Self-Government in Canada
Bruce Clark

5 Unravelling the Franklin Mystery
Inuit Testimony
David C. Woodman

6 Otter Skins, Boston Ships, and China Goods
The Maritime Fur Trade of the Northwest Coast, 1785–1741
James R. Gibson

7 From Wooden Ploughs to Welfare
The Story of the Western Reserves
Helen Buckley

8 In Business for Ourselves
Northern Entrepreneurs
Wanda A. Wuttunee

9 For an Amerindian Autohistory
An Essay on the Foundations of a Social Ethic
Georges E. Sioui

10 Strangers Among Us
David Woodman

11 When the North Was Red
Aboriginal Education in Soviet Siberia
Dennis A. Bartels and Alice L. Bartels

12 From Talking Chiefs to a Native Corporate Elite
The Birth of Class and Nationalism among Canadians
Marybelle Mitchell

13 Cold Comfort
My Love Affair with the Arctic
Graham W. Rowley

14 The True Spirit and
   Original Intent of Treaty 7
   *Treaty 7 Elders and Tribal
   Council with Walter
   Hildebrandt, Dorothy First
   Rider, and Sarah Carter*

15 This Distant and
   Unsurveyed Country
   A Woman's Winter at
   Baffin Island, 1857–1858
   W. Gillies Ross

16 Images of Justice
   Dorothy Harley Eber

17 Capturing Women
   The Manipulation of
   Cultural Imagery in
   Canada's Prairie West
   Sarah A. Carter

18 Social and Environmental
   Impacts of the James Bay
   Hydroelectric Project
   *Edited by
   James F. Hornig*

19 Saqiyuq
   Stories from the Lives
   of Three Inuit Women
   *Nancy Wachowich in
   collaboration with
   Apphia Agalakti Awa,
   Rhoda Kaukjak Katsak,
   and Sandra Pikujak Katsak*

20 Justice in Paradise
   Bruce Clark

21 Aboriginal Rights and
   Self-Government
   The Canadian and
   Mexican Experience
   in North American
   Perspective
   *Edited by Curtis Cook and
   Juan D. Lindau*

22 Harvest of Souls
   The Jesuit Missions and
   Colonialism in North
   America, 1632–1650
   Carole Blackburn

23 Bounty and Benevolence
   A Documentary History
   of Saskatchewan Treaties
   *Arthur J. Ray, Jim Miller,
   and Frank Tough*

24 The People of Denendeh
   Ethnohistory of the
   Indians of Canada's
   Northwest Territories
   June Helm

25 The *Marshall* Decision and
   Native Rights
   Ken Coates

26 The Flying Tiger
   Women Shamans and
   Storytellers of the Amur
   Kira Van Deusen

27 Alone in Silence
European Women in
the Canadian North
Barbara Kelcey

28 The Arctic Voyages
of Martin Frobisher
An Elizabethan Adventure
Robert McGhee

29 Northern Experience and
the Myths of Canadian
Culture
Renée Hulan

30 The White Man's Gonna
Getcha
The Colonial Challenge to the
Crees in Quebec
Toby Morantz

The White Man's Gonna Getcha

The Colonial Challenge to the Crees in Quebec

Toby Morantz

McGill-Queen's University Press
Montreal & Kingston · London · Ithaca

© McGill-Queen's University Press 2002
ISBN 0-7735-2270-0 (cloth)
ISBN 0-7735-2299-9 (paper)
Legal deposit third quarter 2002
Bibliothèque nationale du Québec

Printed in Canada on acid-free paper that is 100% ancient forest free (100% post-consumer recycled), processed chlorine free.

This book has been published with the help of a grant from the Humanities and Social Sciences Federation of Canada, using funds provided by the Social Sciences and Humanities Research Council of Canada.

McGill-Queen's University Press acknowledges the financial support of the Government of Canada through the Book Publishing Industry Development Program (BPIDP) for its activities. It also acknowledges the support of the Canada Council for the Arts for its publishing program.

National Library of Canada Cataloguing in Publication Data

Morantz, Toby Elaine, 1943–
  The white man's gonna getcha:
the colonial challenge to the Crees in Quebec

(McGill-Queen's native and northern series; 30)
Includes bibliographical references and index.
ISBN 0-7735-2270-0 (bound)
ISBN 0-7735-2299-9 (pbk.)
  1. Cree Indians – James Bay Region – History.
2. Cree Indians – Quebec (Province) – Nord-du-Québec – History. 3. Cree Indians – James Bay Region – Government relations. 4. Cree Indians – Quebec (Province) – Nord-du-Québec – Government relations. I. Title. II. Series.
E99.C88M67 2002   971.4'11004973
C2001-904141-1

This book was typeset by Dynagram Inc.
in 10/12 Sabon.

For Gillian, who will help light the world

Contents

Preface xiii

Author's Note xvii

Illustrations following pages xviii and xxviii

1 Introduction: Marking the Trails 3
2 James Bay at the End of the Nineteenth Century 27
3 The Powers of Religion: Christianity Extends the Limits 73
4 Coping with Changes on the Land 97
5 A New Technological and Bureaucratic World: The Confiscation of the Land 131
6 Pale Versions of Southern Institutions 176
7 Conclusion: Despite Government Domination, the Crees Weave Their Own Tapestry 241
8 Epilogue: A New Order 251

Appendices 257

Substantive Notes 279

Reference Notes 317

Bibliography 341

Index 363

Appendices

1 Quantity and Price of Furs Paid by Hudson's Bay Company, James Bay District, 1923–24   259
2 Census   260
   1 Census, 1911   260
   2 Census, 1924–69   261
3 Increase of Beaver in the Rupert House Beaver Sanctuary, 1933–37   262
4 Examples of Department of Indian Affairs Reporting of Beaver Preserves   263
   1 Statement showing Number of Beaver Trapped and Amount Paid Each Trapper on Nottoway Beaver Preserve, Nottoway River 1946   263–4
   2 Statement of Nottoway Beaver Preserve Showing Number of Beaver Trapped and Amount to Each Trapper, Nemaska Post, 1946   265
   3 Beaver Count: A Composite of the Old Factory Beaver and Fur Preserve Annual Reports, 1944 and 1947   266–7
   4 Recapitulation of Beaver Increase between the Years 1942–47   268
   5 Beaver Lodges Counted and Marked on the Waswanipi Division, 1943 and 1944   269
5 Catholic Presence in Five Cree Communities, 1968   270
6 Economic Profiles of Cree Communities, 1968–72   271
   1 Earned Income Living on Reserves/Settlements, 1969   271
   2 Estimated Man Years of Employment, by Type of Employment for Males, Living on Reserve/Settlement, 1969   272

3 Per Capita Income from Beaver Trapping, 1971–1972   273
4 Band Population Living off Reserve/Settlement, 1971   274
5 Social Assistance for June 1972, Number Assisted, by Band   275
6 Enrolment in Schools by Place of Residence 1969   276
7 Quantities of Game Taken by Alfie Matoush Group, August 1953 to early June 1954   277

Preface

I am an ethnohistorian by training and by specialization. Accordingly I have an obligation to two disciplines: anthropology and history. I have tried in this study to serve both masters in a period when anthropology has embraced postmodernism to a greater extent than has history. On the anthropology side, I have been questioning certain of my premises and have acknowledged my inquiry as being subjective. On the history side, I have followed the Western historical tradition of trying to tell a story along a sequential path. Although subjective in its transmission, I did see a story to tell that would lose its coherence without recourse to a chronological order. This history is not intended as the history of the eastern James Bay Crees; its principal raison d'être has always been to provide the Crees with an accounting of people, places, and events on which they could forge their own histories. In the concluding chapter, I return to my anthropological angst, refraining in most instances from explaining why Crees took the decisions they did, though unable to refrain from offering several possible interpretations.

In the introduction I have explained this is a perspective of a history born of Western and personal notions, possibly far removed from the vision of the Crees. To write this particular history I had to spend more time in the archives and libraries rather than in James Bay – my personal loss. The incompleteness of this history struck me when I read Reverend Scanlon's account of his departure from Mistassini in 1957: "The canoes were laden with people and dogs and the dogs that could not crowd in swam after the canoes. The din of outboard motors, the swish of paddles and the howling of dogs were among the sights and sounds of Mistassini we would never forget." I have been unable to paint in the colour and sounds of Cree life, but rest assured I knew they were there.

This twentieth-century history cannot be separated from the centuries of history which preceded it. My earlier research and studies to about 1870 enabled me to see the continuities and discontinuities of the historical processes in eastern James Bay which stretched forward into the 1900s. As I had begun this earlier research in about 1975, my list of persons who worked with me, discussed issues, and unstintingly shared their knowledge is considerable. I hope they will understand if I have allowed my acknowledgments in earlier publications to suffice. A number of these colleagues, though, have continued to help me understand what transpired in eastern James Bay and over the years of our mutual interests we have developed friendships, adding significantly to the rewards I already derive from my research.

I am particularly grateful to six people who generously undertook to read and comment on the manuscript: David Denton, John Long, Alan Penn, Richard Preston, and Adrian Tanner, as well as anonymous reviewers. Their extensive knowledge of James Bay and their wisdom have helped me correct errors, address gaps, and refine my understanding of events, but undoubtedly they could not protect me from all my lapses in fact or judgment. I take full responsibility for those.

Over the years, I have benefited from many who shared their knowledge with me, but I must especially recognize the unsparing generosity of Richard Preston and the late Sarah Preston, who turned over to me their extensive field notes and numerous unpublished reports, which have greatly enhanced this study. Similarly, Jacques Frenette kindly sent me the Maud Watt Papers from the Archives Deschâtelets, also well used here. Daniel Chevrier of Archéotec, long ago, kindly provided me with their field notes, collected by Pierre Trudel at Great Whale River.

I would like to acknowledge the scholarly support of George Wenzel in the Department of Geography and my colleagues in the Department of Anthropology at McGill University, especially Bruce Trigger. Although his understanding of the practice of ethnohistory and his erudition are difficult to match, they have served as a standard for me to strive to emulate. More than that, though, he has always been ready to discuss issues and exchange views and I have benefited greatly from his enthusiastic encouragement of my work. Colleagues in the History Department, Pierre Boulle, Catherine Desbarats, and Catherine LeGrand, as well as their graduate students whose seminars I could sometimes attend, provided me with important critical and comparative issues. With her incomparable knowledge of Cree life dating back to the 1930s when she first visited there as a young doctoral student, Regina Flannery Hertzfeld, Professor Emeritus at Catholic University of America, has taught me a lot about the period I was researching through her wonderfully narrated accounts and her many publications over seventy years.

Teaching both undergraduates and graduates at McGill University has contributed significantly to insights and analyses I cannot imagine developing on my own. I am grateful to the many students, but particularly wish to recognize the following with whom, most recently, I debated issues in tutorials: Cecil Chabot, Lynda Gullason, Rob Hancock, Yumiko Nanaumi, Robbyn Seller, Audra Simpson, Brian Thom, and Masarah Van Eyck. I have also had the good fortune to have had gifted, dedicated research assistants who turned mere suggestions into highly useful quests: Ira Chaikin, Kevin McGee, Kim Nguyen Ngoc, and Trefor Smith. Most recently, Cecil Chabot took a research position in Ottawa, providing me with some vital data to fill in last-minute discovered gaps. I have enjoyed a long association with the staff of the Hudson's Bay Company Archives, particularly Judith Beattie, Anne Morton, and Debra Moore and am much appreciative of the lengths they went to, so willingly, to provide me with my research data and photographs. The composition and clarity of the tables is thanks to the expert work of Diane Mann in the Department of Anthropology.

My gratitude continues to other friends and colleagues who have made a significant contribution to this volume over the years. I am very appreciative of help I received from Asen Balikci, Roland Chamberland, Jim Chism, Brian Craik, Rosalind Halvorsen, Ignatius LaRusic, Susan Marshall, Emily Masty, Gerti Murdoch, John Murdoch, Carolyn Oblin, and Rose Marie Stano.

The editorial staff at McGill-Queen's University Press, particularly Aurèle Parisien and Joan McGilvray, have aided considerably the progression of this work from manuscript to book and I do thank them for their imaginative problem-solving in several instances. Equally, I am indebted to Diane Mew for her excellent editorial guidance and her wise counsel in curbing my tendencies to roam the world. The clarity and instructiveness of the maps are due to their skillful rendering by cartographer Aaron Chang. I also wish to thank Rosa Orlandini of McGill's Walter Hitschfeld Geographic Information Centre who was instrumental in organizing their production.

Some of the earlier research for this book was carried out under the auspices of a research grant I held as a Canada Research Fellow, generously funded by the Social Sciences and Humanities Research Council of Canada. The publication of this book has been made possible through an aid in publication grant of the Humanities and Social Sciences Federation of Canada to whom I am also very grateful.

Last, but definitely not least, I wish to acknowledge the love and support I have received at home. Much of the writing of this book coincided with my daughter Gillian's adolescent years and I am certain she is grateful that I had this preoccupation other than her. I also wish to acknowledge the bucolic retreat that Rick Schultz has shared with me these many years and where pleasant summers were spent writing this history. Additionally, his fine critical mind and first-class cuisine nourished my thinking and my fortitude. I thank him for all that and so much more.

Le Caroubier,
January 2001

Author's Note

PLACE NAMES

The names of the posts and the standardized spelling for them assigned by the Hudson's Bay Company have been employed throughout the book. Some of those names continue today as the names of the Cree villages while others have reverted to the names the Crees have long used, as follows:

Hudson's Bay Company post	Present-day village
Rupert House	Waskaganish
Eastmain	Eastmain
Old Factory/Paint Hills	Wemindji
Fort George	Chisasibi
Great Whale River	Whapmagoostui
Nemiskau	Nemaska
Mistassini	Mistissini
Waswanipi	Waswanipi
–	Ouje-Bougoumou

THE NOTES

In the writing of this book I have used a wide variety of sources, particularly the records of the Hudson's Bay Company. All these sources are listed in full in the bibliography. In the interests of greater readability, it was decided to remove all references from within the body of the text and place them at the end of the book, in two separate sections. Superior roman numerals in the text refer to more substantive notes; arabic numbers indicate a brief source reference.

Native bear feast near Rupert River, Mistassini, Quebec, c.1900. Photographer: J.A. Newnham. (NA PA-135706)

Mr and Mrs Simon Smallboy, oldest couple on the Island. One of the last of the Moose River guides, Simon made many trips to Missanabie from Moose Factory. In 1934 Simon was about eighty-five years of age. Moose Factory, Ontario, 1935. Photographer: Harvery R. Bassett. (HBCA 1987/363-1-83/61, N15129)

Hudson's Bay Company post building at Great Whale River insulated with snow, 1915. (HBCA 1987/363-G-28/8, 1987/335/N415)

Chief Solomon Voyageur wearing medals. (HBCA 1987/363-I-84/1, N82-273A)

Cree children in front of HBC Old Store, built 1924. Children wear rabbit-skin jackets and hold long, pointed snowshoes, the type made by the Cree. Kanaaupscow, James Bay, 1924. (HBCA 1987/363-1-82/32, N15127)

Wash day at Waswanipi, June 1946. Note the tents usually had wood floors with log walls extending upwards for a foot or two. (HBCA 1987/363-W-34/8, N79-208)

Emma Neeposh(?) and Clara Trapper stretching a moose hide, Waswanipi, June 1946. (HBCA 1987/363-W-34/5, N79-210)

The Indians at Great Whale River enjoy a game of chance as a pastime, c.1949. Photographer: R. Bailey (NA PA-27645)

Jimmy Bearskin is the catechist. At the caribou feast small boys shoot at a dummy caribou, Rupert's House, *c.*1947. Photographer G.R. Speers. (HBCA 1987/363-1-83/25, N15128)

Mistassini Post, *c.*1941. A mass wedding is solemnized by Bishop Anderson, seen in the background. Photographer: S.R. Crone. (HBCA 1987/363-M-68/12, N80-132)

J.S.C. Watt supervises a transfer of animals on Charlton Island Preserve, 1939. Lorene Squire Photograph Collection. (HBCA 1981/28/70, N15125)

Indians carrying live beaver in wire netting cages to be set free on the Attawapiskat Preserve, c.1948. Photographer: W.H. Houston. (HBCA 1987/363-B-20.2/2, N15126)

Indians arrive at Mistassini post from their winter hunt, 1941. Note the skins in one canoe. Photographer: S.R. Crone. (HBCA 1987/363-M-68/15, N80-134)

The arrival of the mail plane at Rupert's House, 1968. The post office is in the HBC store. Photographer: Fred Bruemmer. (HBCA 1987/363-R-37/62, 1987/260/NC8933)

J.S. Atkinson, distributor of Gas and Motor Oil, Fort George, Quebec, 1973. Photographer: John Flanders. (NA PA–161633)

Unidentified Cree carrying pails on yoke at Fort George, Quebec, 1973. Photographer: John Flanders. (NA PA–161628)

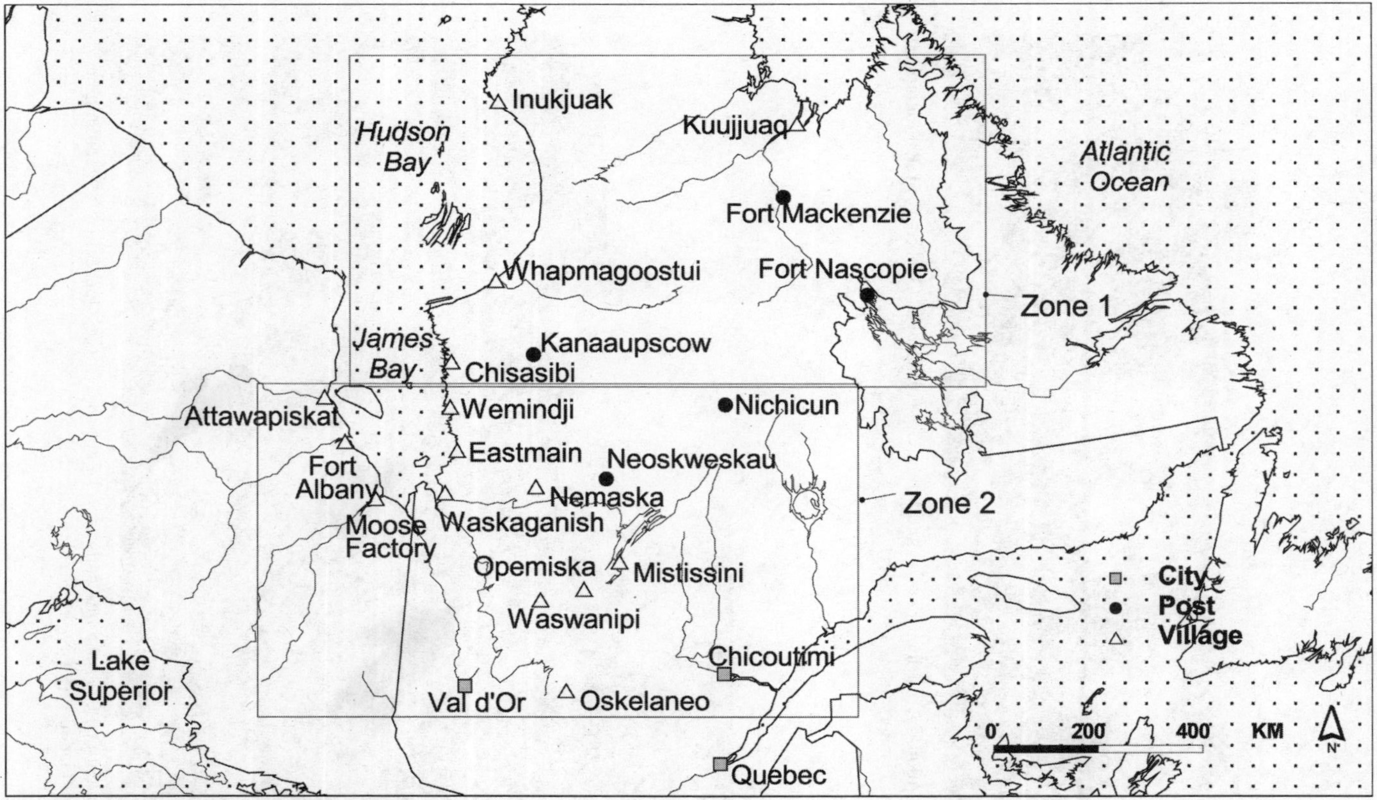

Present-day locations of James Bay Cree villages

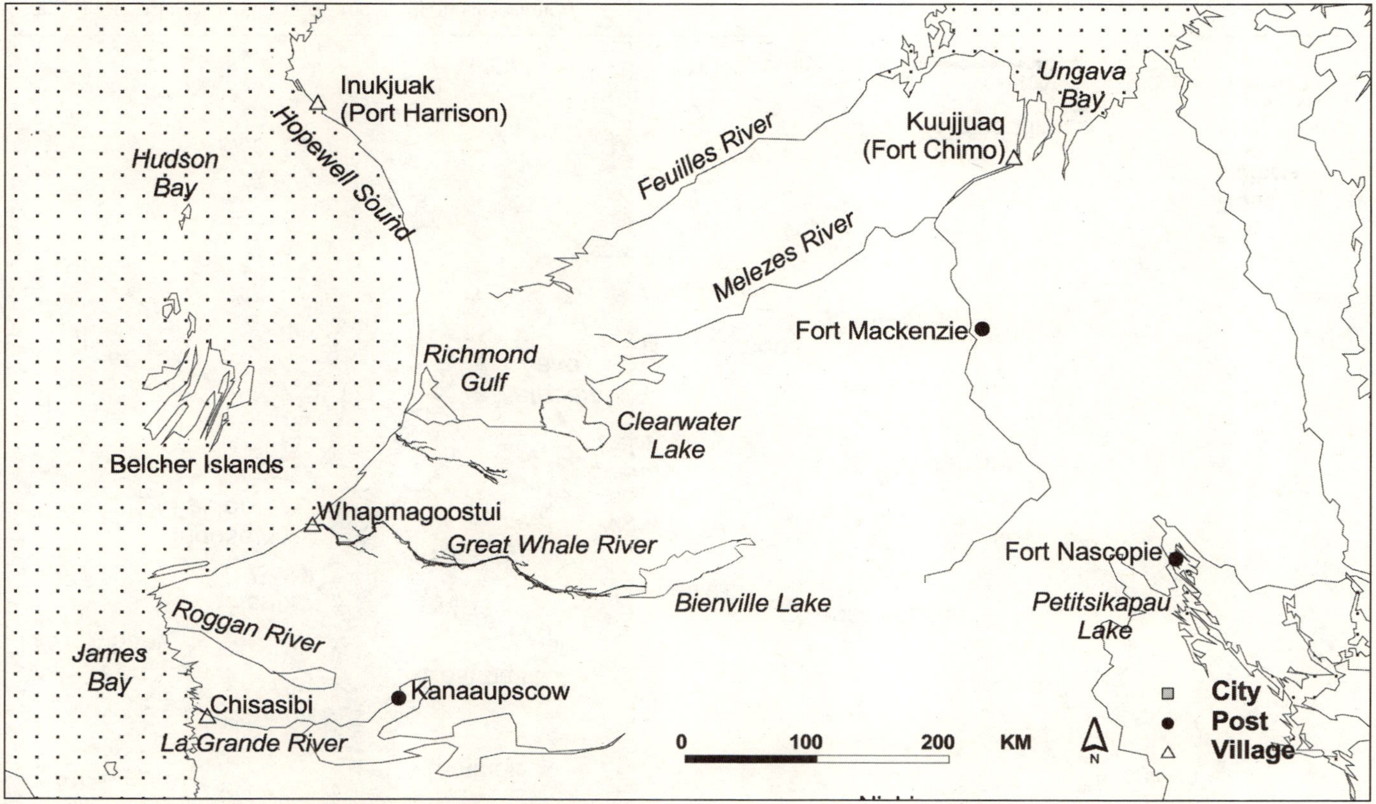

Zone 1: Eastern Hudson Bay, historic and modern place-names

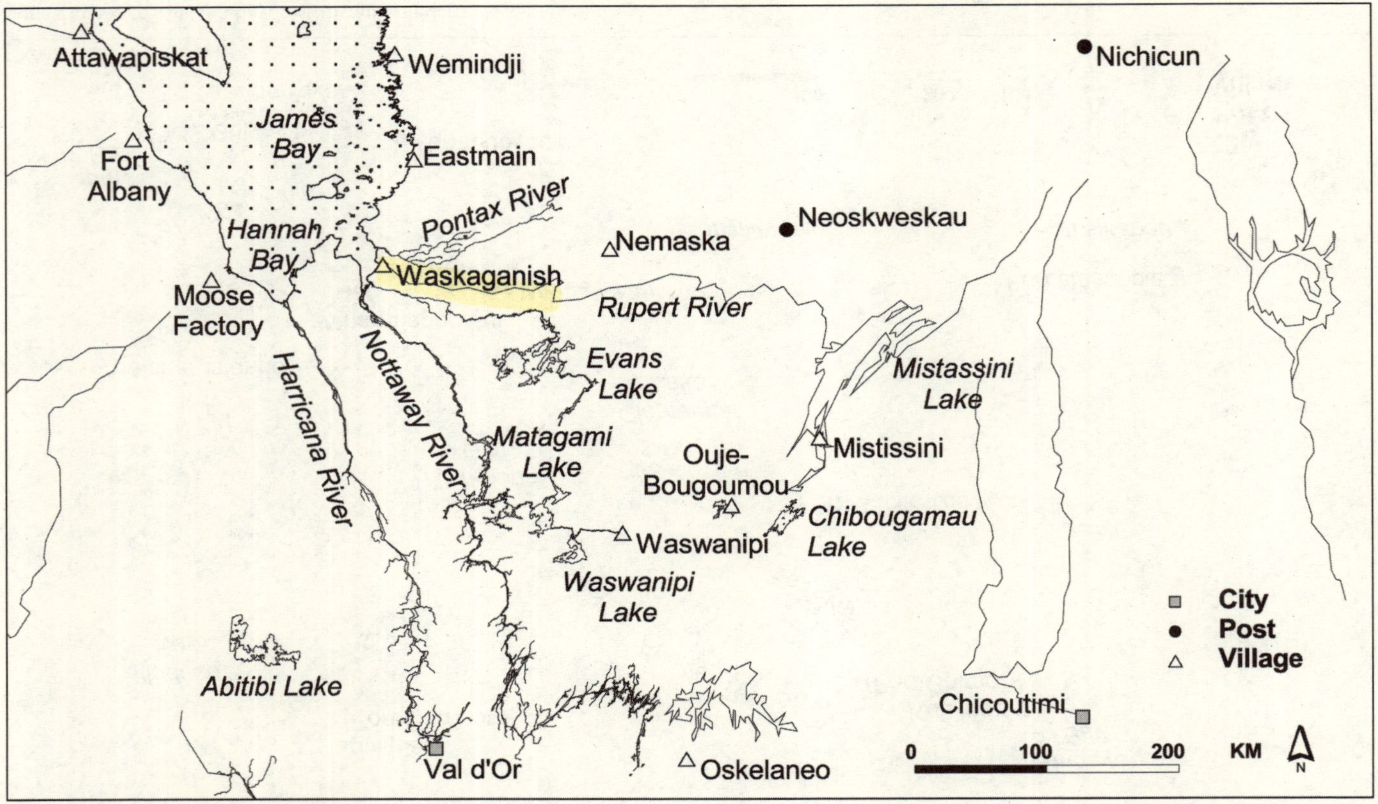

Zone 2: Eastern James Bay, historic and modern place-names

The White Man's Gonna Getcha

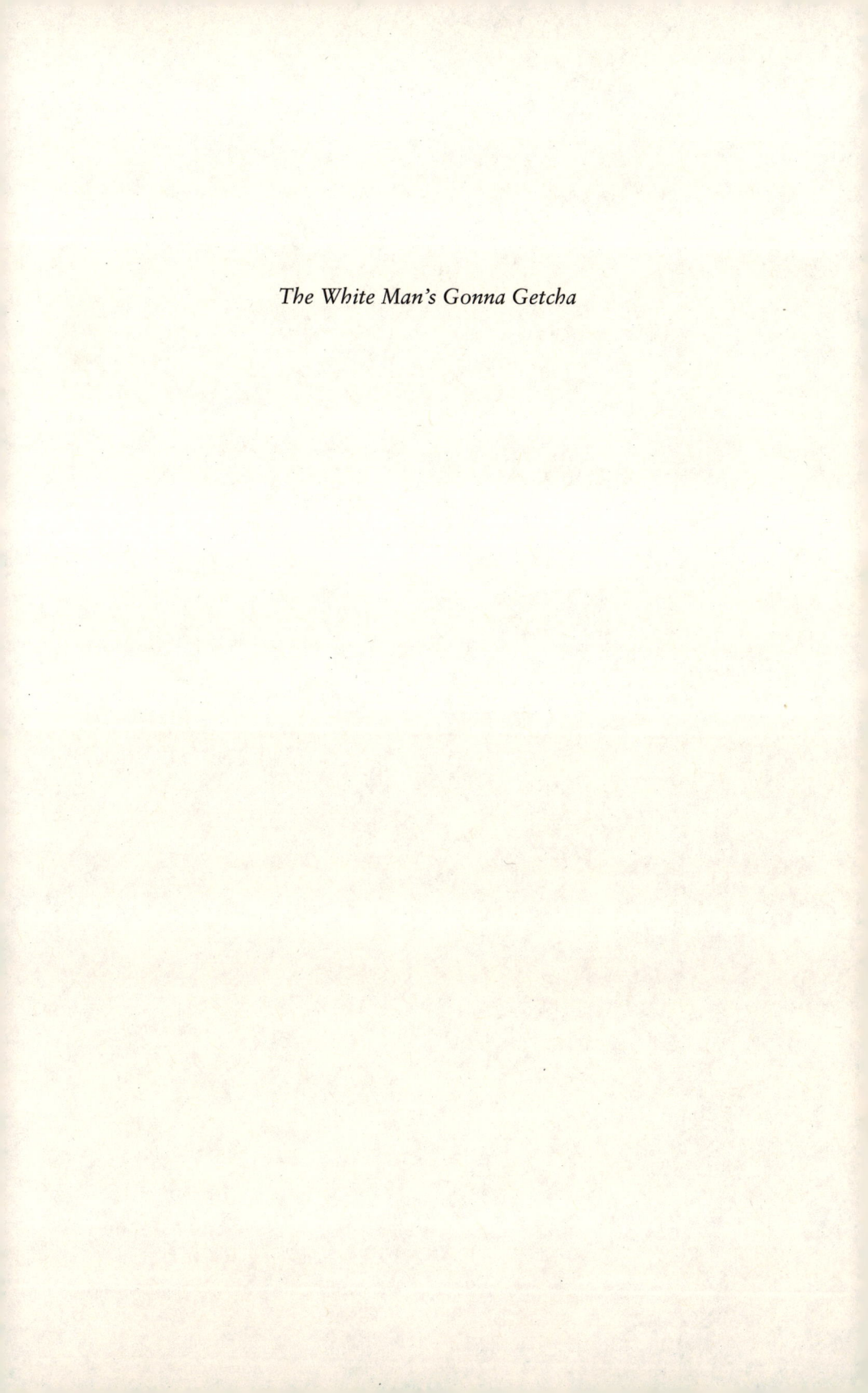

CHAPTER ONE

Introduction: Marking the Trails

This is a braided history of eastern James Bay. Braids, generally, are composed of three strands but this history is composed of only two. One strand is my grasp of the Crees' sense of their history in the first half of the twentieth century. The other tells the story of the gradual overlay of Canadian institutions and principles and the usurpation of Cree ones, what in good old-fashioned parlance is termed "colonialism." The third, missing strand of the braid is a story I cannot tell. It is the Crees' own story: what they, as a people, consider important to remember and in a spoken and symbolic language that is not easily translatable into English or into our Western thinking and cultural forms. The first two strands are the substance of this history. Explaining the absence of the third is the substance of this introduction. The concept of a braided history has been called upon by Natalie Davis to reinforce the notion that the history must tell everyone's story on equal terms, a concept recognized here but impossible to achieve.

The title, "The White Man's Gonna Getcha," is derived from a widely used threat Cree parents for long have held over their children: "Stop! The white man will come and get you."[1] Such an expression conveys the alienation and intimidation they feel from the strange individuals and agencies that have been imposed upon them. The Crees had a vehicle for demonizing and/or distancing themselves from strangers or enemies. They narrated myths which centred on a figure called *pwaat* or *pwaatich* in the plural form and used on the coast.[1] The pwaatich are pseudo-humans who are on the fringes of society and defy its norms, thereby representing behaviour considered anti-social. The pwaatich could represent other Indians[2] but Colin Scott sees the association as most often being Europeans or whites and regards the image presented of the whites a contradictory one. The positive qualities of the whites represent them as partners in exchange, located at the post or along the coast, while the negative quality depicted them as exploiters and situates them in the forest.³

However, whites as the bêtes noires of the Crees is not the dominant theme that runs through their stories; rather it is the Cree theme of preservation. Unlike the eighteenth-century period of great competition in the fur trade and the trading captain phenomenon when the Crees were seemingly dominant in the trade, this is a different story. It is about surviving through periods of great animal depletion and starvation, greater loss of political and economic autonomy, and the dismantling of their world view and of their lifestyles.

To convey both themes in one title would be unwieldy. The colonialism strand was chosen to remind the reader of the progressive takeover by Canadian authorities of Cree institutions, not always apparent, understandably. Reliance only on the Cree life histories or journal entries only provides a portrait of a particular period, the short rather than the long view. That there was, on the part of the Canadian government, an inexorable march towards near total domination of Native Peoples is apparent from the history of the Indian-white relations in Canada[II] and quite evident for James Bay in the correspondence of the Department of Indian Affairs. The dramatic title reminds us of this march by reminding us of the Crees' mistrust of white people, especially those in authority.[III]

WHY THE THEME OF SURVIVAL?

I could have chosen a more esoteric theme for this work, one representing the Crees' interests, perhaps employing the metaphor of the trickster, *tchickabash*, so much a part of their storytelling. However, in telling their stories of survival,[IV] the Crees do not employ literary devices, as they do in others cases. The accounts are straightforward and chilling enough without having to create artifices in which to present them. Not all of the first half of this century was one of deprivation, though the Crees entered it struggling. The competition between the Hudson's Bay Company and the Revillon Frères Company, newly entered into raw fur-buying in 1903, sparked a spending spree for about twenty years that created a bubble economy for the Crees and other hunters across the north. Although spending money on furs and credit, both companies took measures to reduce expenses in such labour-intensive activities as transport, a move which greatly restricted the Crees' opportunities for employment. When the bubble burst in 1929, the Crees were left with a far less paternalistic fur trade; even graver, they found themselves without any economic cushion at a time that all their food animals were at the low point of their cycles. An unknown number died and most were left with the years of privation indelibly marked on their individual and collective consciousness. When asked to tell their life story thirty years later, this is the theme most often told.

I cannot imagine what it is like to be starving over a prolonged period of time, but I can imagine that the search for food would become paramount in one's life, and once over a period of great famine, this obsession with food would continue to dominate one's thinking in a location where the margins of survival are narrow. In a Danish novel, *Smilla's Sense of Snow*, the author, Peter Hoeg, has an eighty-five-year-old Greenlandic woman conclude that "life is better today, since the Inuit very rarely die of hunger nowadays."[4] This is also the sentiment that comes through in some of the Cree oral accounts. So bleak was life for the Crees in the 1930s and 1940s that it is understandable that their hunger for survival would leave them receptive to outsiders usurping their decision-making and taking charge of their society. This history ends about the 1960s but the epilogue is meant to show that, given opportunities, the Crees of the 1970s could seize back the command, just as their ancestors did two centuries earlier.

THE THEME OF COLONIALISM

The Crees' acquiescence, voluntary and involuntary, to outside authority is the story of the progressive development of colonialism in their territory. We scarcely hear the word "colonialism" in Canadian history. It has only come into the Canadian consciousness recently with the development in Canadian literature courses of the genre of postcolonial studies, referring to Canada's past as a colony of Great Britain. Where, though, are our own colonial studies of our internal colonies? It is strange that one can count on one hand the number of Canadian or American anthropologists or historians who discuss Indian-white relations in these terms. A scan of journals and books draws forth very few oriented to a discussion of colonialism, although the number has increased in the 1990s. Palmer Patterson and Harold Hickerson were for a long while about the only scholars writing on Canadian Indian-white relations to establish a colonial context as the setting of this history. Patterson provides comparisons with forms of colonialism in Africa and Hickerson writes of "forest proletariat."[5] More recently, several scholars have written of internal colonialism to describe contemporary conditions for Canadian Native Peoples.[6] Why have so many others ignored this obvious paradigm? We all know North American Indians and the Inuit of the Arctic regions were colonized. If not always directly drawn into labouring for the dominant European settlers, the Indians nevertheless became subjugated peoples. Their societies were dismantled and refashioned in the hopes of making them over into Europeans. They were deprived of the land and resources both of which provided the great wealth on which this Nation was built. For some reason, Canadian historians and anthropologists have chosen not to draw parallels with other colonial situations. Nevertheless, the Canadian example demonstrates significant overlap with the classic examples of colonial societies.

Another discovery I made in the course of my research is that there are only a handful of twentieth-century northern histories focusing on events as they affected Native Peoples in Canada. I found this lack of comparative studies a great disadvantage in developing my own theoretical base. I have identified three equivalent regional histories. All three, though, are of regions in which mining interests, followed by government, early on appropriated the resources and the land. This did not occur in James Bay. In one of these histories by Kenneth Coates of the Yukon,[7] the pressures on the Dene are presented in terms of systematic discrimination. This is a general discussion and not very revealing about the dynamics of the interactions. Coates shies away from conceptualizing the Native-white relations in a comparative framework. This is not my criticism of another history, of northern Manitoba. Here Frank Tough's comparative framework becomes too universalistic and is far more informative about the industrial economy than about the Crees and Ojibwa. We learn very little about how they confronted the takeover of their lands and resources and adapted to these radical changes. The third history, by Kerry Abel,[8] of the Mackenzie drainage system and the expropriation of Dene resources and lands, emphasizes, as does Coates, not the marginalization of the Dene but their adaptability. This overview is not unlike the position I have held regarding the pre-1870 fur trade in James Bay. I hold great admiration for Native Peoples in their ability to have resisted, to the degrees they have, the great attempts to absorb them. However, my research of the twentieth century points to considerable differences in the ability of the Crees to maintain their political and economic autonomy. For this reason, I have turned to the literature on colonialism to help conceptualize their loss of self-determination.

Colonial studies today acknowledge that the focus must be not global histories of colonialism but local ones; each society dealt with this usurpation in its own way.[9] Colonial structures and their rationalizing discourses did not take the same form in James Bay as they did in India or Fiji or West Africa. For instance, we cannot write of colonial relations as shaped "by an economic system that required cheap labour for agriculture" as Warren could of the colonization of Indians in Guatemala.[10] Undoubtedly, the technological and socioeconomic events of the twentieth century which so radically transformed society globally also touched the isolated region of eastern James Bay. This was a region, however, whose inhabitants until the 1970s, were excluded from the modern forms of communications: roads, telephones, electricity, television. The lack of these services until such a late date is emblematic of the absence of Euro-Canadian settlement, moreover of an industrial economy. Twentieth-century James Bay until the 1960s was not, then, a classic case of seizure by the industrial economy.

The Comaroffs distinguish three models of colonialism: state, settler, and civilizing, i.e. missionary.[11] All three models can be found in Canada, and the divisions between them are not entirely sharp. State colonialism, with some aspects of the civilizing model, is what more specifically characterizes the James Bay region. Among the characteristics of the settler model the Comaroffs isolate are domination by force, gradual appropriation of tribal lands, the emasculation of leaders, and native provision of military assistance to the colonial power. Indian societies in southern Canada were specifically subject to these forces, though on a broader scale all Indian societies were eventually affected by how the Canadian settlers established the regulations and procedures to dominate their Indian neighbours. As James Bay was not settled, all aspects of this model do not directly apply here. However, the Crees fell under these rules well before such regulations were applied to the appropriation of their lands. The civilizing or missionary model of which the Comaroffs write is depicted as having as its objective "to reconstruct *totally* African society and culture."[12] Much as missionaries would have held this as an objective for the Crees of James Bay, they soon recognized the impossibility of such a goal. The Crees were hunters; the missionaries' ideal was agricultural society which involved the reorganization of domestic space, of the division of labour, of the family, and of individualism. The Anglican priest E.A. Watkins, sent by the Church Missionary Society to Fort George in 1853, lamented that a permanent settlement at the post was not possible because "If I were to induce Indians to settle here they would depend entirely on the Society for grain which would be a most heavy expense."[13] Nor was it in the interests of the Hudson's Bay Company to encourage its hunters to settle at the post. Needless to say, all recognized the futility of even considering implanting a farming subsistence in this very northern boreal forest region. Thus, over the following century the missionaries had to content themselves with reshaping only the ideological framework of the Crees and ignoring their communal family and economic institutions.

State colonialism is the most applicable of the three models, keeping in mind the significant but still limited colonizing forces of the missionaries. The Comaroffs define the state model in terms of the colonial government overseeing the territory through indirect rule, achieving peace through trade and alliances but not seeing as their mandate "the civilization of the indigenes." Over time, state colonialism changed to limit chiefly authority and impose legalistic and punitive forms of regulation. Likewise in James Bay these aspects were similarly strengthened.[14]

Governance was one of the primary means by which the southern society marked out its domination of the Crees and through which it exercised its controls. In partnership with the church, government officials were also instrumental in impressing upon the Crees the hallmarks of their subordination: powerlessness, racism, cultural degradation. This type of colonialism, the effects without the settlers, I refer to as a "bureaucratic colonialism," a refinement of the state model.[VI] Perhaps in the end it was a more insidious form of colonialism as there was not one perceived colonizer (as a Tswana would view the Boer settler in South Africa) but many colonizers who proclaimed a higher, concealed "boss." Following from the analysis of the Comaroffs one could, in Canada, as in South Africa, point to colonialism not as existing in the singular but having a plurality of forms.[15]

Bureaucratic colonialism is not covered in the literature but it is a concept that I believe begs analysis. It describes perfectly the Canadian history of Indian-white relations. Read a history text such as Olive Dickason's *A History of the First Nations* or J.R. Miller's *Skyscrapers Hide the Heavens* and one cannot help but be astounded by the tremendous number of obstacles the Canadian authorities put in the way of the Indians, even when they were attempting to meet the assimilationist expectations of the government and church. As the Comaroffs so pointedly observe, there is within colonialism "the contradictions of colonialism" caused by the differences among the executors of colonialism.[16] I would add to this the contradictions caused by the various agencies of government's haphazard approach to social engineering. Such a case is described by Sarah Carter in the 1890s when Prairie Indians were trying to become farmers and Hayter Reed, the superintendant general of Indians Affairs, decreed that to protect Indians from the vices of the marketplace they could only be issued with a plow and a cow. Their white neighbours were using labour-saving machinery.

James Bay has its own similar distressing stories, as will be seen, such as classing men who worked for wages more than three months as whites and therefore ineligible to hunt even for their subsistence. However, the government expected the Crees to be both self-sufficient and also to abandon hunting in favour of wage labour – itself a commodity scarcer than beaver. Furthermore, to add to these contradictions, the Department of Indian Affairs was only too eager to allow some of its functions to be carried out by other institutions and it relied on several other departments, such as Health and Welfare, to develop and deliver services. Not having a federal department of education to call on, Indian Affairs turned to the various churches which had rooted themselves in the communities. Within the Department of Indian Affairs, there were a number of different divisions, each with its own fiefdom. Concerted actions do not seem to have been taken. Furthermore, added to the destructive cultural engineering that was forced upon the children in the schools, we are learning today of the atrocities committed.[17] Granted it is with hindsight that we condemn these government policies, but the consequences of these actions are with us today and must be recognized.

Another failing of the government was its paternalism. It knew what was best for Native Peoples without consulting them. Thus, Inuit from eastern Hudson Bay were relocated to the High Arctic and although some consultation with them occurred, the promises the federal government made to convince them of this move never materialized.[18] Not as grave but still demonstrating the government's insensitivity, the Ouje-Bougoumou band was merged with the Mistissini band and only years later were detached at their demand following a lengthy process of negotiation.[19]

Possibly the worst of the bureaucratic colonialism can be found in the government's ineptness and frugality which kept Indians in a state of limbo without the resources to develop along lines they saw possible and desirable. For a federal government that is supposed to have a fiduciary responsibility to Indian peoples in Canada, their only role seemed to be to maintain the status quo. Where provinces stepped on the rights of Indians, the federal government demurred; in the case of hunting and fishing rights it left it to the Hudson's Bay Company to fight it out with the Quebec government.[20] The Crees, for their part, did not challenge. Perhaps they were grateful for whatever help they received in a period when they were struggling to stay alive. This statement underlines another distinction of colonialism as we understand it today. The form it takes in each setting is shaped as much by the political, social, and ideological contests among the colonizers as by the encounter with the colonized.[21]

These are the contours of the colonial structures the Crees faced and to which they reacted. In my mind's eye I see the colonialism as octopoidal, inexorably enveloping all aspects of Cree society. This history tells this story of this particular octopus – colonialism.

Another story that some would say follows from a study of colonialism is the story of the Cree women. I have not been able to fasten onto women as a separate subject of study. Relying as it does, in large measure, on fur trade company, government, and missionary records, they are relatively invisible. The oral tradition, on the other hand, much of it by women, speaks to community interests with little attention to distinguishing men or women or drawing out gender-specific concerns. There is likely enough in these oral traditions to enable me to speak to the issues of women's equality raised by Eleanor Leacock and others, enough to suggest that this 1970s interest is not appropriate and does not seem pertinent to a traditional, family-based hunting society.

THE MISSING STRAND[VII]

There is clearly a Cree story to be told, one that is not a retelling of our Western history. History, as Edmund Leach tells us, is "about the past and the sequence of events that it records are supposed to have actually happened. History is therefore distinguished from legend or myth."[22] At the same time, A.J. Kerr, an ethnographer in Rupert House in 1948, commented that "the Crees did not venerate their past."[23]

The Crees may not venerate their past but they do recount it. As a society that for much of its existence devolved into small, isolated winter hunting groups, it is not expected that the Crees today share a common narrative, an historical consciousness. Rather, their historical past is rendered through a great number of local stories about specific episodes. Despite living in small groups, the themes of this twentieth-century history are strikingly similar, undoubtedly because their local histories were informed by the values and morals of their myths, shared by all the Crees.[24]

To write a history blending both recorded and Cree oral sources is complex because the Cree historical accounts have a time depth of no more than two generations. If I am to respond to Frank Tough's criticisms that my writing downplays the economic factors in the fur trade, resulting in a whitewash of the Hudson's Bay Company's role in the Indians' social and economic spiral downwards,[25] how am I to discover the Crees' thinking for the eighteenth century? Surely how the Crees viewed the Europeans is relevant to this history, especially since not having Cree insights from this era handicaps my own ability to tell this story. On this point alone, writing the history from a Cree perspective becomes difficult, but the problem is considerably more complex than missing data. Herein lies the story of the missing strands of the braid.

Leach has narrowed the definition of history, rightly or wrongly, to a sequence of events that are likely to have happened or, as Appleby and others express it, "explanatory history that arose as a profession in the mid-nineteenth century that enabled the West to understand itself and the rest of the world."²⁶ The Crees, like most non-Western peoples, do not share this tradition, this way of formulating their past. However, if we recast the definition of history, as Elizabeth Tonkin does, as "representations of the past," we can push the discussion further to consider the feasibility of combining Western and Cree traditions of history to produce a history that reflects both outlooks.²⁷

The Crees distinguish between two types of oral tradition, *atiukan* and *tipachiman* stories[VIII] though the demarcation between the two is not always clear, but more of a gradation, according to Richard Preston.²⁸ *Atiukan* stories are what we would call myths, stories concerning the creation of the world when men and animals were not differentiated. Sylvie Vincent refers to these as "foundation stories" which explain putting the world in order²⁹ and Preston calls them "epic stories."³⁰ The *tipachiman*[IX] stories are of real people, either living or their ancestors, but not necessarily without reference to what Western thinking would label the supernatural.[X] The difference between the two types of genres is further explained by Lynn Drapeau, writing of the neighbouring Montagnais/Innu peoples. The *tipachiman* stories use elaborate stylistic and grammatical devices, sometimes painstakingly, to provide the evidence for their story. By contrast, the *atiukan* stories are narrated "exactly as if the speaker had been a witness to the story's events" and as such this genre "dispenses with the evidentiary requirements of the story."³¹

A Cree storyteller will usually state which type of story he is about to relate, but Preston adds he does not believe they would draw the lines between the two as clearly as he does. In his fieldnotes Preston has recorded a story entitled "The Bear Who Stole the Child," which recounts a man's son being taken and raised by a bear, a story foretold in the man's dreams. What is telling is Preston's parenthetical remarks underneath the title which say: "John is not sure of truth of this."³²

The storyteller is usually a skilled historian, as is true in most societies where there is no literacy. As "eyewitness" accounts, *tipachiman* stories cannot refer to a period more than several generations old, for the Crees expect "maximum precision in narration" although they recognize the telling may differ according to the individuals narrating it.³³

Jan Vansina, the historian of the Burundi in Africa, who, in the 1960s convinced Western historians of the value of oral history, does caution us about how we use this oral tradition. He, as others after him, distinguished between a personal and a collective memory. Hastrup reminds us that not all events survive in memory. She notes that "for events to become part of 'history' they have to have been experienced as significant."³⁴ Thus, Vansina distinguishes between personal reminiscences – bits of life history which he labels oral history. It is not to be confused with oral tradition, which has passed from "mouth to mouth for a period beyond the lifetime of the informants."[35] These are messages transmitted beyond the generation that gave rise to them and which he maintains is history on a par with recorded history.

Aspects of Cree epistemology have been discussed by a number of researchers[XI] but the commentary that most directly speaks to the issues examined here is Robin Ridington's writing of the Dunne-za.[XII] Although not Cree epistemology,[XIII] Ridington's analysis alerts us to some of the difficulties in translating cultural forms from the Dunne-za to Western-based cultures. He informs us that a hunter encounters his game first in his dreams and then in a physical reality. He relates that for the Dunne-za their stories about talking animals are equally as true as stories of summer gatherings. He describes the differences in thinking between the two cultures as follows: "In our thought world, myth and reality are opposites ... The language of Western social science assumes an object world independent of individual experience. The language of Indian stories assumes that objectivity can only be approached through experience." Ridington makes his understanding of the differences clear: "When I heard Japasa speak in 1964 about his medicine animals, I knew with absolute certainty that he was neither lying nor deluding himself. It was I who indulged in self-delusion when I persisted in asking for data in a form that could not accommodate Dunne-za reality."[36]

Similarly, writing of the Crees of eastern James Bay in the 1930s, Flannery comments that "the East Cree believed that a hunter's success in securing any form of game was ultimately dependent on the consent of the animals who, in friendship to man, allowed themselves to be taken, and of the spirits believed to influence their behavior, distribution and availability. Dreams were the vehicle for communication with these spirits. The dream visitation occurred under normal conditions of sleep when a spirit 'comes toward the hunter' in his dream and 'appears as a person and talks to him'. This was his *powatakan*."[37] Quoting William Katebetuk in 1938, Flannery adds, "Every animal I killed I dreamed about." According to Norman Chance, dreams are not only classified in the Crees' taxonomic system as a form of reality but are "considered part of the process of revelation by which individuals acquire knowledge about the external behavioural and unseen supernatural world."[38]

Another important aspect of Dunne-za epistemology is the concept of time. To illustrate the differences in thinking about time, Ridington refers to a story he has recounted, told by a Dunne-za elder, and then comments: "their time is different from ours. The old man and the boy circle around to touch one another, just as the hunter circles around to touch his game."³⁹ For the Crees, Preston has identified in the *tipachiman* stories a dual reckoning of time. The stories begin incorporating a linear progression, for they are often situated as having happened "long ago" or "when I was a boy," but the content of the stories is cyclical.⁴⁰

Just as the knowledge that is transmitted through the oral tradition is different from the Western one, so is the means of conveyance. Language is a key factor in understanding Cree oral tradition, though not the entire answer. Just as the knowledge is complex, so is the language. Differences in style, in structure, in nuance all merge to create obstacles for the non-native speaker that do not exist for the native speaker. Cruikshank also demonstrates how the structure of language introduces notions in one that cannot be easily expressed in another.⁴¹ Expert translation would be a partial solution but finding enough people who are perfectly bilingual and bicultural is a pipe dream. Finding the funding for such exacting, time-consuming work is even more of a pipe dream.

With language and knowledge so complex and different, the structures by which the knowledge is transmitted are equally different and complex. Tonkin calls these forms of transmission conventions of discourse, or genres, of oral history. Since the genres are the verbal forms through which the interpretation is organized, she states that one has to learn the genre to understand the message.⁴²

Sarah Preston explains the significance of oral tradition amongst the Crees.

The exactness of statements or precision of memory is not the significant aspect of narrative tradition; rather, it is an ability on the part of the narrator/story-teller to evoke a sense of shared imagery in telling and re-telling stories of two types: *atiukan*, pre-history or legend, and *tipachiman*, history or current events, that the East Cree illustrate competent social interaction, reinforcing the norms of reticence, emotional control, self-reliance and non-interference ... Because belief is expressed in action, it is not necessarily personalities or events with which the narratives are concerned but with actions and interactions, the relationships between characters, which includes human as well as non-human actors.⁴³

An example of one type of genre amongst the Crees is the Nottoway story. This is a story which exists in a number of versions. Having first read in the *Jesuit Relations* of successful Iroquois raids into Cree territory in the 1660s,⁴⁴ I was delighted to learn that the Crees also had an oral tradition of these same encounters. For once, stories matched and I could provide both perspectives. Delight turned to dismay when I read translations of these stories. In the six Cree versions in the Cree Way collection, it is not the Iroquois who are the victors but the Crees. Moreover, it is either an elderly Cree man or a Cree woman who craftily leads the Iroquois warriors to their deaths, over cliffs or in rapids.[xiv] Then I learned that these same stories were widespread amongst Algonquian speakers and were to be found, to cite one example, amongst the Pasmaquoddy living far away on the Atlantic coast.[45]

Julie Cruikshank, whose study of Dene oral tradition has contributed much to our understanding of oral tradition, refers to these constructions as "recognizable formulaic narratives," remarking on their persistence over time, despite considerable changes in every aspect of the lives of the storytellers. She says these narratives are allegorical, depicting cultural ideals in social interaction or confronting difficult issues. They must be understood in the context of the distinct cultural understandings and social relationships.[46] With direct reference to these stories, Sylvie Vincent, who has researched the history of the neighbouring Montagnais/Innu peoples, suggests that the Nottoway stories are not intended to focus on the event so much as on the behaviour one should display towards the enemy.[47]

There are other conventions in Cree oral tradition that are foreign to the Western way of thinking, but one should be able to circumvent these exotic forms by relying on the *tipachiman* stories. Not so. As these are eyewitness accounts, their time depth is at the most several generations, taking us back to the early 1900s. However, one story that is more than 160 years old has retained its *tipachiman* form. In 1832 four Cree men raided the small outpost of Hannah Bay, killing the occupants, the manager, and eight Crees.[48] So horrifying was the event to the Crees trading at Moose Factory and Rupert House that it is not surprising this story, in its retelling, maintains its essential features, paralleling accounts recorded at the time. By contrast, the Nottoway stories, telling of events that occurred over three hundred years ago, have passed from eyewitness reporting to allegory. Nevertheless, the Hannah Bay story encompasses features that are inimical to writing Western history. The Cree oral tradition tells us that messages received through conjuring was the motive for the killings, as well as the hardships the hunters were facing due to the stinginess of this outpost's manager.

What can one learn from the *atiukan*? A number of scholars, Tonkin for one, believe that "sometimes mythic structures encode history" – that is, they register actual happenings.[49] Others, such as Jonathan D. Hill, state that "history is not reducible to 'what really happened' ... but always includes the totality of processes within social orders" and so he sees myth and history as complementary ways of interpreting social processes.[50] While Hill defines history as "giving greater weighting to agency and social action in the present," he sees mythic consciousness as giving "priority to structure and overriding transformational principles that can crosscut, contradict and even negate the sets of relations established through social classifications." Interpretation of these myths is through a reflexive understanding of temporal processes and of the principal metaphors through which the society reproduces itself. Perhaps the best summation of Hill's understanding of mythic histories is their "attempt to reconcile a view of 'what really happened' with an understanding of 'what ought to have happened'"[51] or, as Turner phrases, it "a program for the orientation of action."[52]

These writers argue that in writing history the *aitukan* stories must be taken into account in any analysis of Cree representations of pastness. As other cultural forms of mythic stories, events per se in the Cree *atiukan* stories are not the primary point of the story. Rather, the narratives provide a social charter of how one is to live, to respond, to relate to others.[53] Such an approach is consistent with the increasing importance of cultural history, both in France and North America, with its emphasis on examining a society's "repertoire of interpretive mechanisms and value systems."[54]

In a thoughtful essay on Cree history, Preston[55] has outlined several ways in which the objectives of Cree narratives converge with those of Western history. Preston found that Cree narratives conveyed local knowledge that presented a record of the recent past. They also imparted a sense of continuity, of how the Cree people, through their competency, have been able to maintain their way of life. Their cosmology, describing their environment and their place within it, is another function of the narratives, as are the moral teachings. Preston also sees the notion of evolution embodied within the narratives, though this focus is reserved for explaining how the world of long ago changed into what it is today, explaining the relationship between humans and animals. He further instructs us that one story alone would not suffice to teach all these elements, but a number heard over time would. This convergence in functions between the two historical traditions, he emphasizes, is not necessarily a convergence in substantive themes of the history. In addition, the role of the individual in Cree narratives is much less prominent than in Western history and again there is the issue of time.

Reckoning of time differs in a way other than earlier noted. Instead of the arrival of the white man featuring as a marker in Montagnais history, as popular history would have it, it is the availability of flour or cloth that is of greater consequence. The important marker is "only game, no flour" or "only hides, no cloth."[56]

However, the greatest obstacle to merging these two historical traditions is the receptacle that brings together all the strands: the knowledge, the language in which it is expressed, and the cultural forms in which the thoughts are mediated. All these elements have implicit meanings which are comprehensible to the insider, significantly less so to the outsider. However, the structures in which these elements are embedded, the cognitive models, also carry with them implicit meaning, integral to an understanding of the messages therein conveyed.[57] As David W. Cohen cautions us, to dislodge these narratives from their context is to distort or destroy the meaning. Nor can we use uncritically oral traditions developed in one cultural context as though they can be equated with tangible historical evidence. Doing so, according to Cruikshank, might lead "to misinterpretation of more complex messages in narrative."[58] Examples of this can be found in Marianne Ignace's study of Haida public discourse. What she finds problematic in translating to Western conventions (or simply understanding Haida ones) are the rhetorical devices. She begins with discussing allusion where much of what is meant is not stated. Inversion, another Haida device, is understatement, belittlement of oneself, a value in Haida society, which implies then the opposite. Both repetition and pausing are means by which the importance of something can be conveyed and finally, silence also has meaning for the Haida. By not saying something that is expected is an implicit form of protest or disagreement.[59]

Accordingly, Vincent argues that the two traditions of history cannot be harmonized. She does not see as obstacles the contradictory, irreconcilable interpretations, for those could be presented in the same text, but rather the conceptual and methodological frameworks. In the Innu stories she has analysed, both time and story are fluid and analogous compared to the greater precision of Western history. Moreover, in a combined history, how does one draw in the Cree or Innu relations with the non-human inhabitants, so fundamental to their understanding of their past?[60] This is a view also held by Homi K. Bhabha, who writes that "cultural translation is not simply appropriation or adaptation; it is a process through which cultures are required to revise their own systems of reference, norms and values, by departing from their habitual or 'inbred' rules of transformation."[61]

In 1984 I wrote an article entitled "Oral and Recorded History in James Bay" which begins with this statement: "The purpose of my presentation is to show that a blend of documentary and oral history is essential to writing honest, thorough histories of Algonquian peoples." I further added: "I feel it behooves me to demonstrate the richness and accuracy of the oral tradition by showing how the documentary and oral accounts complement each other to form a more complete, vital portrayal of events."⁶² In the following years, I read and reflected on this objective, more reliable and representative path that I was to follow in producing histories of James Bay. I never made it down this path, nor does this history. I suggest that except for a few individuals, most historians and anthropologists also would be incapable of writing such a blended history.ˣᵛ It needs no belabouring of the point to argue that a history written by Western-trained historians would distort and destroy the depiction of the relationships, the symbolism, the patterning, and the integrity of the oral tradition of the Cree or any other people. In the end, rather than metaphorically put down my pen, I thought a flawed, one-dimensional history would still be useful, although more meaningful to the larger Canadian society than to the Crees. In reading Elizabeth Tonkin's work *Narrating our Pasts. The Social Construction of Oral History*, it became clear to me that I could use the oral tradition in the way she was cautioning us *not* to use it. However, I am not sure historians can do anything else than "scan them [the recollections of the past] for useful facts to pick out, like currants from a cake."⁶³ I believe that, as with other components of our colonial society, we will continue to shape Indian historical perspectives to conform to our historic vision.

Let the plunder begin!

THEORETICAL ANTECEDENTS

The fur trade arrived for the Crees about the turn of the seventeenth century when French ships visited Tadoussac. Champlain in 1603 described a trading route that linked the "Baye du Nord" (James Bay) and Tadoussac, giving all indication that some Cree bands had trade ties with their Montagnais brethren to the east of them.⁶⁴ Direct involvement of the Crees in the fur trade began in the summer of 1668 when an English trading ship, under the direction of Pierre Esprit Radisson of New France, piloted by Captain Zachariah Gillam of Boston, and financed by merchants of the City of London, weighed anchor at the spot the Crees later named Waskaganish and the English named Charles Fort after their sovereign who had given his blessings to this trip of adventure. For most of the fur trade it was known by the Hudson's Bay Company as Rupert House. The Crees' reception was obviously favourable and gave encouragement for the trade in beaver. Two years later the London merchants obtained from Charles II a charter that provided them with a monopoly of the fur trade over the vast lands whose rivers flowed into Hudson Bay. The Hudson's Bay Company owes its start to the interest exhibited by the Crees at Waskaganish in 1668 whom Radisson and Gillam encountered. Evidence of this interaction appears in the testimony Gillam gave to the Royal Society of London in 1670 about his findings during his voyage to Hudson Bay in 1668 and 1670.[65] Radisson must have spoken some Algonquian languages and Gillam may well have understood some of the conversation as he came from the Boston area where distantly related eastern Algonquian languages are spoken.

In 1983 Daniel Francis and I wrote histories of eastern James Bay in which we outlined our understanding and perception of events in this region, from the start of this fur trade period until the 1870s when other outsiders, such as missionaries, were imposing their interests and needs on Cree society. We chose to focus on the relations between the Crees and the Hudson's Bay Company agents, as these relations were played out in the dozen or so posts and outposts the company opened in Cree territory during these two hundred years. Using the journals, correspondence, and account books of the company along with some oral history accounts, we fashioned a history that we believe portrayed the Crees' active participation in the fur trade and the company's sensitivity to the Crees' needs and wishes. Our research was conducted in the 1970s, about the same time others were for the first time making a detailed study of the Hudson's Bay Company archives. Like the others,[66] we came to the conclusion that the Crees had a considerable influence over how they participated in the fur trade and how relations with the company were conducted. We were aware, though, that this favourable positioning of the Crees was representative of a period when the Hudson's Bay Company was opposed, first by French fur trade companies and later by the more vigorous competition of the North West Company that ended only in 1821. Thus, for 150 years of the history of the fur trade in James Bay, the Crees could always go to the company's rivals, even though these rivals were seldom on their doorstep. Undertaking a long journey in the late spring to visit a rival North West Company post south of the continental divide was routine and ordinary for bands of Cree men in the eighteenth century, not the hardship we would think it was. It was a time of year when travel was by canoe and food was more plentiful. It is evident that the Hudson's Bay Company managers did not consider it an idle threat, for why else would the company have financed the trading captain system[XVI] that cost them, some years, up to one-third of the value of the goods traded?[67]

A history that spanned two hundred years, even if it focused on one principal economic activity, the fur trade, is not easily summed up in a few pages. Yet it is necessary to offer some description of earlier Cree society as a prelude to our understanding of the continuity and changes that occurred in the twentieth century, the subject of this present work. In chapter 2 I have tried to capture what life was like for the Crees at the turn of the century and how the monopolistic fur trade functioned then. To summarize the earlier history, I will point to the research findings which sprang from the reconstruction of this two-century history of the fur trade in eastern James Bay.

The anthropological literature on questions of social change resulting from the European fur trade originated with Frank Speck in 1923 and was taken up by Father John Cooper in 1939, who did not see the fur trade as pivotal to explaining Cree socio-political institutions. This stand was later challenged by Eleanor Leacock.[68] Her conclusions about the effects of the fur trade on Montagnais society (but meant to include the Crees as well) were more dramatic than Edward Rogers,[69] writing at about the same time. In fact, Rogers's conclusions were correctly cautious,[XVII] allowing for an array of possibilities. Thus, as I entered this study I had before me a number of Leacock's claims about Cree society for which I have ever since been grateful.

One of the most important claims for the purposes of this study was Leacock's declaration that winter hunting groups were composed of about fifty people[70] and participation in the fur trade constricted the group size as the Crees switched from hunting caribou to hunting beaver, a food resource that provides much less meat. It was puzzling then to find in the records of the 1730s (when the fur trade in James Bay was still a haphazard event and still operating sporadically from a ship moored at Eastmain in the late spring) that the winter hunting group size was described as consisting of three or four families.[71] Furthermore, the daily journals of Eastmain Post, begun in 1736, clearly indicated that the mainstay of the diet of the Crees was not caribou but a variety of the game animals, large and small. Caribou was always considered the Crees' preferred food, but it was difficult to obtain and beaver meat was very much a second but still welcome choice. Thus, the Eastmain Post journals indicated that in the mid-1700s the Crees were not primarily caribou hunters nor were they wintering in hunting groups of fifty – that is, about ten families. Had they changed so much so quickly? I thought not, but fortunately the archaeological studies begun in the mid-1970s was yielding evidence of group size and diet. The precontact record in James Bay, if we focus on the period of about 900 AD, shows that the Crees were availing themselves of a variety of animals, fish, and fowl.[72] Indeed, the James Bay territory, except in its northern, tundra-like reaches, does not support significant herds of caribou that would enable the Crees to have been primarily large-game hunters. Secondly, the precontact winter hunting group size was assessed at about two to four families or ten to twelve individuals.[73] These archaeological findings, coupled with the data in the early eighteenth century archival records,[74] show continuity in Cree social structure and not dramatic change, as Leacock maintained.[XVIII]

Leacock attributed to the fur trade another major transformation in Cree life. She reasoned that, as communal caribou hunters, the Montagnais or Crees would have practised a communal land tenure system, where the territory was held in common by the band. Her foray into this question was provoked by the writings of Frank Speck who, in 1915, proposed that Algonquian-speaking hunters held hunting territories as the property of individual families, calling them "family hunting territories."[75] Moreover, he suggested that these individual hunting territories are of precontact origin because the major hunting strategy was oriented to the hunting of beaver and beaver are sedentary animals. Therefore, it made good sense, to Speck's way of thinking, that a hunter would hunt the same territory year after year since he would know the location of the beaver houses. As the debate was becoming adversarial, both Speck and Leacock were making points that forced them to portray the family hunting territories as fixed and inflexible. Although Speck initially derived his position on family hunting territories from his conversations with hunters and the maps they drew for him, he later became an advocate for Indians and their entitlement to their lands.[76] Leacock, on the other hand, centred these family hunting territories squarely in a Marxist perspective, which regarded property and the family in terms of a primitive communism.

Research in the Hudson's Bay Company's eighteenth- and nineteenth-century records provide ample evidence to support Speck's conclusions about the existence of family hunting territories. However, these data indicated that "ownership" of these territories were more flexible than he portrayed.[77] Travellers through the James Bay region, or to the south of it, in the nineteenth century also provide irrefutable evidence of the long-standing existence of such territories in their narratives of their travels. Daniel Harmon, fur trader and explorer in 1822 in the Abitibi region, was one; the geologist A.P. Low, conducting explorations in central and northern Quebec, was another.

For Leacock,[78] reliance on the fur trade also spelled a dependence on the imported food provided by the post. She reasoned that individualism came to prevail over communalism as hunters dealt individually with the post manager. Again, striking evidence in the post journals demonstrates that her views of the consequences of participation in the fur trade were wrong. In the mid-1700s the journals enumerate the number of beaver pelts brought in to trade by the Coaster* population,

---

* The Crees who lived in the vicinity of the post (within a day or two of travel) were first called "Homeguard" by the Hudson's Bay Company, then later "Coasters." Those who lived far inland and came to the post only once a year were known as "Inlanders." Over the decades, as differences in lifestyle arose, the Crees themselves made the distinction between Coasters and Inlanders (see Kerr 1950:16).

and it was then possible for me to calculate the approximate per capita amount of edible beaver meat. By anyone's calculation, it was not an insignificant amount and demonstrated that hunting for exchange in the fur trade was not in conflict with hunting for subsistence. The records also showed that in the 1700s the Crees were not dependent on imported foods. It is only towards the end of the nineteenth century that small quantities of flour, sugar, baking powder, and tea became trade items.[79] Thus, their subsistence practices were paramount and guided their hunting strategies well into the twentieth century.

The Crees were egalitarian in their practices, sharing the harvest or a common dwelling among three and four nuclear families.[XIX] However, the records show that when the opportunity arose for individuals to have access to power or influence, they seized it; the trading captain system was based on this code. The Hudson's Bay Company promoted the recognition through special dress (a captain's coat, plumed, hat, and pumps) and by awarding gifts of tobacco and brandy according to the number of hunters and their beaver pelts accompanying the captain. It was not, though, an imposed system. The captain was so designated by the company precisely because he conformed to Cree criteria for leadership; Cree hunters did follow their gang captains to the post.[XX] More importantly, this practice, which endured over a number of generations of Crees, also attests to the fact that the Crees supported leaders. The notion that there are leaderless societies is unfathomable, yet Leacock[80] made this claim for Cree and Montagnais society, saying that leaders were irrelevant. Admittedly, the leadership is founded on influence rather than power or authority, "primus inter pares" as Rogers described it,[81] but there were definite, recognizable leaders exercising influence in the place of authority. Moreover, there were leaders that chose to aggrandize their positions when they could, as did the trading captains.

Another finding of James Bay research is that the Crees were discriminating consumers and the company went to a great deal of trouble to meet their needs and demands, particularly during the period of greatest competition. The company paid attention to the complaints of the Crees and asked London for better-quality goods and ordered custom-made tools according to Cree specifications.[82]

Those of us mining the Hudson's Bay Company records in the 1970s had before us Harold Hickerson's view of the consequences that awaited Indian hunters when they were drawn into the fur trade. He portrayed the hunters as a forest proletariat subject to the whims of the post manager. I have read the records of about a dozen posts, covering now close to three hundred years, and scarcely is there any indication that the company could command the hunters to live in the image they would have liked to fashion for them. Furthermore, there are no condescending comments; the post managers consistently wrote respectfully of the Cree hunters. This stands in contrast to the work of Alan Cooke[83] who found the opposite; and in fact, he cites several examples of derogatory statements by the Fort Chimo post managers regarding the Naskapis who came there to trade. Even here, the worst comment is the managers' depiction of them as lazy and indolent. The explanation for the discrepancy between the two types of reporting lies in the fact that the Crees brought in beaver pelts. The Naskapis, living above the treeline, rarely brought in beaver or any other marketable goods, thus provoking such outbursts by the fur traders.

The tenor of the history of eastern James Bay to 1870 is one of active participation by the Crees in the fur trade established in their territory by the Hudson's Bay Company in 1670. I could not have imagined when I was preparing for this research in the early 1970s that my study would have been so oriented. I knew ahead of time that it was going to be a story about the little guys up against an international trading company, and I was sure it would have a good-guy versus bad-guy scenario. It did not turn out that way. Using the records of the company and some recorded oral history interviews, I found that the fur trade, although managed by a few Englishmen, was in fact orchestrated by the Crees. Despite pressure by company managers, each Cree hunter brought in to trade the number of pelts he needed to transform into imported goods and no more.[xxi] It was the Crees who provided the labour, not only in supplying pelts but also in transporting the goods and furs and maintaining the Englishmen at the post. They provided them with country food, firewood, clothing, male and female companionship and family life. Nor did the Crees feel bullied by the company; it seems the other way around. As one company manager, B.R. Ross, said despairingly: "I do not believe that the natives ever consider their presents in the light of payment for anything, regarding them more as gift-offerings to their own importance and superiority."[84]

Frank Tough[85] considers that economic inequality lies at the root of the serious problems of underemployment and demoralization afflicting Native Peoples today. I do not see the fur trade, at least as shown in the company records to 1870, as having so undermined the Native economy that it could be interpreted as one of victimization. After all, I do not see in contemporary histories of Canadian society an underlying premise that we are all exploited by the usurious banks. I believe we all know that, just as we know that the Hudson's Bay and the North West companies were in Canada to serve their own interests, not those of the Indians. As it happens, the interests of both parties happened to converge, which made the fur trade possible. The chopping of trees with stone axes, the cooking of meat in birchbark containers with red-hot stones, or taking forty hours to tan one hide, could not have been welcome labour. The pelts that were furnished to obtain iron axes, copper kettles, and duffle cloth required an exhausting expenditure of human energy and hands, arms, and feet plunged in freezing water; but once the beaver was taken, the meat was consumed by the family and the excess pelts were traded. Earlier, the beaver would have been transformed into tasty meals and their pelts burned as surplus to their needs.[86] Once the Europeans expressed an interest in the skins, the beaver pelts became valuable commodities.[XXII] Note the words of a Montagnais man quoted by Father Le Jeune in 1634: "The beaver does everything perfectly well, it makes kettles, hatchets, swords, knives, bread; and, in short, it makes everything. The English have no sense; they give us twenty knives like this for one Beaver skin."[87]

An interdependence arose. Hunters incorporated this new technology into their daily life and could not have permitted themselves to lose access to it. At the same time, European men's fashions in haberdashery were dependent on the beaver pelt until the 1830s when silk hats replaced beaver hats.[88] Towns in Scotland and northern England fed off the fur trade, providing iron-manufactured goods and cloth.[89] The colonies in the southern United States (along with the Portugese colonies in Brazil) supplied tobacco for the fur trade and the Orkney Islands provided cheap labour. Everyone suffered when the fur trade ended, Indians and Europeans alike.

In sum, I do not believe that every contact history need be a history written from a destructive perspective. Change need not be devastating to a culture, particularly when that change is directed from within the culture. During the fur trade period, the Crees still had the means and the power to define themselves. The anthropologist Kay Warren,[90] writing of Indian identity in Guatemala, chides her colleagues for having portrayed change as a loss or impoverishment of the culture, thereby creating a passive rather than an active role for the populations. Similarly, Stephen Hugh-Jones reminds us: "Tribal peoples did not only suffer history, they also made it and continue to do so."[91] The Crees seized opportunities and maximized their social and cultural options. Furthermore, they could not have imagined the wealth the fur trade produced for a few merchant families in England. What they saw of the Hudson's Bay Company surroundings, except for a few of the large posts such as Moose Factory, Rupert House, and Fort George, were very middling living conditions, sometimes bordering on starvation for those company men in the outlying posts. There was no justification, based on the evidence, to write this history from the perspective of subordination or powerlessness. Quite the contrary.

Despite how deeply the fur trade dug into Cree society, I have maintained that the dependence was more a technological one than a loss of economic and political autonomy. All the while the Crees were supplying the Hudson's Bay Company with beaver pelts they remained foremost subsistence hunters, providing their own food and thus in control of their economic and political strategies. It is only in the twentieth century that they became trappers working for exchange; this change was determined by modern developments in the market system and by transportation and communication, along with the greater access to cheaper imported foods such as flour. Certainly, the Hudson's Bay Company controlled a number of the realms affecting them, such as the price paid for the pelts and the prices charged for the goods. However, for three-quarters of this two-hundred-year period, northern hunters could always threaten to take their trade elsewhere, giving the Crees some degree of control over the trade. Even trading at a neighbouring Hudson's Bay Company post proved to make the post manager more compliant. In short, I rejected depicting the history of the fur trade in James Bay as part of the world systems theory,[92] the kind of history that paints marginal peoples as a universal type of victim. Despite the valuable contribution Eric Wolf made to our understanding of colonial peoples in his book *People Without a History*, he is implying, as Talal Asad[93] would formulate it, that their involvement with industrial capitalism transformed not only their mode of production but also their kinds of knowledge and lifestyles. This did not happen in James Bay. In criticizing Wolf's universalism, Kirsten Hastrup rightly comments that these indigenous peoples to whom Wolf gives a history "should not be admitted to history only by being implicated in ours. They should be allowed to have their own."[94] I see my responsibility as demonstrating how the culture of the Crees mediated this global history of dominance and exploitation by contorting it to suit their needs. I reject those hypotheses founded on societal transformation to characterize the fur trade prior to this century because my reading of the historical evidence does not convince me that the fur trade was so dominant that it transformed the relations the Crees had with each other, with the land, or with how they made a living.

Coasters were more dependent on the post than Inlanders, since living on the coastal plain produced fewer furs. Coasters made up the difference by selling their labour or provisioning the post. Being tied more tightly economically to the post did not, though, transform them into a forest proletariat. As will be seen in chapter 6, when the company drastically reduced the employment opportunities at the post in the last century, Coasters went inland and became full-time hunters again. Although many aspects of their lives were interconnected with the fur trade, the Crees, who lived for something like 349 days a year far removed from the post, maintained an autonomy that, for the most part, enabled them to pursue their own objectives. For several hundreds of years they were able to exploit, shape, or negotiate the circumstances of the fur trade that impinged on their lives. The circumstances were to change in the twentieth century and this forms the raison d'être of this history.

Arthur Ray[95] introduced the notion of equating the debt system in the fur trade with welfare. It is a juxtaposition I have resisted. I fail to see how the Crees would view the credit they received from the company as welfare. Primarily, there was the expectation of repayment of the debt. In the period in which Ray's analysis takes place (the end of the nineteenth century), welfare was unknown to everyone in Canada. Moreover, the Crees, as other Indians, have a very sound principle called reciprocity which enables them to receive, and to expect to receive, knowing that down the line they had to return in kind to the individual what they have received from him. Was not the fur trade an example of reciprocity? Did the Crees not bring in food – that is, geese, fish, and caribou meat – for the Englishmen at the post, as well as valuable furs? Did they not also provide fuel and transport? Did they not provide women and have children in common? Why would not the debt system have been one additional undertaking that fitted into this pattern? Each individual helps in the ways he or she can, with the expectation that this help will be returned when needed. Welfare, on the other hand, is the opposite of reciprocity. It implies receiving without the expectation of returning in kind. Welfare is a mid-twentieth-century phenomenon that, as we now know, has sapped the energies and desires of millions of Canadians, not only Indians. Although not always possible, the Crees believed they had to repay the fur trade debt. J.W. Anderson, a post manager in James Bay in the early 1900s, noted that "despite the absence of legal compulsion, they invariably paid their debts."[96] This is not the behaviour or thinking associated with welfare; the Crees had not internalized receiving debt or credit in this way.

This mentality, as well as the conduct of the fur trade, was to change for the Crees and the company as they entered the twentieth century. The end of fierce competition with the Revillon Frères Company and new forms of communication and transport all had their effect on changing the conduct of the fur trade and the Crees' role in it. World events, such as market forces, for the first time impinged on regions as remote as James Bay. Changes in lifestyle were being forced on them from the outside, as the interests of such agents as missionaries and government began remaking the Crees in their own image. These new institutions were tolerated by the Crees because the fur trade was no longer a viable enterprise for them. Undoubtedly, when the Crees in 1668 took a hatchet and some twine in exchange for their beaver skins, this set off a chain of events that two hundred years later was to entrap them in events over which they had no control. Their work in the fur trade may have been what enabled them to be drawn into the Canadian sphere; far more was to befall them in the twentieth century that yanked them from their cultural base than had occurred in the two previous centuries when the fur trade was the sole outside agency. In this study I contend it was not the fur trade which radically transformed Cree society, spiritually, socially, economically, or politically. It was events in the twentieth century, especially the imposition of extensive powers and the financial supremacy of the Canadian government, that inexorably overwhelmed Cree society, sapping it of its ability to administer itself. It is here that an unequal economic relationship becomes a classic dependent or colonial relationship. The following chapters offer evidence of the Crees' descent into colonialism.

CHAPTER TWO

James Bay at the End of the Nineteenth Century

INTRODUCTION

The years of the late 1860s and onward challenged the Crees in terms of their survival. This era ushered in an unprecedented decline in food resources[1] that eventually led the Crees to alter some of their social and ideological forms into those we see today. Complaints of starvation or near starvation abound in the Hudson's Bay Company journals and the Crees everywhere had to get used to depleted sources of food and reduced goods for exchange. Food was uppermost in their minds, while dwindling fur returns preoccupied the company traders.

These years mark another watershed in the lives of the Crees – one that began more slowly and less harmfully than food shortages but one that nevertheless, by the early 1900s required major changes in Cree society. Those years saw the start of the inexorable march towards the imposition of the Canadian state on their society and their lands. In the two previous centuries only the fur trade had intruded into their lives but this was to change. For the people of eastern James and Hudson Bays, fifty or more years would pass before they had to confront, in the 1930s, relatively large numbers of outsiders living in their midst.[II] Even before then, they had to contend with the social, economic, and political effects radiating from both settlement to the south and west of them, and governmental policies and directives born in Ottawa and Quebec.

How much and in what ways the Crees of eastern James Bay were affected by their diminished food and fur supplies and encroachment from the south is one of the key issues in the analyses of the history of the area. The focus on food, or rather the scarcity of it, must also take into account the larger social and economic context, namely the fur trade and Cree–Hudson's Bay Company relations. The trade itself was to change considerably in the twentieth century; the changes in the company operations thus necessitated changes within Cree society and vice versa.

THE LAND

The Crees of eastern James Bay once occupied a vast territory of something like 400,000 square kilometres, twice the size of England and one-fifth of the whole of Quebec.[1] This land fell under Canadian command in reality only after the Second World War, though Canada had exercised controls in arenas such as fledgling medical and education services prior to the 1940s. The province of Quebec began imposing its jurisdiction only at the start of the 1960s. At the turn of the century, the province had enacted game legislation which, if enforced, would have regulated the Crees' hunting practices; but James Bay was far away and out of the reach, for the most part, of the few game wardens. Administratively this land was not seen as Cree territory until 1975 when both the federal and provincial governments recognized the Crees' aboriginal rights and negotiated a modern treaty. By this time, their territory had shrunk drastically but the Crees were acknowledged as holding legal and usufructory rights over portions of it, sharing the rest with Quebec; sharing with a state government, the proverbial elephant and the mouse, has continued to erode these rights and holdings.

In a previous work my co-author and I described the land as inhospitable, a description I quickly came to regret once I saw it in print. The land is inhospitable from my sedentary, urban point of view, but from the perspective of a hunting society it is fecund, familiar, and accessible. Besides, it is home. The traders wrote of the vagaries of animal numbers, the deluge of mosquitoes in the summer, soggy travel and inclement weather, but the Crees saw it as a provision store of delicious wild foods that provided them with the means to live autonomously. The Crees' cultural values and religious ideology that issued from living on this land is testament to its richness.

This vast territory ranges from coastal plane, including the coastlines of James and Hudson Bays, from the treeline at Richmond Gulf in the north to Rupert Bay in the south (roughly from 52° to 56° latitude); it embraces the land fronting on this shoreline inland to the lakes and headwaters of the rivers which drain it (roughly 69° to 80° longitude). Most of eastern James Bay falls within Canada's subarctic region and forms part of the Canadian Shield.

The present contours of Hudson and James Bays took shape about two thousand years ago from the receding Tyrell Sea, although the isostatic rebound is a continuing process. This water-strewn land, the result of extremely poor drainage resulting from the glacial coverage, is host to a variety of vegetation covers. Jean-Pierre Ducruc and his associates have schematized the area into five major ecological zones (see figure 1) although there are numerous other regions within each zone. Another diagram used to depict this diversity presents four zones, divided into a total of nineteen ecological regions in James Bay.[2] This diversity is due to the interplay of the glacial history, the soil and type of drainage, the microclimates, and the exploitation by the animal and human populations. The use here of forest cover as the main variable is because most of the animal resources on which the Crees live inhabited forested regions (except for the barren ground caribou). What Ducruc terms closed crown-forest (zone 5) is really only found in the southern portions. At about the latitude of the Eastmain River the forest cover has significantly opened up and north of the La Grande River it is sparsely wooded. The treeline, just south of Richmond Gulf (today renamed Lake Guillaume Delisle)[III] marks the traditional end of the Cree territory and the start of the Inuit one. The animals living in this varying forest cover include caribou, beaver, bear, and a host of small mammals found throughout Canada's north as well as fish and waterfowl. Neither vegetation nor animals or fish are equally distributed. There is not a simple correlation between ecological zones and animals so that distribution of the animals is related to the distribution of nutrient-rich islands of productive habitats.[3]

As food resources are sparsely distributed, the productivity of the land decreases as one goes north.[4] Consequently, Cree hunting groups were small and dispersed making communication and group solidarity difficult. The earliest dated occupation in the James Bay territory, 3,500 years ago, was in the northern reaches, at the headwaters of the La Grande and Caniapiscau rivers,[5] an area now flooded. It is presumed that human occupation predates this site by about two thousand years, when the earlier taiga vegetation was replaced by the more diversified boreal forest.[6] In precontact times, several Cree bands would meet in the summer at good fishing spots.[7] Fur trade posts, beginning in the late seventeenth century, sprang up along well-travelled waterways and became one of the summer meeting places that brought together the Cree bands hunting in the area. As the opportunities to meet increased and as the outside world created a collective consciousness of common interests, it was not difficult for these local bands to unite formally into a national or ethnic group.

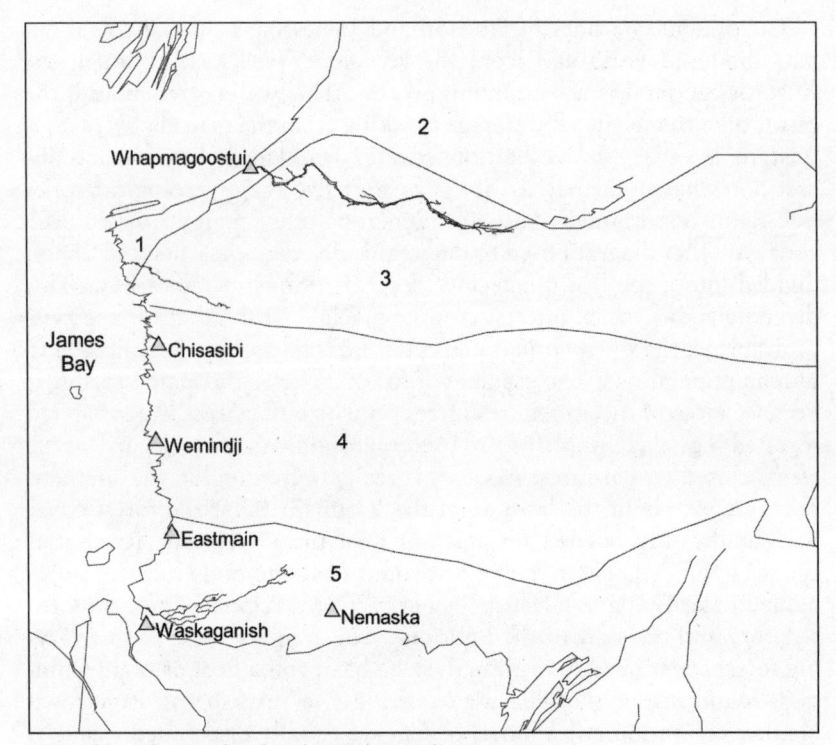

Legend: 1 barren lands (above the treeline)
2 lichen barren grounds (less than 5% forest)
3 lichen woodland (5–25% forest)
4 open forest (25–40% forest)
5 closed crown-forest (40–80% forest)

Figure 1   Ecological Zones of the Eastern James Bay Territory

SOURCE: based on Ducruc et al 1976: 372–6.

LIFE BEFORE THE TWENTIETH CENTURY

In all the lands inland from James and Hudson Bays, hunting for subsistence was still the dominant Cree economic activity in the 1870s, followed by trading furs and other country products to the Hudson's Bay Company. At this time the Crees were still hunters rather than trappers. The trade in furs, primarily beaver and marten, was, of course, the raison d'être for the presence of the Hudson's Bay Company. In broad outline the late nineteenth-century trade does not appear too different from that carried on in the early eighteenth century when a debt system was first instituted and widely subscribed to by the Crees.[IV]

The extension of credit to the hunters was not a charitable act by the company for it protected its own interests. Given that the animal populations fluctuated and climatic conditions often limited hunting success, the company recognized that there were times when the ability of the hunter to obtain furs was beyond his control. To have denied him essential items such as metal tools, twine, or cloth would have meant the hunters had to devote greater time to hunting such game as fish, ptarmigan, and caribou for food and clothing. Without these essential tools, in poor fur years, the hunter might have starved. A dead hunter could not produce furs for the company, nor could one who had to pursue caribou or fish all the time, using old methods and tools, such as stone-tipped bows and arrows or spears. By making an advance to a hunter against the following year's hunt, the company was able to keep him gathering furs and retain his loyalty in times of competition. With a run of a few difficult years, a hunter's debt did accumulate but the rule was to advance for the amount of furs they brought in.[8] In the case of poor hunters or a string of bad luck, the company did allow the debt to amount to far more than a year's hunt. When it looked as though the debt would never be repaid, it was reduced or cancelled, on occasion called a "donation."[9] However J.W. Anderson,[V] who began his long service to the company in 1910, suggests this was not the norm. As cited previously, he claimed the Crees repaid their debts "invariably."[10]

All hunters used the debt system whether they needed it or not, in all likelihood viewing debt as part of their complex of social obligations.[11] The Cree hunter trapped for the company and in turn the company assumed the responsibility to look after him.[12] With such a perspective, we might detach ourselves from our twentieth-century Protestant view of equating debt with economic or social dependence for the period in which the Crees had a viable economy.

Although the company's system of bookkeeping maintained the debt system for many years, it was the Crees who turned the system into one of social status, thereby ensuring its continuation. Writing of the late 1940s, A.J. Kerr found[13] that the Crees at Rupert House used the amount of debt granted to each hunter as an important gauge of the hunter's success.[VI] That being so, there was little incentive to clear the debt; in fact hunters asked for debt even if they had a credit balance on the books of the company. One hunter told Kerr that not needing debt from the company did not deserve much respect. Given the ways in which the Crees themselves viewed and used debt, Tanner suggests distinguishing between the ordinary debt system and what the company viewed as their burden of debt whereby they "carried" a hunter for many years.[14]

The system gave the company considerable monetary advantages over the hunters and was able to exercise control over them. Yet the hunters, too, had advantages, well known to the traders. The Crees were relatively demanding consumers and exercised control over the quality and kind of goods and even prices according to a complaint of D.C. McTavish, a Rupert's River district manager in 1896.[15] Competition between fur trade companies – the Hudson's Bay Company with the French and North West companies in the past, and Revillon Frères and independent traders to come in the next century – all helped to strengthen the hunter's hand. The company imposed its will best when this competition was not so evident, though on the southeastern reaches of the James Bay region, Mistassini and Waswanipi Crees could benefit from the rival trade to be found in the Lake St Jean settlements. The Crees' relatively modest and fixed needs also gave the hunter some measure of control over the Hudson's Bay Company, for the company always strove to encourage greater fur hunting and tried to increase a hunter's production.

MARKET DECLINE

Despite the company's incentives and the hunters' needs for a certain quantity of store goods, the trade in the last decades of the nineteenth century satisfied neither side. For the company, Arthur Ray has shown that these years, coinciding with a world depression, hit the fur markets hard. More significantly, the fur market was changing throughout the north of Canada. Whereas in the several hundred years before, beaver had been the prime fur traded, now it was muskrat, with beaver second in importance until 1890, and then displaced by marten and mink until about 1910. As to whether fashion or decreasing beaver numbers dictated the change in fur markets, there is evidence from James Bay and elsewhere in Canada to indicate that beaver stocks were in decline by the end of the century.[16] Hunting the much smaller muskrat meant a drastic decline in earnings for the Crees. In addition, they were forced to plan their hunting strategies around harvesting muskrats, not hunting for food. As the fur trade switched to an emphasis on small animals, the Crees suffered economic hardship and a down-sizing of their winter hunting groups and/or a shortening of the period when larger groups could winter together. These changes were gradual, as was the decline in the bush resources. For a while in the late 1800s, the Crees were still able to support themselves and their fur-trapping strategies through living off caribou.

An excellent reminder of the vast size and variation within the territory we call eastern James Bay is that all Crees did not experience the same years of bounty or deprivation. While the Crees living inland from the coast suffered greatly, those in the Mistassini and Waswanipi regions did not. In 1892 the district manager of Rupert's River wrote of "the heavy falling off that has taken place chiefly in Beaver and Otter" and noted that in the past three years "fully 20% of the Ruperts House Inland Indians having perished, the majority from starvation."[17] By contrast Low, the geological surveyor in the Mistassini region, commented on the availability of beaver still "found in considerable numbers" as were marten and mink.[18]

Caribou, the hunt and the meat, were the object of the Crees' premier hunting activity and food preference. Until the mid-1800s, Crees living near the limits of the treeline and blessed by a relative abundance of caribou[VII] were little involved in the fur trade, preferring to live off the by-products of the barren ground caribou herds. Then, for reasons still unclear, they began trading more regularly for furs which required them to spend more winters south in the forested regions. Thus by the late 1800s all the Indian hunters of the James and Hudson Bay region were full participants in the fur trade.

A major change in the trade items in the late 1800s was the addition of European foodstuffs, such as flour, sugar, oatmeal, and tea. Relatively little of these foods were traded though, because transportation costs made them expensive. In general, these items were used by the Coasters as opposed to Inlanders. For example, in the winter of 1864–5, Chizzo, a Coaster trading at Rupert House, left with two pounds of biscuits, three pounds of flour, and five pounds of oatmeal, while Diamin, identified as an Inlander, ordered two pounds of sugar, the only food charged to his account that year, and Cheemuttawaish purchased one and one-half pounds of biscuits. Both men, though, took out a considerable list of the other categories of store goods.[19] Moreover, the Coaster reliance on English foods is underestimated here as Coasters were paid in foodstuffs for their manual labour at the post. Coasters brought to the posts large supplies of country food such as caribou, fish, and ptarmigan, against which they took out supplies of flour, sugar, and oatmeal as well as ammunition, twine, and so on, often listed as "gratuities" in the account books.

What did the Crees of 1870 want from the Hudsons' Bay Company? The list, interestingly, is too lengthy to reproduce; in fact, it runs about 20 folios, but the most commonly traded ones are given below:

Manufactured Goods Traded at Fort George Post, 1870 (selected)	
Blankets, white 3 pt.	Guns, common NW flint
Capots, blanket, 3 ells	Gun powder TPF
Cloth: Cloth, coloured	Gun shot, asstd.
Coburg	Handkerchiefs, common cotton
Cotton, fancy printed	Kettles, tin, asstd. sizes
Cotton, grey shirting	Knives, roach, small
Cotton, white shirting	Mufflers, men fine woolen
Duffle, white	Needles, glovers
Druggets, striped	Ribbons, silk
Flannel, fine white	Shawls, asstd.
Hudson's Bay Blue Strouds	Shirts, mens common cotton
Hudson's Bay White "	Shirts, boys " "
Tartan, comm'n stuart	Spoons, tinned iron
Drawers, swanskin, long	Sugar crushed
Flour	Soap, yellow
Files	Threads, reels, coloured
Flints	Trousers, mens
Garters, worsted	Twine, Holland no. 1
Gun caps	Vests, mens plaid

Source: HBCA B.77/d/21, fos. 1d–12, 1870.

Omitted from this list are some of the more exotic items traded by only a few Crees, such as blue buck beads, a belt, a man's cap, essence of peppermint, powder horns, peppermint lozenges, tin pans, rings (finger) and tea. Tea soon became a prized commodity and a staple. To understand this we look to the comments of a Waswanipi Cree who referred to the "time before tea," when in the morning "we just drank the broth from what we cooked ... beaver, moose, rabbit, partridge and fish."[20] Anderson explained that for the Indians whose only beverage was a bouillon from meat or fish and water, tea was a "wonderful" drink and on the winter trail it became a "veritable nectar."[21] Axes, chisels, and traps (beaver and spring) are listed under "made up works" – that is, manufactured at the post – but only a few were traded of each item. By the turn of the century, new items turn up in circulation, such as canvas and Winchester rifles.[22] Without having precise accounting for the 1870s, it appears that the greatest expenditure was on cloth and/or clothing, with ammunition second. The value of all other items was significantly less.

The labour carried out by the Coasters was vital to the operation of the post and enabled the company to restrict the numbers of its overseas employees who had to be transported, fed, and clothed. The country food the hunters and their wives produced for the company was considerable and served the company well in reducing their shipments from England. Numerous jobs had to be performed to keep the post going: work such as logging, building, gardening, haying,[VIII] blacksmithing, manning boats, manufacture of canoes, sleighs, snowshoes and clothing, provisioning and transportation. Although for much of its history the company paid the Indian labourers for each task they performed, by the 1860s they had switched to a system of hiring Cree men and boys for a month at a time, usually during the summer months, and in 1888 began requiring the men to sign monthly engagements.[23] In these cases, the employees were given wages, such as ten or twelve MB ("made beaver")[IX] per month which could be converted into goods at the post. With these wages, advances were given, in some cases up to half the value of the month's wage.[24] Some years the labour needs were filled by bringing men from one post to work at another, as ten Fort George Crees were sent to Rupert House in the summer of 1895. Although difficult now to comment on wages in James Bay a century earlier, it is noteworthy that in the 1920s a district manager for the Hudson's Bay Company, George Ray, was critical of the "pitiful" wages paid at Fort George, which helps to understand why George McLeod, a hunter and monthly contract employee at Rupert House, quit in 1901 because of the low wages.[25] For most Coasters these wages, paid in imported foods and goods, were an additional, necessary support. The coastal lowlands were always poor in food resources and the increasing number of Crees who chose to hunt closer to the fur trade posts created additional strains on the land and people.

Most Crees, both men and women, worked for the post as provisioners. The women were either widows of hunters who camped close to the post or the wives of company servants. Undoubtedly, many other Cree women, traditionally the "fishermen" and snarers of small game, produced food for the post and castorum for trade, but they were not listed in the account books. Their goods and products would have been traded to the company under their husbands' names.

The payment to the Coasters was almost always in the form of European foodstuffs or ammunition, since the company had a long-standing policy to trade essential items (twine, clothing, guns) only for furs.[26] It was reasoned that the Coasters or Inlanders would neglect fur hunting, particularly of the small non-food animals, if they could obtain their supplies in other, less arduous ways. In this way, the Coaster population came to be reliant on supplies of flour, oatmeal, sugar, tobacco,

36 The White Man's Gonna Getcha

and pipes.[x] However, speaking of his early married life, with a young family, about 1900, Matthew Cowboy said he took inland 150 to 200 lbs. flour which he shared with his father-in-law's family. They ate a little flour every day "until by January it was gone. As long as we had matches and ammunition we did not care."[27]

The company store also sold trade goods to the post's servants and their families of whom there were about a half a dozen each year and usually all of them "country born" – of mixed ancestry – families with names such as Louttit, Wiegand, Chilton, McLeod, and Moar. These families did not generally remain at the same post but were moved around within and outside the company's districts. The company provisioned these people through the families' own efforts, as the servants' wives and children also hunted and fished for the post. For example, in 1881 the Mistassini journal reports that the "wives returned from Pepuneshawin with lots of fish which is a very good job for us."[28]

All the goods had a standard mark-up. In a 1858 account book the cost of each item was listed along with its price at a 33 1/3 percent mark-up and a 50 percent mark-up. The first was the price charged to servants, the second to Indians. Thus, a gun that cost the company 35 shillings was sold to the servants at 46s.8d and to the Cree hunters at 52s.6d. This differential treatment[xi] raised the ire of the Crees. When Père Guinard began visiting Waswanipi in 1907 and witnessed the arrival of the store goods by canoe brigade, he observed that the company servants were given the first opportunity to select and purchase the merchandise. It was only then that the hunters were invited into the store. This discrimination, Guinard said, produced discontent amongst the Crees who grumbled amongst themselves but did not take any action.[29]

Needless to say, the company was buying furs at one price and generally selling them higher on the world markets. However, with poor communication between London and the posts, until the advent of the telegraph the company was unable to alter the prices it paid the hunters to reflect the fluctuations in the market. Thus, during these final years of the nineteenth century the fur prices appear stable from one year to the next.

A commonly held view is that the Hudson's Bay Company exploited the Indians in the sense they made large profits from the furs.[30] To tackle this issue for the eastern James Bay region would require a full accounting of prices, sales, and costs, well beyond the parameters of this inquiry. To his credit, Arthur Ray took on this daunting task and investigated profitability in the context of the finances of the whole of the Hudson's Bay Company's fur trade operation from 1870 to 1885. He learned that in 1876 the company suffered a loss, but in the remaining years it earned what he deems a very modest return on investment. Accordingly, Ray sees a conservatism in their outlook that he suggests caused them to lag behind as new competitors were gaining ground.[31] Undoubtedly the company, over the long run, did turn a profit, for it was able to withstand competition in the first half of the twentieth century. However, the profits were relatively small and, unlike other extractive companies operating in mining or agriculture, the company incurred social costs to maintain its involvement in the fur business, a fact recognized by Tough in his several discussions of the company paternalism.[32]

CREE–COMPANY RELATIONS

The most significant social cost was the sharing of food and throughout most of the company's history, until well into the twentieth century, it worked both ways. When Crees from inland were starving and were able to send camp members to the post, the company gave them food. Food-sharing was a strong Cree principle to which the company men adhered, for they, too, were very often beneficiaries. Some Crees were simply helped, as this directive indicates: "There are a few widows and orphans and one or two old men in the district who should receive a net and a little ammunition annually to prevent them starving, but only those who have no relations able to help them, are entitled to the above."[33]

Handouts of food were given, but these same men and women were also residing in the vicinity of the post and supplying it with fish, eggs, and berries. In company parlance they were known as the dependants and never numbered very many. Even in the 1930s, as bleak a period as ever documented for the Crees, David Cooter, trader then at Mistassini, commented that there were never more than ten elderly men receiving assistance and two of them were former employees.[34] Even by the standards of the day, the level of assistance the company provided was meagre. E.B. Borron, an Ontario magistrate, was sent on several expeditions, beginning in the late 1870s, to report on the conditions of the "natives and others" in the Moose River basin as part of Ontario's claim to this northern territory. In his 1890 report he is critical of the Hudson's Bay Company's seeming unwillingness "to promote their temporal welfare comfort and happiness" and he pitied the widows and children of the company servants. On the other hand, his comments remind us that for the company "trade, not government or the administration of justice, was their chief or only function."[35] One should inquire whether in the 1890s British companies in the home country were expected to provide economic security for their employees or producers. What the company did, in terms of food handouts and other necessities, it did in the knowledge that dead hunters do not provide furs. However, by providing for the non-hunters, it also created expectations and a practice from which the company would later find it difficult to extricate themselves. As Rosemary Ommer pointed out, a necessary interdependent relationship developed between merchants and indigenous peoples which was mediated through the credit system and helped form the staple economies of the New World.[36]

THE POSTS

There were either seven or eight posts operating at any one time in eastern James and Hudson Bays in the last three decades of the nineteenth century. Little Whale River continued serving mainly Inuit, but in 1870 it received an increased number of Crees. They had been trading at Great Whale River before its closure that year because of the failed whaling (belugas) venture. However, in 1880 the company officials decided to close Little Whale River and reopen the one at Great Whale River. The mainland Inuit (as opposed to the ones on the Belcher Islands) objected to this proposed change because of distance and threatened to go to Fort Chimo on Ungava Bay which was reopened in 1867.[XII] Finally, in 1889 the company reported they were able to proceed with these plans and Little Whale River closed in 1890.[37]

Fort George was upgraded to a trading post again in 1870, drawing back the Crees to the north of this post who had been trading at Great Whale River. Similarly, Eastmain, which had been a central post in the region from 1717 to 1837 and had been closed in favour of Fort George, reopened following a decision by the southern council of the company at their meeting at Moose Factory in 1870. Furs were not the motivating factor; this action was taken because of Eastmain's favourable location for raising cattle and procuring geese. Those Crees whose hunting lands lay to the south of the post and had been trading at Rupert House switched back – for example, families such as Georgeskish and Chizzo who a generation or two earlier been associated with Eastmain before it was closed.[38] There was some consideration to closing it again in 1891 because of poor fur returns and because the countryside was poor in food resources. Instead, the company decided to maintain it as a refuge for Rupert House people who hunted in that vicinity but phased out the livestock by sending the cattle to other posts.[39]

Rupert House did not undergo any changes at this time and in fact maintained its central role as the supply post for the more southern and inland posts of Mistassini and Waswanipi. An outpost of Waswanipi was Migiskan, which had opened in 1828 to stem rival traders from the south.[40] It was closed in 1891 because of poor fur returns and in the expectation that the company could send a trader from Waswanipi to meet the Migiskan hunters there in the spring.[41] The other post that drew interior peoples was Nichikun, Fort Nascopie having been closed about 1870.[42] The company did consider relocating Nichikun because they found it extremely costly to operate. They were then paying each voyageur about fifty made beavers and found it difficult to recruit men at that price.

The Rupert House to Nichikun supply route was by far the most difficult, a total of over five hundred miles. The canoe trips were extremely arduous and dangerous; over the centuries of operations, numbers of Cree men died from the strain of the work or from drowning, and desertion was a constant problem.[43] Nevertheless, Nichikun continued operation until 1913 when it was closed because of transportation difficulties. It reopened in 1937 when independent traders began flying into the area and continued as a post until 1953.[44] In 1940 the Nichikun and the Neoskewskau Crees were encouraged by the Department of Indian Affairs to move to Mistassini during the summer months. To replace Nichikun in 1913 Neoskweskau, a post that had been abandoned in 1821 with the merger of the North West Company, was reopened; it was located one hundred and fifty miles closer to Rupert House and easier to supply. It was closed in 1940.[45] In 1891 the company had to abandon plans to reopen the outpost at Lake Nemiscau as there were "not enough Indians to man the brigade." Finally, at the end of February 1902 four men were sent there by dog team with building materials to erect a small store.[46]

NEW INTRUDERS

In the declining years of the nineteenth century, the Hudson's Bay Company held its monopoly over the trade in much of the James Bay region. In the south, hunters who normally traded at Mistassini and Waswanipi had the option of bartering their furs in the Lake St Jean region. Settlement in the region, based on logging and sawmills, had expanded in the mid-1800s, as a result of a combination of the gradual move northwards of the forest industry and the building of a Quebec–Lake St Jean Railway in the 1880s.[47] Competition in this region was not a new situation because the Mistassini and Waswanipi Crees had long taken advantage of the posts on the other side of the height of land, be they competitors' or other company posts. These posts were too far from the heart of the James Bay trade for their managers to maintain effective communication and could inform each other of a hunter acquiring debt at two posts. However, now this competition was different, based as it was on permanent settlement. Nor was it necessary for the Crees to travel to Lake St Jean; free traders now came into Mistassini territory, including St John Indians who "do a good deal of petty trading."[48] In this region, the Crees were also in touch with other Indians, principally the Algonquins and Montagnais who traded at the posts in settled areas, such as Abitibi and Bersimis.[49] To develop easier communication with regions to the south, by 1892 the company was attempting to find a route to Lake Chamouchouane, on the other side of the height of land, that would permit it to bring in provisions from Lake St Jean.[50]

East of Waswanipi and Mistassini, the region was more isolated from the economic activities of southern Canada. The only threat to the company's monopoly was the occasional, informal trade that individual Cree hunters made with others, such as The Mink and Caunashesh, who traded with some Bersimis people they met in the winter.[51] Aside from the resident traders and missionaries there was no reason for others to travel through the territory. However, this isolation came to an end with two related developments.

The fledgling country of Canada was made up of four provinces in 1867. It recognized the economic potential of its untapped resources of the hinterland. Enormous political pressure was brought on the Hudson's Bay Company to surrender its vast holdings, known as Rupert's Land. In 1870 the company's subarctic lands were unilaterally transferred to the government of Canada; the Indian, Metis, and Inuit residents were neither consulted nor informed. The Dominion government gradually turned over the northern territories to Ontario (1897 and 1902) and Quebec (1898 and 1912). Although each province was required in acts of Parliament to validate this transfer of lands by obtaining surrender of the aboriginal right to it, only Ontario entered into a treaty (No. 9) with its Indian population in 1905–6. Quebec did not, as it was believed that as aboriginal title had not been recognized in New France, it was forever extinguished.[XIII] Thus, for the period of this history the James Bay territory was unceded Indian land, albeit more a Cree perspective than a Euro-Canadian one, as will be seen. The final episode in establishing Quebec's boundaries occurred in 1927 when the Judicial Committee of the Privy Council in Britain ruled that a large inland chunk of the Quebec-Labrador Peninsula belonged to Newfoundland, thereby creating political boundaries for several bands of Montagnais/Innu, Naskapis, and Inuit.

The second development was the opening of the Canadian Pacific Railway line in 1886, located a mere ten-day journey south of Moose Factory. Hand-in-hand with the development of the railway was the advent of the telegraph. The first to make use of this easier access to

James Bay were surveyors for the Geological Survey of Canada, founded in 1842. Their activities of exploration and surveying began in James Bay in 1877, marked by a bland entry in the Rupert House records: "July 13, The Geological Survey depart for Little Whale River."[52] The next year the area was surveyed by Robert Bell, the veteran explorer, geologist, naturalist, and physician.[53] On that first expedition he travelled to Portland Point in the vicinity of Great Whale River. Ten years later he was succeeded by A.P. Low and three others who were there for a "short look around." Miles Spencer, the post manager at Fort George, was glad to see them "as we have not had a stranger here since summer 1877, and we enjoy the company."[54]

Albert P. Low, more than any other surveyor, is identified with the charting of the Quebec-Labrador peninsula. In this region he achieved the plotting of three great rivers – the Eastmain, Koksoak, and Hamilton – and described the movement of the ice sheets and the iron deposits along the Koksoak River.[55] Although a number of scientists explored the Quebec-Labrador peninsula, it was not until Jacques Rousseau's scientific studies in the 1940s and 1950s that fresh information would be provided.[XIV]

Low's first arrival in James Bay must have created a sensation, given that he appeared at Mistassini in the evening of 23 December 1884 with a party of twelve men. The surveyors used the post as a base, with Low living at the manager's house. Throughout the winter two surveying parties came and went led either by Low or F.H. Bignell. Each time they departed or returned to the post, Mr Miller, the post manager, gave a feast in their honour, as on 13 May 1885, when he inscribed in his journal that it was "very nice bear meat."[56] According to Zaslow there were disputes between the two, with Low going south to Ottawa in the spring and returning with instructions to complete the survey.[XV]

As is usually the case, little is known of the men who guided and advised Low and the other surveyors. At Mistassini, on his first expedition, Charley guided Low while two men, Chechwish and Isaac, were the guides for Burgess, another of the surveyors. As well, Mr Wigand, a company servant, spent some time with the Bignell party surveying Little Mistassini Lake. Also serving Bignell was Wigand's wife who was "washing for the Old Gentleman."[57] Then in 1888, on his way through Fort George, Low asked Rupert and his brother Waskyagan to take his boat to Great Whale River while the surveyors travelled there in "wooden" canoes.[58] A few years later Low used the services of two Iroquois canoemen on the Great and Little Whale rivers and found that because of the centuries-old fear of the Iroquois, he had difficulty in engaging Cree men to join the surveying party, though they eventually did.[59]

The next geological team through the east coast region was a party of four from the University of Wisconsin on their way to Richmond Gulf in 1909. They were accompanied to Fort George by an "Eastmain Indian," Achinaya, and taken north by John Fireman and his family. The Firemans were inland hunters trading at Great Whale River. This expedition is well documented in a book by the two brothers who headed the geological team, Charles and Arthur Leith, entitled *A Summer and Winter on Hudson Bay*. It has been drawn upon here for some insights into early twentieth-century life.

Inuit[XVI] were also involved in guiding strangers north along the James and Hudson bay coasts. Hence a cryptic comment from the Rupert House records indicates that on 18 February 1898 a "husky" (Inuit)[XVII] and the Americans arrived at Rupert House. Five days later mention was made of their being off to Moose Factory, having hired the company dog team to take them for $25. A year later an entry states that a Mr Jones, having arrived by sailboat from Moose Factory, was anxious to leave for Whale River to take up some mining claims on the coast before some Americans could.[60] Thus, eagerly seeking their fortune and not always accounted for in the post journals, adventurous but mercenary men were traversing the territory by canoe.[XVIII] So numerous were the men coming in to the entire James Bay region that one anthropologist, Alanson Skinner,[XIX] had great difficulty in arranging for a canoe to Moose Factory and complained that "the country is so overrun with prospectors." A few days later, he wrote from Missinabie, that his was the first of twenty parties heading up to Moose Factory for various reasons.[61]

Others entered the James Bay territory through the southeast. Their mission was not always clear, though sometimes it was just for adventure. The Labrador region hosted a number of "explorers," usually from the northeast of the United States, such as Mina Benson Hubbard, the widow of Leonidas Hubbard, who in 1905 retraced the route of her husband's ill-fated expedition through Labrador.[62] Earlier, in 1881 a Professor Galbraith arrived from Lake St Jean but his purpose was not identified.[63] On the other hand, Mr Edward G. Bell was a tourist, for he was described in the Mistassini records as "A Gentleman from the States … on a pleasure trip to the Bay and home by Moose River … he is to stay here until Monday as he wants to get Bread made and washing done."[64] Similarly, the same post journals two years later make note of "a Gentleman that came here yesterday on a pleasure walk all the way from Boston," adding that he was stopping because he had a sore leg.[65] This intrepid walker was William Brooks Cabot who made this winter overland trek from Lake St Jean in the company of two Indian companions, one of whom was John Bastian. This was his first of many journeys throughout the Quebec-Labrador peninsula that he undertook until 1920, sometimes alone, sometimes in the company of Montagnais or Naskapi families.[66] Unfortunately we do not know the identity of the "gentleman and his lady [who] came from lake St John."[67] Mistakenly, J.W. Anderson, the Mistassini post manager, reported his guests in 1916 were "probably the first tourists ever to visit." They were not, but the two, Mr Justice Ramsey and Mr Milo R.M. Chamberlain of New York, arrived in relative luxury, accompanied in two canoes with "six French Canadian and Metis guides," stayed one day and returned south.[68]

To late twentieth-century urban dwellers, accounts of these Euro-Canadian and American travellers of a century ago conjure up images of heroism and adventure. Perhaps, for the Crees, too, they were objects of fascination: different in their activities, dress, and manner than the few Hudson's Bay Company traders who lived among them. As much as they served as curiosities for the Crees and as beneficial in terms of bringing in other interests that challenged the monopolistic control of the company, their presence ultimately spelled doom for an unknown number of Crees. These early trail-blazers unwittingly provided the passage by which disease could enter this hitherto isolated region.

LITANY OF EPIDEMIC DISEASES

Whooping cough had hit the coastal people in 1858 from Moose Factory to Little Whale River. Bishop Horden had commented that this epidemic had caused greater mortality amongst the children of the company servants than the Indian children,[69] presumably because the Cree children were off in the bush. A whooping cough epidemic struck again in 1884 with less grave consequences but the same year a skin disease laid up most of the hunters in the fall. The following spring, Miles Spencer of Fort George in a letter to his superior, James Cotter at Moose Factory, head of the Southern Department, remarked that most of the Indians and Inuit had suffered from a "a great deal of sickness."[70] An epidemic described variously as a cold or "la grippe" made life miserable for people in Rupert House in 1891 and two died.[71] On 19 June 1895 whooping cough was once again reported at Moose Factory and by 3 August many at Rupert House had it and were dying.[72] Three years later, Rupert House people, as elsewhere, suffered from scrofula and that same month chicken pox made its appearance.[73] In 1900 influenza struck and was said to have "decimated the hunters attached to Fort George." One reason given for these twenty-nine deaths was that the Cree were already much weakened by being "riddled with scrofula" (tuberculosis of the lymph nodes). The influenza epidemic continued into the following winter and was compounded by a scarcity of caribou, so people trading at both Fort George and Nichikun died of starvation.[74] Further south at Rupert House, a measles epidemic invaded from Moose Factory where nineteen had died. Consequently, in January 1901 the company offered the carpenter's shed as a quarantine but the journals make no comments about the results. By 1902 a devastating measles epidemic was raging along the coast, leaving many dead and others considerably weakened. W.G. Walton, the Anglican minister, described it as a cruel time when there was not a tent where they were not mourning; he estimated one hundred had died at Great Whale River and Fort George. Walton's wife and four children came down with the measles and the eldest child died.[75] At Rupert House there were more than sixty cases and fourteen deaths by the fall.

This tragic tale of sickness and death continued. By 1906 people had to be buried outside the cemetery at Fort George; it was too full.[76] In Leith's recounting of the 1903 measles epidemic, which he must have heard about but also read in the post's Great Whale River journals for that year, he also commented that tuberculosis was prevalent but practically ignored by the Crees. He told of people in advanced stages of the disease, "working without murmur ... They literally die in harness."[77] In 1908 at Rupert House, Alanson Skinner was readying to return to Moose Factory but was detained because "a violent pestilence" broke out at Moose Factory among the five to six hundred people assembled there and "they began to die off." He never identified this illness but remarked that "even whites died" as there was no medical attention.[78]

Whatever was in the arsenal of both the Cree shamans and the English traders and missionaries was obviously not powerful enough to stop the deaths. Cree medicines were primarily derived from plants and animals products, but it is not known what specifically was tried in these cases. Nor could the traders or missionaries offer much more than consolation. They did dispense pills and had a relatively up-to-date collection of so-called cures at the post. The list of treatments and medicines at Little Whale River in the 1860s is impressive, including pill machines, numerous powders, salts, acids, and ointments and even strychnine, opium, and chloroform,[79] none of which was effective against these deadly pathogens. There were no doctors or any other kind of professional medical help at the posts, a fact which the Leiths decried as "One of the most astonishing features of the control of the Hudson's Bay Company,"[80] though it is unlikely early twentieth-century medicine could have stopped the epidemics.

The illnesses and deaths in this period are almost certainly attributable to the increased flow of outsiders coming to James Bay, the longer summer visits to the post by the Crees, and possibly the change in diet which resulted in a weakened and more vulnerable population. Moose Factory was the entry point and illnesses seem to have spread from there. The people at the posts were aware that diseases were spread in this way. The 1901 epidemic of influenza was blamed on mining prospectors and in 1904 it came into Fort George with the winter mail. In fact, two Cree men who arrived at Eastmain with a supply of ducks in 1902 were immediately sent away to prevent their contracting measles.[81] The writer of the 1902–3 report for Mistassini feared the epidemics would "now become more or less a feature of the Indian trade as civilization extends north and travel through the Indian country becomes common."[82] Of course, the disease was not spread only by outsiders; the Crees also became carriers. In John Kawapit's Great Whale River narrative of the early 1900s he recalled his family's meeting with others who had been at Fort Chimo where they had fallen ill and now the Kawapit family was stricken "with the sickness [the flu he thought] that the men had brought back with them from the post."[83]

Unquestionably, the Crees suffered great hardship in this period. The scarcity of caribou and the resulting periods of starvation must have left them more susceptible to disease without even considering the "virgin soil" phenomenon.[xx] How grave starvation was is summed up in the remark that in the three years from 1889 to 1891, "fully 20% of the Ruperts House Indians have perished, the majority from starvation."[84] Conversely, the sickness and deaths would have left them very weakened and demoralized, thereby impeding their ability to hunt and feed themselves, not to mention their inability to gather firewood for cooking and heating. This weakened state also affected the trader and his family at Great Whale River, for while they were laid up in bed with the measles, their house burned down.[85] Despite tragic episodes, life in James Bay carried on, thanks to Cree resilience and fortitude and the flexibility of their social institutions.

GLIMPSES OF CREE LIFE IN THE LATE NINETEENTH CENTURY

Depicting Cree life in eastern James Bay in this late-nineteenth-century period relies on two ethnographic accounts. Lucien Turner, identified as a naturalist, was at Fort Chimo from 1882 to 1884 keeping meteorological records for the US Signal Corps. Little is known about him but he did produce an ethnographic account of the Ungava district which the Smithsonian Institution published in 1894. Turner's descriptions of material culture and folklore are of both the Inuit and the Naskapi. Although there are valuable observations, his comments about the people, certainly of the Indians, have to be read with caution.

Turner was not an admirer of the people he wrote about so his accounts, besides being questionable, are devoid, for the most part, of interesting narratives or insights. On the assumption that he could not converse with too many Crees or Naskapis in English, it is doubtful he carried out much credible research, as he could not speak Cree. For example, he reports: "Owing to the impossibility of getting a reliable person to teach me the language of these people I was able to procure but few words."[86] One can only presume that in matters other than descriptions of material objects or hunting techniques, Turner obtained most of his information from the Hudson's Bay Company trader at Fort Chimo who, according to the geographer Alan Cooke,[87] made a practice of making derogatory comments about the Naskapis.

Anthropologists in Quebec are not decided on whether the Crees-Montagnais-Naskapis had at one time been the same people even though the three groups had different experiences in their contact with non-natives. In Turner's view there were three Indian groups, with distinct boundaries, inhabiting the Ungava region who, differed "but slightly in speech, and even less in habits." These three he identified as the Mountaineers or Montagnais, the Indians to the southwest of the Ungava who differed the most in speech from the Montagnais, and, the Ne né not, whose customs and speech differed slightly from their neighbours. Further, he observed that members of the second group, those whom he only names once as Little Whale River Indians, had in recent years moved eastward to dwell near or with the Naskapis because the caribou had become so scarce in the vicinity of Fort George.[88] Even more intriguing is Turner's recounting of the Naskapi tradition that they originated north of an immense river (the St Lawrence, he suggests) but remnants of them were driven farther north by Iroquois attacks before the advent of the white traders. They moved into the land of the Inuit which initiated armed conflicts that only in the nineteenth century were waning, leaving them with a mutual fear of each other.[89] Some of these details are found in the Jesuit Relations, which inform us that the northern area in 1660 had become a refuge "where various Algonquin Nations sought a retreat, fleeing from the Iroquois,"[90] and indeed, until the mid-1800s the Crees and Inuit regularly raided each others' camps, terrorizing each other in what the company men referred to as the Esquimaux hunts.[91] Clearly, the early relations of the people of James Bay and elsewhere in the Quebec-Labrador peninsula is a subject that needs further attention.

Linguists working on dialects in this region have, as Turner, divided them into three dialects of the language they refer to as Montagnais or East Cree.[92] However, within these very general categories, there were differences first documented by the linguist Truman Michelson following his research along the coast in 1935. Focusing on a hunter, Oliver Loutit, born at Fort George, Michelson reported he could understand the Great Whale River dialect better than Eastmain's. For Loutit, the Rupert House dialect was intelligible but Eastmain's easier to understand. The Fort Chimo speakers were hard to understand. As for differences between Fort George and Great Whale River, David Masty (from Great Whale River) told him "with his eyes closed and disregarding the voices which he might recognize, he could tell whether a man was speaking Ft. George dialect or G.W.R." Masty also said he could understand only a little of the Nichikun dialect. When he shifted his research to Rupert House and interviewed Andrew Wapatchee, born upriver from there, Michelson learned that Waswanipi and Mistassini Cree are very close to the Rupert House dialect although Eastmain is a little closer.[93]

At the time Turner was living in Ungava the Naskapis were still fashioning their tools, dwellings, and clothing from the resources obtained from the land and these he describes in great detail. He reported that they, "like all other Indians ... are inordinately fond of tobacco for smoking, chewing and snuff."[94] The men considered it as essential in hunting as ammunition and expected a gift of it on arriving at the trading post.

Turner's monograph is an important description of late-nineteenth-century material culture and an offering of some of the stories told, a good number of which connect back to accounts in the seventeenth-century Jesuit Relations, such as eat-all feasts with eating-all showing respect for the caribou and the men feasting first, followed by the women. In connection with this feasting, Turner posits that it is held by one who has been unusually successful in the hunting of fur-bearing animals, so the purpose of the feast is to display his wealth. This reference to wealth is also to be found in Turner's mention of hunters keeping parts of prized kills, such as a claw or the tip of an ear[XXI] which serve as a "token of the wealth."[95] However, the anthropologist Adrian Tanner suggests that Turner was likely told these tokens were prized as representing a hunter's "power."[96] On the other hand, he could be making assumptions about the feast celebrating wealth that were more characteristic of his European society rather than Cree or Naskapi.

A different account of the same period comes from a chronicle of one woman's life. Ellen Smallboy, born sometime in the 1850s, lived to the south of James Bay (today in Ontario). The anthropologist Regina Flannery first met her at Moose Factory in 1933 where she recorded her life history. This account primarily focuses on her early married years with Simon Smallboy, her husband of fifty years. This takes us back to the 1880s and 1890s. She provided detailed information about the Indians' material culture: making nets, birchbark baskets, fish traps, rabbit-skin weaving. The history, though, is really an account of coping under a variety of situations, all the more interesting because it provides a woman's perspective.

When she was about twelve, Ellen's father became weak from an unspecified illness, so her mother and two sisters had to run the winter camp. Although Ellen and her sisters were very proficient at women's work, they needed to transport their father by toboggan to the lake edge for him to instruct them in the arduous task of setting nets beneath the ice. After his death, Ellen, her mother, and sister lived with her older married sister. However, the women provided as much as possible for themselves. Over time, Ellen became adept at using a gun and would track and stalk caribou.[97]

Ellen enjoyed especially the springtime when several winter hunting groups would gather to fish and share their catch. It was a time when those arriving "poor and starving" would get fat again. She explained[98] that on a diet only of rabbits one would starve but "to live on fish alone you can be healthy."[XXII]

The roles between men and women were not as strictly defined as introductory anthropology texts lead us to believe. Ellen spoke of her significant role in securing food and attributed this to the help she received from her father-in-law and his mother, now elderly (in 1899), who remained at the camp with the children. She spoke warmly of her father-in-law, missing him terribly when he died and this rare insight into personal relations is further enriched with her speaking so affectionately of her father to whom she felt closer than to her "short-tempered" mother.[99]

Ellen Smallboy was also an ethnologist, pointing out that some practices of the Moose Factory Crees differed from those at Rupert House. At a caribou feast held at Hannah Bay, halfway between the two posts, she felt sorry for the Rupert House women who were proscribed from eating the choicest parts of the animal, namely the head and foreparts. No such prohibition governed her eating and she invited the women to her tent to feast on all parts of the animal. According to her, their husbands were amused by this because "it wasn't their hunt." She also reported that sharing food was a strong Cree ethic. She mentioned it several times and spoke disapprovingly of times when this tradition was disregarded, either when parents appropriated all the food instead of sharing it with their children or when a husband did so alone.[XXIII] Similarly, she condemned other Crees who mistreated orphans.[100]

As one reads of Ellen Smallboy's life as a youngster and then a young woman, one is struck by how few of her recollections were about the Moose Factory post. Flannery had asked her to speak of her life, leaving it up to her to choose her subjects. Seemingly, Ellen thought the stories regarding her life at French River (her husband's hunting grounds) of more consequence than what transpired at the post. Such a disregard for the activities at the post is not at all surprising but serves as a reminder of how sadly Eurocentric our histories of northern life are, reliant as they are on the post journals.

The quality of life on the land portrayed in Ellen Smallboy's account should not be construed as descriptive of the situation in all of eastern James Bay. The Smallboy camp was on French River close to Moose Factory, a region that presumably was somewhat densely populated and thus without sufficient animal resources for everyone. More importantly, different regions produced varying quantities of game and this produced differences in how comfortable life was for the Crees of specific regions.

Ellen Smallboy's life history also served as one of the testimonies Flannery collected which enabled her to publish an article in 1935 on the contemporary position of women in James Bay. She writes that although women were not considered to be owners of hunting territories, except in special cases, a wife did enjoy "full disposition of everything her husband provides," referring to game, and in this respect she judged women as having "equal rights with the man." Socially, Cree men were said to look down on women and considered their affairs trivial, but in practice they were left alone to conduct such activities as child-rearing, food-procuring, and managing the household as they pleased. Politically and religiously the men were the leaders, although the women could and did take positions, depending on their ability and personality, since neither religion nor political leadership were institutionalized. No formality pertained to divorce and the women were as free as the men to leave. As women were also important food providers, Flannery judges that their status was "fairly equal to that of the man."[101]

Thirty years later another anthropologist at Rupert House wrote of the more pliant gender lines. Although Crees recalled for him that in the early part of this century women set traps for fine furs and joined in the caribou drives, they were less likely to do so in the 1960s due to improved technology and better forms of transport. However, he observed that due to the increased number of children a woman now had, the younger and middle-aged married men were regularly preparing bottles and changing diapers, along with chopping firewood. Certainly they were always helping out with the wife's chores when she was pregnant, sick, or old. There were limits to this blurring of gender roles; Knight remarked that when a Cree from Moose Factory accompanied his wife on a visit to Rupert House and, walking with her, carried the baby, the village consensus was that he was being "overly English." The way the local people explained to him the differences in male and female roles was in terms of "practicality rather than appropriateness." Thus he was told that men did not dry skins; if they did they would not have the time to trap.[102]

DWINDLING ANIMAL RESOURCES

The Anglican minister, the Reverend W.G. Walton, resident at Fort George from 1892 to 1924, was struck by how much the native peoples' living conditions deteriorated during his thirty-two-year residence, particularly for the Inuit. He became so wedded to the idea of introducing a small herd of domesticated reindeer to the barren grounds, as had been done in Alaska, that he was nicknamed "Reindeer Walton."[103] He seems to have had the support of the federal government, but the logistics defeated him and the reindeer got no farther than southern Baffin Island, where they wandered and mingled with the caribou.[104]

From information he learned from Natives, company men, and surveyors, Walton attributed the decline of the immense herds of barren ground caribou to the east of Hudson Bay either to fires that spread about 1883 or some widespread disease. By contrast, Low and Flaherty deduce that the drastic decline was caused when the main herd shifted from their usual summering in the highlands of the northeast coast of Hudson Bay to the eastern slope of Ungava Bay.[105] William Duncan Strong, an anthropologist who spent part of the winter of 1927 with the Naskapis of the Labrador coast, wrote that the caribou had greatly decreased in the past ten to fifteen years. His hosts had several explanations for this decline, including recent over-hunting by the Indians[XXIV] and disrespect for the caribou by "long-dead Indians" who, having killed large numbers of caribou, did not take proper care of their bones, leaving them in piles. The caribou smelled these bones and did not return.[106] Recent investigations into caribou behaviour indicate that about every generation or so the barren ground caribou undergo dramatic oscillations in numbers.[107] The Crees, particularly those living in the northern reaches of their territory close to the treeline, repeatedly told of the hardship caused by the loss of their principal food resource.

John Kawapit's account of the caribou takes us through the process of the dwindling numbers. John Kawapit, a hunter at Great Whale River, was born around 1903 and ascribes his story to the time when he was old enough to have killed four caribou on the lake (Chagoonobin) on which they lived but was still too young to know how to cut them up. "That was the beginning of the decline of the tundra caribou. We waited around all winter for them where they used to come during their migrations. We had a few from time to time and soon we did not see any caribou."[108] It is a striking account of the disappearance of the caribou when compared to his previous several hours of stories relating caribou kills of ten, even forty caribou in one day and large gatherings of people. Whether stories of starvation dominated the internal mind set of the Crees prior to the late 1800s is not known, but it certainly came to dominate it, understandably, for the next century.

The declining years of the nineteenth century and those of the early twentieth century were, for many Crees, years of misery and starvation. Hannah Natachequon, born in the 1890s into a family trading at Great Whale River, remembered Reverend Walton wiping away tears at one of the prayer meetings as he talked of people he loved dearly who had died one of the most awful deaths by starvation.[109] Walton noted that 150 people starved to death in 1892-3 south of Fort Chimo and seven from the Cape Jones area, over on the Hudson Bay side.[110]

Fort George people, too, have recollections from grandparents of times when the caribou had been more plentiful but then disappeared. They also learned that the Crees survived because families in the early 1900s altered their winter hunting strategies. Whereas formerly they had wintered in larger hunting groups, they now formed smaller groups of one and two families and looked to fish, ptarmigan, and hare[xxv] as their main food sources. Or, as John Kawapit expressed it, "Then the people were sure that the caribou were not coming around this area like they used to. We parted there to look for a good fishing area."[111]

As one travelled southwards in the James Bay territory, it seems as though food sources during these latter years of the 1800s were more reliable than in the north. John Blackned[xxvi] at Rupert House talked of the time during his youth in the early 1900s. He believed the Fort George people were the poorest then, followed by Eastmain and Rupert House, with Inlanders faring better than Coasters.[112] These differences were presumably due to the changing ecological conditions as one moved south. The fewer caribou in the north, the less reliance the Cree hunters placed on them as a staple food in favour of a more mixed harvest of small animals. Nevertheless there were years of great deprivation also in the south, some of it presumably aggravated by the epidemics that were coming in from the south.

If one goes back to almost a generation before John Blackned's birth in 1894 and his eyewitness accounts, one finds in the journals of the early 1880s that the Inlanders trading at Rupert House suffered terribly. A number lost their furs because they were reduced to singeing and eating the skins. One starving woman was said not only to have eaten her family's and others' cache of furs but also to have killed her children and eaten them.[113] This phenomenon came up again in the post journals in 1900 when a hunter was said to have hanged himself after he had gone mad and tried to kill and eat his children. McTavish uttered some suspicious comments at the end of March of that year suggesting that his sons had killed the man, as they were afraid to stay alone and were refusing to bring in his body. The following year, Frank confided to McTavish his concern that if he went far from the post he was fearful, "as he feels like turning cannibal."[114] No more was said of this but 1900–1 was a very harsh winter with a number of deaths due to sickness and starvation.

Cannibalism is one aspect of the Cree/Algonquian complex *witiko* phenomenon. The *witiko* (or *windigo* in Ojibwa dialect) is a monster-like creature that may eat humans or possess them spiritually so that they become cannibals. Writers distinguish witiko from starvation cannibalism, the difference being that witikos crave human flesh when there is other food available. The killing of such a person, so possessed, was considered justifiable.[115] It has been questioned whether it described an actual phenomenon, a psychotic state, or a form of social control. Preston, writing of eastern James Bay, discounts the belief as being anything more than of a non-specifiable figure, akin to the notion of the Christian devil.[116] However, Flannery, working amongst the western James Bay Cree in the 1930s, collected twelve accounts of the witiko, including three from Rupert House, a number of which she accepts as having occurred as they were *tipachiman* stories and the narrators recognized the difference between witiko and starvation cannibalism. Furthermore, she commented that east coast people did not readily volunteer details of cannibalistic behaviour, attributing this reticence to the fact that a Cree man from either Eastmain or Rupert House who had killed someone with such cannibalistic cravings was still living and would have feared legal retribution.[117]

These few cases from the Hudson's Bay Company records do not provide an actual witness to killings by such a possessed individual. That the Cree believed in a cannibalistic spirit is, of course, testimony to the dread that the thought of starvation held for them. Flannery informs us that "the winter component of the seasonal round produces stressful situations which are dealt with on both practical and symbolic levels ... For the Cree the witiko complex functions as both a symbolic expression of the dangers and isolation inherent in a subarctic existence and as a means of rationalizing fear and explaining deviant behavior."[118]

The years 1882 and 1883 also were harsh ones. The Coasters at Rupert House were said to be very hard up for food though not furs. Had

53 James Bay at the End of the Nineteenth Century

a Rupert House Coaster, John Neeshapees, remained at the coast, he too might have been starving. Instead he wintered with some Whale River Indians and perished with twelve others.[119] As for the most southerly regions, the Waswanipi and Mistassini Crees may not have suffered to the same extent. Waswanipi, according to the early records, had been one of the poorest regions, devoid of caribou. In 1827 the post manager noted that "people die each season."[120] The Crees were forced to resort to hare and fish for their food and clothing, an indication of impoverishment by Cree standards. Yet by the next century, in contrast to other Cree bands, their fortunes had improved. This reversal is attributable to the arrival of the moose in their hunting territories; the oral narratives date events according to before and after the moose.[121]

Moose had been absent from the James Bay region from the earliest days of the Hudson's Bay Company's post journals that began in the early eighteenth century, though we know of their earlier presence through the Jesuit Relations; indeed, Father Charles Albanel in 1671-2[122] and the Crees had designated the area as "Moosonee." Moose began to reappear in the southern portions only in the late 1800s, which is why Low described them in 1896 as almost extinct.[123] The first actual killing of a moose at a post and thus a dated record of moose hunting was in the Mistassini journals of 1909[XXVII] with the notation "the boys have killed one moose Deer."[124] It is this turn of events that Andrew Ottereyes mentioned, recalling that moose came to the Waswanipi area when he was a young man and Maria Otter commented that before moose, people lived on grouse and fish.[125] In 1949 it was reported that Rupert House hunters were taking moose, the first time in thirty years, though large numbers of moose were hunted in 1938-9 at Nemiskau.[126] In her letter to L.A. Richard, deputy minister of the Quebec Ministère de la chasse et de la pêche, Maud Watt, a resident of Rupert House, was asking that some restrictions be placed on the hunting. Moose were not north of the Rupert River and the Cree hunters from there were selling the hides to others at Eastmain and Old Factory River for $20 to $30 each.[127] One explanation for the northward migration of the moose earlier in the century was given by the Leiths who suggested it was a consequence of the building of the Grand Trunk Railway.[128] Joe Ottereyes attributed the appearance of the moose to the white man's clearing of the land for towns and Pien suggested that the fires drove them north.[129] In the 1960s the harvesting of moose on Rupert House hunting lands was attributed to fires, although eliminating large feed tracks for caribou had opened up extensive new niches for moose.[130] A moose was killed as far north as Great Whale River in 1970 and Andrew Kawapit noted that it "was the first time in the history of Great Whale River."[131] Moose was highly valued as it gave much more meat than deer or caribou.

STRATEGIES OF LIVING AND HUNTING

The material culture[XXVIII] of the Inlanders was modified, sometimes by necessity and sometimes by the introduction of new imported trade items. Once cold weather set in, the summer canvas tent was exchanged for the *miichiwaahp* or wigwam, ten to twelve feet in diameter on the ground with the poles set in a cone shape six to eight inches apart and banked on the ground with snow. This cone was covered with "cotton cloths, sheets of birchbark, or dressed deer [caribou] skin, often in part by all three" and a space was left at the top, two feet in diameter for the escape of the smoke. Inside the floor was covered with a thick bed of green boughs. In the centre was a hearth of stones though, at the time of his writing, Low noted that many of the southern Indians had small stoves made out of sheet-iron, thereby avoiding the constant smoke from the open fires.[XXIX] These home-made stoves did not give off enough light and so people made candles from long strips of dry sap from the trees. Low also commented that, unlike the others, the Nichikun people were using cotton for their *miichiwaahp* covers because of the disappearance of the caribou and scarcity of birch trees in their region.[132]

Whereas in the 1960s men went hunting from a main camp for as long as ten to twelve days, sixty years earlier the men tried to return with their catch in the evening; in the days before supplies of flour the margin of food did not allow them to stay away much longer. In the late 1940s the Crees started building wood houses at their main camps whereas earlier Cowboy explained that the camps were moved five to six times in one winter.[133]

Guns were used at the time of open water for shooting from canoes in hunting for beaver, otter, mink, and muskrats. Caribou hunting, though, on the tundra, was still by spearing at the river crossings. Once freeze-up set in, the fur hunt was made with traps, either steel or deadfalls of wood. Thus, even at the end of the nineteenth century, guns had not assumed a central place in the hunting arsenal of the Crees as they were to do later. Joe Ottereyes claimed that "bows and arrows were as good as guns," one could sneak up on the animal.[134] Muskets were commonly used and preferred by the Cree hunters over the breech-loading rifle. According to Anderson, muzzle-loading guns were lighter to carry, had fewer parts to break down, and needed few accessories such as powder and shot or ball. The ball could be home-made from the lead lining of tea chests and the wadding made from grass or moss.

The relative absence of large game meant that rifles were only gradually introduced into James Bay.[135] On the other hand, Knight, at Rupert House in 1961, suggested that the Crees may well have wanted to use rifles rather than muskets but "modern arms were not introduced to the area" until the Revillon Frères Company arrived in 1903.[136] Whether or not he had a choice, it seems that William J. Stewart of Old Factory River continued to use his old musket loader until the fall of 1940 when the entry in the company journal reads that he decided it "was no longer safe to use" and D.G. Boyd, the manager, added: "He must be the only Indian around here who still has one of those kinds of guns," although George Georgekiss from Rupert House arrived at Nemiskau Post in 1939 looking for parts for his muzzle-loading gun. The parts were in stock at the post.[137]

Fires were purposely set, in part as a hunting strategy to bring in new young growth of berries and thus attract bears, Low reported. Similarly, Andrew Ottereyes noted that the aftermath of fires resulted in moose coming in to the Waswanipi area.[138] Another hunting technique the Crees had perfected was the use of decoy calling. The Crees imitated animal sounds from hawks to seals and were particularly adept at attracting foxes with their imitation of the squeak of a field mouse. As for geese, the Leiths reported that each hunter brought in over one hundred a day, no doubt in large measure through their calling and decoys.[139]

As for clothing, Low said that except for the eastern Nauscapees inhabiting the interior north of a line drawn westward from Hamilton Inlet to the headwaters of the St Maurice River, all the Indians dressed in European-style clothing. Tartan shawls covered the women's dresses and were even used as a measure of wealth. The footgear worn by the Crees were caribou moccasins which Low said soaked up moisture like a blotter and were responsible for their high incidence of pulmonary diseases, while Turner pointed out that they last only two to three weeks, so that an adult needed fifteen to twenty-five pairs over a year. It was at this time, as Inuit were gradually becoming incorporated into the post economy, that the more waterproof sealskin boots became available in the Cree trade at the posts. The Leiths, who conducted geological surveying in the Richmond Gulf area in the winter of 1909, were very grateful for the warmth and dryness of the "husky boots," but noted they were inadequate for walking over rugged terrain unless they also wore several pairs of duffle socks and a pair of sealskin slippers. It is not known what boots the geologists brought with them from home, but given their enthusiasm for the boots they purchased at Great Whale River their American – made ones must have been inferior. The boots were made by the Inuit women from sealskin they and their children chewed. The Leiths felt they were getting a bargain at $2.50 to $4 per pair.[140] These sealskin boots were marketed by the Hudson's Bay Company and traded at posts on western James Bay, as far away as Fort Albany and Atawapiskat.[141] Eventually the Crees began making their own sealskin boots.[xxx]

Transport was by canoe in summer and a small toboggan for hauling goods in winter, especially the items purchased from the Hudson's Bay Company. One man at Wemindji said he used to haul seven to eight hundred pounds of food and other items by toboggan.[142] A few Mistassini men were still making birchbark canoes in 1913 but by then most were of canvas. Andrew Ottereyes recalled the Waswanipi using birchbark canoes when he was young, but later they switched to canvas. For winter travel, the Coasters maintained small dog teams and sleds for their several visits to the post but the Inlanders relied on hand-drawn toboggans. The use of sleds drawn by dog teams was relatively recent and had been copied from the Inuit tomatuks. They were, according to John Kawapit, made "exactly like them down to the frozen peat iced runners."[143] The husky dogs had been used by the Crees only about the turn of the century. Matthew Cowboy, who was born about 1876, remembered them being adopted in his youth.[144] Dog sleds were not a comfortable mode of transport; the Leiths relate how strenuous it was to haul, heave, and push the sled over rocks and other obstacles, not to mention the complication of having to provide food for the dogs. For the Leiths the most wondrous Cree mode of winter travel was the snowshoe and they thrilled at being able to identify a person's origins from his snowshoe tracks.[145]

RELATIONS AT THE POST SETTLEMENTS

Around the turn of the century, the rhythm of life for the Coasters at the post followed the earlier general patterns. They were still dependent on country food[xxxi] but were able to supplement this with imported foods gained from wage labour or obtained through their trade of country food such as fish and geese. During the summer months Coaster families performed a host of jobs around the post. Little is known about their living conditions, particularly in the summer when larger numbers were in residence at the post. Low[146] did observe in 1896 that the majority lived in cotton tents but the most successful among them had log houses there.[xxxii]

The summer months brought together all the Coasters and some Inlanders so the post was a lively place, the sparse buildings and yards being surrounded by Cree tents and tipis. One can imagine the echoes of laughter emanating from the tipis as the Crees were said always to be on the lookout for some kind of joke or fun. The men engaged in various sports such as cricket, soccer, and hockey and these sports made up a large degree of the entertainment at Moose Factory. Baseball came there in the mid-1920s.[147] Football would have been played, using a blown-up sealskin. Church services were held several times a day and there was a considerable amount of visiting, dancing, and feasting. Feasts were held in the summer on the occasion of the Crees' annual trading visit. By 1898 this feast was taken over by the Hudson's Bay Company as an annual feast for both Coasters and Inlanders. Even the four Inuit families at the Fort George post were included. Those Inlanders who arrived afterwards were given another feast, as happened in 1898. The numbers were considerable; at the 26 June 1899 feast 250 men, women, and children were present and a second feast was held on 7 July. Such feasts at trading time were held at all the posts though at Mistassini they seem to have been given at departure rather than arrival.[148]

The social scene at the larger coastal posts was obviously more animated than at the smaller inland ones, but even these took on a more lively air with the arrivals and departures of people. Father Guinard, who was at Waswanipi in the early years of the twentieth century, has left us a description. Arriving there early in the summer of 1907, he commented on the emptiness at the post. The shelves were practically bare and it was only with the arrival of the canoe brigades from Rupert House in August that the store filled up with goods and the settlement came to life. The day after the canoes arrived the company manager held a feast outdoors for all. The meal was served on a large sheet on the ground and consisted of raisin bread fried in fat, accompanied with tea and sugar. The first to eat were the manager, the missionaries, the company servants, and the Cree men; the women and children ate at a second setting. After sunset the dancing began with drums, violins, singing, the clomping of dancing feet, and the barking of dogs all fusing into a concert that lasted long into the night.[149] These Hudson's Bay Company feasts lasted into the 1940s when the records end. At this time, beaver sanctuaries were in operation and feasts were part of the ceremonies at the annual gathering. By 1924 the feasts had generally become more elaborate affairs with speech making and dancing. In 1920 a feast was even given to celebrate the company's 250th anniversary.[150]

The end of winter and trading time were not the only occasions feasted by Crees. On 27 November 1872 Henry Namacoose brought a bear into Rupert House and that day McTavish entered a complaint in his journal that the people were feasting instead of hunting. The killing of a bear was an even more sacred event than other game, at least in the 1950s,[151] or as it had been in the time of the Reverend Walton in

1894;[152] such a ritual was often practised by the Crees throughout the James Bay region. One Waswanipi hunter was praised for his great successes at bear hunting. It is said that when he started out in the morning he would go straight to the bear because "God led him that way. He would find him in his cave, dig a place and tell him to come out. The bear then comes out, he thinks like a person."[153] The onset of fall trapping was another occasion that warranted a feast. The high regard the people held for beaver is seen in its prominence in feasts but also in Gilbert Dick's comment that "a beaver sometimes puts a stick in your trap so you get the stick by mistake ... We think the beaver got a bit of human mind, he works like a human because he knows how to make a dam, how to make a house, how to get some supplies, ... He knows there is a trap there too."[154]

Since a feast marked an important Cree occasion, it is not surprising that formal marriages, introduced by Christianity, retained feasting as a celebration. So, on 28 June 1897 the chief of the Rupert House band held a feast at the time of his daughter's marriage to Joseph Waupatchee's son. Sometimes the company contributed food as they did so for Rat's son's wedding at Fort George. He supplied the deer fat and the company provided the rest, presumably cakes and biscuits. That summer, manager Owen Griffiths decided to merge the feast celebrating the wedding of Peter Cox with the annual company feast since he suspected the company would end up providing most of the provisions.[155] Of course, weddings were seldom single events, multiple marriages being the standard. We read that on 26 August 1887 at Mistassini Post, "no less than three weddings today."[156] Only a few marriages in the twentieth century in James Bay were not held in the summer at the post with a clergyman officiating. In one instance, four couples at Great Whale River were married on 15 July 1938 "by civil contract." Bishop Fleming had been at Great Whale three weeks earlier, therefore one must assume that the couples had missed his visit, presumably because of the poor weather that seems to have persisted throughout June, and the post manager, Ross,[XXXIII] took over these duties.[157] These accounts in the records of marriages, regrettably, miss out on informing the readers of the negotiations and intricacies of arranged marriages which continued for much of the twentieth century but can be found in Sarah Preston's moving account of the life history of Alice Jacobs.

The dances were held to the tune of fiddles and an Indian drum and perhaps an accordion. Favoured was the old Red River jig as well as Indian rabbit and duck dances, quadrilles, and square dances. Other dances enjoyed were the straight dance, eightsome reel, thrashing dance and round-up.[158] Dances began at eight in the evening and could last until at least three in the next morning. All at the post were invited.ˣˣˣᴵⱽ This is a company journal account of the dance that took place at the small inland post of Nichikun in 1939, on the eve of the departure of the hunters and their families. "We held a dance tonight seeing that the Indians were leaving the next day. The orchestra consisting of a fiddler and a drummer complained that there were no strings on the violin. However with the help of an old banjo string, a piece of snare wire and 1 piece of radio wire, the fiddler was soon scraping out a tune on three strings while the drummer was knocking the gong around, the gong happened to be an old basin; it was a real swing time in the raw."¹⁵⁹

There was also a winter feast at the posts, held on New Year's Day. From the earliest fur trade days there were usually some Coasters around the post during the Christmas and New Year's season but no mention in the journals of celebration other than that the day "was observed." As best as can be discerned, it seems that a gathering of Coasters began only in the 1870s. The post manager at Rupert House, D.C. McTavish, seems to suggest this in his entry of 30 December 1872, for he says: "Nearly all the homeguard in to pass New Year's. I gave each a regale for New Year's Day as this is the first time they have come in at New Year's or Christmas since I have been here [circa 1870]."¹⁶⁰ Thereafter, annually, there was some way of marking New Year's Day at the coastal posts; at the inland ones this practice arose somewhat later.

Another very important ceremony at the post was the departure of the Inlanders, vividly described by Anderson. Once the tent was struck, the campsite tidied, and the canoes loaded, the whole family would proceed for a ceremonial farewell with the trader, the head of the family leading his wife and children. The hunter would ask for a statement of his account and for the price of furs for the coming winter.ˣˣˣⱽ Then they would shake hands first with the trader and then with every other person at the post.¹⁶¹

The social life at the post was marked by a class/racial distinction which can best be seen in the company's different celebrations for the servants of the post (European and mixed-blood) and the Indians. Such was the case at Rupert House on New Year's Day of 1874, when Miles Spencer wrote that he "gave each Indian a day's ration and our men and their wives got a dinner from us instead of cakes and wine which used to be given formerly."¹⁶² More commonly, the Indians were given a feast of cakes, tea, and coffee while the company servants and their families were given a dinner of beef and vegetables with tea, coffee, and cakes.

There were, however, local variations to the celebration. At Great Whale River the men engaged in shooting at targets, with a pound of tea as the first prize, while at Rupert House they held a dance in the evening.¹⁶³ Sometimes, as when there had been a number of deaths in the community, the festivities were subdued. In 1897 the company journal read: "some of the young people may have danced ... but no grand ball out of sympathy for those who were in mourning."¹⁶⁴

The type and intensity of celebration was obviously guided by the managers as well as the number of people at the posts. Not surprisingly, D.C. McTavish initiated a Scottish celebration at Rupert House on 30 November on St Andrew's Day. In 1898 he marked the occasion with a supper for the company servants, at that time about half a dozen men and their families. The highlight of this day was a magic lantern show that the Reverend Ascah held as he did periodically throughout the several years he was at Rupert House.¹⁶⁵

The first specific reference to the Indians coming in for Christmas at Rupert House was for 1891 and thereafter it was a regular entry at some of the posts. However it was not until 1914 that we learn of church services on this holiday; the Reverend Walton gleefully reported that "our Fort George Indians are at last giving up the New Years tea drinking feast, an old custom of the H.B.Co Scotch traders and are now coming in for the Christmas Holy Comm. Service."¹⁶⁶ Presumably, the food sources at or near the post did not permit large numbers of Crees to congregate there over a period covering both holidays; naturally, for the Anglican ministers, observing Christmas was more important. As for other church services, we do know that at Fort George services were held on Sundays in the summer when large numbers were congregated: one for the whites, two for the Indians, and one for the Inuit.¹⁶⁷

We can only surmise how much socializing there was between the Coasters and the company employees during leisure hours at the post. Many of the servants were either descended from Cree mothers or were co-habiting or married to Cree women. How much socializing was permitted by the company is difficult to ascertain. Although the company divided the "Indians" from the "servants" at the New Year's dinners, it is unlikely that this separation occurred in other of the festivities, particularly the dancing, the servants numbering too few to hold dances themselves. It is clear that Coasters living at the post were included in the post's social activities.

I would argue that the distinction of "Indian" used by the company here is an economic one. In 1878 the head of the Southern Department, W. Parsons, expressed regret that he would have to let James Linklater go, for with a large family he could not find a place for him. The terminology Parsons used was "he must go free as an Indian." This was also applied to Alexander Moar at Mistassini in 1878.¹⁶⁸ Several years earlier Sam Atkinson, a company servant at Rupert House, was dismissed from the service but would be "employed as an Indian from time to time."[169] The Anglicans also thought of "Indian" as an occupational category, for that is what they entered in the church registers.[170] This distinction may well have been a Cree one too. In an oral account from Rupert House, Willie Jacob applied the term *wemstukshiokan* or "made into white people"[xxxvi] to the mixed-ancestry post servants. The use of "country born," it must be said, is to be found only in reference to place of birth in lists of company servants and does not appear in the narratives in the journals. Not until the census of 1911 (see Appendix 2) are the Cree/white offspring referred to as "mixed."[171] During his field research at Rupert House in 1947–8, A.J. Kerr found in the missionary records "a sharp distinction between the 'English' section of the community (including metis servants) and the Indians" but he also commented that Indians, "to some extent ... were considered a separate group, outside the status system of the Company servants" and were not simply a group located "at the bottom of the heap."[172] Earlier, though, the Reverend Thomas Vincent, himself of mixed ancestry, writing of the diocese of Mosoonee, claimed that such a person, having been born there and speaking the language, "is in all respects considered a brother." This is a curious statement coming from Vincent because Long documents how Bishop Horden, a holder of odd racial views, passed over him for the office of bishop and that throughout his career he was a victim of discriminatory racial views.[173]

This classification of individuals according to their livelihood rather than by some racial designation (a concept that likely did not enter the consciousness of the people of James Bay until the last few decades), prohibited the development of a distinct cultural group such as the Metis in Western Canada. So did their exclusion from any treaty process. On the west coast of James Bay the mixed-bloods or halfbreeds were relegated to a type of caste when in 1905 the government commissioners for Treaty No. 9 decided to exclude them, though they had admitted halfbreeds to the same treaty at Fort Albany a week earlier. At Moose Factory five of them petitioned the Dominion government for some sort of compensation: "We have been born and brought up in the country, and are thus by our birth and training unfit to obtain a livelihood in the civilized world. Should the fur traders at any time not require our services we should be obliged to support ourselves by hunting."[174]

The government responded that "they were refused treaty by the Commissioners on the grounds that they were not living the Indian mode of life." Eventually the province of Ontario accepted in 1906 to allow "these halfbreeds ... 160 acres of land, reserving minerals"[175] but that the lands be in the district in which they reside and in no way interfere with Hudson's Bay Company posts or Indian reserves or railways. Long suggests this provincial offer of land may never have been conveyed to the claimants.[176]

In eastern James Bay there was no treaty, hence no government-imposed classification of the Crees. As statuses were more or less "achieved" rather than "ascribed," it meant that the men and women (through marriage) could move back and forth. Once the Department of Indian Affairs began compiling band lists[xxxvii] and using them as the bases of restricted access to services, the classification gradually became more rigid, as at Moose Factory. However, the large numbers of servants at Rupert House began dwindling; by the 1930s the company was relying on mechanized transport and imported materials and, as will be seen, these former company servants resumed Indian lifestyles, living off hunting and trapping.

The company more than the Crees had a vested interest in keeping track of the daughters of company servants, for they seemed to think they had an obligation to marry them to company servants. Long before it was official policy to regulate the marriage of the company managers to native women, which was forbidden in 1940[177] and remained in effect through the 1970s,[178] there was a stringent policy in the Southern District. A directive from Macdonald at Moose Factory to Cotter at Fort George in 1875 stated: "I am very sorry to learn [illegible] into proposing marriage to the girl you allude to – were there not servants' daughters in the country, she would doubtless be one of the most eligible of the Indian girls; so long however as there are so many of the former unmarried in the Bay, I shall countenance the marriage of no Comp's servant with an Indian woman – a trip either in the summer to this place or in the winter to Ruperts House would have given him an opportunity of selecting another wife – should he insist on marrying this girl, you will at once dismiss him and let him go free on the spot, when of course he will live beyond the establishment."[179] Furthermore, the company required that its employees receive permission to marry. For example, in 1878 David Hester was granted permission to marry Mary Moar,[180] both being of families descended from two Englishmen and Cree wives in the mid and late 1700s. This was a policy that had been initiated in the early 1800s when the company was becoming alarmed at the number of dependants it was supporting at the posts.[181]

Although no tally was kept, it seems that there were few English women[xxxviii] in the James–Hudson Bay region during this period; the first, in 1830, was the wife of John George McTavish, head of the Southern District at Moose Factory. With the encouragement of Governor George Simpson, McTavish distanced his English wife from the mixed-ancestry wives of the post traders.[182] The traders' wives had to endure being snubbed for five years until the McTavishes were transferred to Lake of Two Mountains, close to Montreal. Another European woman, the wife of the Reverend George Barnley, whom he brought to Moose Factory in 1844, also put on airs, but she and her husband were rebuffed by the traders and their country-born wives.[183] Despite Governor Simpson's misgivings in the late 1840s about bringing "European Ladies" to Hudson Bay, missionary wives did continue to settle in James Bay, but their stay was usually not very long because of health problems.

More successful, it seems, were the Englishmen whose wives were country-born. Thus Miles Spencer, the trader at Fort George and head of the Eastmain District for twenty-three years from 1876 to 1899, was married to a woman of mixed ancestry as had been his father.[184] Furthermore, his daughter, Daisy Alice, married the Reverend W.G. Walton, who arrived in 1896 and stayed until 1924.[185] In the same period, the wife of the Fort George post manager, Griffiths, was the daughter of Alan Nicholson at Rupert House and also Nicholson had been married to the daughter of Archdeacon Thomas Vincent, himself country-born.[186] Another of Nicholson's daughters was married to Alick Louttit, Hudson's Bay Company servant who took up his duties at Eastmain.[187] Daughters of inland managers also married company employees, as did the daughter of William Miller who married Thomas Moar, the post carpenter at Mistassini.[188]

One group of people with whom there seems to have been very little fraternization was the Inuit. Turner says of those at Fort Chimo that they were "more or less directly in contact" but "here as elsewhere, they do not intermix."[189] The Crees and Inuit encountered each other at Great Whale River more than at any other post but not en masse. The Inuit tended to come in to trade in the spring, camping for several months on the offshore islands to hunt the seals. Only the Cree men and women working at the post would have been there at the same time. The Indian hunters arrived in June after the Inuit had left for caribou hunting out on the tundra. Even years later, in 1935, W. Anderson, the Revillon Frères trader at Great Whale River, observed that the two peoples avoided each other, noting that the Crees would pay one dollar extra per pair of Inuit-made sealskin boots by buying them from the trader rather than directly from the Inuit.[190] The enmity between the Crees and Inuit has a long, not readily understood history. By way of explanation, we learn from a story told by Beatrice Fairies of her paternal uncle who, working at Fort Chimo, was invited by an Inuk to marry his daughter but her grandfather refused to sanction this marriage for he feared "the Eskimo powers." Despite this objection, the grandfather out hunting one day fell into a crevice which further confirmed for him the Eskimo powers.[191] As well, we learn from this story that the Crees believed the Inuit life hard, living as they did "out in the cold where there's no trees or anything."

Communication between the three language groups at Great Whale River would not have been a problem for much of the sixty years Harold Udgarten[xxxix] worked at the post. He was born in Moose Factory of mixed ancestry and his wife, whose language he learned, was an Inuk. Moreover, many Inuit working at the posts spoke Cree but the Leiths did not encounter one Cree who spoke Inuktitut.[192]

The Crees and Inuit were thrown together as employees at Fort George and Rupert House in addition to Great Whale River and much later in the 1930s at Old Factory. In the 1890s the company encouraged a number to settle on the coastal islands so they could do the "snow works" at the post. That meant building up snow around the buildings in December, running the team of dogs, building and maintaining the sleighs, and hunting seals for the post.[193] It is certain that the Crees and the few Inuit were put on work teams together at Fort George and when feasts or celebrations were mentioned the two were brought together. There were some marriages between the two groups along the coast; five were counted in the 1940s.[194] Not surprisingly, there was some cultural exchange, at least Truman Michelson, a linguist who visited Fort George in 1935, thought so, as he wrote that "Indians at hunt like Huskies; kill seals, sometimes walrus. Their women know how to make Husky boots ... They never go far inland."[195]

The number of Inuit families frequenting the Fort George region would have remained few, perhaps three or four families, had it not been for the arrival in 1903 of the Hudson Bay Company's energetic competitor, the Revillon Frères Company, who transformed the operations of the fur trade there. This new company began providing mid-winter supplies to the Inlanders and fetching their furs, thereby requiring the services of Inuit teamsters who, with their sleds and dogs, travelled up the frozen waterways. Needless to say, the Hudson's Bay Company soon took up this practice as well as continuing to employ the Inuit for other transport work and their wives to make the much-coveted boots.[XL]

Inuit, who had come to dwell on the Cape Hope Islands, were also employed at Eastmain and later at Old Factory River when it opened in the late 1930s. The Old Factory River settlement of Inuit predates the fur trade post there although the company did invite them to the region in 1847 to seal for the company and produce the blubber. Inuit were also sealing for the company at Eastmain in the 1890s.[196] There were also a few Inuit at Rupert House, though farther removed from the activities of the post. They lived on an island located off Sherrock's Mount and at Charlton Island. The company had invited the "two sleds of Eskimos" from Little Whale River in 1871 to "see what can be done at seals, porpoises, etc."[197] It was expected that if worthwhile they would remain there. In the meantime, a young Inuk lad was assigned to the Rupert House post in the hopes they could teach him English and use him as an interpreter at Little Whale River. Just how new this area was to the Inuit is demonstrated by Thomas Fleming's account of how he had killed some rabbits on Charlton Island but did not know how to kill the beaver in the lodge, for this was "the first he had ever seen."[198] The Inuit stayed on the islands off Rupert House, particularly at Charlton.

The number of Inuit working for Rupert House remained small as the competition with the Revillon Frères never materialized; they disappeared from the records in 1911, although Charlton Island was closed as a depot about 1931 when the rail connection to Moosonee supplanted it as a shipping point. Relations between Crees and Inuit at Old Factory were obviously very good; in the late 1940s the Cree Old Factory band "voted unanimously to permit the Cape Hope Island Eskimos to take a beaver quota from the Old Factory Preserve."[199] These Inuit families living both at Paint Hills (the name for the new village of the Old Factory band) and Cape Hope were transferred by the government in 1960 to Great Whale River, although most had been born at Cape Hope. Their departure from Paint Hills was lamented by the district manager who commented "we are all sorry to see these happy people leave ... some of them are expert canoe builders."[200]

The Inuit were treated differently by the company than the Crees. The amount of credit extended to them was very little or none.[201] This distrust is also to be seen in an account in the Leiths' book of 1912. The geologists were told by Mrs Walton that in her father's time as factor at Fort George the Inuit were not allowed to come nearer than Eskimo Point, two miles north. There they camped and were allowed to come in to the post to trade on certain days by twos only.[202] These restrictions are not apparent from the company records, other than an entry that the encampment of Inuit was away from the post on islands. This was understood to be so the Inuit could carry out their sealing. It is not inconceivable that the Hudson's Bay Company maintained a lingering mistrust of the Inuit after two fatal incidents, one in 1754 and another in 1791.[203]

As for Cree relations with the Hudson's Bay Company factors or managers, they were probably as variable as the personalities of the individuals. Not surprisingly, little on this subject is said in the records, so when a particular manager complains or makes derogatory statements one runs the risk of generalizing about possible harsh treatment of the Crees. Such a manager was D.C. McTavish who arrived at Rupert House on 27 September 1892 and left on 19 July 1901,²⁰⁴ to be replaced by Alan Nicholson.ˣᴸᴵ

Unlike his predecessors, McTavish was highly opinionated and seemingly disliked the Crees. In a lengthy tirade in 1893 against a company servant (presumably of mixed ancestry from the west side of James Bay)ˣᴸᴵᴵ one of his denunciations against him was that he "was fond of low company."²⁰⁵ He made many other derogatory remarks towards the Crees (though they diminish over the years), such as, Jimmiken called "lazy"; the Hester gang being a "lot of trash" and "gifted with the tongue"; Andrew Butterfly was "a dirt" and Matilda Moar "won't die out of spite," though she did, two weeks later, at about age ninety-four.²⁰⁶ In a presumed reference to the Coasters, McTavish wrote in his 25 October 1898 journal that "the rubbish are gathering from all sides ... they are not grateful for what they get" and a few days later he called them "useless." These uncharitable comments need not necessarily have translated into harsh treatment, for balancing these comments is his acknowledgment that Ruben Namacoose turned out to be right several days after doubting something Namacoose told him. On the other hand, McTavish does admit to punishing an Indian. In response to a story about a break-in at the outpost of Michiskun in 1891, he wrote to Robertson at Waswanipi that he had once jailed a man for a year for taking "only a little flour" and advised Robertson to tell the story as a warning, "to see that they can be punished." He offered to send his handcuffs but had lent them to the hunter, Picatao.²⁰⁷ However, McTavish just as easily complimented individuals, so we learn that an Indian named Vincent was one of the best hunters, and Old Namacoose was a "true and faithful Indian for the Company."²⁰⁸ More than any of the other post managers of his time, McTavish sponsored dances, as on St Andrew's Day of 1895 when he commented that they had "so few amusements. Those people who try and deprive them from joining in these happy gatherings do more harm than good."²⁰⁹ He also threw dances at the holidays and sometimes in the summer.

The dances were likely a reaction to the attitude of the Anglican ministers who denounced dancing. Walton was the most vigilant in this; in his 1905 report he decries the fact that when the Indians arrive at the post to celebrate New Year's they dance there with all the servants, two of the communicants being the fiddlers. He goes on to say: "Every one knows the evil results of this dancing." The Crees, for their part, seemed perplexed by Walton's attitude, for they pointed out that it is not a sin to dance and that they had known "even ministers" to do so. Alcohol was not Walton's concern in his condemnation of dancing because he also noted that to date "drinking has not been introduced much here."[210] Donald Gillies, in his 1909 journal for Fort George, records this outburst. "Went to church ... got his Reverences ideas on dancing, condemning utterly our little jollification of Friday evening."[211] It was also government policy to discourage dancing. The deputy superintendent general of Indian Affairs, Duncan Campbell Scott, wrote to the Indian agents in 1921: "You should suppress any dances which cause waste of time, interfere with occupations of Indians, unsettle them for serious work, injure their health or encourage them in sloth and idleness."[212]

Existing writings are not always helpful in determining the relations between post managers and the Crees. For example, J.W. Anderson, who served as Alan Nicholson's assistant at Rupert House in 1918, stated he would have been honoured to have been named successor to the "famous" Alan Nicholson[213] yet in the book on Maud Watt,[XLIII] both the Nicholsons are portrayed as part of the "old breed that looked with contempt on the natives."[214] Perhaps the last word should go to Willie Jacob, who recounted that "Mr Nicholson was a very good HBC manager. Very often he would give a person food even when they didn't have fur to sell. He used to say that he hoped he would get some fur from them in the future, that's why he did this to the Indian people."[215] Nicholson's wife, it should be remembered, was the daughter of the Archdeacon Thomas Vincent, a native of mixed ancestry from Albany. However, Maud Watt herself was denounced by the Anglicans as "unspeakable" and "a menace to the other sojourners at the place."[216] On the other hand, in their description of the manager and his surroundings by the geologists, Charles and Arthur Leith wrote of "the comfortable house of the manager with its well-kept yard, hewn picket fence, huge gate, usually a garden plot for potatoes and other hardy vegetables, and buildings and pens for cows and chicken, form the central feature of most of the posts ... The complete control of the post manager over the affairs of his subordinates and dependent Indians ... give an air of a certain military precision."[217]

The Leiths also remarked that "the attitude of the Company toward the Indian is a curious combination of stern, relentless control[XLIV] with a sort of furtive kindliness." Anderson had a different view, for what it is worth. He described the majority of managers as "men of character ... going forth with honest purposes" and the best of them were "friendly and fair, scrupulously honest, understanding, courteous and respectful."[218] However, the public image of the Hudson's Bay Company was of a more officious nature, more akin to Philip Godsell's depiction of the company domain at Norway House being a "semi-feudal state," while he claimed the chief factor at York Factory "practically ruled the country and the Indians."[219] Interestingly, that chief factor was George Ray, later to become the district manager for the southern James Bay trade. As will be seen through the excerpts of his reports in the 1920s, Ray vigorously championed the welfare of the Cree hunters. So if he "ruled," it was as a benign ruler rather than as an advocate solely of the company's welfare. Clearly, we should be making a distinction between the larger posts, the factories, and the smaller posts. At the larger ones such as Moose Factory, or even Rupert House, the chief factor oversaw a large number of employees[XLV] and a whole range of activities, including responsibility for distribution over a vast geographical area, running a sawmill, a store, provision of food rations for the employees and their dependants, maintaining buildings, manufacturing of tools, boats, and so on.[220] The other posts, however, were much more modest enterprises of only a few employees and their families, who contributed much of their own food. Many of them suffered from a shortage of food, along with the Cree hunters when hunting was poor. Mr Foreman was delighted to see the transport canoes approaching Nemiskau in 1938, relishing the food he would be receiving which would be "a treat after tea and toast for ten days." At the same post, Mr and Mrs D.G. Boyd found the house so draughty that they scrounged the material to make two storm windows from the abandoned Revillon Frères house, using chewed chewing gum in place of putty to afix the glass.[221] In these posts it would be difficult to imagine the manager running a feudal operation especially since the men in charge were of mixed ancestry, having been raised in the country. Thus, when we learn that in 1916 the Hudson's Bay Company required that its post manager and his assistant had to be in the store "to attend personally to the wants of the natives" rather than remain in his office,[222] we can only assume that this had been the long-standing practice in the smaller posts.

Regarding the relations between the Crees and the post managers of small posts, on the whole, whatever their real feelings, the managers display a sense of respect for the hunters. It may be an observation as straightforward as D.G. Boyd's, writing of one family at Nemiskau: "Indians are certainly tough. One of George Jolly's children is only 4 months old and they are travelling in below zero weather."[223] Mostly, it is the respectful way in which almost all the journal entries are written. The basis of the relations between trader and hunters was naturally confrontational. The hunters brought a product to trade where the price was dependent on size and quality. The amount of credit they received was also subject to discussion. Thus, understandably, the trader would find certain individuals "nuisances" or perhaps

69   James Bay at the End of the Nineteenth Century

"demanding," maybe even at times "deceitful." Unfortunately, the Cree reactions to the traders at these times are not recorded. Only one trader in the 1900s stands out as being generally contemptuous of the Crees. Mr Black took over from Mr Corston, the country-born manager of the small inland post of Nemiskau in 1929. Reading his journal was distressing; one wonders how the Nemiskau Crees worked with him. We find such comments as "they are the biggest bunch of bums," and he turfed a family out of the servants' quarters where Corston had allowed them to live.[224] With Corston's permission some people were storing their belongings in the shed but Black "cleaned most of their junk ... they have been accustomed to leaving their rags." Other unusual derogatory comments are "we kicked him off pretty quick. He is a useless sort of fellow anywhere," or "a few stray Indians arrived today." Black complained that some of the Nemiskau hunters were taking their trade to Waswanipi. His explanation is that "McLeod who is in charge ... they say is very good to them, he is a half-breed."[225] One wonders if Black ever figured out why he lost customers.

At larger posts, such a Rupert House and Fort George, the manager maintained a relatively privileged southern lifestyle complete with servants and cooks until the 1920s when the company stopped supporting deficit-ridden posts. Although the Hudson's Bay Company came to rely on mixed-bloods to run their smaller posts and the outposts, this policy seems to have changed after the First World War. Except for brief interludes, gone are the Iserhoffs, the Marks, the Louttits, the McLeods from the ranks of management. Instead these posts were staffed by outsiders because twentieth-century management demanded more skills than the James Bay country-born men could acquire on their home territories (and also because the company wanted to distance itself from its growing burden of family dependants). Although far from representative of the mid-1900s management, David Cooter, who arrived as post manager at Nichikun in 1940, was a graduate of Oxford University and went on to teach linguistics at the Université du Quebec à Chicoutimi in the late 1960s.[XLVI]

At these smaller, isolated posts we can only surmise that for some men, fresh from England or, more rarely, from southern Canada, their isolation might have affected their mental state which, in turn, could well have rebounded on the well-being of the Crees. The Crees, being too polite, do not recount incidences of such difficult managers. However, Ross at Great Whale River gives us clues of potential mental problems. Bryce Merrill was the clerk in charge of the outpost on the Belcher Islands, having been sent there suddenly in March 1939 as a replacement. Two months later he sent a message to Ross that he would like "to see a tree again." Ross replied to the effect that, rather than worrying about trees he should "worry about when he gets the first sight of the *M.K.* Fort Churchill and runs for the hills with the shock of civilized contact."²²⁶ One perhaps might understand the loneliness of foreign-born managers, particularly in the small posts, cut off by language from socializing and from cultural activities. At Mistassini in 1926, J. Hurley sounds sorrowful that a radio was sent there. It was a doubtful blessing since when it did not work, which seemed often, "the dumbness of the radio also serves to make the winter long." A few years later it was the reading material that he missed, for he commented "rather tough luck to be out of reading material ... I am reading a novel for the third time." However, he also occupied his time by "studying French."²²⁷

The white Hudson's Bay Company personnel did socialize with the company families in their homes but their relations with the hunters seem to have been more distant. Anderson broached the subject, saying "Many of the Indians and their families were cleanly enough and worthy of entertainment in your home, but you had to draw the line here, for there were too many of them."ˣᴸⱽᴵᴵ He offers yet another explanation suggesting that as manager he could not favour one customer over another; they all had to be treated equally or the manager "would be looking for trouble."²²⁸ Such distancing of the whites from the Indians was also a phenomenon in the 1940s, described as a caste system where Indians entering a white person's house was expected to use the back door and rarely got beyond the kitchen.²²⁹ One exception was Solomon Voyageur, the highly respected chief guide who "was honoured by having tea at the manager's house."²³⁰

A perceptive comment by A.J. Kerr enables us to recognize the strength of ties that company employees from the British Isles must have held for each other as well as their strong loyalty to the company, for he points out that coming from abroad they would not have had any ties to families or institutions in the south of Canada.²³¹

As for Cree thinking about the Europeans, it was probably as varied as the European views and treatment of the Crees. However the oral accounts are silent on this subject. That some Englishmen remained in James Bay for fifty years suggests that some had good relations with the Cree. Anderson thought the popular wisdom that the managers or missionaries or government agents could dictate to the Crees was preposterous, for he says "it is unreasonable to suggest that one white man (and many of the posts were one-man posts) in a remote community, far removed in time and distance from the other white men or the white man's law, and surrounded by three or four hundred Indians, could exercise any unfair or domineering influence over the tribesmen. If he tried to, things would not go well with him."²³² He goes on

71   James Bay at the End of the Nineteenth Century

to say that the Crees, particularly the chiefs and leaders, were men of importance in their respective communities and the company men depended on their active cooperation. Whatever leadership the whites might achieve was by virtue of their character and their ability to deal equitably with the Indians. Likely under many conditions, when a white person overstepped cultural bounds or reasoning, the Crees ignored him. There is one incidence of a post manager being replaced because some Cree men at Moose Factory complained "he was no good." Harris[233] attributes this assertiveness on the part of Harvey Smallboy and others as having experienced the wider world through serving in the Canadian army in the First World War. In truth, for much of this period living conditions were very restrained and the Crees had few options; there was no alternative to working with the company. The Hudson's Bay Company was the outside "universe" in which the Crees operated; even government transfer payments were funnelled through the manager until well into the 1960s. It is not surprising, therefore, to find Willard Walker, at Great Whale River in 1952, pointing out that the Crees ascribed price changes to the caprices and vindictiveness of the post managers. While on the subject of Cree views of the whites, Walker also claimed that the whites did not readily share food and the local people thought of them as stingy despite the teachings in the Bible. In terms of collective behaviour, they also found the whites "over emotional and addicted to uncalled for petulance and anger."[234]

OVERVIEW

This lengthy report of the people provides some idea of the external forces that rained down on the Crees from the 1870s to the early years of the next century. Those most affected were the post people and the Coasters who came to the company post at least several times a year. Their lives were inextricably woven with the routines of the post and the changes that the trade were gradually undergoing. The Inlanders remained in the bush, far removed, for much of the year. However, with their month-long summer residence at the post came the devastating effects of epidemics, the observance of Christian practices, and their contact with foreigners – all of which whittled away at the integrity of their culture. Yet during this period we must remember that the Crees, both Inlanders and Coasters, lived out their lives on the land, getting food, marrying, giving birth, interacting without external direction or control despite their involvement with the company. They were preoccupied with daily life, with finding enough food, and with security of mind and body. In these circumstances, the fur trade itself must have seemed distant and peripheral in the bush, though central at the times they were in at the post. Nevertheless, during this period external agencies were taking root; the missionaries, government, and settlers to the south were imposing their priorities and agendas over the resources of the land and ultimately its people. The next chapter will examine the degree to which these new institutions burrowed into existing Cree society and will attempt to assess the extent of change.

CHAPTER THREE

The Powers of Religion: Christianity Extends the Limits

I will argue here that the fur trade per se did not transform Cree society. The Crees' participation in it did not alter significantly their institutions or their perceptions of the world. Trapping for exchange purposes was secondary; they were still preoccupied with securing their food, thereby maintaining their institutions geared to survival. Their cosmology would have remained more or less intact, continuing to guide them as hunters and members of small hunting groups. However, diminution in their preoccupation with hunting of large game and beaver, the animal spirits they most revered, would logically weaken their traditional beliefs; that was yet to come. That they were involved in exchange, and had acquired certain wants and needs, obviously left them susceptible to other pressures and forces that challenged this security and world view. These outside influences arrived in the form of missionaries, government agencies, tourists, changed world economy, and so forth, and were combined with the pressures already described, such as animal depletion and disease.

The tremendous social changes that befell Native Peoples in Canada is popularly attributed to the missionary as the agent, par excellence, of Western society. Thus this chapter is devoted to looking at the beginnings of the Christian church in James Bay. Why did the Crees became Christian and Anglicans? Clara Sue Kidwell writes that "Christianity (in all its complexity) cannot be taken by itself as a causal agent of cultural change."[1] Christian missionaries and the religion itself also reinforced values of family and self-sufficiency. Accordingly, it is my belief that the Crees took from Christianity what they needed to help them survive in a changing society. At the time that Christianity was taking root James Bay was not a settler society, nor was there government interference or involvement. The Anglican missionaries certainly had support from the British managers of the local fur trade posts, but it was not in the interests of the company to intervene and threaten a fur hunter with reduced credit if he did not convert. In fact, conforming to the demands of the Christian church, such as shedding extra wives, or spending much of the summer at the post learning the Christian teachings, was seen by company officials as a drain on their resources. The one time a company official intervened[1] was to take on what seems might have been a threatening tone to those hunters flirting with Catholicism.[2]

It is not possible to ascertain the depth of commitment the Crees felt to this new religion except to say that it expanded from the time the Anglicans began bringing their message to the east coast in the 1850s. There are only the missionary accounts on which to base some understanding of what Christianity might have meant to the Crees in the early part of this century. Anthropologists have been more interested in documenting the traditional culture, despite indigenous peoples' deep embrace of Christianity at the time of ethnographic research. Such an attitude even slanted the work of the priest-anthropologist Father John Cooper, who began his work in James Bay in 1932. Although focusing on such issues as land tenure and hunting practices, Cooper did write on the *witiko* phenomenon and the concept of the supreme being[3] but not on their combined attachment to traditional Cree practices and Christianity. Similarly, Adrian Tanner's revealing study of Cree ritual as he observed it in the 1960s and 1970s does not situate this belief system alongside the Christian one, despite the fact that the Crees were by then Christians. Tanner has separated the two, associating Christianity with settlement life and Cree shamanistic religion with bush life.[4] It was a biologist-anthropologist, Jacques Rousseau, who, in writing of the persistence of Cree ancestral beliefs, did acknowledge that the Mistassini people in 1952 were "devout Anglicans."[5]

People convert for a variety of reasons and it would be difficult to give primacy to any one. We can say that it was a process that had a starting date in 1840 when George Barnley, the Methodist missionary based at Moose Factory who arrived at Rupert House, blessed the Cree residents with baptismal and marriage rituals.[6] By 1870 there were established missions and churches at Moose Factory, Rupert House, and Fort George, occasionally also serving Great Whale River. For a brief time in the late 1850s even the post at Little Whale River had a resident minister. However, by the 1860s the Church Missionary Society, the missionary arm of the Anglican Church, was experiencing increasing difficulty finding ministers for these distant lands. During the years leading up to 1870, the Reverend John Horden, based at Moose Factory, travelled along the east coast performing ministerial duties.

75   The Powers of Religion

Rupert House was sent its first resident minister in 1875 and Little Whale River in 1876. Fort George was second to Rupert House in economic importance as a fur trade post, and it drew on an even larger number of hunters. Yet its first resident missionary, James Peck, only moved his mission there from Little Whale River in 1884 following his marriage to an English woman – the event which prompted him to change his residence to more southern climes.[7] His Anglican predecessor at Fort George in the mid-1850s, E.A. Watkins, never fooled himself that he was having much success among the Crees who "feel no interest whatever in the sacred truths which it is my duty to proclaim."[8] He was removed after four years and sent to the Red River Colony. This Cree lack of interest in Christianity's offerings seemingly parallels the Rainy River Ojibwas' minimal enthusiasm at the same period.[9]

The Anglicans outlasted the Cree disinterest in their religion and eventually found the means to achieve some measure of success. In the 1860s the Church Missionary Society had come under the influence of its honorary clerical secretary, Henry Venn, whose plan for England's far-flung colonies was to establish Native churches operated by Native clergy. He called for the white missionaries "to seek their own euthanasia" by training Native clergy and at the same time asked that the non-Native clergy working for the Church Missionary Society "respect the national habits and identity of their charges."[10] As Nock further tells us, the Church Missionary Society sought to make Christianity indigenous, not exotic. As will be seen, these principles seem to have guided the Anglicans in the James Bay area, for Cree deacons and several Cree priests were invested from the earliest of days.

The Catholics were also represented, mainly at Waswanipi and its outpost of Migiskan in about 1850, when Governor Simpson had given permission to the Catholics to construct chapels.[11] Simpson's policy was not to permit the "collision of creeds" at posts, which he considered detrimental both to the Indians and the trade, but to reserve some posts as Protestant and others as Catholic. Thus the coastal posts of eastern James Bay were to become Protestant while in the regions to the south, such as Abitibi, Temiskaming, Waswanipi, all on inland routes, the Catholics were permitted to construct chapels which were sometimes underwritten by the company.[12] The Crees at Mistassini encountered Catholic priests in their travels to other posts and regions over the height of land such as at Lake St Jean. The Catholic priests also travelled there and Mistassini was visited several times between 1844 and 1861. Beginning in about 1852, Waswanipi was also visited most summers by priests coming from other posts such as Grand Lake Victoria or from the Upper St Maurice.[13] We also learn from the parish history that at some point the Anglicans began sending "one of the Christian Indians" inland from Rupert House. In 1884 a Waswanipi man, Robert Iserhoff, trained as a catechist by Archdeacon Thomas Vincent, held services for company employees and the hunters. Being given the sacraments by a resident Native person was short-lived for the Waswanipi Crees at this time, as Iserhoff died in 1886.[14] The Anglicans at the interior posts were also served by visiting ministers or by the Crees themselves travelling to the larger posts at the coast, particularly Rupert House.[15]

However, at Waswanipi at the turn of the century it was Catholicism that had the greater number of adherents,[II] according to Canon Samuel Iserhoff's recollections of his birthplace. He was born in 1885 to a Cree mother and a company employee of mixed ancestry[III] and observed that "in my boyhood days, nearly all the people there were Roman Catholics, with maybe three or four families of us being Anglicans."[16] If we are to believe the parish history, the people of Waswanipi were at first Roman Catholic "more by accident of geography and necessity than by choice. However, their family and economic and religious ties were really with James Bay and … they were not long in changing churches when the opportunity arose." Scanlon further writes that in 1907 a petition was presented to the (Anglican) Bishop Holmes signed by twenty-two heads of families in which they renounced the Roman Catholic faith and "sought admission into the purer sphere of the Church Catholic."[17] Similarly, a 1911 census prepared by the Reverend J. E. Woodall at Rupert House shows that of 138 Crees associated with the Waswanipi post, forty-three were deemed to be Protestants.[18] In this period, rather than sending a minister to Waswanipi, a Rupert House Cree and catechist, William Wapatchee, visited the post with the canoe brigade in order to conduct services. He was deemed by the Catholics to have greater influence amongst the hunters for he spoke their language rather than the Montagnais the priests spoke and he was "one of theirs."[19]

Wapachee[IV] was known as *aiamié okima* translated by the priest as "the king of prayer."[20] Despite the stature Wapachee held, the priest, Father Joseph-Etienne Guinard, questioned his right to preach and what he preached and insisted that he, Guinard, as a "black robe" held the truth of the religion of Jesus Christ, not to mention that the Catholics were at Waswanipi before the Protestants. Few came to his services that night or for the next twenty years until he left the mission in 1928. In fact, on a day in 1907 when he rang the bell for services he claimed that the son of the Waswanipi post manager and other youths stopped people along the path to the chapel, intimidating those wishing to attend his services.[V] At a later date, he charged that the clerk, Stuart, made him ill by putting something in his food. In his memoirs, Guinard also expressed his surprise and frustration at not being offered lodging or dinner on the evening of his arrival at Waswanipi at the home of the company manager (actually clerk), C.J.R. Jobson, despite this being the practice at all the posts. Guinard went without dinner but the next day he surprised the clerk by appearing there and confronting him. In his defence, Jobson explained that Father Georges Lemoine, a visiting priest at Waswanipi from 1901 to 1905, had counselled the Crees to demand higher prices for their furs and told them the company was stealing from them. Father Guinard assured Jobson that he was there only to preach the word of God. On his first mission there in 1899 the priest seemingly enjoyed better relations with the clerk, David Baxter, who arranged to saw lumber for him with which to construct a chapel.[21]

As for the Anglicans, Bishop Anderson visited Waswanipi in the summers of 1912 and 1913 to prepare forty-one people for confirmation. Guinard was also there, carrying out his religious duties. Once again, the Waswanipi people were subject to great displays of religious factionalism and probably "badgering" from both sides, for Scanlon writes that the priest warned the Catholics of "evil that befall them for resorting to 'heretical teachers'."[22] Thus one can only speculate at the joy the Anglican establishment felt when, in 1913, shortly after the priest left Waswanipi, the Catholic chapel was overturned in a squall.[VI] Scanlon quotes Harry Cartlidge, the Anglican missionary who arrived there in 1914, as saying: "This incident made a great impression upon the Indians, specially when all the other buildings escaped unharmed."[23] By the 1920s and by Cartlidge's figures, there were 173 Cree men trading at Waswanipi, made up of forty-four families of whom thirty-six were Anglican and the rest Roman Catholic. These figures accord with Guinard's, who wrote that he always had about the same number of Catholics, thirty.[24] Guinard admitted defeat in 1928 when he abandoned "cette impossible mission" for reasons of health. Thereafter Waswanipi Crees who were Catholic were expected to meet the priest at Senneterre, but these tended to be only the men out on supply trips; the women and children stayed back at the post.[25] The Waswanipi people, as other Crees, embraced their new Christian religion wholeheartedly, to the chagrin of the post manager who wrote in 1922: "Looks as if I'll never get them [the supply brigades] off until the blinking church is burned down. Services all the time and no work done."[26]

Despite the acrimony between the officials of both religions, the Crees seem to have practised tolerance towards each other. That was Father Guinard's assessment. In his writing of the trips he made with the Waswanipi men to Senneterre he commented that the Catholics amongst them prayed in peace without being ridiculed. He himself suppressed his zeal. When he slipped in this endeavour, the Crees' demeanour changed from high spiritedness to indifference and he corrected himself. At their rest stops the men were more interested in plying him with questions about such subjects as the stars, electricity, wheat, and asked him for books on these matters.[27]

Guinard left an analysis of why he thought the Catholics failed at Waswanipi. He suggested that the problem dated back to about 1901–6 when the priests, Lemoine and Blanchin, served at Waswanipi only a few days in the summer and did not await the return of the men on the canoe brigades. He felt that had they done so they would have been able to combat the influence of the Protestants at Rupert House. Interestingly, Father Guinard also gives us some insights into some objections to the contents of his preaching. He informs the reader that sometimes in his sermons he attacked Protestantism as having been founded by an apostate, a lewd and murderous king, and he was accused by the Crees of speaking only of misery, eternal damnation, and a thousand terrible things. They told him he must speak of beauty, of the "grand nuage."[28]

Despite each church's attempt to portray itself as embodying the "true word," the Crees, not uncharacteristically, had their own way of responding to these competing attempts to win over their souls. Writing in 1935, the anthropologist Frank G. Speck remarked: "Evangelization rests very lightly upon their moral conscience. The case of the Waswanipi Lake Indians affords a good example. They are both Catholic and Protestant. When a priest comes to administer his service, the people take their prayerbook and attend; when the Protestant minister comes to hold service, they take their books and assemble for him – for they have both."[29] Speck's observations were corroborated. Years later, one Waswanipi woman, Caroline Diamond Oblin, made a chance comment to me that she did not know who baptized her in the 1950s, and that her mother was not aware of the differences between the Catholics and Protestants.

The religious wars were not as marked at Mistassini as at Waswanipi. Possibly once the Anglicans became visible within the summer community at the post, people may have accepted the religion offered them there rather than travelling to Pointe Bleue or other settlements in the region to participate in Catholic rites. It was in 1903 that Bishop Newnham visited the post and by 1910 the Anglicans had built a church there that lasted until 1960. In place of a bell at the original church, a saw blade and stick were used to call the worshippers to church.[30]

Christianity, as preached by the Anglicans through the Church Missionary Society, evidently had appeal for the Crees back in the mid-

1800s as numbers of them accepted Christian baptism and marriage. Between the years 1853 and 1871, the registers of St Philip's parish, which included Fort George and Great Whale River, recorded twenty-nine baptisms, while in the four years from 1852 to 1856 there were twenty-one marriages officiated by an Anglican priest. Incidentally, most of those marrying were listed only with Cree names, suggesting they had not been previously baptized. Later church records indicate the Cree children were given Christian names and for the most part their parents also bore Christian names and surnames.³¹

At the time the two denominations were fighting over Cree souls, the Waswanipi people managed to maintain a number of their own religious practices, or "superstitions" as Guinard termed them. He describes the bones of bear and beaver hung on adorned perches, of how the door of the lodge had to be closed while they were eating bear for fear the animal's soul would forewarn other bears to flee. The surveyor A.P. Low also noted that they continued to hold "a sneaking regard for the windago and other evil spirits of their forefathers."³²

However, it was Lucien Turner, the naturalist who resided in Ungava from 1882 to1884, speaking of the Little Whale River Crees, who observed that "while they are Christians externally, they are so only as long as they are within the reach of the missionary."³³ To illustrate his point, he noted that one time when the Reverend Peck visited among them the priest noticed some men with several wives and berated them until they sent the second wives away. Once the missionary was gone, Turner tells us, the men took back these wives. Similarly, for a later period, Speck suggests that "subordination to sacerdotal authority – which means only the abolishment of polygyny, conjuring and the performance of individual pagan rites of divination, dream control, drumming and dancing – holds sway only for limited periods."³⁴ On the other hand Low, writing in the early 1890s of the whole Labrador peninsula, observed that most of the Indians were Christian at the time he was carrying out his studies and he commented that they were "devoutly religious, noting that despite long absences from the 'eye of the missionary' while in the woods they kept track of the days in order to observe Sundays properly by abstaining from work."³⁵ Writing of their geological expedition in James Bay in 1909, the Leiths claimed that "the natives delight in attending church services as often as possible.ᵛᴵᴵ Morning and evening prayers are commonly observed in their tents, not only when at the posts but when in the wilderness."³⁶

The Crees kept track of the days by ticking them off on a rough calendar; later proper calendars were issued to them by both the Anglican and Catholic churches. Those distributed by the Catholics were first circulated in 1893 by Father Fafard, using a simple mimeograph machine and written in Cree syllabics. It was called "Pisimo-Masinaigan," meaning "book of the moons" (the Crees, as other Algonquian-speakers called months moons). The calendars began in June and ended in September because, as Father Guinard pointed out, it was in the summer months that the missionaries saw them, not on 1 January. Besides Sundays, other holy days were clearly marked with crosses. The Catholics and Crees produced special names for each of the months; for example, January was the month (or moon) when "the branches are bare" and November, when "all is suspended because of the cold." Apparently the Protestant Crees abandoned these names and were using the English ones. The calendars served another purpose; out on the land the families would mark significant events such as births and deaths and then show their calendars to the priest when they saw him in the summer. Accordingly, he was able to record the dates.[37] So fastidious were some Cree people in marking their calendars that at Nichikun in 1940 they were able to prove Stevenson wrong. He writes: "It is rather strange that every Indian that comes in figures he is a day ahead of us, we are beginning to have a sneaking suspicion that we have missed a day somewhere." This was confirmed for him on 14 December when a supply plane landed.[38]

The Leiths also learned a lot about the Cree practice of conjuring and remarked that their "superstitious spirit" is seldom noticed by the traveller but "nearly always lurks beneath the surface."[39] Presumably they were writing of the northernmost Crees, people they met on their travels, but Anderson also found this for the Mistassini people when he worked there from 1913 to 1918. Besides describing the shaking tent ceremony, he had this to say: "Although the Mistassini Indians were a very devout people, carried prayer books to church and reciting family prayers daily, the Christianity never seemed to interfere with their conjuring seances. The willow frames of conjuring tents were to be seen on most of the portages on the river route and occasionally a seance would take place right at the post, usually in the autumn when all the voyageurs had returned from the coast and all were at the post prior to departure to the trapping lands. It is difficult for the white man to understand what brings about these seances, for they seem to happen spontaneously."[40]

Despite the increasing involvement with Christianity and the loss of some practices and beliefs,[41] the shaking tent ceremony could still be observed in the 1960s by anthropologists at Rupert House[42] and at Waswanipi.[43] Likewise, the work of Adrian Tanner in the 1960s at Nichikun-Mistassini and his observation of the continued practice of hunting rituals intended to influence the animal bosses had already alerted students of Cree society to a persistence in the belief of traditional supernatural forces. So it is with no great surprise that one finds the elders at Mistassini accounting for an especially good moose hunt in the summer of 1942 as being due to the women and children having returned to the "Indian habit" of beating the drums until the men returned.[44] Twenty years later, at Rupert House, Knight heard from both Billy Jolly (born circa 1901) and John Minister (born circa 1901) that in hunting, drum singing was more powerful than bones, and Minister told him: "You sing and listen to what you sing and then you hear your voice coming from a certain direction. Sometimes he sees how far to go ... not many older men who can do this anymore." Then he added: "It would be as good now as in the past if there were as many moose and caribou as there were in the past."[45] One can wonder whether it was the missionaries or the loss of game that propelled Christianity to the forefront of Cree lives.

Although whites seem perplexed by this duality in religious practices, the Crees obviously were not. David Cooter, writing in his journal from Nichikun Post in the spring of 1941, left us this glimpse into a Cree view of the supernatural: "Bertie Jimikin's religious principles prevent him from working on Sunday but do not prevent him believing in witchcraft. He was supposed to marry Kitty, Sam Rabbitskin's step daughter, but broke off the engagement to marry Annie Longchap in the spring. After a dream the other night he seems convinced that Sam Rabbitskin had been conjuring him and that as a result he will die before the snow disappears. No one seems to have realized, when the marriage was first proposed, that Kitty and Bertie are first cousins and therefore cannot legally marry."[46]

An initial enthusiasm for what the Anglicans were saying may have ebbed for the Crees. The Reverend Woodall in a 1911 report expresses some dissatisfaction with the commitment to Christianity and Christian morals amongst the Rupert House people. He lamented that there was a "failing of respect for the 7th day and 7th Commandment that is becoming pretty general ... All this is very depressing to those who knew Ruperts House previous to 1907."[47] Similarly, he commented about the moral suasion that William Wapachee, the catechist, had at Nemiskau, saying he was "doing what he can but his word is not the law it was a little while ago."[VIII] To add to the difficulty for the Anglicans there, Wapachee had no shelter in which to hold classes or services, for the tent they had used since 1907 had been demolished in a gale.

John Horden first arrived with his wife at Moose Factory in 1851 under the auspices of the Church Missionary Society and, according to a diocesan history, threw himself into the mission work with great enthusiasm. He reportedly had considerable talent for the varied demands of the ministry both spiritual and practical, and tackled such tasks as carpentry and printing. He was seen by the society as having considerable success with the Crees and the next year was ordained a minister. Twenty years later, his indefatigability having stretched even further with his taking on a larger and larger territory when one by one each of the missions lost their cleric, Horden was elevated to bishop of the newly formed diocese of Moosonee. One of Horden's greatest achievements was his prodigious output of religious pamphlets and tracts, written materials that the Crees could take with them to their camps.

A magical form of communication in James Bay had originated in the 1830s at Norway House in Manitoba and quickly spread throughout the subarctic, in part aided by the missionaries. The Reverend James Evans had produced for his Cree parishioners at Norway House a syllabary by which they could write their language. It was an ingeniously devised writing system that took little time to learn[ix] and thus was easily passed on at meeting places in the bush. As the missionaries established permanent ministries in various places they translated prayers, hymns, and a portion of the gospels which they printed on presses imported from England, Horden was the first to introduce the system at Moose Factory in 1852, eventually producing no fewer than sixteen hundred books in three dialects.[x] This syllabary was used by the Crees not only for reading religious tracts but also to communicate with each other, so that in writing of the area Low comments that "all the Christian Indians can read and write." He explained that letters written with charcoal on birchbark "are commonly seen on the portages along various routes."[48] The available printed materials were all of a religious nature. At Great Whale River in 1949, the literature furnished by the missionary included prayer books and hymnals, the Ten Commandments, the New Testament, the Sermon on the Mount, *Pilgrim's Progress*, and "Peep of the Day." Additionally, the Hudson's Bay Company calendar was written in syllabics.[49] In the days before acquiring literacy the Crees would have had to make arrangements for meeting in the spring before they split into smaller hunting groups for winter, agreeing to meet when the ice leaves the rivers or when the fur of the otter becomes common. Sometimes they would leave signs such as broken twigs along the route.[50] Being able to leave written messages simplified making these arrangements. Romance was also greatly aided with syllabics; the young people would leave love letters in "their private post-offices" in trees and other hiding places.[51]

There were two ministers of mixed ancestry amongst the Rupert House people at various times and one wonders what additional influence they may have had over the Crees. Certainly, Reverend Thomas

Vincent, himself country born, in a lengthy reply to the Church Missionary Society insisted that Native clergy would be more acceptable to the Indians than Europeans.[52] Vincent, ordained as a priest and sent to Albany in 1865,[XI] married Eliza Gladman, a mixed-ancestry daughter of a Rupert House factor. He is described as having "waged a vigorous and fiercely energetic campaign to win souls for God" until his death in 1907. Evidently, his favourite motto was "Compel them to come in."[53] Compelling, it seems, he was. Bishop Renison claimed that Vincent, whom he described as a "magnificent patriarch with a jaw like a dreadnought and shoulders like a buffalo ... made Christians of every tribe from Osnaburgh to Winisk River; from the source of the Albany River in the west to the most northerly Indian settlement in the diocese." According to Renison, the last lone Indian conjuror at Albany managed to avoid conversion by living on fish and clothing himself in rabbit skins in order to keep away from the post.[54] Long's analysis is that Vincent was the victim of Victorian prejudices and did not receive the recognition from Bishop Horden he deserved.[55] The Reverend Edward Richards, another of Horden's pupils and a native of Moose Factory, served for ten years at Rupert House before being sent to take up a mission at Moose Factory. His work there is not chronicled, but Bishop Renison later noted that he was known affectionately as "Uncle Ned."[56]

The weakness of the men of the Church Missionary Society sent out to convert the Crees may well have worked in the Anglican Church's favour. The church had to rely on Native catechists, often hastily elevated to deacons and even ordained as ministers despite not spending the years at St John's College in Winnipeg that others did. Their lack of academic qualifications is not a criticism of their abilities, for like their fellow parishioners, they had formed their own blend of Christianity. Undoubtedly these were the best men to transmit the teachings and messages of Christianity and in a fluent Cree tongue.[XII] Thus, the early catechists in James Bay were William Wapatchee and his sons; Redfern Louttit; Robert, Joseph, Charles, and Samuel Iserhoff; John Gull; Edward Richards and Second Bearskin.[XIII] They implanted the Anglican religion into the hearts and minds of their Cree brethren and helped them graft it onto their Cree religion. No doubt a good number of these men were originally recognized as being imbued with supernatural powers. For instance, George Kechekapo held daily services at Eastmain in the early 1900s and Woodall felt that "his consistent character is having a splendid influence on the Indians. They are quiet and tractable and making good progress."[57] The historian Morris Zaslow reminds us of another reason the Anglican Church benefited from employing Cree catechists and deacons. Their efforts, he notes, were powerfully aided by the Hudson's Bay Company whose "support was cemented by marriage ties between fur trading and clerical families, and extended downward to the employees of the company whose numerous progeny afforded a continuing nucleus of supporters and workers."[58]

One outsider is said to have achieved the same results – W.G. Walton, the "reindeer man." Walton arrived as a deacon in Fort George from England in 1892, becoming a priest two years later, and remained there for the next thirty-two years. He left an enduring and respected impression on the Crees of Fort George, Great Whale River, and Old Factory (Wemindji). He was remembered fondly years later by the Crees for his pivotal role in bringing them Christianity. Rupert George, born about 1890 and living in Great Whale River in 1974, told the anthropologist Lucy Turner that "I must have been fifteen when people started going to church. Right away, I listened and believed what was being taught to us. [Mr Walton] was the first one to teach us."[59] Similarly, Sam Masty, speaking in 1974 at Great Whale River, said Walton was the "first man to tell people to put away the things they believed; the first to change many people." Masty explained that the people lost the supernatural powers "when they heard about Jesus Christ from the missionaries ... The people willfully lost these powers because Reverend Walton said to do so. They listened to him and now today no one has any powers like that ... Reverend Walton didn't think it was all that bad to have powers like that but he still didn't want people to practice this, also he didn't want people to practice the 'shaking tent' ... Reverend Walton preached that everyone should love each other, no matter who they were."[60] When Richard Preston, asked on his visit to Fort George about why they should have such an enduring memory of Walton, especially when most whites are not remembered, he was told that Walton "came, baptized us, learned our language and preached to us in Cree and was still there to baptize our children. And if he had something to say to us, and he knew we wouldn't like it, but he thought it was true, he would say it anyway."[61] Fikret Berkes was struck by the richness of the stories about this missionary, ascribing it in large measure to his tolerance of the open discussion of Cree practices and legends.[62]

Walton was a small man but evidently very authoritarian. The Leiths describe him as exercising a "benevolent despotism ... which extends beyond spiritual affairs,"[63] while one Cree man remembered that Walton was very strict with them, making the boys sit for many hours with their hands behind their back, learning the Bible. As well, he shouted at them, which Sun reminds us was "an unCree act," seen as a loss of self-control.[64] Why was Walton tolerated and, in fact, seemingly held in esteem both then and now? The Reverend Griffin provides an explanation similar to Preston's. He comments that Walton's knowledge of the Indian language and character gave him an influence and command that most of the missionaries of the Bay lacked.[65] Walton did take his learning of both Cree and Inuktitut very seriously, mentioning it several times in his few extant letters. In one, believed to be dated 1900, he expressed his thankfulness that he no longer had to use an interpreter for Cree but added: "still I am far from knowing their language."[66]

Undoubtedly Walton's learning of Cree and Cree ways was helped immeasurably by his wife. Daisy Alice Spencer, whom he married in the spring of 1896,[67] was the daughter of Miles Spencer, the Hudson's Bay Company manager for the Eastmain District, stationed in Fort George and himself of mixed ancestry. Daisy Walton spoke Cree, for Walton is quoted as writing: "I think about the only time my wife and I spoke in English was at the dining-room table. The rest of the time was spent in conversing with the Indians, the services for them, or in translation work."[68] Her Cree family connections were certainly useful to him.

Walton was also a vigorous defender of the Crees' rights and well-being. His eloquent arguments to the government regarding their initiating a reindeer management scheme attests to this, as well as Walton's championing their cause before the American Wildlife Association. In an article in the 1920 *Bulletin of the American Game Protective Association* he assured the readers that the Crees could not be responsible for the diminishing number of game birds, as alleged, but he also warned them regarding the game laws "that when human life is at stake, we will not keep the law."[69]

Although he did not tolerate Cree religious rites, more significantly, Walton defended some Cree practices. In 1908 the Inlander Noonoosh apparently went insane and became violent. According to the Inlanders who arrived at the post in June, Noonoosh was killed by his own people, which included his son. Walton delivered a sermon about the death of Noonoosh which, according to Gillies, the post manager, "practically amounted to a defence of patricide." Gillies was again critical of Walton when he set out the next day for his annual trip to Whale River, taking Noonoosh's son along as part of his crew.[70]

Another Walton characteristic was his willingness to trek through the bush and canoe the waters just as the Crees did and in the same clothing as they wore. In his thirty-two years of service he must have covered thousands of miles to visit Cree camps to discuss religion and tend to medical needs. At the post, one of Walton's techniques was to invite three or four Cree men to his home to talk and he believed the "most good was done" this way.[71] The post journals also indicate his selflessness in making special trips through the bush to visit a sick or injured person.[72] In fact, the first introduction the reader has to him in the Fort George post journals is his response to an appeal of David Cox, who in November 1893 came looking for someone to see his brother-in-law, John, ill at his camp. Walton left, returned the next day, and reported John better.[73] Thereafter the company men at Fort George left all medical care to Walton. However, he saw his role as doctor as subordinate to his role as a missionary. For example, in 1902, in the middle of a devastating measles epidemic the post manager at Fort George, A.A. Chesterfield, criticized Walton for not sending Crees living at the post out into the bush to avoid the disease.[74]

Walton did not always win people over by being generous, sacrificing, and selfless. In his study of Christianity amongst the Wemindji Cree, Sun demonstrates that Walton was often critical of Cree ways and was persistent in demanding they give up their "superstitious" practices. For example, he objected to the first fish of the spring being returned to the water, declaring it was a "sacrifice" and wrong because "it was not made to God." Similarly, he complained of their respect for the beaver, declaring that man and animals were different and therefore man was "permitted to kill the animals for food."[75] In his writings, Walton scorned other "foolish ideas," such as thinking of the black bear as their god. "I have gathered the Indians together and spoken very plainly about these very foolish ideas and one old man was perfectly convinced, but I am afraid that it will be a very long time before many of their ideas will be given up."[76] Some company men thought him interfering when he castigated them for their behaviour. Gillies complained in his journal entry of 21 February 1909 that: "all hands went to church and as usual got it in the neck on the Drink question. It is getting monotonous as a text for sermons at this place where there is less promiscuous drinking than at any Coast Post on the Bay, G.W.R. excepted."[77]

Even amusements such as dancing and music were condemned by Walton. In a 1905 letter to an unknown recipient, Walton wrote that "we almost dread the coming of summer," explaining that the people would be tea drinking and dancing to fiddle music. He goes on to say: "Every one knows the evil results of this dancing but they want to persist in it because they say it is not a sin to dance and that they have known even ministers to do it."[78] Walton displays elation in 1914 when he reported to his superiors that the Fort George Indians had given up the "New Years tea drinking feast – an old custom of the H.B.Co. Scotch traders – and are now coming in for the Christmas Holy Communion Service. This made our last Christmas service very joyous."[79]

Despite his interfering ways, the Crees recall Walton in a more positive light; even at the time, he obviously commanded their respect and attention. A more important consideration is what message from him drew them into the Christian sphere. Walton's personality alone could not have been responsible.

Christianity contains within it a richness of messages and symbols that has appealed to a great diversity of peoples and world views. The Crees were a profoundly spiritual people; their whole world, material and non-material – animals, plants, rocks, clothes, doorways of tents – was infused with spirits and spiritual powers.[80] As John Webster Grant, the historian of Canadian church missions, observed, the Indians could find in Christianity some elements which their own traditions lacked.[81] From this perspective, then, it is not surprising the Crees were open to additional religious thoughts and concepts. Obviously there was a selection process in play, for there must have been aspects of Christianity that they could not accept. Rather than holding an appeal for them, some of these beliefs must have left them confused. For a more or less egalitarian, consensual society, it must have seemed strange to learn of hierarchy and authoritarianism, of a highly structured patriarchal society, as one does in Christianity. Another problem would have been the Christian attitude towards animals. Even though flocks and shepherds might be seen as respect for animals, domesticating, controlling, and killing them was not consistent with the Cree view that they and the animals were guided by their "attending spirits," and that the animals gave themselves to the hunter.[82] The notion that a man would dominate an animal, rather than the other way around, as in the hunt leading up to the kill, must have seemed alien. So would have the Christian obsession with sin, a concept which, at the time, likely did not have a Cree counterpart.[XIV] The prominence of Mary in the New Testament might also have seemed unusual, especially to a hunting society rather than an agricultural one, yet this imagery might have been submerged within the notion of family life. How a discussion of transubstantiation would have been presented by Walton or viewed by the Crees is speculative but nevertheless would have produced some relatively significant views in the minds of the Crees, given their belief in, and fear of, *witiko*. John Long doubts the Crees accepted Christian notions of heaven and hell; their soul lingered nearby the living.[83] The concept of Christian love of Jesus Christ and one's fellow man, so central to this religion, must have baffled Crees however it was explained to them. One could sympathize with the Crees when an exasperated Walton writes: "Even such a simple text as 'if you love me, keep my commandment' is all dark to them."[84]

There would have been many more contradictions for the Crees as basic tenets in Christianity were being explained. One might also ask how the Crees were able to ignore the verbal abuse hurled at their traditional beliefs. Missionaries denigrated their heathen practices as savage. They did not target only their religious practices but strove hard to alter their daily habits.

Despite all these contradictions and belittlement, the Crees obviously found aspects of Christianity highly meaningful. It is clear that Walton won them over through words, the literal message of God. This is the hallmark of Protestant conversions rather than Catholic ones, the latter relying also on rituals and ceremony.[85] Walton saw the benefits of discussing Christianity with small numbers of Crees, for in acknowledging that the most good was done by talking to them he sees these gains in terms of their "beginning to see the practical side of religion."[86] Not only did Walton invite Cree hunters to his home to discuss texts, he also was concerned that he might not have enough time to instruct people at Great Whale River during his brief visits so he could baptize them. Accordingly, he worked hard to print a large number of hymn books and almanacs.[XV]

Religion does not fulfill one's need for logic or rationality; it meets an individual's emotional and psychological needs and helps locate one's place in the world.[87] One's understanding of religion and observance of its rituals are highly individual, as are the reasons for coming to believe in a specific creed or continuing to believe in the religion in which one is raised. Furthermore, it is difficult for all but those schooled in theology to articulate one's beliefs and reasons. Therefore it is surprising that Cree individuals or any other lay person would be able to discuss their religious views sufficiently to explain why, at about the turn of the century, they chose to incorporate Christianity in their ideological system. Not surprisingly, Speck, in his book on Montagnais-Naskapi religion,[XVI] commented they cared not "a whit about the character of the deity, the nature of retribution, the problem of trinity, the virgin birth."[88] Of course, the Crees likely would not have thought of their spiritual practices as a religion; they would not have thought of them in the abstract. They were part and parcel of life. The whole issue of syncretism, the fact that the Crees blended or merged both Christianity and their own animistic religious beliefs and practices or maintained them as parallel systems[XVII] will not be demonstrated or argued here as it is sufficiently covered in the literature.[89]

The acceptance of Christianity came at a juncture for both religions. At the turn of the century, life was changing for the Crees in ways that must have strained the range of domains covered by their traditional religion. New agents from the south were not only importing new ideas and ways; most importantly, they were importing serious epidemic diseases at the same time as there were critical animal depletions. The epidemics that raged well into the 1900s, with hundreds dying, must have demoralized the Crees, making them all the more vulnerable to a religion that preached an after-life and reunification with family. For the Anglicans, the doctrinal homogeneity of the Anglican Church and the relationship between the sacred and the secular were being undermined and refashioned with "Protestant notions of self-construction through rational improvement and the bourgeois ideal of accumulation through hard work."[90] These changes in the relationship of church and state, along with the anti-slavery, anti-colonial sentiments taking hold in England, provided new opportunities for the Christians there to extend the reaches of their church; Africa, India, Australia, New Zealand, and Canada provided potentially rich missionary fields for them.

One of the keys to understanding Cree acceptance would be to know what part of Anglican doctrine was presented to Cree churchgoers in the form of sermons and teachings. This is not information that has survived other than occasional references.[XVIII] Nor do we know how Christian terminology was translated so as to be meaningful to the Crees. Conversion to Christianity could not have been a simple cognitive operation; it would have required a change in the content of an individual's thinking.[91] Possibly Christianity evoked in the Crees sentiments which might not have been present in their traditional religion, such as Christianity's emphasis on love. The cognitive would have required a change in "operational" thinking, in devising new answers to old questions. The internalization of new ways of thinking and feeling was not easily discernible by the missionaries. However, the remaining area in which Christian conversion took place – the moral sphere – was quite within the view of the missionaries, who often felt betrayed by the Crees, particularly those who served as catechists. Adultery was the "vile sin" which the missionaries seemed to single out as most offended them.[92]

Speck's earlier comments about the Montagnais-Naskapi who, in his opinion, were oblivious to the theological aspects of Christianity, therefore led him to a sociological explanation of why Christianity was adopted. He appears to link it to the conditions of their physical world. He tells us that "the one yearning of the Naskapi mind is for subsistence while living and postponement of death," this at a time when both were difficult. He seems to be suggesting that to achieve subsistence, they must rely on the "traditional agencies," for Christianity cannot help them kill animals. As for the postponement of death, Christianity does teach of the immortality of the soul and the rewards of the Christian heaven. It is this that "accounts for the liberal acceptance of Catholicism so widely throughout the peninsula," remarks Speck.[93] Certainly, at the end of the nineteenth century when Walton was actively proselytizing, the Crees were facing a drastic decline in the caribou herds. At the same time they were suffering from epidemics which seriously aggravated this famine. Those who survived were often too weak to hunt and this, along with the tragic losses of family members, must have generated a deep psychological depression, perhaps making them attentive to promises of a God that would take care of them and give them hope of an everlasting life. At this time the Crees were spending more time near the post and congregating in larger numbers and for longer periods than they had before. Perhaps Christianity also helped them cope with larger group living, providing a code for regulating relations with non-family members while their own religion continued to govern their lives in the bush, both in hunting and hunting group relations. Although speculation, if one accepts that sociological factors as well as ideological/cosmological ones must be involved in the conversion process, that seems a reasonable supposition.

Long's work takes us back to looking for common principles between Cree and Christian elements and he found in the Cree tradition that power was an important element. He saw the Cree religion as conferring personal power and found in Christianity the means by which the Crees could add to their personal power. This democratization, the ability to influence the power through prayer, meant that each one could overcome situations that threatened their security: the food quest, *witiko*, illness, perils of travel, and threatening shamans. Long notes that it was not a reckless abandonment of their traditional beliefs but a selection and incorporation process through which they chose to adopt other channels to manitu and power.[94] Christianity, then, became another source of power which would permit them to interact with their environment, so crucial to their way of life.

The oral histories from Great Whale River also attest to the importance of these supernatural powers at the time the Crees were incorporating Christianity into their belief system. Sam Masty, born in about 1906, told the anthropologist Lucy Turner of how a man saved his wife from attack by putting her into a deep sleep and from that story he went on to say that the Reverend Walton did not condemn people having those powers but suggested it was bad to harm people. Sam Masty thought that people lost those powers when they heard about Jesus Christ but attributed it to Walton's persuasion, saying "they completely forgot the powers."[95] Similarly, Rupert George said that Walton had told them that God could do anything for them, so they stopped "practising their powers" and, accordingly ceased their drumming and singing. When Turner was interviewing the Crees in Great Whale River in the 1970s she was told, regarding this power that "they just didn't use it and now it's completely forgotten."[96] Their abandonment of drumming and singing may not have been as benign as suggested; Sun reports a Cree informant telling him that on Walton's hearing the drums, one evening he stormed into the tent and angrily threw the drum onto the fire."[97]

These powers were not completely abandoned but as conditions changed for the Crees, so did the nature of these powers. Comparing her 1930s study at Rupert House to Richard Preston's thirty years later, Flannery found that of the pantheon of spirits the Crees called upon to help them subsist in the bush, it was the Cree hunter's *mistabeo*, attending spirit, a kind of "master of ceremonies" that survived to the detriment of their *powatakanak* their dream-helpers, those spirits which helped the hunter with foreknowledge of the location of the animals. By the 1960s what survived of the old power complex centred on the *mistabeo* concept[98] or *mistaapew* at Mistassini.[99]

Sun's explanation does not centre on the theology but on understanding the aspects that led the Cree of Wemindji to follow the teachings of Walton. Central to this explanation is the fact that elements of Christianity and Cree religion were permitted to exist side by side on two distinct but overlapping levels, yet harmonious and unproblematic.[100] Sun shows how a number of hunting rituals were observed, though "not condoned officially by the church" and he concludes that by allowing the parallel existence of traditional practices the missionaries enabled the Crees to accept Christianity as a complementary religion to their own traditional one.[101] This compartmentalization was not only possible but necessary for Cree hunters, "whose experience of spiritual communion was cast in metaphors that were for the most part personalized symbols of moral relationships to the animals they hunted."[102] Sun also noted corresponding ideals in the two belief systems. He specifically mentioned the ethical concepts such as "cooperation, sharing, reciprocity and benevolence" which facilitated making the two religions fit together. There were other similarities, such as the age-old one of Manitu and God, but although Sun discusses them, he does point out the similarities were superficial. Manitu is a "boss/maker" while God is a "maker/creator."[103]

The emphasis on pre-Christian ritual may be another explanation for conversion. The Leiths commented on the great importance the Crees attached to attending church services several times a day, prayer meetings in their tents, and an individual's recitation of prayers on rising and going to sleep. At first the brothers thought this behaviour incongruous but then decided that "this strict observance of religious form is undoubtedly, for many of the natives, merely an expression of their desire for ceremony, form and social intercourse."[104] This point is also made by Preston when he commented that the Crees valued highly the services of priests or ministers in baptism and dying, "among other rituals that have some enduring hopes built into them." Preston had earlier learned from an alarmed Anglican minister at Fort George in the 1970s that "when the Cree catechists baptized a child, it was thought to be a protection against sorcery."[105]

In addition to the rituals and beliefs, Sun also found some compelling sociological reasons why the Crees would find Christianity attractive. He stresses that the improved technology provided by the fur trade weakened the dependence the Crees had on the animal spirits. The introduction of the repeater rifle made hunting more accurate and deadly. Small quantities of store-bought food were being taken inland which made the difference between a family starving and not. All this enabled the Crees to be less religious in the traditional sense.[106] For if the animals, principally the caribou, were dwindling in number, and then fish and small game became the mainstay of Cree life, the need to placate or cajole the animals spirits also diminished.

Preston sees the importance of Cree songs as one medium that helped Christianity fit in. He finds correspondences between the styles of word use in Cree songs and Christian hymns and between the expression of hope in songs and in hymns and prayers. Additionally he recognizes that there would have also been a fit between the old beliefs held by the Crees and the missionaries' preaching of moral precepts, principally the important ethic of looking after another.[107]

It needs reiterating that conversion, religious beliefs, and similar subjects defy simple explanation and are multi-causal and multi-dimensional. Undoubtedly, all the reasons given above were in play in the case of the Cree conversions in W.G. Walton's parishes. With Christian religiosity seeming to have taken a firm hold first in Fort George due, in part to Walton's special gifts and abilities, it may be that Christianity spread to other northern settlements. In 1912 Charles Iserhoff, the Native catechist at Mistassini[XIX] wrote to Woodall at Ruperts House that "it is a good thing to hear that the Fort George Indians are coming to East Main and holding services there and that they are causing many to give up their Old ways ... and how thankful I am to hear that some of the People at Rupert House are beginning to awake up and to think of the never ending eternity." The next year, when nineteen families of Fort Chimo Indians arrived at Great Whale River to see him, Walton commented on "how earnest the people [presumably Native lay people] must be in their inland work."[108]

Other communities, such as Rupert House, Waswanipi, and Mistassini received Anglican ministers only sporadically, yet these people, too, turned to Christianity at about the same time as the northern posts ministered to by Walton. The southern posts often had only sporadic visits by Anglican missionaries, but religious services were provided by

Crees or men of mixed ancestry who knew the language and their traditional spirituality. No Walton there; yet they converted. In other words, the time was ripe; the Crees, for a host of reasons, were receptive to incorporating elements of Christianity.

To try to explain conversion to Christianity throughout James Bay, another factor is worth considering, another weapon that Christianity had in its arsenal. It is the magic or power of the written word and what was available to the Crees once they could read the Bible in their own language. Sun interviewed a Cree at Wemindji in the late 1970s. In response to the question, "Have you always been a Christian?" he replied: "I believed in God right away as soon as I heard about the Bible … After I heard about the Bible I really began to wonder about God and the people." Another interviewee said: "I always used the Bible. I never was sent to school and I taught myself to read." In response to his meeting the missionaries, he replied. "He was the first one that taught me the Bible – William Walton from Fort George."[109]

Looking at the importance of the Bible to these two men[xx] brings into sharper focus some of the writings of Walton. His letters back to his superiors always discuss the progress he is making in writing prayer and hymn books. By 1905 Walton was proudly writing of having produced "an almanack and prayer for every am and pm for one week" and referred to one man's pride in telling visitors to the post about their books, explaining, "you know, it is our minister who makes them himself." Walton saw the printing of these books as providing inestimable good for his mission. In his 1902 letter to Reverend Gould he commented that "it is impossible to over estimate the good that has been done in this way and is a very great joy to me. If the poor people forget, as they may do, what they have heard in church still I can testify to the fact that they have become a praying people during the past 4 or 5 years … It is true that they first learned how to pray from some books I printed for them still they have made them so much their own by altering them so that they are more idiomatic."[110]

Walton was aware that the Bible was his most important tool. Sun tells us that he found a 1943 article by Walton in which he wrote: "If you can show to the Indians that something is 'in the book' right there and then, he will believe."[111] He was sensitive to the importance of the language used in the books. For the Inuit, he could call on books in Inuktitut written by his predecessor, Peck, but for the Crees he and the other Anglicans were using books produced in the Moose Factory dialect, originally translated by the Reverend John Horden in the late nineteenth century, making it a liturgical language for east James Bay Crees.[xxi] In 1904 Walton was lamenting that the people at Fort George and Great Whale River had "no book yet in their own dialect and only a very few understand a little of the 4 gospels in the Moose dialect. We have been doing all we can towards giving some small books, such as a few hymns."[112] It is clear that translation of the Bible for the Crees on the east coast of James Bay was yet to come but it seems that Walton accomplished this early in the twentieth century. In a 1914 letter to the bishop at Moosonee he mentions working on the translation of the Gospel of St Matthew and then proceeding to the "other two synoptic gospels" in addition to other books, such as commentaries on the ten commandments.[113]

"The power of the written word." How would this apply to the Crees and their acceptance of Christianity? The Crees had already a long-established practice of telling stories, particularly during the winter months when they were spending long hours in their tipis, captives to the inclement weather. Participation in prayer and hymn-singing fitted into this pattern and was admirably suited for small-group living. Once the Bible could be read, it opened up an immense new store of stories that touched Cree lives and gave importance and perhaps new meaning to them. There may also have been a magical quality about the written word. Walton was aware of how important illustrations could be in conveying the message and had brought back from England five hundred illustrations of the Testaments to use in printing his books. How much store do we place in Walton's declarations regarding his use of the magic lantern? Writing in 1901 of the services he had been holding in the "little iron church" at Great Whale River, where he used the magic lantern a little each time, he declared that his communicants told him: "Now we shall believe because we see what Jesus did is all true."[114] Was writing like the images of the magic lantern? Did it enable people to "see" and believe because the nature of the printed word was such to conjure up the same stories and same images – and with an authority of something distant and removed?

Was there a feeling of magic or even power in the fact that the Crees could read, that they could reproduce and transmit knowledge or a text in the same form they had first heard of it?[XXII] Walton commented: "They help and teach each other and they honour their teachers. Last year one went to Fort Chimo where he obtained new hymns which he learnt. By the time he reached Great Whale River every one he met on the way set out and copied them so that I was quite surprised to hear the whole congregation start singing ... 'In the sweet by and by' after our service one Sunday."[115]

A wider perspective on the significance of the written word is provided in the writings of the British anthropologist Jack Goody. It is here that we learn that it was only with alphabetic writing that some religions broke through their national frontiers to become religions of conversion. Goody explains that the written word of God was seen as more effective than the purely oral one because of the "evident performative force of that channel of communication and the hierarchical status of its practitioners" but also because of its static nature compared to the local variations in beliefs and actions among non-literate religions. Furthermore, a religion of conversion is propelled towards ethical universalism since its norms must apply to more than one society. Being written down aids in this process of generalization. The injunction "thou shall not kill" is sufficient when written. If delivered in a face-to-face situation it is likely to be embedded in more particular phraseology such as "thou shall not kill except under the orders of leader, party or of nation."[116] Thus Christianity, as a literate religion, would have been attractive to the Crees for the effectiveness, and therefore authority, in communicating its messages and for the universalism of these messages.

On another level, Goody suggests that writing provides privileged access to the sacred texts which thus provide "a unique link to God." Furthermore, since literacy is intrinsic to these "religions of the Book,"[117] so is the teaching of the skills of reading and writing. Recall Walton's comments about helping and teaching each other and honouring their teachers. Thus, the Crees derived from their incorporation of Christianity not only the sacred texts, a unique link to God, but also the magical powers of literacy, the supremacy of written communication over oral.

There is one more explanation to add. In other societies, women were seen to have had a considerable role in speeding along this conversion because of the opportunities of power and prestige that opened up for them[118] but such a focus could not be perceived in the oral or archival sources.[XXIII] Similarly, there is not enough substance to the records to suggest the role the missionaries might have had in refashioning Cree conceptions of cleanliness or housekeeping during the worst of the epidemics. We can only surmise how the gradual embracing of Christianity modified the Crees' vision of the world, its mix of the natural and supernatural, their own self-identity, as well as transforming their social and ritual practices. Yet there is no indication that Christianity brought with it abrupt changes in thinking or behaving. That the missionaries did not seek to turn the Cree pantheon of animal spirits into "devils" as they did elsewhere in the world[119] suggests to me that the missionaries did not see such traditions menacing Christian beliefs; the two religions served different needs and were observed in different non-conflicting and non-threatening ways. Each religion had its rituals but each operated in different spheres of Cree life: the processional in the church, the prayer in the lodge, while the respect of the animal spirit was manifest outdoors, at the kill, in the trees outside the lodge. As for the shamans, the men who held the spiritual knowledge of the Crees, they too were readily absorbed by the Anglicans as deacons and catechists, thereby speeding along and smoothing over the Cree incorporation of Christianity. These were men who had already delved more deeply into "spiritual seeking" and became more at ease with the missionary's words.[120] Through them might well have occurred a kind of evolving synthesis, or syncretism, an equivalency of the two religions in the minds of the Crees, to be called upon as the situation demanded. Long suggests that as long as hunting and trapping remained viable and before Cree children were forcefully resocialized in schools, the Crees were able to make intelligent choices, easily modifying the effects of Christianity. Moreover, by separating their religious life into the spheres of bush and town they could avoid confrontation with the missionaries and preserve or revitalize their traditional beliefs. Furthermore, the Crees sought protective powers.[121] One account which highlights this blending of the two religions is Andrew Ottereyes' statement that in bear hunting, "God led him to the bear."[122] As the Crees manoeuvred themselves through the twentieth century and as their social and economic situations changed away from a subsistence hunting society with its periods of starvation and death, their Christian beliefs might have provided greater security and understanding of the ongoing changes. Although not a combative society, the Christian messages of love, peace, and unity may have had great appeal and served the Crees well as they moved into ever larger social spheres. In the end, it mattered not, as we know from the Catholic Crees on the western side of James Bay or the Montagnais to the east, whether the religious agents in each settlement were Catholic or Protestant. The message, the themes of Christianity, addressed needs of the Crees and they did not resist. They embraced its spirituality, interpreting it in their own Cree way. Although Ronald Niezen suggests that "missions, medicine and education acted together as complementary institutions to conversion"[123] in James Bay, this is not so. By the early decades of the twentieth century when most Crees had incorporated Christianity, they were not yet being schooled,[XXIV] and although Walton took over from the post manager as a kind of "barefoot" doctor, this could not have been an important factor. In the 1920s the Catholics arrived in Fort George, offering superior medical services to the Crees who willingly accepted them but did not convert to Catholicism.

An understanding of their conversion may elude us but the reality of Cree acceptance of Christianity is real. They integrated Christian beliefs and practices into their culture to the extent that Christianity came to form the bedrock of the society in terms of its values and direction.

CHAPTER FOUR

Coping with Changes on the Land

"Competition was the life of the trade." So Sydney Augustus Keighley described his life as a Hudson's Bay Company trader out west in the late 1920s and he bemoaned the loss of it.[1] Certainly his bosses at the company headquarters in Winnipeg or his peers in James Bay in 1928[1] would not have agreed with him. One wonders what judgment the Crees of James Bay would have given this turn of events, for competition did not appear alone. It was embedded within a host of interconnected worldwide phenomena: vastly improved land, air and telecommunications, devastating epidemics, recessions following a Great War and proceeding another one, and an economic boom in the 1920s that permitted North Americans and Europeans to indulge themselves in such fineries as white and silver fox furs. There were other more regional interests, such as explorations for minerals and the federal and provincial governments' awakening interest and intrusion into their northern territories. As a simple response, one might say that the Crees both won and lost in this flood of events that eventually changed their society and their relationship to the land.

It is a mistaken belief that the Hudson's Bay Company has long been a monopoly. On the contrary, it established itself on James Bay in 1670, through the "back door" as a means of draining off furs from the French company operating out of New France. The French were never vigorous opponents to the company's trade, which at one time drew in all the northern lands of Canada. Close on the heels of the surrender of New France in 1760, the mainly Scottish merchants operating out of Montreal began financing fur-trade ventures by using the knowledge of the French coureurs-de-bois. In 1779 the North West Company was formed as a partnership of eight of these merchant concerns trading above and beyond Lake Superior. They proved to be highly aggressive and forced the Hudson's Bay Company to establish inland posts to meet their Indian fur suppliers rather than await them "asleep by the frozen sea," as charged their detractors in England in 1749.² By 1821 the North West Company had expended all its resources and could call on no more. It merged with the Hudson's Bay Company.

In much of its vast region, the Hudson's Bay Company would enjoy a monopoly for the rest of the nineteenth century.ᴵᴵ Although it reorganized certain aspects of its trade by closing posts, decreasing credit, and becoming more authoritarian towards the hunters,ᴵᴵᴵ it is my contention that these changes alone did not transform the Inlander Cree from a subsistence-oriented hunter to a market fur trapper. Over time, though, this symbiotic relationship between hunters and company continued to develop. When the company was forced to make use of improved means of transport to cut labour costs at a time when world markets were forcibly impinging on prices and costs of imported goods and when their country food resources were dwindling, the Crees themselves had to restructure and regroup. Some of these changes remained, others turned out to be short-term until their economy re-established itself. This is the story of this chapter.

CHANGES IN THE FUR TRADE

Opposition arrived in James and Hudson Bays in 1903. The entry in the Rupert House journal is quite bland, given its unique character, so evidently the news had preceded it from Moose Factory. Alan Nicholson writes: "opposition canoe arrived from Moose presumably to locate and meet the inland Indians."³ On 17 July, A.A. Chesterfield,ᴵⱽ filling in as post manager at Fort George for the absent Donald Gillies, wrote that the "Great Opposition" arrived in a "peterboro" canoe from the southward. He also recorded that the Indians and the House people "seem very much excited." The opposition boss, a Mr Landin, told Chesterfield they were on their way north to either of the Whale Rivers or Richmond Gulf to meet their steamer. Before Landin and his crew departed they traded a few skins with several of the hunters. Not surprisingly, within ten days, Mr Mackenzie, the Hudson's Bay Company's district manager stationed at Charlton Island, arrived at Fort George to announce changes to the fur tariffs paid to the Fort George hunters. Now they would be paid more, the same as the Rupert House hunters.⁴ The Rupert House Crees were also to have the advantages of competition, for although the opposition had passed through in June of 1903, they were back in September, said to be camping above the Rupert House post.⁵ In 1907 they erected a post there.⁶

The opposition steamer, the *Eldorado*, that Mackenzie had gone to meet got only as far as the Loon Islands off the coast of Fort George, where it ran aground. The forty-seven men made it ashore and asked Gillies for help. He agreed as long as they did not engage in any trading activity. Walton, too, said his mission helped the men, and their man in charge did his best to "keep the 'drink' away from the sailors and our Indians," not allowing any of the crew to come to the post. Most of the crew embarked in the vessels belonging to the steamer and made their way to Moose Factory, guided by Cree and Inuit men, and from there via the Abitibi River to the rail line. Four men remained behind with the cargo, one of whom was a Frenchman named Gaston Herodier.[v] They erected a rudimentary post two miles away which eventually became their post of Fort George.[7]

The opposition or "Frenchmen" as the company traders persisted in calling them, we now know as the Revillon Frères Company, a French fur house based in Paris since 1839. One of the founders' descendants, Victor Revillon, was in charge of the New York operation which purchased raw furs and sold the finished products. He dreamed of engaging in a head-on competition with the Hudson's Bay Company and buying the raw furs directly. In 1901 he received the approval of his associates in Paris and by 1903 had launched his campaign in eastern Canada.[8]

Walton wrote of the excitement amongst everyone "as each company is trying to get ahead of the other. All sorts of libel are circulated ... till the poor Indian does not know what to think or who to believe." Walton was pleased, though, as through it all the Crees, both employees and hunters, were even more regular in their church attendance and the company was holding to its promise not to sell alcohol and not to hunt on Sunday.[9]

At Fort George the new trading company under Herodier hired runners, also known as trippers, the first being Richard Matthew. Thus began a pattern of each company going out with dog teams and hired men to the various camps to collect the furs and supply the hunters. It had not been the previous practice of the company; both Coasters and Inlanders brought their furs in to the post and transported their own supplies. This new mid-winter pick-up and delivery also increased the number of times some hunters came to the post for supplies, who had never done so before, prompting Gillies to write that "the Indians have been much more troublesome than usual." Already in 1905 the company was running two dog teams to visit the various camps, north and south of the post.[10] It must have been an exasperated post manager, who penned these remarks in his journal of 1906: "Damn these Opposition men they are an undiluted nuisance and we can get no work done at the Post from continually chasing them. No doubt they feel left out as the inland Indians still give the lion's share of their hunts to the old Co."[11]

The Crees did patronize the Revillon Frères post; several hunters later that month traded their otter skins there. This is not surprising; the previous year Gillies reported that the opposition were paying double the price for otter.[12] News travelled quickly along the coast whenever a hunter trapped a highly valued animal, such as a silver fox.[VI] Once known, each company raced out to the camp to try to purchase the skin. Thus in January 1910 word was received at the Hudson's Bay Company post that Sandy Kapusso had caught his second silver fox of the season. Richard Matthew (Esquinamow) was dispatched to his camp to obtain it. Instead Sandy Kapusso came in to the post the next day saying he was intending to keep his silver fox at his camp for some time. Owen Griffiths, the post manager, commented that "I have hopes that he may give it to the Company yet."[13] One would like to think that the Coasters savoured the situation, one they had not seen since the North West Company was disbanded in 1821. Perhaps they enjoyed it in other ways, too, for in 1909 Tom Snowboy at Fort George traded his silver fox for a phonograph and records. His brother William also made the same trade later that winter. This surprised the Leiths because the two brothers shared a tipi.[14]

Elsewhere in eastern James Bay, the competition between the Revillon Frères and the Hudson's Bay Company was not as marked as at Fort George. By 1915 the Revillon Frères operated also at Rupert House (more because of their depot on Strutton Island)[VII] Eastmain, Mistassini,[VIII] and Nemiskau. However, their headquarters were considered to be Fort George[15] and it is in those company records one finds most of the complaints and commentary about this opposition. In fact, with the new Revillon Frères post at Nemiskau, the Hudson's Bay Company decided in 1908 to re-establish a post there which they had abandoned in 1809, and this store was not closed until 1970.[16]

As the competition became rooted in Fort George, there developed, at least from the Hudson's Bay Company's perspective (the sole source for this information), two camps of Cree hunters, those who were "opposition Indians" and those who were on their own. The opposition Cree included runners as well as hunters. Some of the hunters were Old Cook, Noah Kepsu (Kapusso), Passenequon, and Moses Snowboy; the runners were: Richard Matthew, David Louttit, and (Inuk) Bill Fleming. At Rupert House some of the opposition hunters were Willie and Bertie Morrison, Sidney, and Charlie and Joe Hester.[17] In their oral accounts, Matthew Cowboy describes the freighting he did for Revillon Frères from Nemiskau to Rupert House and David Salt recalled how his elderly father was fired from the Hudson's Bay Company and was then employed as an interpreter by Revillon Frères.[18]

Coping with Changes on the Land

The Hudson's Bay Company always had the fear that men would "defect," as they called it. Thus in 1906 Donald Gillies informed his superiors at Moose Factory that they had better re-engage Matthew Esquinamow[IX] as labourer at Fort George and increase his wages, as there is the distinct possibility that he could succumb to Revillon Frères' attempts to lure him away. Gillies explained that "more than half the southard Indians are related by blood or marriage to Matthew. Out of say 21 hunters two are brothers-in-law each with married sons, nieces, nephews or nephews sons and it is quite possible he might do the Company a good deal of harm even if he did not drag all or most of his relatives into the Opposition camp."[19] Matthew Esquinamow must have become vindicated in the eyes of the company, for his death in 1935 brought an obituary in *The Beaver*, the company magazine, noting that he was one of the company's oldest pensioners and his forty-five years of service earned him a gold medal and three bars which he "always proudly displayed to visitors."[20]

It is believed that Richard Matthew was Matthew Esquinamow's brother and his employment with the rival traders was not viewed kindly, as Gillies angrily referred to him as "a little abortion."[21] The language of the records during this period of keen competition is the most biting since the early 1800s when the North West Company was in their midst, with words such as "molest" appearing again. Whenever a Cree returned to the Hudson's Bay Company's trading sphere, it was bound to be noted gloatingly. In 1907 Achewanahum's brother wanted to return to the "old Company" because he found "the yoke too heavy"; in 1920 Sam Atkinson returned to the company "having got tired of Revillon Frères." Those who were "fired" by the opposition were happily welcomed back as hunters attached to the post.[22]

Besides being able to demand the best possible prices for their furs and increased advances, the Cree hunters also expected to be treated fairly and reasonably by the traders. If they disliked the trader the records show that they gave their furs to the other company, as happened in 1928 when the Rupert House hunters switched to Revillon Frères because Mr Harris was unpopular.[23]

As had happened one hundred years earlier, the Crees benefited enormously from this competition throughout the 1920s. The Hudson's Bay Company official reports complain of Revillon Frères "seducing" the Indians with advances of $300 as opposed to its advances of $100 in 1915.[24] The prices of furs went up as well and the company managers said they had no choice but to pay these prices, even though there were times they evidently did not. In 1921 Ernest Renouf[X] feared they would lose most of their spring trade because Revillon Frères were paying extremely high prices for a marten skin – anything from $40 to $50.²⁵ To give some idea of the wealth in furs that was taken out in the 1920s, the total the Hudson's Bay Company paid for furs in the James Bay District^XI was $264,020.²⁶ The breakdown of prices paid, per fur, is found in appendix 1.^XII As a contrast, it is reported that in 1928 in the south of Canada more than half the workers had an income of less than $1,000 per annum.²⁷ In addition, the companies regularly carried out the trade at the winter camps, even transporting provisions there for the hunters. If they were missing certain supplies in mid-winter, all they needed was to send for them.^XIII

Individuals also profited as employees of either company, receiving higher wages. Undoubtedly a number of extra men were hired to provide the tripping out to the camps. When it was reported that William Spence was being engaged for four months in the spring of 1921, Renouf said that if they did not hire him they would lose some of the Inlanders' trade. Spence had been hired away, at high wages, from the Hudson's Bay Company by the Belcher Fur Company in January of 1921 and his position at the Fort George post was assumed by Richard Matthew. It is not clear why Spence chose to leave the new company. Perhaps it had something to do with the "principals" being away until the end of June and he had not been paid. However, it is clear that Renouf was prying him away; had Spence stayed on with the Belcher Fur Company, we are told all the Inlanders would have "put a few pelts there."²⁸ Later, in the post-Revillon Frères period but with a number of free traders operating throughout James Bay, the Hudson's Bay Company engaged a number of Cree men and their wives to run a small trade out of their camps. Thus, Samuel Gull was trading for them at Opatawika camp,²⁹ Tommy Neacappo at the store [actually a scaffolding] at Opemiska Lake in 1950,^XIV and William Spence at Cape Jones, to name but a few.³⁰ The arrangement in 1939 was for the person who ran the camp to collect a full 10 percent in royalties. Since the Waswanipi trading camp collected $420.60 on furs in January and had also taken in a total of $854.80 at the end of December, Gull's royalties would have been about $120.³¹

There were also occasions when the Hudson's Bay Company bosses appealed to the hunters to remain loyal to them. In the summer of 1921 George Ray, district manager, was on his annual inspection tour to Fort George. He found that the post was low in stock, that the supply ship was not to arrive for some time, and that the Crees were ready to take advances from the well-stocked Revillon Frères store at Fort George. Ray addressed the men, called on their loyalty, and assured them that the supplies they needed would be sent from other posts.³² This arrangement had never been made before. In the past, if the company's supply ship did not arrive before the hunters were ready to travel inland, the hunters did without or waited until the ship did come.

The proliferation of new posts established by both the Revillon Frères and the Hudson's Bay Company also benefited the Crees. There were salaried positions for those wishing to supplement their family's income, and the new posts, both on the coast and the interior, reduced travel time, especially in mid-winter when supplies became short. The posts also proved to be a place of refuge where emergency rations could usually be had in periods of starvation. As of 1921, Revillon Frères posts on the eastern side of James and Hudson Bays,[XV] could be found at Rupert House,[XVI] Eastmain, Nemiskau Fort George, and Great Whale River[33] and later inland at Waswanipi and Neoskweskau.[34] In 1910, with the help of David Louttit, they established a post at Port Harrison,[35] a development that surprised Gillies, but in 1921 the Hudson's Bay Company opened one there as well to obtain some of the trade in white foxes. The company charged that Revillon then opened a post at Great Whale River that year in retaliation. Both companies also opened posts at Richmond Gulf in 1922.[36] There was criticism of this establishment only eighty-five miles north of the company's post at Great Whale River. The two posts continued until 1955, and the Crees and Inuit then traded at Great Whale River.[37]

While the Coaster trade was demanding for the post managers because of the frequency of Crees arriving at the post seeking supplies or credit, the trade with the Inlanders, under competition, was even more difficult, necessitating the transport of them and their supplies up the various rivers. Owen Griffiths, the Fort George manager, expressed his frustration in these remarks from his annual report for 1909: "Each summer it is becoming more and more difficult to get the inlanders away from the Post with their supplies. I am kept working continually with two large canoes taking their provisions etc. up this and other rivers, besides sending a boat to Great Whale River with the supplies of those indians who prefer to get to their lands by that route."[38] In addition, Griffiths was being pressed by the Inlanders to establish a winter post up the Chisasibi (the Grande) River, for they had been telling him that the Frenchmen were making all kinds of promises if the Crees would give them their furs.

As a consequence, a small post was built at Kanaaupscow, 150 miles upriver from the post at Fort George in 1921. That June five freight canoes[XVII] left Fort George to establish the outpost. Their departure was preceded the night before by a feast.[39] The manager of the new outpost, Richard Matthew,[XVIII] took leave from it in early August, once the buildings were completed.[40] It was an inauspicious start as Matthew was back the following January reporting that the fur collection had not been one of "abundance ... owing to the country having been extensively burned last summer."[XIX] Revillon Frères never did counter with an inland post and, in fact, in 1932 the company reported its opposition had had little dealing with the Inlanders.[41] These Inlanders[XX] were not drawn to the Kanaaupscow region for fur trapping; the post was located there to supply them on the lands they had long occupied. It was considered these hunters were on the fringes of real fur country. The supplies available at Kanaaupscow obviated the necessity of the hunters having to take their families all the way to Fort George.[42]

The outpost at Kanauupscow continued until 1949, then becoming a trade camp; a clerk from Fort George opened the store twice a year in January and March. According to Clifford Bearskin, the post went out of business gradually though it was still operating in 1958.[43] The threat from Revillon Frères did not materialize, so why did they maintain the post? In 1925 Ray, the James Bay district manager, addressed this issue in his annual report. He remarked that "the actual importance of the outpost either to the Indian or to the Company, anything approaching its real worth to either will be impossible to estimate as the value of the Indian's being able to obtain assistance in the shape of ammunition and food in times of emergency is incalculable in light of its relation to Returns."[44] The success of this post was important to Ray and he sought similar support from the Inlanders in 1925. With this objective in mind, he asked Bishop Anderson "to make one of the prominent Inland Indians a catechist to officiate at Kanaaupscow." This was likely Jimmy Bearskin, listed as the catechist in 1938 and also reported in the account of Sydney Rat.[45]

Altruism was not likely the only consideration.[XXI] The Hudson's Bay Company was faced with another competitor at Fort George, Jack Palmquist,[XXII] a free trader, who started operating out of Moose Factory in 1926 and began trading in the Fort George area in 1929. He also opened a store at Old Factory River in 1935.[46] George Papp is often mentioned in the Great Whale River records for his inability to work with his Cree assistants.[XXIII] In 1934 Anderson wrote: "Kanaaupscow is an outpost of Fort George which is maintained for the purpose of securing the hunts of the inland Indians before they come down to the coast; for we are alone at the outpost whereas both Revillon Frères and Palmquist are located at Fort George. In the trade war which took place in Outfit 264 [1934], naturally our efforts were directed in maintaining our position at Kanaaupscow and this we have been entirely successful in doing."[47]

Competition seems an insufficient reason for the company to underwrite the expenses of maintaining and supplying an inland post. The commentary of Elijah Blackboy, of an Inlander family, touches on an issue that probably underlay the continuation of the post. His view is that the Hudson's Bay Company opened Kanaaupscow to encourage people to move farther inland after the caribou had moved farther east. He said the Crees were willing to go but needed the assurance that if they ran out of food they would be able to reach a store to get supplies.[48] The outpost at Kanaaupscow did not draw them into the interior but assured them supplies so they could remain there. Similarly, Betsy Pachano said she and her husband, David Pachano,[XXIV] when they were first married, hunted on the coast in the Fort George area. In the mid-1930s, when one daughter married an Inlander, the whole Pachano family moved inland because of poor hunting on the coast.[49]

The opposition of Jack Palmquist at Old Factory in 1935 motivated the Hudson's Bay Company to establish a post there in 1936, and with the two trading operations there, both the Catholics in 1937 and the Anglicans in 1940 also established a presence. For the Hudson's Bay Company, Thomas Mark, the interpreter at Eastmain, was first sent in to man the post. Old Factory drew on the Cree hunters whose lands lay south of Fort George and north of Eastmain. In the summer a village of tents sprang up of about two hundred people.[50] As an aside, Thomas Mark's sojourn at Old Factory was marked by a terrible tragedy in 1939, for his young daughter Emily was set upon and "torn-up" by the dogs. The wind was blowing fiercely and no one heard her cries. She was taken to Eastmain for burial and there is a touching account of the funeral in the journal.[51]

What did the Crees think of the Revillon Frères Company? It is difficult to say since the oral accounts are relatively silent on this subject. What there is, are generally reflections on the dynamics between the two companies or of the Hudson's Bay Company and any of its competitors. According to Ray, it was the custom for the Inlanders to have the furs of their unmarried sons taken to Revillon Frères so that they could have "a foot in each camp."[52] Similarly, Willie Jacob and Charlie Blackned, from Rupert House, commented that many of the men would sell their furs to Revillon Frères but they used to sell most of their furs at the Hudson's Bay Company. For instance, in 1915 Kapat sold to the Revillon Frères one silver fox for $200 and two others to Owen Griffiths, manager of the Hudson's Bay Company's Fort George post for $175 each.[53] This practice of trading at the two companies was an old Cree strategy, one they employed in the early 1700s with the New France trading companies and then the North West Company in the 1800s.

The Crees were also able to take advantage of a communication problem at the inland posts. For the company, the problem lay in trying to harmonize its fur tariffs among posts. The Crees knew the different tariffs at each post, which sometimes forced company managers to deviate from the standards set at their post. At Neoskweskau the trader there in 1938 was paying $20 for a good dark otter skin but at Nemiskau the set price was $16, prompting Foreman to complain in his journal that it is too bad such a thing happens as it makes him look as though he were deliberately "putting it over them [sic]."[54]

According to company figures in 1924, Revillon Frères was taking in about 27 percent of the furs in the James Bay District.[55] Despite the opposition's aggressive policies, the Crees remained loyal to the old company as they had in previous centuries.[xxv] According to the Leiths, loyalty to the company was a "watchword more effective than money. Natives take pride in telling of the number of years they and their ancestors have been in the Company's service."[56] This loyalty was explained by James Anderson as a consequence of the Crees' honesty in repaying their debts. According to him, each year a hunter went inland with an outfit of supplies which had been advanced to him by the company in the fall. The next spring he would bring his furs down river to the Hudson's Bay Company post, pay his debt, and spend the surplus at the store there. Then he would present himself to the opposition and ask for an advance for the next year, "without a farthing to his name." This confounded the early Revillon Frères traders who had expected the Cree to "jump" their debts and trade with them.[57] Cree loyalty[xxvi] might also be explained by their mistrusting the permanence of the new company.[58]

Eventually the high prices paid would wear some down; examples have already been given of the wrath that this incurred amongst the Hudson's Bay Company managers, especially Donald Gillies at Fort George. Louis Romanet, the Hudson's Bay Company's district inspector who had been recruited from Revillon Frères credited the Crees with having nourished this competitiveness: "It is a masterpiece of Indian diplomacy to arrive every year to break down an agreement between companies, to make every Firm suspicious of the other, and to force to a fight, to the sole advantage of the Indians, the most peaceful opponents. There is not a trader worth the name who has not experienced the power of Indian Gossip."[59]

The oral accounts of this subject tend to discuss the relations between the two companies. Thus John Kawapit, at Great Whale River in the 1970s, talked of the time there were two companies who wanted the fur from the hunters; these people waited for the hunters on the way to make their trade, wooing them with gifts of tea, sugar, and flour with which to make a bannock meal.[60] Other stories referred to some verbal and physical confrontations between the two companies.[xxvii]

107   Coping with Changes on the Land

Despite the tirades in the journals about the opposition, relations between them were obviously not always bitter. It is not unusual, even in the early years of their rivalry, to find evidence of their having helped each other. For example, the Fort George post received its mail from Rupert House via the Revillon boat and Bobish's son and Napesh's boy got a lift to the post with some of the "French Company's men" but brought their muskrats to the Hudson's Bay Company.[61] There was even a concession in the 1918 annual company report that "on the whole, their competition is straight and honourable, and we might have very much worse opponents."[62] Moreover, post managers did socialize. In 1924 Renouf mentions in his Fort George journal that Mr Williams, manager, and Mr Cameron, clerk, of the Revillon Frères Company visited the post, while Anderson wrote of his year in 1919 at Rupert House that Thomas Bell, the Revillon Frères manager, "was a very agreeable neighbour and an excellent organist who could entertain us on many a winter evening with music and song."[63] In the judgment of an "outsider," the men of the two companies were "on friendly terms[XXVIII] ... that is, socially speaking, but in business matters there is keen rivalry and it is amusing ... to watch the various maneuvers to obtain some advantage."[64] One such manoeuvre was termed by J.W. Anderson as a traditional strategem. One January afternoon in 1911 when he was an apprentice at Moose Factory, they heard by moccasin telegraph that a hunter had trapped a silver fox. They hoped to keep the news quiet and send off men and a dog team the following day. In order to "throw the rival traders completely off the scent," the Hudson's Bay Company threw a gala dance that night, inviting the Revillon Frères personnel and, "most important, their dog drivers." It worked, except that Cheena, the hunter, had already moved on from his camp sixty miles away which took them six days to reach.[65]

The competition over furs between these two companies did not last beyond the mid-1930s, by which time a number of ex-Revillon Frères men had opened stores at Fort George, Cape Jones, Roggan River and Old Factory, and Richmond Gulf.[66] The Hudson's Bay Company also reopened Nichikun post in 1937 and a former Hudson's Bay Company manager at Neoskweskau opened a post at Mistassini. The company also opened a new post at Old Factory River in 1936. Crees who hunted north of Eastmain, traded and settled there in the summer. Although far from main transport centres, the Nichikun region still was attractive enough for independent traders who visited the hunters' camps by plane and often the first plane to arrive got the furs.[67] The independents did not restrict themselves to the Nichikun hunters but also traded with Mistassini and Chibougamau hunters.[68] At various times, traders Olav Brieve, Sandy Lorimer and Emmett McLeod[XXIX] were cited in the journals; occasionally their appearance provoked an outburst of anger, such as Stevenson's reference to Lorimer as being "about as welcome as a skunk at a garden party."[69]

A major opponent was the "line," the railway. As early as 1929 the Hudson's Bay Company officials were complaining that more than the usual number of James Bay natives were getting advances at "line" posts.[70] According to one district manager, the Church of England missions, particularly at Moose Factory, were also regarded as the opposition. Rackham accused the mission of "preaching sermons of a strong socialistic character ... holding up the Company as an example of tyranny and oppression. Our servants are also spoken to privately and told that although they are styled 'servants' they are in reality slaves."[71]

Both companies weathered the slump in prices and problems of transport during the First World War, though it is not known how, as the Hudson's Bay Company annual reports for the James Bay District are filled with complaints and gloomy forecasts about the trade. In 1920 the news of a slump in fur prices did not reach the posts until after they had paid the hunters higher fur tariffs and advanced them for the winter hunt based on these inflated tariffs. Foxes, the mainstay of the Coaster trade, were also scarce.[72] Obviously Revillon Frères were also hurting and at Fort George their store manager, McLeod, operating on his own or by instructions, suggested to his Hudson's Bay opposite, Renouf, that they agree to a fur-buying tariff. Apparently the approach ended unsuccessfully.[73]

The next year both companies chose to expand their operations, increasing the number of their posts, particularly northward, along the coast, into fox country. Even by 1923 Revillon Frères had fur-trade operations all through the north of Canada,[xxx] with James Bay proving to be one of their strongest regions.[74] There they were able to maintain a high gross profit margin on the goods they sold in addition to selling their furs at double the amount they paid for them.[75] The Hudson's Bay Company was feeling at a competitive disadvantage in their physical assets, as one district manager in 1927 remarked that the "Revillon Frères buildings are better maintained in appearance and fittings."[76] It is difficult to know the circumstances that made Revillon Frères take the drastic step in 1923 of asking for a working arrangement with the Hudson's Bay Company. This agreement involved the elimination of the trade in unprime fur, the combination of transport, the free interchange of information, and the elimination of unnecessary outposts, camp traders, and tripping.

For whatever reason, it seems that the Hudson's Bay Company was not anxious to eliminate the Revillon Frères operation completely but rather to permit it to carry on as a separate entity with its own managers even though it had secured 51 percent of the Revillon stock.⁷⁷ Perhaps it deemed that having a "sane and reasonable competitor" protected it from others who were not. These measures saved Revillon Frères for a little while but in 1936, in a depressed world economy, its fur-buying operations in Canada were taken over by the Hudson's Bay Company.⁷⁸ In any case, the advantageous position that the Crees had held for thirty-three years in a competitive market was diminished because by this time other rival traders had arrived and competition continued, though not with the same vigour.ˣˣˣⁱ

A DIMINISHED LAND

It would be hard to imagine the James Bay fur trade as vigorous in the late 1920s and early 1930s, despite the decline of the Revillon Frères Company. During this period the number of food and fur animals dwindled drastically. It is the singularly most important event for the Crees in this period; it impoverished and demoralized them, and left them with few alternatives in their attempt to cope with the onslaught of external forces and agencies. They could only recoil. They could not resist. They could not react.

It is difficult to assess how common the Cree experience was in the 1930s. Fortunately, the terrible scarcity of country food was not shared across the north – at least not in the posts and region the fur trader Sydney Keighley travelled. Writing of 1931, Keighley commented that Caribou Post in Chipewyan country was overstocked in unwanted imported foods because the Chipewyan and Inuit "had all the grease and fat they wanted from the caribou."⁷⁹ In 1929, in neighbouring Ontario at the post of Big Trout Lake, Keighley writes of "a considerable stock [of furs] ... mostly of otter, beaver and mink" coming from one of the outposts and the following winter that "otter, marten, fisher and beaver were plentiful."⁸⁰ Such comments are in stark contrast to the situation for the Crees in James Bay at that time.

The first story was told by Samuel Mayappo, born around 1902. His narrative was recorded at Wemindji in 1979, but when he was a young hunter he traded at Eastmain; the post at Wemindji (Old Factory River Post), was not opened until the late 1930s.

As far as I can remember from the first time I learned to hunt, sometimes everything that the peoples' lives depended on was so scarce. Most of the time, the only thing that the people depended on was fish. I didn't like what I saw while I was out in the bush, starvation. All of my late brothers died from starvation. Two of them were older than I was. One of them who died out in the bush lay there for three days and the other one who also died in the bush lay there for one day. I always look back at the time that this tragedy took place ... All my late brothers were nothing but bones when they died from starvation ... Also people didn't have any ammunition to hunt with. Because it was so sad in the past that a whole family including his children who left Eastmain, never returned from the bush. It's hard for a person who has nothing to provide for his children ... Many times in the past, I had to go out with nothing to eat or drink, all day. Even when I slept out in the bush, I didn't have any tea to drink. The only thing that I could drink was water. (MC Scott Collection 1979, tape III–D–108T)

One observer of these dire, tragic times was Maud Watt, wife of the Rupert House company manager, J.S.C. Watt. Considered by William A. Anderson as the "Angel of Hudson Bay," she became the subject of his book, published in 1961 and, one assumes, his chief informant. We learn there that thirteen children of Simon and Mary Katapaituk died of starvation or malnutrition as did ten of the twelve Blackned children. Amongst the voyageurs, the Jolly family lost six children and the Edwards family four. In referring to these times and the catastrophe, the author writes: "it was like a slow creeping mold that brought paralysis and the hush of death along the shores and into the forest." To try to mitigate the suffering at Rupert House he reported that the Watts went on short rations and shared their food allowance with the people in the community. Those who had the strength moved together into the bush, fearing to be alone. Since game were scarce they dug up roots and ate the soft inner bark of the birch tree.[81]

The worst years were from 1929 to 1932 according to J.W. Anderson, whose district report reads: "The native population have been experiencing difficult times for three years now, for the decline in fur values has been coincident with a downward cycle of scarcity in their country foods ... Through a combination of sickness and starvation seventeen Indians died at Great Whale River in March 1932 ... There was also a case of starvation at Neoskweskau Post."[82] There is no reason to suspect that starving Crees arriving at the post were denied food. The company was able to charge the federal government's "sickness and destitute" account for these supplies. According to the post journals, food was sent out whenever they heard about the need. At Great Whale River in 1927 two families were saved, though that year, one man died within five miles of the post.[83] There were years at the small inland posts of Neoskweskau and Nichikun when food was not always available for hunters or company employees.

The James Bay territory of the Crees is a vast region. Not all areas and people were similarly stricken with impoverishment. John Blackned told

III Coping with Changes on the Land

Rolf Knight in 1961 that in his youth (Blackned was born about 1896) the Fort George people were poorer than those at Eastmain and the Eastmain people were poorer than those at Rupert House.[XXXII] As well, Inlanders were better off than the Coasters at Rupert House.[84] The greater disparity, though, lies between these posts and those far inland, such as Waswanipi and Mistassini. In Waswanipi, the Crees were enjoying bear and moose feasts and a reading of the journals from the turn of the century does not turn up evidence of anything like the degree of scarcity suffered elsewhere. At Mistassini the people there were also eating moose meat, though one has the impression that it was not as frequent a delicacy as in the Waswanipi region.[85] There were, needless to say, times of deprivation even at Mistassini. The spring of 1928 was said to be "unsettling times" as exceptionally high water made hunting difficult. They were unable to get fish even at the post and were gratefully surviving on oatmeal.[86] On the whole, though, their fur hunts were not the subject of constant complaints. For instance, the entry for 12 June 1929 reads "the hunts look very good from the north end of [Lake] Mistassini" and several days later Gabriel Fleury[XXXIII] paid Samuel Voyageur $75 for a fisher while J. Hurley at the Hudson's Bay Company post only offered him $60 for it.[87] At both these posts there was much more cash available than at the other Cree posts as numbers of prospectors were exploring for minerals, hiring Crees to prospect, guide, and supply them.[XXIV] The money earned need not have been spent at the Hudson's Bay Company post or for the purchase of supplies from Gabriel Fleury or D.C Bremner (an ex-company clerk) or a number of other free traders in the area; the Crees at Waswanipi and Mistassini could go down to the line to make their purchases more cheaply. Perhaps this extract from the Mistassini journals of 1937 also highlights the relative prosperity the Mistassini people were experiencing. It is recorded that on 16 June 1937 Matthew Shecapio left for the line to travel to Quebec City to see a government minister, to ask for aid for the Mistassini people. Jeffery's reaction to this event is that it would be a joke for the Indian agent to visit Mistassini where he would find "the majority at Oskelaneo buying provisions for the next winter and a good many of those left getting rations."[88]

Competition shattered the symbiosis that existed between the Crees and the Hudson's Bay Company. As James Anderson was to write in his memoirs, "Before World War 1 the Crees of James Bay could still claim the country largely as their own. There were no railways, no telegraph or telephone, no wireless and no aeroplanes. The only resident whites were the missionaries and the traders, and white travellers were very few and far between. The only commercial activity was the fur trade, for which the Indians were the indispensable primary producers."[89]

112   The White Man's Gonna Getcha

This was all about to change. With the end of isolation came the end of the simple economy in which company and Crees had nourished and protected each other, a relationship that developed and grew from the mid-1800s when each had only the other. Even had the Revillon Frères Company not burst on the scene in James Bay, the makeup of the economy would still have changed, for the people of the north would have been at the mercy of the world economy. The development of the telegraph and the telephone would have ensured that ease of communication caused fur prices in James Bay to fluctuate dramatically even from one month to another, whereas previously, with mail infrequent, they remained stable throughout the season.

In the 1890s a hunter taking out a certain amount of debt at the company knew how many furs he needed to repay it. He did not in the 1920s. Similarly, the post manager formerly had some idea of the credit he could advance, given the hunter's production in previous years. This changed state is exemplified in F.D. Wilson's district report of 1915. The First World War had caused a fall in fur prices with these consequences at Moose Factory: "As most of the Indians trading at this Post have their hunting grounds some distance from the Post, it is usual for them to be allowed to take their advances in July and August, so that before we had news of the War and the slump in the fur market, the most of them had been equipped ... and as a consequence of the low prices and small hunts, very few were able to pay their debts."[90] Those Crees who did hear about the lower prices evidently "took up their traps ... and devoted all their time to hunting country food."[xxxv] Silver foxes had been high in demand in the 1920s, but following the stock market crash this demand declined, bringing down prices.[xxxvi]

RESTRUCTURED CREE–COMPANY RELATIONS

In the late 1800s the Coaster population grew with the fortunes of the Hudson's Bay Company in James Bay. Not only were post managers, clerks, labourers, coopers, and other craftsmen needed, but this growing number of servants and their families needed food and fuel which the company supplied.[xxxvii] When the voyageurs set out in the summer to transport the goods inland, their families were similarly supplied with food rations. In the summer there were special labours to be performed at the post such as haying, gardening, building fences, rebuilding the post buildings, or building transport canoes. For these jobs the Cree men received weekly rations of flour, pork, oatmeal, and suet.[91] Ronnie Cowboy remembers the men were given "one scoop that was about six pounds of flour to last them for a week" and they had a bakery for them, the women baking bannock and bread.[92] Thus, a whole

113 Coping with Changes on the Land

industry developed to maintain the fur trade. Although still responsible for their own subsistence, the Coaster population that lived in the shadows of the post might well have been content to live in both worlds – the bush in the winter and near the post in the summer. They hunted for their own food, trapped what they could from the strained fur resources on the coast and, in order to purchase imported goods, made up the difference with their labours at the post. Such a lifestyle meant they were not far removed from food supplies at the post or from other Crees, should their own sources fail them. The coast of James Bay was always less plentiful in food and now even more so. Both fur animals and also food animals[xxxviii] went into rapid decline in the late 1920s. By 1929 the low point had been reached; the drop in the number of food animals such as ptarmigan, grouse, and hare caused by harsh winter conditions made hunting and even fishing difficult, and this was combined with over-hunting.[xxxix] Accordingly, J.S.C. Watt, manager at Rupert House in 1929, wrote that "the fear of starvation prevents the coast Indians from going far inland."[93] This is also echoed in the federal government's report for the James Bay agency in 1931 in which it was said that "the fear of starvation is what impels so many of the Northern Indians of this district to inhabit the Coastal Region … The Coaster is given more to dependency on the white people in threatening times. At these periods he is readily susceptible to a tendency to beg."[94]

There is also evidence that the Inlanders were fearful of starvation and tried to remain within some reasonable distance from the post. The comments of Elijah Blackboy in the context of the opening of Kanauupscow post supports this. It suggests that people were willing to spread out more, farther away from Fort George, but needed the assurance of a stock of food and supplies. This is also the conclusion of Adrian Tanner who researched this question in 1978–9.[xl] Similarly, A.P. Low commented that the presence of a trading post in the interior, such as at Nichikun, was an absolute necessity in seasons of starvation. Without Nichikun, he added, "it is doubtful if the country would support half the present population."[95] There were animal resources farther inland. The Crees trading at Neoskweskau were forced, because of forest fires, to hunt in virgin territory and were repaid for their trouble and hardships by largely increased hunts.[96] Likewise, the fur hunters at Kanaaupscow were said to be hunting "at present on the fringe of real fur country" in the view of the district manager in 1927, Innes Wilson, who also remarked on the "great fur territories away at the back of Eastmain and Fort George – far past Neoskweskau and Kanaaupscow – that are awaiting development and expansion." Accordingly, he suggested that the hunter must "be driven more and more into the wilder and remoter parts of the country."⁹⁷ However, the Inlanders, according to J.W. Anderson, "looked askance at one of the number who accepted permanent employment with the white man,"⁹⁸ so it is doubtful whether large numbers married into Coaster families, thereby abandoning the Inlander society and economy.

In the 1930s it was Coasters who were joining inland society. Rolf Knight's research in 1961 at Rupert House points to a number of Coasters who moved inland. For example, Charlie Wiestchee (born 1901) went inland to trap with Matthew Cowboy (born 1876).ˣᴸᴵ Harriet Whiskeychan (born 1879) and her husband, who began married life hunting on the coast, within two to three years had moved inland up the Rupert River to the northeast of Nemiskau.⁹⁹ Charlie Hester (born 1887) thought there were considerably more women from Rupert House marrying men of inland posts than inland women coming to Rupert House, inland people being very desirous of sons-in-law.¹⁰⁰ It was one of the solutions that the company thought was obvious but it was clearly not easy to implement, according to George Ray:

> ... whenever a poor fox year occurs the coast Indian is in a very bad way indeed there being little else to hunt. At least 70% of these Indian debts is owing by coast Indians. From this it might appear that it would be wise to encourage these men to shift their locale or enterprise and go inland. But experience has taught managers that coast Indians are quite useless in the bush and vice-versa, and there are good and sound reasons for these failures ... A solitary Indian family is seldom found either in the bush or on the coast; almost always they are found in camps of at least four or five families and with very little distance between their own and neighbouring camps. So it is easy to understand that a newcomer, unless he is prepared to go far afield, would have little chance of finding any territory that had not been trapped out or found unprofitable. Furthermore, he would be strange to the locality and conditions and be quite at a loss as where to find the necessary country produce for food and clothing.¹⁰¹

It is clear that the Inlanders suffered from great deprivation early in this century, particularly the years 1929 to 1932, but the Coasters endured yet greater hardship. Why? Part of the answer lies in the poor resources on the coast, increasing population, and restricted hunting lands. The rest of this complex answer follows from the Coasters' relationship to the Hudson's Bay Company and world events that shattered this relationship.

Both Coasters and Inlanders were advanced credit each summer and expected to repay it following the winter's hunt. As the poor hunting years increased, these debts grew and at times were written off by the company when it became obvious they could not collect.[102] Prior to competition, this would not have been a hardship to the company, for they needed only to raise the price of the imported goods.[XLII] The post manager of Waswanipi, D.H. Learmonth, obviously did not approve of this and similar business practices. In his post journal of 1923 he wrote disdainfully: "Inspection completed. Mr Watt seems quite satisfied. $5,000 loss on Indian debts evidently a matter of little moment in this District. Policy evidently accepted on James Bay 'buy furs at a big margin of profit then lose it all again in Indian Debts and expenses'. Fear I must be an old timer with conservative stick in the mud ideas."[103]

Dudley Copland, fur trader for the company from 1923 to 1939, on coming to Fort Chimo in 1932 commented that "benefits had been granted to staff and natives that were still in effect and were draining the resources of the Company in that area."[104] However, in his study of the financial structure of the Hudson's Bay Company, Arthur Ray concludes that "in reality, the bad-debt problem was never as serious as it seemed to those in the commissioner's office" and he went on to explain that, viewed as an inevitable expense of collecting furs, the cost was very low.[105] However, with energetic competition and a much more volatile fur market in the 1920s, the post and district managers were under increasing pressure to cut their costs.[XLIII] The debt balance for each post and the district was the subject of much discussion in the annual district reports and it is evident the district managers were expected to reduce them or keep them in check, a seemingly losing battle as wars, depressions, competition, and diminished food animals wreaked havoc – a far cry from the dependable barter economy the Crees and the company enjoyed to 1902.[XLIV]

It is unclear whether it was the pressure on the company managers to run a profitable fur trade or a nasty, mean-tempered disposition that prompted the Mistassini assistant manager, possibly Hurley, to enter the following in his journal: "Mon. June 18, 1928. John Awash arrived yesterday – his wife died this Spring. He has no fur, so as far as we are concerned it would be more profitable were he also to die soon as we will almost have to give him more supplies this Fall."[106] Balancing this outburst are several defences by district managers of the necessity of granting the Crees credit. Ray, always writing in a humanitarian vein, presented to the Winnipeg office this argument. "If we continue, as I propose, the debt system as a means of keeping the natives alive during the lean years, the Company may – in small measure – be reimbursed by the amounts the natives may be persuaded to pay when fat years shall come again and in the main, I imagine it will be more easily handled than any system of gratuity we may devise."[107]

From the company's perspective, one of the posts hardest hit by the economic downturn was Rupert House. It was a very high-debt post with very low fur yields.^XLV Its returns were largely those of the Coasters, for most of the Inlanders were drawn off by the inland posts of Neoskweskau and Nemiskau and, perhaps, Mistassini. In addition, Rupert House was a supply centre for other posts and therefore required a larger labour force and costs associated with inland transport. With much of the Hudson's Bay Company discussion focused on this coast, Rupert House will serve as the example of the restructuring of the fur trade.

The company took a number of measures that were severe, given the times. Although under credit constraints since the beginning of the competition, directives to post managers from the district managers became more specific. In 1927 a memo from V.W. West directed that "advances to each native or white on account of his Fall hunt must not exceed 50% of his customary Fall hunt value. If not paid no further advances can be made, unless it be a very small amount to enable the hunter to have matches, tobacco, tea and ammunition to enable him to make his Spring hunt."[108] West went on to say that a native would get advances just "as long as his conduct warrants it ... his standing with the Company is entirely in his own hands." Watt was also under orders that year not "to give summer debt."[109]

Managers and district managers who had direct experience with the Crees in James Bay tended to ignore the chain of command. Writing directly to Charles V. Sale, the governor in London, Watt complained of the inconsiderate attitude at the Winnipeg office which would destroy the goodwill of the Indian.[110] He obviously felt obliged to lecture the governor on the history of company-Cree relations:^XLVI

> Until recently, the Company has carried on in very much the old patriarchal style. For probably over one hundred years employment during Summer has been found for everyone able and willing to work ... There can be no doubt that the Company's system of advancing Indians is to a very large extent the reason the Company has continued to prosper for such a lengthy period; the Indian regards the Company as "insurance", and being naturally improvident looks to the Company to carry him over a year of famine; so long as the Indian can depend on the Company doing so, he is usually willing to pay more for his supplies and accept less for his furs, than he could get from rival traders.[111]

Credit was never eliminated at the posts; the company's district reports of subsequent years contain discussion of their annual losses on debts, while the journals of later years show credit was still being granted.[112]

117 Coping with Changes on the Land

Nevertheless, the reduction in credit ensured that the Hudson's Bay Company and other free traders were forced to continue the system of mid-winter supply inasmuch as the Crees were now expected to turn over furs for purchases throughout the winter rather than once a year. On balance, the company benefited; it was able to adjust the price of furs as its managers received news of increases or reductions.

Over the years the company had come to depend more on local labour than men from the old country. This dependence on native labour for outside work prompted district manager West to complain in 1929 that this system may have worked in times gone by but the company was now paying heavily for this practice. He complained that the staff had been trained "to think and act along lines since obsolete"[XLVII] and suggested that new apprentices were perfectly willing to do "whatever work is allotted to them."[113] Obviously this outside labour was cut back.[XLVIII]

The summer activities of haying and inland transport by canoe were discontinued in the late 1920s. The haying [XLIX] was a form of summer employment for the Crees at all the coastal posts that dated back to at least the 1780s. The amounts paid for this summer work were said to be barely sufficient, at least at Fort George, where rations were not dispensed. Writing in 1922, Ray seems to be appalled at the $1.50 per day[L] and no rations earned by the men, especially those with large families to feed. It was insufficient and required them to take debt "almost daily throughout the summer to stay alive."[114] Of course, if they were working all day for the post they were unable to hunt and fish to support their families, relying instead on store food. Ray tried to remedy their impoverishment by raising the wage to $2.50 per day which he hoped would decrease the Indians' debt. It was to be a short-term measure; in 1927, to cut costs, the company killed off the cattle and the "natives were deprived of their chief source of income."[115]

Inland transport was extremely arduous work and in past decades the company had to cajole and amply reward men to undertake it. This cajoling is missing from the records of the early 1900s. It may be, as Ray wrote in 1921, that "the very precarious life of these men makes them less independent and more amenable to discipline.[LI] Consequently it is they who do nine-tenths of the inland transport work."[116] It was arduous, back-breaking work with a high degree of risk of injury and death. One account of the life is told by Willie Jacob and Charlie Blackned in which they talk of hauling the supplies upriver to Nemiskau. There were five men in one canoe, one of whom used to do the cooking. It was his responsibility to look after all the food, including the hauling of it, the utensils, the tent, sleeping bags, tarps, paddles and poles. For this he was paid $25. The other men were responsible for five-hundred-pound loads. Some insight into the hardships of the inland transport is imparted in this excerpt from their story:

Sometimes on rapids where the current is so swift the men used a long rope to pull the canoe from the shore line. Sometimes they had to wade in the water to pull the rope because the water in the river was so high. Sometimes the men were very tired from all the pulling and poling up the strong current in one day. They used to carry heavy loads on their back on portages. One man had to carry two hundred pounds on one trip. Sometimes these portages would be about one mile long. The trails were not all smooth and good. There were many obstacles on their way, such as sticks and trees fallen across the path making it rough walking and sometimes they had to walk on slippery mud and they had to watch their step so they wouldn't fall with their load and then they had to paddle the heavy loaded canoes up the stream.[117]

Sometimes a man would make four trips to Nemiskau in one summer and when he did he would receive a $25 bonus. In terms of the hardships, one feature not mentioned in this account were the thick cloud of mosquitoes that descended on the men in camp. Dudley Copland, the Hudson's Bay Company chief trader at Fort Chimo, once accompanied the Fort Mackenzie brigade back home with supplies and although glad, despite the gruelling work, for having experienced river freighting before the airplane took it over, he said the mosquitoes "were so numerous that they filled our nostrils with each breath."[118]

George Georgekish, also of Rupert House, told how about fifty years earlier, roughly about 1935, he and other men canoed to Mistassini, Waswanipi, and Neoskweskau. It took them a little over a month to reach Mistassini from Rupert House paddling in long boats that held six men. Mistassini men arrived from the post carrying the furs and returned with them to bring up the supplies. The Mistassini men were paid $60 each for the trip and the Rupert House men were paid $50. "At that time the men thought this was big money and besides the company donated food."[119]

Doubtless there were many heroes of the brigades, but two men are immortalized in the *Beaver*. One was John Iserhoff who was in charge of the Waswanipi brigade from 1880 to 1889. Working under his direction were thirty-six men in six canoes for fifty days on a five-hundred-mile round trip to Rupert House.[120] The other leading voyageur was Solomon Voyageur.[LII] He was the head guide of the Mistassini–Rupert House canoe brigade for thirty years. Recollecting his years at Mistassini (from 1913 to 1918) Anderson, had nothing but praise for him. He described him as "a man of strong character, a real leader of his people[LIII] and outstanding guide and trapper."[121]

The canoe brigade was a vital part of the lives of the Inlanders; it brought them the tools, clothing, and a few luxury items that contributed to their subsistence. It was also of great consequence[LIV] to both Coasters and Inlanders, for this arduous work provided them with one of the very few employment opportunities in James Bay in the early twentieth century. The money paid to the voyageurs was considered good money and it is obvious that the Crees, the Coasters in particular, were much in need of this summer employment to stave off starvation in the winter months. However, as the Hudson's Bay Company reduced the amount of credit, so did they also the number of men employed in the inland transport. Their labour costs were high, resulting in high-priced goods at inland posts. For a long time the company had no options but to incur these expenses. However, competition, infusion of money, opening of rail lines, and new technology all conspired to produce cheaper means of transport and fewer wage-earning opportunities in James Bay, felt most severely at Rupert House. An interesting point is made by Anderson, who said the company were loathe to give up the canoe brigades because the money they paid out was then spent at the posts.[122] Nevertheless, another compelling reason for reducing transport costs was inflation. The rising value of raw furs on the world markets translated into more store goods being needed to buy these furs, thereby taxing an already expensive, arduous, and under-manned system of transport, the canoe brigades.

The changes began when Revillon Frères tried a winter transport in 1912–13 from Rupert House to Nemiskau using horse teams. They brought in four "French-Canadian horsemen, horses, sleighs, feed and equipment" and cut or improved a winter road along which they built stables and bunkhouses roughly twenty miles apart. Given the heavy snowfall and the small tonnage, they found it too expensive and quickly abandoned it in 1915.[123] This had not been the first such experiment. When at Rupert House, Alan Nicholson, had tried a winter transport but with oxen in 1904–5 and he quickly abandoned it. About the same time the Hudson's Bay Company initiated the freighting of some of its goods in from the south, not inland from Rupert House, but to southern posts such as Waswanipi, using a warehouse at Nottoway Station on Bell River. By 1922 the company was seeking to arrange with the Quebec Fisheries of Senneterre Company for it to transport its cargo to the end of Chibougamau Lake. This would shorten the canoe route to Waswanipi by eight days, thereby lowering costs. In addition, it would stop the Cree voyageurs from travelling to the line.[124] Crees coming to the line in Senneterre were able to compare prices of furs and goods which were much more favourable there. Not only were these men saving part of their furs to trade in Senneterre but they were advertising the rates amongst other Crees. The company also objected to having to freight, at its expense, the goods the Waswanipi men were purchasing in Senneterre, for they transported them back with them in the freight canoes. Their solution to keep Indians away from the line was to establish warehouses – for example, another at Matagami Lake, 150 miles below Senneterre – and have the goods hauled there.[125] Rupert House crews were also eliminated from inland transport to Waswanipi when the latter post was administratively removed from the James Bay District and placed with the company's Lake Huron District. Mistassini transport, too, eventually switched from Rupert House to Oskelaneo. Southern transport to Mistassini was begun during Anderson's posting there. The heavy cargo, such as flour and pork, was transported by a white contractor from Lake St Jean who took it off the train, then partway by horse team and then dog team to Lake Chibougamau, on a winter road first built in the early 1900s between St Felicien and Lake Chibougamau.[126] There it was stored until the summer and brought in the remaining sixty-five miles by canoe.[127] The last of the brigades paddled out about the start of the Second World War although when the post journals end at Nemiskau in 1941, freighting by canoe is still the mode of transport for that inland post.[128] However, in the south of the territory where motorized canoes were used, the crew size was cut because the same load of merchandise could be carried on smaller canoes more easily managed by two men; with one motor, one could also tow two canoes.[129]

Winter transport did eventually take over much of the summer freighting, especially from the towns along the line. Even for inland posts, some combination of winter and summer transport was used. Thus, in 1922 two freight canoes set out from Fort George to dump supplies at the new winter trail in order to be freighted in winter to Kanaaupscow.[130] This winter freighting was likely by sleds and dogs and run by Inuit who, since the turn of the century, had been charged with running much of the winter transport out of Fort George. However, technological advances brought another means of winter transport – the tractor over a winter road. These tractors were modified with front skis that drew a "train" – that is, sleighs on which the goods, packed in wooden boxes, were lashed, also known as "motor sleighs."[131] The company experimented with them in 1923 on the inland routes from Rupert House and by 1929 tractors made regular runs to Nemiskau with freight from Rupert House.[132] The independent traders, less committed to incorporating Crees into wage labour, principally used these new modes of transport. For example, the trader Palmquist was taking up a tractor with supplies from Moosonee to Fort George, a trip that would take ten to fifteen days. Tractors required winter roads/trails that Crees worked on.[133]

121   Coping with Changes on the Land

Teams of horses drawing sleighs do not seem to have been a common mode of transportation in James Bay though it may have been in the southern reaches of the territory.[LV] Certainly horse teams were used around the Hudson's Bay Company posts for hauling logs and firewood, though horses were introduced late to James Bay. Horse and wagon were also used to haul the supplies from the dock at Rupert House. After witnessing how they were handled, Cree men at Rupert House took over their handling and began using the horses with sleighs for transporting their wood. Horses evidently provided some type of fascination for the Crees. Willie Jacob and Charlie Blackned recalled that older people at Rupert House watched horses for omens. "If a horse sits up like a dog, that meant he brings bad news to the settlement ... sure to hear a death of someone."[134]

COPING STRATEGIES

The Inlanders

When the Crees talk about the late 1920s and 1930s, they recount how they survived. They talk of specific episodes where two families might have dined out on the remains of one squirrel or on a broth made from boiling lichens scraped off rocks. A number recount the horror of finding whole tipis of relatives and friends starved to death. In setting the scene for these grim accounts they also talk of where they lived, with whom they camped, and what they ate. It is from these details that we can identify significant changes to Inlander society.

Prior to the disappearance of the caribou and the beaver, the Crees wintered in hunting groups of three to five households.[LVI] This changed when there was no longer sufficient large game to feed twelve to twenty people on a daily basis. What becomes evident from their reports of their suffering, as John Kawapit told Adrian Tanner, is that hunting groups now began spreading out, practically one family per lake. Several families would be on lakes a short walking distance apart so that they could share catches of fish.[135] This is also how "KG'"s family coped:

A long time ago before my time (I was young during that time) was when this story happened. Food was scarce at that time. I guess there was not any Whiteman food at that time. People would move from spot to spot in the winter-time when there was nothing left to eat at the spot they stayed. While travelling, some of the people would walk. The ones that couldn't walk would be pulled on the sled by the others that were still strong enough to travel. They would look for a lake that had a lot of fish to eat.[136]

Looking at Samson Neacappo's life history (he is said to be old in 1977) tells us much the same story. He began hunting at the age of ten. At the time his father was hunting with Pipabano. This would have had to be before September 1909, as the Fort George journal mentions that Pipabano died there then.[137] The animals the two hunters killed at that time were caribou, bear, beaver, porcupine, and fish. As Samson got older the hunting got worse. First the caribou became scarce; there was one year his father killed only one. Bear were also difficult to find. Later the beaver started to decline. At the time he was still living with his parents and they hunted with his mother's brother. If the hunting was bad the families would split up.[138]

With fish being the mainstay of the diet, as it was likely much of the time in the first half of the century, Inlanders and Coasters had to resort to wintering in smaller groups, usually single households. It is not accurate to depict this as change, for this flexibility in social organization, this ability to fragment and regroup according to resources, is the hallmark of the success of northern Algonquian society. The twentieth century was not the first time the Cree social system had to devolve in the face of a food crisis. Needless to say, there had been many times before. Nor was starvation unknown to the Crees early in the twentieth century. The Anglican Church burial registers from Rupert House list James Miller and John Katapatuk from Mistassini as having died of starvation in 1906, and several more in 1911.[139] A severe three-year down-cycle of hare and ptarmigan, plus a difficulty in catching fish, also occurred from 1880 to 1882, leaving the Crees of Rupert House undergoing great hardships, with twenty-one having died.[140] Stories from this period would certainly have been part of the Cree oral tradition in the early 1900s. However, they were still unprepared for the widespread deprivation they suffered from 1929 to 1932.

Wintering in single households or families was not the preferred lifestyle[141] nor was it a practical means of ensuring food and survival; the sickness and/or death of either the mother or father endangered the lives of the rest. Also a single hunter was not the most efficient way to maximize the chances of killing game. Moreover, the sociability inherent in larger group living is important in human society. John Blackned told Richard Preston that the strategy of spreading out on the land in scarce times was not a wise one, that it felt "intuitively wrong to him." From what he learned from the stories of his elders and from his own experience, he felt there was a better chance of obtaining at least a little to eat with a larger number of hunters. He was also concerned that in times of hardship people might doubt the judgment of their leaders and set off on their own, a practice that he did not sanction. Preston comments that for Blackned, "maintaining their personal community proves more precious than following an optimal foraging strategy."[142]

123 Coping with Changes on the Land

The reduced size of the winter hunting group did not become a lasting feature of James Bay Cree social organization, nor was it likely a year-round feature. Once game numbers recovered, such as beaver in the 1940s, it is obvious that three and four families were wintering together, the norm discovered by social anthropologists beginning fieldwork amongst the Crees in the 1950s.[143]

What did change was their orientation, their primary objective in living off the land. Prior to competition and market pressures brought on by the fur fashions of the 1920s, the inland Cree likely did not think of themselves as fur trappers but as subsistence hunters whose main objective was to feed their families. The furs were only important to provide them with essentials such as cloth and ammunition; they were not the means of putting food on the table. That the land provided. When the land offered up meagre food resources the Crees could usually eke out a living by subsisting on fish or ptarmigan. When the land offered up only meagre fur resources then the Hudson's Bay Company could be relied upon to continue to advance them the imported goods on which they had come to rely, even though their previous debts had remained unpaid. When the company failed to underwrite their trapping due to its own financial squeeze, the Inlanders became impoverished and had to adapt to the demands of the market. Had food animals been abundant they might have resisted being drawn in primarily as trappers serving the market, but even that is disputable.

After the First World War, North America was undergoing a technological boom. There were now repeater rifles, outboard motors, and sewing machines that improved their hunting productivity and made life easier. One can only surmise the Crees wanted them. To be able to purchase these goods as well as afford the regular provisions, now at higher costs, the Cree hunter had to serve the market. The market wanted foxes and other small furs and, besides, there were no more beaver. The hunter of yore who captured beaver, feasted on the meat, and traded the pelt was out of date. He was now hunting marten, mink, fox, muskrat, animals taken for their pelts not their food. Subsistence hunting and trapping for these furs was incompatible, as D.C. McTavish counselled in 1882. "It is impossible for Indians to trap when time is employed searching for food."[144] Without country food to subsidize the fur trapping, the Inlanders turned to imported foods: flour, sugar, lard, baking powder and the much-favoured tea.[LVII] Consequently, in the last century the Inlanders became tied into the world market in a much more fundamental way than they had previously. They now depended on it for their subsistence, as a much-needed safety valve that would stave off starvation and enable them to be primarily fur trappers rather than food hunters. When the Crees set out in the early fall to their winter hunting grounds, it is assumed that much of their hunting strategy and plans centred on their ability to secure furs, for these furs could be transformed into food. These were the days before welfare. As "MJ" from Wemindji tells it, "Nowadays it is easier for the people, they have everything they need for hunting. It is easier today, people have money to support themselves that they did not have in the olden days."[145]

For a short period the Crees enjoyed a boom in the 1920s. Their furs were much in demand to satisfy the needs of the flapper era; they could get $126 for a silver fox, $52 for a fisher, $24 for an otter, even 80 cents for a muskrat (26,000 were trapped).[146] This newly gained wealth enabled them to rely even more on store food beyond what they had taken into the bush at the turn of the century.[147] This changed. "GD" from Wemindji reported that he pulled seven hundred pounds of groceries on his toboggan from the coast to his hunting territory two hundred miles away. Since this was a winter transport, he would have taken in supplies in the fall as well. His hauling of groceries began "when his sons were grown up" (about the 1940s) whereas "way back when I first got married, I never went to the coast for groceries."[148]

Throughout the 1920s the Inlanders and the company were locked into the midwinter supply system. Usually the company or free traders provided this provisioning, making it easier for the Inlanders to obtain store food. This was another modification to the fur trade that drew them away from reliance on the land to reliance on the store. And then the boom ended. The 1929 crash, of markets and animals, forced the Inlanders to draw on their inner resources.

This analysis is wanting on at least two significant issues. Inasmuch as the Inlanders were veering away from a subsistence economy based on caribou, beaver, and bear, it is assumed that certain beliefs or practices such as conjuring, drumming, and interpreting dreams were modified or lapsed, but it is not possible to reconstruct these changes. It would also be worthwhile to inquire into the changes in their views of their hunting territories at the time when few beaver were being harvested. A discussion in the following chapter will show the contradictory statements about them anthropologists heard but the remarks were recorded at least thirty to forty years after the economy had changed.

The Coasters

More is known about the Coasters than the Inlanders. The post journals from the coast are more informative about them because they were frequent visitors to the post but also because reporting from the coastal posts was more extensive than the inland ones. Thus there is the danger of attributing more dramatic change to them than to the Inlanders. As well, much of the accounts I have drawn upon were collected at the posts on the coast, without a distinction made between Coasters and Inlanders. One suspects that Coasters were more likely to be at the post and perhaps more willing to be interviewed.

The Coasters were, in many ways, products of the fur trade and their economy was highly dependent on it. Once the company reduced its dependence on the labour provided by the Coasters, the Crees had to find other sources of food. They could not, like the Inlanders, spread out over their land. It was already overcrowded and naturally devoid of a viable food base.[LVIII] The solution was varied. Some remained on their lands, presumably those whose hunting territories had provided some minimum standard of living. Others joined Inlanders to work their hunting territory with them and eventually take over territories that were left vacant, as Pachano acquired the lands of English Shoes. Billy Jolly (born 1901) thought that many people moved into the Mistassini area to hunt because the prices of goods were cheaper there. He also thought people moved away from Rupert House because they had too big a debt there. According to Jolly, their debt would be forwarded to the new post but they still would receive an additional credit.[149] For example, one family of Diamins [Joseph] from Rupert House was encouraged to move in 1942 to Waswanipi as his hunting lands were now within the Waswanipi section of the Nottoway Preserve, though for a number of years he had been living and trading at Senneterre, close to his lands.[150] It may be that, as a result of the mining activity in the Mistassini area, lands were freed up or at least more wage opportunities were available. As well, some women became attached to different posts even though they married men trapping in the same quarters as their fathers. Alice Butterfly (born 1914) was the daughter of Abraham Esau, a Rupert House Coaster, and Elizabeth Gilpin (of Eastmain). Alice met her husband on the family hunting territory, in the Hannah Bay region, but he traded at Moose Factory. Consequently, Alice Butterfly became a winter resident of his settlement when their children were in school and, of course, stayed on there.[151]

Coasters also headed south to the line, for example at La Sarre or Amos, lured in part, by the attractions of the larger towns, perhaps, as West wrote, "by the proximity of 'bootleggers.'"[152] Presumably there they combined a trapping life with whatever wage employment could be obtained, perhaps work in the sawmills at La Sarre, Quebec.[153] In this regard, Beatrice Fairies' account is instructive. Her father was Joseph Trapper (died 1961 at Moose Factory), son of Peter Trapper, and her mother's father was Reuben Namagoose, both families associated with Rupert House.[LIX] Her father had hunted up the Harricana in the

Rupert House area but then often moved south to La Sarre in the summer. There he sold his fur at the Hudson's Bay Company and obtained work at the company store or the local hotel. He had also worked on the boat going to Great Whale River and before he was married he worked on the company's dog team. Beatrice was sent to the residential school at Chapleau in the 1930s, where she stayed two winters and one summer. When her mother got sick and was taken to the hospital in Cochrane, her father and brother went to the bush and she ended up living and working in the home of the Indian agent, Dr T.J. Orford, in Moose Factory. He later arranged for her to work in the home of the Reynolds family [LX] in North Bay, which she did for two years. Beatrice married Ed Fairies of Moose Factory.[154]

Aside from the Fairies' account illustrating one family's move out of Rupert House, it also raises another theme – that of the employment opportunities for women that drew them away from hunting lives. In the 1930s this employment was mainly domestic,[LXI] but later other opportunities arose such as the work in laundry at Moose Factory. As with other Indian communities, the people who moved away from the villages have not been sufficiently studied. There is today a sizable community of Crees from eastern James Bay at Moose Factory who call themselves "MoCreebec." Some moved there in the 1920s and 1930s, women more than men, but it is assumed the larger exodus came in the 1950s with the establishment of the hospital and increased economic opportunities because of the railway and the town of Moosonee.

It is difficult to generalize about the changed social organization among the Coasters since circumstances and economic opportunities determined each family's living arrangements. A general comment about the Coasters in the 1920s and 1930s is that, like their ancestors, they seized opportunities. On the whole, though, the main adaptation should probably be characterized as a "back to the land movement," drawing some to the interior regions and others to more prolonged occupation of their hunting lands on the coast.

Company Families

They were the Crees who by design or happenstance became year-round employees of the Hudson's Bay Company. Originally, perhaps more than one hundred years earlier, they had one English or Scottish ancestor working for the company (such as George Atkinson, James Hester, Andrew Moar or John Loutitt). The Crees distinguished between the company servants and other Crees by referring to them as *wemstukshiokan* ("made into white people"), presumably because their lifestyle at the post was more akin to that of the whites. As for the company, originally it refused to acknowledge the offspring of their employees at the posts but in the early 1800s recognized them as a "small Colony of very useful Hands" which ultimately would lessen the need to recruit men in England.[155] Not all the men of mixed ancestry chose careers with the company but those who did because of their knowledge of the people and the Cree language, English and sometimes writing, as well as their bush skills, became valuable employees, especially at the outposts in the interior. In 1919 the posts at Eastmain, Nemiskau, and Neoskweskau were under the charge of "native traders"[LXII] and have "done fairly well."[156] Over the years, several others were praised. In addition to the native traders, a large number were labourers at the post. In the 1920s the company was trying to downsize and consideration was given the "general servants." George Ray wrote in 1922, that they "are far in excess of the number required, yet what are we to do with them? They are sons of generations of Hudson's Bay Company servants. We cannot give their fathers medals for long service and then send them (the children) out into the world. They are in reality products of the Company and the Company must carry them until such time as a railway or something comes into the country and absorbs them. Of course in taking this view I am governed by sentiment, but no business can be completely soulless."[157]

In 1929 the company had still not resolved this dilemma. West raised it again in his report:

At some posts we are still paying for past carelessness in the matter of native labour. Men have been engaged in capacities where they were not absolutely necessary, with the direct result that we now have a surplus of employees on hand. This problem will gradually right itself and care will be taken to prevent recurrence. A point which may seem to be of little importance to the casual observer is the placing on pension of native servants. In this District, there are some who, although receiving a pension, are also engaged from time to time as temporary labourers, and in addition to their usual rations, they are given their house, their fuel and minor gratuities. So far as post expenses are concerned, therefore the situation remains unchanged.[158]

Eliminating native employees came to be a policy of the company. The eastern James Bay inspection report of 1925 regarding Fort George states that "if a good Apprentice Clerk had been available for Fort George, two native employees could have been dispensed with. They would than have been released for hunting, and, most important of all, their families would not grow up accustomed to living at a Post."[159]

Company families at Moose Factory became crystallized as a separate social category because the 1905 James Bay Treaty excluded them.[160] Without a treaty in James Bay until 1975,[LXIII] there were no legal barriers to movement back and forth between Coasters and company families. We learn something of this movement from the field notes of Rolf Knight recorded at Rupert House in 1961. An interesting issue springs from Knight's findings which has a bearing on the discussion here. Using the information obtained from his interviews, Knight came to the conclusion that the Crees had not had a long-standing system of family hunting territories. His conclusions did not ring true for a number of people who had either studied Cree society or the historical documentation or read Knight's field notes filled with contradictory statements about hunting territories. Twenty years later, Sarah Preston demonstrated why Knight had obtained the kind of information he did. She documents that a good number of the Rupert House Crees he interviewed had been working for the company (or Revillon Frères) and had only begun hunting later in life and hence had no hunting territories. Watt also said this in a letter to Dr Tyrer, the Indian agent, telling him that "Coast Indians who have never hunted beaver are going inland with experienced men and consequently will have something to trade around New Year."[161] It was Watt's policy to encourage Coasters to change from temporary servants to independent hunters.[162] During his fieldwork Knight recognized that where once there had been three occupational groups of Crees at Rupert House, now there were two. He writes: "The former importance of Métis as intermediaries, straw bosses and artisans have vanished. Even men who were formerly in the Métis groups are now considered 'Indian' by Indians."[163] It is the Knight interviews that are used here to provide some insights into the choices people made when the company reorganized its labour requirements.

David Salt was born in 1896 at Rupert House where his father was a clerk. Salt was about thirteen or fourteen when his father was fired because he was too old. For a while his father and mother worked for the Catholic mission at "Rupert House"[LXIV] but this also did not last and they "moved to Rupert House" where the father acted as an interpreter for Revillon Frères. The younger Salt married an Eastmain woman and he worked there for the Hudson's Bay Company until he was thirty-two years old when he was put on the mail run, making four trips between Fort George and Moose Factory during the winter. During the summer "he and his dogs were kept." With the coming of air transport, Salt lost this employment about 1943. He moved his family (he was now married to a second Eastmain woman, probably Daisy Mayappo) back to Rupert House and began trapping. He trapped with Andrew Whiskeychan, considered an old man at the time. At first Salt did not own any of his own traps but received a share of Whiskeychan's furs. Eventually, in about 1959, under the registered trapline system, he and his son Ronnie were assigned a section of land that Charlie Hester had "wanted to close down" for two years and so was forced to forfeit this land. Salt's three sons from his first marriage were not on the land with him in 1961. They had jobs, two in Rupert House; Billy worked as caretaker of the nursing station, Isaiah was a Hudson's Bay Company clerk, while Henry held the same job in Chibougamau.[164]

Another life history is similarly illustrative of some of the choices these former company servants made. Frank Moar, born about 1903, was the son of Daniel Moar, who had been born and raised at Mistassini, working there on the mail run to La Sarre without the benefit of a dog team, dragging the toboggan himself. About 1900 Daniel Moar was transferred to Eastmain where he worked as an interpreter, and it was there that Frank Moar was born. Knight believed that Moar's mother was from Eastmain. According to Knight's notes, Daniel Moar had not done any trapping and Frank had to learn it from his wife's family at the age of twenty-five. Until then he had managed to support himself in other ways. Although his wife (Nellie Stephens) took up winter residence at Rupert House in 1954, Frank Moar continued hunting-trapping until 1958 when he gave his beaver quota to his youngest son. Frank Moar was the first Rupert House elected chief,[LXV] about 1947. However, Knight carries on in his notes to comment that "possibly some pressure had been exerted by the Agent because Frank was not re-elected, to the disconcertment of the white community then resident." Moreover, we are told that Frank Moar was the only member of the community that Knight heard vociferously criticized by another member of the community.[165]

The government did distinguish between those of mixed ancestry and the Indians. The ones who did not make it onto the band lists because the agent deemed them not "living an Indian life" at the time the list was drawn up were singled out from any entitlement to hunt in the boundaries of the beaver sanctuaries, but they were not excluded from hunting. Mixed ancestry and white persons married into the band and "leading the life of an Indian" could obtain a licence to trap beaver as long as they had been residents in the region for three years.[166] However, in 1942 when licences to hunt were required, only males whose names were on the band roll were eligible.[167] The number of individuals at any post listed as "non-Indian" or "not Indian" was very small.

As for the women of company families, some married Inlanders; for example, Daisy Hester to Billy Jolly (Nemiskau), Josephine McLeod to Bertie Diamond (Rupert House).[168] They also (and more likely) married Coasters, for example, Marion MacDonald whose father worked for Revillon Frères at Fort George, who married Wesley from Moose Factory.[169] These women also married men of company families or company managers: Daisy Spencer's marriage to the Reverend Walton, Annie Iserhoff's to Edward Corston, and Jane Harper's to Thomas Iserhoff.[170] There were also the Mistassini marriages of Winnifred Iserhoff, daughter of Willie Iserhoff, to trader A.S. Ritchie and Winnie Matoosh to trader E. MacLeod.[171]

Thus a combination of exogamy and a return to the land reduced the number of company servants in James Bay and blurred the distinction between them and the Coasters. When the 1975 James Bay agreement was signed the old company families were therefore not excluded as they had been at Moose Factory in 1905.[172]

SUMMARY

This analysis has centred on change or adaptation and in doing so it has brought the story of Cree adaptation to the fur trade up to more contemporary times. When I began my studies in the mid-1970s of events in James Bay, I rejected earlier hypotheses of significant change, arguing that eighteenth- and nineteenth-century Crees were still essentially subsistence hunters who had to make very little accommodation to the European fur trade that began in the late 1600s. I saw significant continuity in their economic, political, and social institutions with their forebears of pre-fur trade days. This work, though, carries the study further into the twentieth century and here I have shown the Crees changing from being first and foremost subsistence hunters to trapping for exchange. In the early 1900s the Crees, particularly the Inlanders, were able to exercise the flexibility their social organization permitted them by resorting to dependence, primarily on the nuclear or small extended family rather than the larger three- and four-family winter hunting groups. Ordinarily, as it had over the centuries, this social organization would have reverted to the preferred, and larger, winter hunting groups when food resources became more abundant. Other circumstances occurring at the same time built on this retreat from communal living – influences such as the church's conception of the family, wage employment, schooling, and government bureaucracy. In sum, the options for the Crees to organize their daily lives had become much more restricted.

CHAPTER FIVE

A New Technological and Bureaucratic World: The Confiscation of the Land

The world after the First World War changed, James Bay included. As elsewhere, the economy, fuelled by technological changes, had dramatic effects on the society. James Bay had remained isolated for longer than the more settled parts of Canada. But it would no more be sheltered from the global forces. Industrial development, made possible by technological changes in transport and telecommunications, opened up the north of Canada for mineral extraction.[1] The correlation, demonstrated elsewhere in Canada, of the government following closely on the heels of mining development is true also for James Bay. O.S. Finnie, director of the Northwest Territories Branch of the federal government, recognized this about government policy in the 1920s. He wrote: "The Canadian government subsidizes the Territories, not altogether in the spirit of philanthropy, but as an investment from which it will draw ample dividends."[1] This chapter chronicles the development of government interest in this region and its gradual burrowing into Cree society. It begins with the technological changes that drew the Crees, unwittingly, into the political and economic agendas of the south. Some of this appropriation of Cree society is a familiar Canadian story, based as it was on the national Indian policy such as the Indian Act and Department of Indian Affairs. Another significant part of it developed from the particular social, economic, and environmental circumstances in James Bay. The creation of beaver preserves and registered traplines was of predominant interest to the people of James Bay in the 1930s and 1940s. However, the Cree emphasis would not be on the programs imposed on them, but on survival. Their struggle during these particularly harsh ecological and economic times was exacerbated by traders, missionaries, and government agents bombarding them with views on how they should be living. Consequently, the story that unfolds also includes a tale of competition from other than of fur trade companies – of competing churches, governments, and agencies who knew what was best for the Indians in a part of the country that had become highly impoverished.

HIJACKING OF THE LAND

The "sucking in" of native societies into the Canadian polity took place throughout the country at different times and in different ways. Needless to say, the southern regions, followed by the prairies, first bore the brunt of settlement by foreigners, who imposed their institutions and values on the indigenous peoples, drawing them into a sphere of poverty, loss of cultural identity, dependency, segregation, isolation, and a sense of being overwhelmed.[2] The northern peoples eventually were drawn into this undertow of dependency. Those areas rich in mineral resources or timber or hydroelectric potential (such as the Ontario James Bay) were affected sooner than others, while the expropriation of the resources on Cree land in eastern James Bay came relatively late for most in the Cree territory. Without significant Euro-Canadian settlement or business interests in eastern James Bay, the undermining of the old Cree ways was more gradual and more imperceptible than elsewhere in Canada. It began for the southern Crees, such as those of Waswanipi and Mistassini, in stops and starts early in the century, but large settlements did not spring up on their land until the 1950s.[11] Most Cree settlements, particularly the coastal ones, were far removed from such industrial expansion. This absence of economic development also ensured the government's lack of interest in building north-south roads or railways. Hence most of the Crees were quite isolated, especially since universal electrification, long-distance telephones, and highways had to await a trade-off with the James Bay hydroelectric project in the 1970s.

A significant feature of colonialism is the colonial society's domination over the land. For the Crees that began in the 1870s with the transfer to the Canadian government of the immense territory known as Rupert's Land which the Hudson's Bay Company had long considered its fiefdom. To a Cree, this possession would have aroused some mirth, for it is highly doubtful whether anyone, including the post managers in James Bay, saw themselves as governing anything other than the particulars of the trade. Nevertheless, the Hudson's Bay Company and the government came to an arrangement in 1869–70. With the transfer of land went the requirements that the government would arrange with the Indians for the cession of their rights to their ancestral lands. This is stated in the order-in-council of 1870: "Any claims of Indians to compensation for lands required for purposes of Settlement shall be disposed of by the Canadian government in communication with the Imperial Government."[3]

When the Dominion government turned over vast tracts of these northwest lands to Ontario in 1897 and Quebec in 1898, no mention was made of the recognition of these land rights which is deemed an omission rather than an abrogation of these rights. By the Quebec Boundaries Extension Act of 1898, Quebec's northern boundaries were set along the Eastmain River and thence roughly eastward to the western border of Labrador. A further land transfer in 1902 to Ontario and 1912 to Quebec did provide for a land cession by the Indians. The Quebec Boundaries Extension Act of 1912 reads:

(c) That the Province of Quebec will recognize the rights of the Indian inhabitants in the territory above described to the same extent, and will obtain surrenders of such rights in the same manner, as the Government of Canada has heretofore recognized such rights and has obtained surrender thereof, and the said province shall bear and satisfy all charges and expenditures in connection or arising out of such surrenders;

(d) That no such surrender shall be made or obtained except with the approval of the Governor in Council;

(e) That the trusteeship of the Indians in the said territory, and the management of any lands now or hereafter reserved for their use, shall remain in the Government of Canada subject to the control of Parliament.[4]

Ontario met this requirement with the signing of Treaty 9 by Crees, Ojibwa, and Algonquin societies in 1905–6. Those bands that were omitted until the final settling of the northern boundaries in 1912 were visited by a commission in 1929–30 when they signed adhesions.[5] Quebec never undertook to extinguish aboriginal claims to the land, neither in James Bay nor anywhere else in the province. It chose to ignore the requirements of 1870 and 1912, as well as the Royal Proclamation of 1763 which granted to the Indians, living in unsettled lands, the right to continue to occupy those lands "unmolested" until such time as the government and the government alone "purchas'd" their lands. The Quebec position has long been that since New France had acquired its land without treaties (and presumably, by conquest) it was not incumbent on them to sign treaties.[6]

The Quebec decision was a political and bureaucratic one, never subjected to a legal opinion through a hearing process. As a result of petitions for a treaty by Indians in Ontario and Quebec, a memo to Clifford Sifton, minister of the interior, sets out this position in 1903:

As far as the Indians of Quebec are concerned, it is suggested that no treaty should be made with them or that any Quebec Indians living temporarily in Ontario should be included in the Ontario treaty but we should endeavour to obtain an understanding from the Province of Quebec that as claims are made by the outlying tribes ... the Province should be willing to set apart at proper times suitable reserves. The Indian title in the Province of Quebec has never been recognized or surrendered as in the Province of Ontario and, I presume, that it is not proposed to change the policy in that regard.[7]

Thirty years later this arbitrary position regarding Quebec's obligation to obtain title for Indian lands was reinforced by another Indian Affairs declaration. A letter from the secretary of Indian affairs to the Indian agent at Moose Factory, Dr W.L. Tyrer, reads: "You are apparently under the impression that as the Indians of the Rupert House district are not in treaty they have some aboriginal title to the lands in the province of Quebec. This is not the case as that province has complete control of the lands within its boundaries, free of any Indian title, as the Indian interest, in so far as lands are concerned, was provided under the statute of 14 & 15 Victoria."[8] Although the Quebec government failed to deal with aboriginal rights, it is also a failure of the federal government which retains the underlying power to extinguish aboriginal title and constitutionally has held the Indian bands as wards of the state.

Although Quebec had unilaterally established jurisdiction over Cree lands, it was for many years only a paper declaration. However, the federal government has gradually asserted its domination over this region. It is a story of bureaucratic colonialism that has choked a people's resourcefulness and initiative.

EFFECTS OF THE FIRST WORLD WAR

The First World War was not unknown to the Crees of James Bay who, according to Anderson, "developed a surprising interest in it."[9] Some had direct experience, enlisting to go overseas. Several of them were from Fort George, according to a history of the Catholic presence in James Bay.[10] These vague claims are not substantiated in a listing of native soldiers who served in the war,[11] although four men are recorded as coming from Moose Factory.[III] Many followed the progress of the war along with the post managers, as best as they could in those days, having only the mail and newspapers from the company packet on which to rely.[IV] After the war, Crees visiting Fort George might have heard anecdotes from Ernest Renouf. He had been a clerk at Great Whale River when he enlisted in 1917. He was back at Fort George in 1919, presumably full of stories of war-related events. A roving veteran was Louis Romanet,[V] who rejoined his French regiment in 1916 when he first learned of the war and returned in 1919. As inspector for the Hudson's Bay Company in James Bay he would have had occasions to recount his overseas experiences at a number of different posts. It is doubtful if too many other company men served in the war because Renouf, now manager at Fort George, declared 11 November 1920 a holiday, but also declared that "the men have been given a holiday – though their part in the disturbance was conspicuous by its absence."[12]

The Crees were also affected materially by the war in Europe. Griffiths at Fort George first heard of the outbreak of war from the Revillon Frères supply boat on 12 September 1914. Along with the news came instructions to him from company officials that he was to give out supplies sparingly and encourage the Indians to live on country food as much as possible.[13] No more was said, but in 1919 the Rupert House hunters were complaining about the quality and price of goods that were now being imported from Canada. William Rackham, the district manager, writes: "In my opinion, however, the goods are not altogether unsuitable for trade, but the people have become so accustomed to the British goods supplied previously, that they continually find fault, not only with the price, but also with the quality of the Canadian goods which we have been obliged to substitute."[14]

As elsewhere in rural and northern regions of Canada, the end of the war brought home men and, with their stories, exposure to new places, peoples, things. Soon after the James Bay population, Crees and whites, had to contend with more than ideas because technological items, only recently in use in the south, were now making their way north.

NEW TECHNOLOGY IN TRANSPORT AND COMMUNICATION

Boating in Canada was mechanized about the turn of the century. The first reference in eastern James Bay was in Renouf's Fort George journal of 1920.[VI] He had taken over as post manager two days earlier and apparently took the chief and councillors out for a run in the *Kelly*, his motorboat, commenting that "they were frightfully pleased."[15] Nellie Moar recalls her first time out trapping with her husband Frank. They left from Rupert House about the middle of October in a "motorized canoe."[16] It may be recalled that Frank Moar had been the son of a company servant and this trip inland, with his in-laws, was his first time trapping. Their use of a motorized boat to go thirty miles upriver seems anomalous as there is no mention of a Cree hunter's purchase of outboard motors in the journals in the 1930s. They were highly expensive items for hunters to own, especially in the 1930s, and one questions as to how useful they were on trips far inland with numbers of portages and no gasoline depots. Nevertheless, there may be another explanation of why Cree Coasters were not using them. The Hudson's Bay Company may not have been promoted them for sale, since this would permit the Crees easier access to the stores along the line.[VII] They were in use, though, by the company. A 1925 entry in the Waswanipi journal noted: "J. Miller and Jacob Gull with motor canoe to help Joseph Ottereyes' crews ... all down with influenza."[17] It was only in the 1950s that outboard motors became available to the Crees at Rupert House, requiring a change in the construction of the canoes that were manufactured there.[18] However, there are a number of references to the company or missionaries engaging Crees to transport them along the coast.[VIII]

In the 1920s most Canadians in the south were listening to American radio broadcasts either because they preferred the more polished American programs or because they could not receive the few low-powered Canadian ones. Radio came to James Bay in the winter of 1922–3. It was a battery-operated three-tube set that Westinghouse had sent to Watt at Rupert House for experimental purposes. The first transmission was from the Reverend Hugh Kerr of the Shadyside Presbyterian Church from radio station KDKA in Pittsburgh. However, months went by before a message sent by dog sled from Watt confirmed that the message had been received.[19] J.W. Anderson, then at Albany post on the west coast of James Bay, received the second set in 1924. He expressed difficulty in conveying fully the impact of radio on the isolated fur trade posts of 1924: "Just think of the news value alone – every day from far and near, the latest happenings around the world! You can say what you like about your first kiss, but when I put on the earphones on a cool autumn day in 1924 and heard voices coming in from hundreds of miles away – why that was one of the great thrills of my life!"[20]

Radio may have come to James Bay but, much to everyone's annoyance, it often did not work.[IX] Writing of the late 1920s, Reverend Cartlidge at Waswanipi commented: "radio was being pioneered, but most of the time the batteries were dead." At other times the reception was poor and they missed their messages.[21] When it did work, the radio at Fort George became a focus of socializing for the whites living there in the 1920s. They would often get together at the home of the Anglican missionary. Absent from these gatherings were the occupants of the Catholic mission. However, it was the Catholics who established the first two-way broadcasting station at Fort George in 1938.[22] By 1940 the company began its own system of two-way radio communications in the north whereby posts along the coasts of James and Hudson Bays were linked by broadcasting stations.[23] Previously they had only short-wave radios with which they were able to hear but not transmit, something the Great Whale River manager in 1938 found highly limiting.[24] The company formed its own "radio department" and in 1940 Mr Horner, in charge of radio transmission for the company, came to the coast to install radio stations at all the posts, linking Belcher Island, Great Whale River, Fort George, Eastmain, Old Factory and Rupert House. Within a few months inland posts such as Mistassini were also hooked into the Hudson's Bay Company's network.[25] These radio stations were powered by windchargers erected on towers.[x]

Having the radio was a great boon to the white population, feeling very isolated as they did. The Great Whale River manager, Carmichael, always wrote exuberantly in his journal when he reported on hearing a broadcast on his radio, whether it was the World Series, President Roosevelt, or updates on the war.[26] The Hudson's Bay Company's radio network throughout the north of Canada was put to use in the Second World War. It played a strategic role in the war, providing vital weather data, sometime hourly, for the use of military aircraft. As well, at fifty-six of the posts, fur traders were trained to recognize and report enemy ships and planes. Also of importance was the cooperation they gained from the "isolated bands of Indians and Eskimos."[27]

Not having generators at their camps, the Crees would not have had radios, but occasionally there is mention of their being able to listen in when at the post. At Old Factory in 1938, D.G. Boyd got their radio working and noted "the whole village was around listening to the new radio in the evening."[28] Over at Great Whale River on Christmas Eve of 1940, P.M. Carmichael said they listened to a broadcast called "Bringing Canada to the Frontier" in which messages were read. He added that "the Eskimos[XI] were all in to listen to this broadcast and the evening was topped off by the taking of flash pictures."[29] Momentous occasions such as the death of King George V came in via radio.[30] The company practice of flying flags at half mast on such important occasions was bound to ensure that the news spread. Although radio was not a general entertainment or communication medium for the Crees, its use in James Bay drew them more completely into the world economy by throwing them at the mercy of the ever-changing market prices for furs.

138   The White Man's Gonna Getcha

It is not known when electricity, via the generator, first came to James Bay. When it did it would have been used only by the white agencies. The hospital at Fort George, built in 1930, had electricity, and stores and churches would presumably have had electric lights earlier. It does not seem to have been a subject that merited anyone's attention except for one. J.M. Stevenson was the Hudson's Bay Company clerk at Nichikun Post in 1939 and he received, in his shipment, a windcharger which he mounted and connected to a battery. On 20 September 1939 he remarked: "We had the comfort of electric lights in the evening much to the amusement of the Indians who had never seen them before."[31] Finally, we find that the Anglican Church at Rupert House had an electric light for the first time on Christmas 1944.[32] Electric lights at Rupert House in the 1960s were still operating off a bank of six-volt batteries.[33]

Air travel was another technological advance that eventually recast economic and social life in James Bay. The Fort George journals provide the most descriptive view of its advent on 4 July 1929. Obviously planes had been going through the southern posts earlier[XII] and seemed already commonplace when it was recorded on 1 August 1929 that a doctor had landed by plane at the inland post of Nemiskau.[34] In fact, some part of Watt's inspection tour of posts for the Hudson's Bay Company brought him into Waswanipi by plane in the summer of 1923.[35]

In 1933 the company began periodically using bush planes for inspection tours in James Bay but did not come to rely on them for transport or supplying Cree camps until their rivals in James Bay forced them to do so in the 1940s.[XIII] The company dragged its feet on plane transport for the same reason they held to the canoe brigades: the summer employment of Crees that reinjected the monies paid them for transport back into the company store.[36]

There must have been a great deal of excitement when the first planes invaded Cree territory. In his memoirs the trader Keighley told how the first plane flying over Stanley (northern Saskatchewan) in July of 1924 caused a flurry of excitement. One Cree man, Mist-a-kusk, came running from his tipi with a loaded shotgun "to shoot the devil from the air."[37] Similarly, Daniel Saganash of Waswanipi remembered seeing his first plane and remembered throwing a rock at it.[38] The stunts the pilot of General Airways did for everyone's benefit before departing from Waswanipi on Christmas Eve of 1934 amazed one old man, who thought the plane would provide an easy "way of getting to Heaven."[39] A Carnegie Museum expedition under Arthur Twomey was scheduled in 1938 to take a month-long dog-sled trip from Moose Factory to Great Whale River. Instead they flew in, prompting the dog-sled

139 The Confiscation of the Land

driver who was watching the passing ground from the plane remark every fifteen minutes that "another day's journey had just gone by."[40] Yet there is no story like the one R.H.G. Bonnycastle reported when he was in Aklavik in 1929 and the first plane landed. There the pilot, Punch Dickins, took five Inuit at a time for a ten-minute excursion, charging them $10 for the flying experience. He made seven flights that day.[41] The presumed commotion provoked by the first view of an airplane likely occurred not only amongst the Inuit and Crees but also the white men, who would never have seen one, though probably heard about them in the stories of the war.

Eventually, with an improved financial situation, the Crees would charter airplanes, first to transport their food, household goods, and hunting equipment which were left cached at their camps inland,[42] and later to fly themselves as well. Emma Neacappo pointed out that she and her husband were the first of the Fort George people to charter a plane to their territory but she also commented that they "went the furthest inland of the Fort George people," to the Caniapiscau River region.[43] The flying time in 1931 from Fort George to Moose Factory took two hours and fifteen minutes; by dog team it took twelve to fourteen days.[44] Similarly, the 120-mile trip from Rupert House to Josephine McLeod Diamond's hunting territory took two weeks by canoe but just over an hour by plane.[45]

When bush plane travel and transport became a regular feature in James Bay, arrangements were made in the fall for a mid-winter pick-up of furs and a drop of supplies. Those whose camps were close to each other met at one camp to await the arrival of the plane from either the Hudson's Bay Company or an independent trader. According to Richard Blackned, he and other Wemindji trappers met at Old Factory River, his camp, to await the plane. The others were George Kakabat, William Asquabaneskum, Atsynias, Hughboys, and Sam Visitor. This particular winter the pick-up netted the Hudson's Bay Company five hundred pelts. The plane would go on to other camps and meeting places. If people needed additional supplies not asked for on the list they left behind in the fall, they could request a return trip of the plane, the cost of which was deducted from their fur sales.[46] Clearly, all transport was charged to the Crees, whether as an added or a hidden charge. Some of the private companies that operated the bush planes in the James Bay territory were Dominion Skyways, Quebec Airways, and Canadian Airways.[47]

An older form of transport was to have renewed impact on Cree life in the early 1930s. Although the Canadian Pacific Railway was completed in the 1880s, it was still ten days' journey by canoe from Moose Factory, the port of entry to James Bay. The National Transcontinental

Railway through central Quebec and Ontario, eventually to form part of the Canadian National Railway, was completed in 1914. This was the line, through the towns of Senneterre, Oskelaneo, and Cochrane, that caused the Hudson's Bay Company post managers so much aggravation because Crees in the southern part of the James Bay territory would regularly travel there to trade, the lure being lower prices and frontier town attractions. Still, it was too distant from most of the Cree settlements. This would have changed had the plans for a railway from Senneterre to the mouth of the Nottoway River on James Bay materialized. The North Railway Company was formed in 1912 to oversee this project and had dispatched a steamer to Charlton Island and Rupert House with supplies for the surveyors. The following summer, though, the projected line was cancelled.[48] However, in 1932 the Temiskaming and Northern Ontario Railway (later named the Ontario Northland Railway) opened up easy access to James Bay. The railway was built through the rich Timmins-Porcupine mining and forestry region and through to James Bay, stopping at the new town of Moosonee[XIV] across from the island of Moose Factory, Ontario's only saltwater port.[49]

NEGATIVE EFFECTS OF THESE TECHNOLOGICAL ADVANCES

With such a technological advantage, the Hudson's Bay Company had to reorganize its transportation. It could no longer afford to supply the James Bay posts by ship from Montreal and it closed down the depot at Charlton Island, using the railway at Moosonee as the point of departure for the motor schooners still needed to supply the posts along the coasts of James Bay.[50] The closing of the depot at Charlton naturally reduced the company's labour requirements both there and at Rupert House. The posts a greater distance from Moose Factory, such as Great Whale River, continued to be supplied by ships from Montreal on the same voyages to the Inuit posts in Arctic Quebec.[51]

In industrial societies, the railways and airplanes spell progress. Not so for the Cree hunters of James Bay. They gained as a result of ease of transport with cheaper and more plentiful goods, but the social costs were high. The restructuring of the fur trade resulted in the downsizing and streamlining of the company's operations, with the result that the Crees lost their relatively generous advances and, more importantly, their summer employment.

A railway to James Bay and bush plane travel brought even more outsiders. With the completion of the first railway in the 1880s, the men who came into the territory were surveyors and mining prospectors. In the late 1920s and early 1930s those who seized the opportunities of cheaper, swifter travel and transport were, in addition to surveyors and miners, white trappers. The Crees and the whites were not operating on an even playing field. The Crees were both trappers and subsistence hunters with strong notions of husbanding and conserving resources. They needed to combine hunting for food and furs so they could continue to feed their families while taking pelts for trade. As a hunting society, they had developed a harmonious relationship with nature so that as each generation of hunters died there would be food and game left for the next. Their hunting territory and how they harvested it was their children's legacy. Not so the white trappers. They came in supplied with provisions for the winter so they could be full-time trappers. Their interest was not in future generations but in clearing out the fur-bearing animals in one area and moving onto the next. The advent of the train and the plane enabled these white trappers to travel farther into the interior with full provisions, permitting them to devote all their energies to trapping.

White-Indian conflict came later to James Bay because it was an isolated region. By 1924 there were complaints by the Hudson's Bay Company of whites trapping out the lands of the Atikamekw at Manouane. The correspondence states that the white trappers "have in many instances seriously depleted the Beaver, as their usual practice has been to kill every beaver in each colony ... instead of leaving a certain number which is the Indian practice."[52] There were a very large number of such complaints that year. Presumably fur prices were high, making it very attractive to whites. Affecting the James Bay people directly was the construction of the Canadian National Railway though it was not until the 1930s that a massive influx of settlers began to arrive.[53] The main concern of the various advocates – Indian agents, health officers, clergy – was the insensitive disregard by whites for the native hunting practices. An Indian Affairs official, Auget, wrote that "whitemen kill everything, including the breeding stock. Therefore the Indians feel they cannot leave anything."[54] Also, the white trappers, unskilled and uncaring, were taking animals not in their prime. "The white man's hunt will be at least half unprime skins or else he has absolutely stripped the territory of fur bearing animals," complained one Indian Affairs inspector in 1926.[55]

By 1927 there were complaints emanating from the southern portions of James Bay, Waswanipi, and Mistassini. The Reverend Cartlidge wrote a long, impassioned letter to D.C. Scott, deputy superintendent general of Indian Affairs. He wrote that until recently only Indians were in these territories hunting and being self-supporting. Now large gangs of men working for Quebec Fisheries out of Senneterre were trapping along the Nottoway River and Lake Mattagami and had practically killed all the fur-bearers. These company men were not all the trappers in the area, for Cartlidge knew of at least ten other white men, Americans included, engaged in trapping that past winter, as it happened on the lands of the chief of the Waswanipi band. He attributed the influx of whites in part to a recent Ontario law prohibiting white men from trapping beaver and otter there. Furthermore, Cartlidge identified another serious aspect of the problem which would have long been known to Scott. The white trappers were using poison (strychnine),[56] which not only killed fur-bearing animals but also entered the food chain.

The anthropologist Father John Cooper[XV] described the Crees in 1933 as demoralized due to the lack of game in James Bay and their distress at the way the animal spirits upon which they depended and which they so respected were tormented. No doubt demoralization would also be an appropriate way to characterize what Indian hunters felt on finding their camps pillaged by whites, their food, traps, canoes, taken.[57] The late 1920s and early 1930s was one of the bleakest periods for the Crees in much of James Bay. Faced with serious depletions of their food animals and depressed fur markets, they also had to contend with the plunder of their lands and had few resources to control this encroachment. A later memo written in 1942 by Hugh R. Conn, head of Reserves and Trusts for Indian Affairs, suggests that Indians tended to withdraw when up against white trappers and unwittingly contributed to the depletion of resources. He writes that "it is a well known fact that an Indian will not or cannot compete with a white trapper. When a white encroaches on his grounds the Indian in most cases simply gives up and moves over onto his neighbor's ground and the movement gathers force as it progresses until the Indians are crowded into a small corner of their former area which is depleted by them as fast as their rightful lands are cleaned out by the whites."[58]

In another discussion of the apparent Indian withdrawal in the face of competition with white trappers, the unidentified person finds this reaction perfectly reasonable, saying that "an Indian who has practised conservation only to have the fruits of his labour taken by some white man is certainly not going to practice any more than a farmer is going to leave livestock in a field constantly raided by black market operators."[59] At least the farmer had recourse to the law; the Indian trapper had none.

The northern regions of James Bay were not spared this competition. In 1929 the Revillon Frères general manager, S. Coward, complained to Indian Affairs that two "Swedes" had been trapping, using poison, in the Fort George district the past winter and the Crees had found "many marten carcasses partially eaten by other animals."[60] Of course,

143 The Confiscation of the Land

poisoned bait was also a threat to the health of the Cree people. They had complained for some time to the RCMP as they were concerned about eating the country food caught where poison was being used.[61] In 1931 Dr J.J. Wall, the Indian agent, claimed there were "eighteen trappers, mainly Swedes" in the area of Eastmain but added that the Moose Factory Indians had refused "to be a party to ravaging and plundering the hunting grounds of their people by refusing to assist the transport of this equipment."[62]

Another trapper, also trading, was Louis Martineau. He had located himself during the winter of 1930–1 on the Bishop Roggan River between Fort George and Cape Chidley and with a large family of adult sons (making up a party of eleven) was evidently depleting the fur animals. Some Cree men complained to E.S. Covell, the RCMP constable, on his visit there from the Moose Factory detachment. It was stated that Martineau did not hold a Quebec trapper's licence, at least as of 4 December 1931.[63] There was little that Covell could have done in this matter, other than write the reports he did, for he had no authority under either the Ontario or Quebec game laws, nor was the area under the jurisdiction of a game warden.[64] Louis Martineau's name shows up in the records again that October. He wrote to the Hudson's Bay Company that "he has been appointed Game Warden for the Province of Quebec ... his intention is to curb the suspected illegal trapping activities of the white trappers ... taken in to the Eastmain country." The following March it was announced that he had been deprived of his game warden's badge,[65] though no reasons were given.[XVI]

THE PROVINCE IMPOSES ITS NOTION ★ OF CONSERVATION ★

Following the lead of Ontario, Quebec also passed an order-in-council setting aside the trapping rights of "practically the whole of the unsettled areas of the Province for the exclusive benefits of the Eskimos and Indians. Trapping by whites within that area is totally prohibited."[66] Although the government authorities and the traders saw the desperate need for this prohibition on trapping by non-aboriginals, evidently the Canadian public did not. An inkling of the prejudice, or the ignorance, towards Indians is summed up in a headline in the *Montreal Star* of 5 February 1940. The article reported on a further five-year extension of the ban on killing beaver. Only Indians "in extreme need of food" were to be exempt. The headline reads: "Quebec Bars Killing of Beaver Except by Privileged Indians."[67]

Quebec's first Game Act was enacted in July 1895.[68] It was not the first attempt by government to regulate wildlife in the province as the federal government had intervened in the salmon fishery along the St Lawrence in 1855.⁶⁹ Concern to support the growing interest in sports hunting led the province in 1873 to permit private sporting clubs, a means also by which poaching could be kept in check as these private interests employed their own wardens.⁷⁰ Even the forests which housed these animals came under provincial jurisdiction in 1868 with the appointment of the first commissioner of crown lands. It was intended to control the many forest fires that had been set by settlers.⁷¹

The 1895 Game Act was a consolidation of earlier developments and a product of the times, since conservation and sports hunting were extreme preoccupations in the late 1800s in the United States.⁷² The same year as the Quebec Game Act, the provincial legislature also established Park Laurentide, a seven-thousand-square-mile preserve in which hunting was regulated through the issuance of permits. The act proscribed hunting seasons, hunting methods, and set bag limits for large game and fur-bearing animals. It also imposed a "close season" [sic] on beaver trapping for five years until 1 November 1900. There was no mention of Indians in the act.

In 1895 the boundaries of the province of Quebec extended to the Abitibi region; the Crees would not have been affected by these game laws although there were still great numbers of other Indians who were: Algonquins, Abenaquis, Mohawks, Montagnais, Atikamekw, Micmacs, Malecites. Three years later the southern territory of James Bay was affected by the legislation and in 1912 the rest of the Quebec-Labrador peninsula that was granted to Quebec.

The restrictions on hunting were first challenged by Indians in the south of the province who were directly affected. They complained to Indian Affairs who advised the St Regis Mohawks to comply with provincial regulations as the department had "no power to interfere in any way."⁷³ The Hudson's Bay Company, as threatened as the Indian hunters by these restrictions, applied pressure on Indian Affairs at the highest levels to do something. In response the federal government asked the province whether the Quebec Game Act applied to Indians. It also asked the same question of the Justice Department, receiving the reply that the "game laws of Quebec ... were within the legislative authority of the local legislature." The province replied through its assistant commissioner of crown lands, E.E. Taché, that it was its intention to enforce the provisions of the law but a special permit could be granted to "any Indian whose poverty would be well established and who would require hunting the beaver as a means of subsistence."⁷⁴ The Hudson's Bay Company's response was predictable. It protested the law and wrote to Indian Affairs that the list of Indian hunters in need would include all adult hunters. Then Taché reversed his position on granting special permits because his game wardens were issuing unfavourable reports on the number of beaver.[XVII] The Department of Indian Affairs recognized this legislation was causing the Indians much hardship, and so committed itself "to extend some assistance to them out of the ordinary appropriation for the relief of the Indians of the Province of Quebec."[75]

The tensions aroused by the provincial game laws stemmed from the fact that the provinces were responsible for the wild game in an era of scientific approaches to conservation, backed by popular support in the larger society[XVIII] while the Dominion government was responsible for the status Indian and Inuit populations dependent on that game. Other provinces and other jurisdictions also began requiring licences and levying royalties on furs. Indians who had signed treaties in other provinces generally had some guarantees about hunting, but Quebec Indians had no such guarantees and thus no protection from the law. The Crees' isolation countered any intentions the Quebec game and fisheries departments might have had in regulating hunting in their territory.

It has not been possible to trace through all the developments regarding the ban on hunting beaver, but a reading of the Hudson's Bay Company journals and correspondence indicate that if the province had intended the game laws to apply to James Bay, it was not enforcing them. The trade carried on as before until encroachment by the whites in the 1920s and 1930s. Although technically a part of the province of Quebec only in 1912, the northern region – Nouveau Québec, as it became known in the 1960s – was considered an unsettled area and ignored.

The year 1932 seems to mark the beginning of Quebec's attempt to control Indian hunting and trapping in James Bay. That year the province declared the whole of the northern regions a game preserve; while regulating Indian and Inuit hunting and trapping, it banned such activities by non-natives. This ban was obviously not monitored; in the Hudson's Bay Company's Waswanipi records of 29 December 1934 we read that four prospectors flew into Waswanipi, one of whom had "a fair hunt" which the company bought.[76] Evidently the Indian Affairs branch thought Indians in Quebec fared much better than those resident in Ontario. Writing in 1942 to the commissioner of the RCMP, the deputy minister of Indian Affairs remarked that in Quebec, Indians are permitted to have "wild meat" all year round for their own use but Ontario "has decided that he must observe the letter of the law and their decision has been upheld by the Courts."[77] As well, L.A. Richard, the deputy minister of Quebec's Ministère de la chasse et de la pêche, was praised for his "sincere desire to help the Indians" which "has been proven time after time."[78] The Crees extended to Richard the honour of naming him Chief White Beaver.[79]

FEDERAL GOVERNMENT INSERTS ITSELF IN JAMES BAY

What drew the federal government into the northern territories of Quebec? Of all the services that the federal government was later to provide, it was relief or assistance that launched the government's involvement in this region. Helpless in overturning provincial legislation that gravely affected the welfare of its Indian wards, the federal government offered minimal assistance in the form of relief payments. Government officials had, over the years, seen accounts of the destitution, as in E.B. Borron's report for western James Bay. In this 1890 report, based on his inquiries at Moose Factory, Borron remarked that "I know of absolutely nothing that has been expended on, or anything that has been done for the natives and others in this territory – unless it be to tax them."[80] Sometime between that year[XIX] and 1905 the federal government began issuing so-called S&D rations, explained in a letter to the district manager of the Hudson's Bay Company as supplies issued to "Sick and Destitute Indians at this Post for the six months ending 31st December 1908."[81] The purpose of these rations was to assist a hunter and his family secure a living when they were in difficult circumstances. The rations included food and other supplies such as twine and shot. The administration of this aid was left up to the discretion of the traders. The supplies were taken from the company's inventory and charged to the government. Forms in triplicate, justifying these expenses, were sent in, at first twice annually and later monthly, to the government. The relief was originally distributed only by the Hudson's Bay Company. After Indian Affairs discovered in 1905 that the company was using these payments as "a trade lever," it extended this service to the other traders.[82] Little is said of relief in either the fur trade or government records but the following table should indicate the increasing importance it seemingly took in the communities.[83]

A rough calculation indicates a great variation in the per capita amount of relief payments, which also had increased dramatically over the years. Thus, using 1911 census figures (see Appendix 2) but 1913 relief payments, the Crees at Rupert House received, per capita, $6.38, Fort George $4.87, Eastmain, $2.38, Waswanipi, $4.57, but Mistassini $1.02. It is not surprising that the larger posts of Fort George and Rupert House received the greater amount. These were coastal posts with inferior food resources but with more activities, posts, and missions that might have attracted more dependants. In this context, it is difficult to explain the relatively high relief payments for Waswanipi. Another figure with which to try to assess the amount of relief given in 1913 is Walton's report of the church collection at Fort George made by the Crees from August to Christmas 1913. It was $425.23 "in spite of the very poor fur hunts."[84]

	1905	1911–12	1912–13
Rupert House	$362.35	$948.51	$2,478.49
Mistassini	33.09	–	174.16
Waswanipi	94.89	–	632.82
Eastmain	67.71	245.96	343.32
Fort George	330.84	679.13	2,093.46
Great Whale River	39.93	347.75	1,559.39

Over the years the Indian Affairs Branch tried to put a ceiling on these payments, suggesting, for example, a maximum allotment to Rupert House of $1,800 in 1918 or of $2,500 for Fort George.[85] Ray indicates this was a policy that extended beyond James Bay.[86] These maximums of relief payments must have been put into effect and remained unchanged over subsequent years. The Reverend Harry Cartlidge, writing from Waswanipi, complained to the Department of Indian Affairs in 1925 that the Hudson's Bay Company claimed to be unable to help Mrs A. Blacksmith because their total relief budget was too small; they had only $300 to allot.[87] This was the same amount Waswanipi was allocated in 1918.

The purpose of these ceilings on the sick and destitute rations was Indian Affairs' attempt to curb the abuses of the system by both Cree hunters and traders. In an anonymous report of the James Bay agency in 1931, the writer claimed that "many Indians were not ambitious to secure a wealth of this world's possessions." Thus able to obtain a minimum of foodstuffs on the excuse of illness, many Indians, it was thought, would not make the necessary effort to provide for their needs. This writer, to give credence to his comments, quoted George Quartermaster (Fort George) who recalled with pride his younger days when the hunters of the district were "real men who had to support themselves entirely by their own efforts."[88] It was felt that more judicious administration of relief by the traders would reduce the numbers on the relief list.[xx]

The second abuse was the practice of the post managers. At the end of the year some of them, in tallying the outstanding debts of their post, charged the government relief fund with some of these debts as S&D rations, thereby lowering the debts against their own post's record. This practice was verified by government officials asking hunters at Fort George about some rations recorded as having been given them by the Revillon Frères company manager. The hunters let it be known that it had been their understanding these supplies in question were to be charged against their account and to be paid back in the next winter's hunt.[89]

In order to check these irregularities, the Department of Indian Affairs considered requiring each hunter to sign a receipt for the goods issued as rations. This appears to have been rejected as a solution because hunters could be convinced to sign blank forms, to be filled in at later dates. However, the writer of the report was not suggesting the Crees would knowingly "act in collusion with any white man to swindle the Government in relief supplies ... The native would readily become too tyrannical a master for any such individual who would so foolishly place himself thus in the native's hands."[90]

This official attempted to persuade each trader not to give rations in "undeserving" cases. He argued that the profits made by the two companies from distributing government relief were minuscule and suggested that the Indians be encouraged to stay away from the posts. Those going into the bush were to be supplied with the necessities for hunting and trapping although the official recognized that old people with no one to support them would have to be on relief. He seemed able to control the relief expenses by refusing to certify accounts for several months. This he did at Eastmain, saying that the accounts were entirely out of proportion to what was justly warranted and the post manager responsible was dismissed. The Eastmain list of recipients was quickly reduced from thirty-eight to nine with an anticipated decrease in the cost of relief. In this circumstance, the hunter would realize he must make reasonable efforts to support himself and "that laziness disguised under various pretexts will not be subsidized."[91] These harsh measures were instituted in 1931, in the midst of the terrible three-year famine through which the Crees were suffering, and two years into the depression. The historian Arthur Ray has observed that government expenditures across the country for relief, medical assistance, and education had increased until the onset of the depression "when they were reduced for the sake of fiscal restraint."[92]

Another form of assistance was called "widows' rations," first mentioned in the 1938 journals.[93] According to Richard Blackned, these were weekly rations. Even with a number of children, "they didn't receive very much. All the widow received was a bagful of flour in a size 10 paper bag for a week."[94] If the widow was going off to fish she would receive a month's rations. Blackned also told of the time a widow with two children was living with him and his family. It was when the animals were very scarce and this widow had more store food than he or his partner despite the fact they were actively trapping. It is clear that throughout the 1930s relief was an emergency measure only.

The issue of relief was a serious problem as the Crees and Inuit in James and Hudson Bays were starving. The government obviously did not see its role in the 1930s as the provisioner to the native peoples and

149 The Confiscation of the Land

the Hudson's Bay Company officials held conflicting views. The company old-timers saw credit or advances, even though uncollectible, as a moral claim[95] on the Crees, and George Ray and James Watt argued passionately for continuing their system of advances, which they saw as retainers for which the company would be repaid. Others saw it only as a heavy debt burden and sought to reduce it, which they did with new rules and regulations issued in 1927. Commissioner French wrote that "should he [the Indian] wish to be regarded as ... honourable and upright ... he must live the part and pay his debt when due."[96] The traders in the field resented this way of thinking by company men they considered ignorant and they objected to young college men being put into responsible positions "instead of promoting the men who learned the trade from the bottom."[97] The men in charge of the stores presumably could not help but be moved by the starving condition of the hunters. When he left off his Nichikun journal on 20 June 1940, J.M. Stevenson noted: "I really don't know what to do with them [the hunters], they are absolutely in rags and look like the very devil."[98] The running of the post was taken up by David Cooter in the fall and he was pressed to write: "I have never seen such poverty among Indians as there is here. They have practically nothing to eat now but fish and frostbitten berries. Before they received their small advances some were going barefoot and half naked although there was snow on the ground already."[99]

The scarcity of food was compounded by the fact that supplies to the post, via air transport, often did not come in on time and the hunters were unable to get items they needed such as matches, tobacco, twine, etcetera: "If there is no lard we cannot expect to sell flour."[100] Thus, company traders were said to hand out credit liberally, especially when faced with such conditions. The same is said to have been the practice of Revillon Frères. Then the agents would use what was known as a "hip-pocket ledger," a special account book separate from the regular debt one where the agents took it upon themselves to advance credit to certain hunters without the knowledge or consent of the Revillon head office.[101]

Nevertheless, the Hudson's Bay Company revised its manner of operation. The federal government pled fiscal restraint. The Crees starved, some to death.

As for the provincial government, its interest in the Indians revolved around land and game issues, not welfare. Understandably, the province would not be expected to play a role, as Indians were a federal matter. An indicator of how each level of government tried hard to avoid being held responsible for native peoples was played out in northern Quebec. There, by arrangement between 1929 and 1932, the federal government provided relief to Inuit in desperate need and were reimbursed by the Quebec government to the amount of nine dollars per person. In 1932 the province reconsidered its position and objected to having to reimburse the federal government for the care of people whom they deemed Indians and thus a federal responsibility under the British North America Act. The federal government claimed Inuit (or Eskimos) were ordinary citizens and both governments looked to the Supreme Court for clarification. Their decision, handed down in 1939, determined that Eskimos were Indians[XXI] and therefore under the jurisdiction of the federal government.[102]

What more should the federal government have done? In the context of today we would argue much more. However, in the 1930s the federal government was not even supposed to be in the business of social assistance. According to the British North America Act, health and education and eleemosynary services were the responsibility of the provincial and municipal governments. Furthermore, during the 1920s the federal government was generally timid about spending money because of the heavy debts it had incurred in the First World War.[103] It was, of course, the great unemployment and destitution of the 1930s that eventually led the federal government to institute special programs of social assistance in the late 1940s and early 1950s. This form of help was to come for the next generation of the Crees, but in the 1930s they were subject to the moral views of the day. Relief was given in the south of Canada not as hand-outs but as indirect relief in compensation for some form of labour which would be psychologically and socially more useful.[104] Spending in the south was aimed at generating jobs; no such thinking would have been entertained for the north. Except for the churches, the destitute Crees were far removed from the wealthy strata of Canadian society; the destitution of the Crees in James Bay was probably little known in the south or of interest in the dirty thirties. The government, traders, and missionaries certainly knew about their plight. The missionaries might have spoken out, but it was not in the interest of the government or Hudson's Bay Company officials to draw attention to what was happening in their domain.

THE ARRIVAL OF RIVAL MISSIONARIES

The Crees were not without missionaries; they might be excused for perhaps suggesting they had a superfluity of missionaries in those days. They had barely come to an acceptance of Christianity, introduced to them by Anglicans, and found the means to integrate those beliefs with their own, when a new set of missionaries approached them exhorting them to reorder their religious thinking. This happened in 1922 with the arrival at Fort George of Father Philippe Boisseau and Brother Jean-Paul Hébert, accompanied by their Attawapiskat Cree housekeeper, Nancy Wabano. They had come on the Revillon Frères' schooner from Albany where their order, the Oblates of Mary Immaculate, had established a mission in the latter part of the nineteenth century.[105] There the Catholics had established a strong presence[106] and the Cree population of Attawapiskat and Winisk were predominantly Catholic, while Albany remained mainly Protestant.[XXII] At Fort George on that day of the priests' arrival in July of 1922, the shore was lined by Cree families who greeted the docking of any boat as a significant event. The priests had chosen Fort George as their site on the east coast of James Bay on a reconnaissance mission the year before because it had a large population. They named this mission St Joseph and used for their residence a cabin put at their disposal by William McLeod, the Revillon manager. Their first mass was held the next day in the Revillon Frères store to which they drew about forty curious Indians with the number increasing at the evening services.[107] The assistance of the Revillon Frères Company was not an isolated occurrence and not directed only to the Catholics. It was the policy of the company to encourage missionaries to settle at the post and it provided them with transportation and temporary lodging. They helped both Anglicans and Catholics get established, carried their mail, provided supplies, and so on.[108]

"Curiosity" is probably an apt description of the Crees' motivation, for by this time they were devoted followers of the Reverend Walton and his brand of Christianity. The priests arrived when Walton was absent with his family for several months at missions on the west coast of James Bay, but Walton hastened back when he heard of their intrusion, arriving seven days after them. According to Sister Paul-Emile, the writer of a history of the James Bay missions, he called his parishioners together the next day to explain to them how there were Catholic priests at Fort George. He is said to have told them that "S'il y a encore des prêtres catholiques dans le monde c'est ... qu'ils ne sont pas allés à la guerre qui vient de se terminer."[109] Thus began the ferocious battle between Catholics and Protestants at Fort George. As best as can be determined, the Crees were bystanders in this, but they were also able to turn this competition to their advantage. Although Catholics and Anglicans shared other communities and were rivals for souls, one source claims that Fort George was the exception in the degree of acrimony engendered.[110]

There were good practical reasons for the Crees to attach themselves to the Catholics. However, they did not do so for religious reasons but to use the services provided by the Catholics. Father Boisseau had more medical knowledge than the traders, and Crees came to him for such matters as dental extractions or remedies for their illnesses. Even the Hudson's Bay Company manager conceded his superior knowledge and referred sick people to him. Father Boisseau travelled to the camps during a flu epidemic in 1925 and grateful people came to his chapel, although this happened after the departure of Walton. Undoubtedly Father Boisseau and the brothers guardedly hoped that with his departure in July 1924 the Crees could become convinced to join the Catholic Church. Their hope was short-lived; they found that Ernest Renouf, the Hudson's Bay Company manager, carried out a vigorous anti-Catholic campaign.[111]

Renouf, post manager since his return from the war in 1919, had been on furlough from his Fort George duties beginning in September 1924. So it was on his return in March of 1925, in the absence of Walton, that he stepped up the campaign.[112] As Sister Paul-Emile writes, the company had a hands-off policy with regard to the religion of their employees, but Renouf was far removed from their sight and ignored such directives.[113] According to her, he made known his views through the offices of Peter House, a Coaster whose hunting lands lay on Ruperts Bay, twelve miles north of Fort George.[XXIII] He warned his "compatriots" about straying from the "faith of their ancestors" and pronounced that the Catholic Church was the church of the devil. Allegedly, House also threatened that whoever took up Catholicism would lose his wife, as she would go to live with the priest and moreover the company would not trade with them. That Renouf was a self-appointed guardian of Anglicanism during the period Fort George was without a minister is evident from one of his journal entries, gloatingly written. Dated 21 November 1925, it reads: "Roman Catholic Mission got their first family of converts in the shape of Sam Atkins and his old wife – both in the dotage and irresponsible."[114] Atkins had developed a fever and Boisseau had visited him on his hunting grounds to treat him so that on his recovery the seventy-five-year-old Cree headed for the Catholic mission.[115]

Despite the spirited attacks on Catholicism in 1925, Crees suffering from the flu did visit Father Boisseau. On one day in July it is said he had as many as fifty seek his help, despite the remonstrances of Peter House. However that summer the Anglican bishop, John Anderson, arrived to announce that the Crees would be "orphans" no more. The deacon, Fred Mark, would be arriving to take up the mission.[116] The Anglican Church was having trouble finding a replacement for Walton, one of the last links with the Church Missionary Society[117] which withdrew from the missionary field in Canada in 1921.[XXIV] Fred Mark was a Cree catechist[XXV] whom Bishop Anderson ordained a deacon in 1925 before sending him to Fort George. In 1928 as a priest he was put in charge of the Eastmain mission where he died in 1945.[118] The Reverend Redfern E. Louttit, also native from Albany,[XXVI] was sent to work at Eastmain in 1940, holding services there with David Tamatuk. He was also charged with establishing the mission at the new post-settlement of Old Factory River,[119] where he supervised and helped build a log church with a seating capacity of 150. Its communion table and chairs were considered a work of art and had been crafted by "Old Wetaltuk"[120] who, according to Bishop Renison, had carved the chairs, which were copies of King George VI's coronation chair, from a photo in the *Illustrated London News*.[121]

Henry Gilpin was another Cree lay preacher, who held Christmas services at Eastmain in 1938 for about fifty Indians.[122] David Jimmiken was the lay preacher at Nemiskau performing baptisms and marriages,[123] and Joseph Hester served as a catechist at Rupert House, retiring in about the 1950s when his eyesight began failing him.[124] The Anglicans relied on Matthew Shecapio at Mistassini to serve as the preacher there, taking over from Charles Iserhoff who died suddenly in 1930. Shecapio, first as lay reader, then as catechist, and finally as deacon in 1953, served the church at Mistassini until his death in 1958 at the age of eighty-four, a passing that was lamented by "all who knew him."[125]

Aside from the flying visits by the bishop every few years, the Anglican Church relied on their indigenous preachers. Undoubtedly the Catholics were up against fierce competition in the naming of Cree men to head the missions. These men held obvious advantages over the priests, aside from the fact that the Crees had already accepted Christianity in its Anglican variant. To the Catholic thinking, they obviously questioned and resented the naming of these native ministers. In such a discussion of Reverend Samuel Iserhoff, it is noted that he had been a clerk in an outpost, then interpreter for the Anglican mission at Fort George. This, it was said, was the origin of his calling and at Eastmain, Bishop Renison ordained him. Since they considered Iserhoff a strong opponent, it is no wonder the Oblates looked for ways to denigrate him. The priests also resented Louttit's presence at Old Factory, claiming that he waged a defamatory campaign against the Catholics and raged against those Crees who sent their children to the Catholic school. They felt that a good number of the Crees and Inuit were sympathetic to Catholicism but did not dare declare so openly.[126]

At Fort George, Fred Mark was assisted by Richard Matthew, a native from Fort George and a company employee. Only Father Boisseau's account is extant, so it must be read guardedly. As already seen, Boisseau found the company manager highly interfering. When Mark was named as deacon, Boisseau suggests that Renouf was furious, especially after Fred Mark had gone to dine with the priests; thereafter

Renouf mistrusted him. Accordingly, Renouf managed to convince Bishop Anderson to permit George Cotter, the newly named manager of the Revillon Frères store, to lead the services. As a result, Fred Mark became, according to Boisseau, a "simple assistant."[127] Cotter had been a lay reader at Cumberland House (Saskatchewan River) before coming to Fort George in 1925. From Boisseau's correspondence we also learn that Mark's English was not good and that Cotter, with Mark, was to serve the employees of the two companies.[128]

Since his arrival at Fort George, Boisseau had difficult relations with the manager of the Hudson's Bay Company, but now he was finding that even the Revillon Frères Company was mixing business and religion. Accordingly, he complained to that company and in February 1926 Cotter was sent a letter of reprimand by the secretary-treasurer, E. Mellor, for his "openly appearing antagonistic not only to the priest but to the Roman Catholic Church."[129] Boisseau seemed to think that it was as a result of his complaints to both companies that the two managers were transferred in the summer of 1926.[130] Although Mark stayed on until 1927, the Reverend George Morrow was sent to Fort George in September 1926. Both of them left the following year and were replaced by the Reverend John Thomas Griffin, who had assisted Walton at Fort George in 1917.[131] Griffin, an Orangeman from Ireland, was married to Susan Quartermain, whose family were hunters in the Fort George area.[132]

Not only did the Catholic priests run into conflict with the managers of both companies but evidently they also found their wives meddlesome. Brother Beaudoin of Moosonee suggested that Cotter himself "was not too bad" but "it was Mrs Cotter who was hard on the mission."[133] As for Griffin's wife, Boisseau suggested that she decided herself to be a doctor, with poor results, so that sick Crees had to sneak around to see him for medicines.[134] Later, in 1930, when the Catholic mission established its first residential school, Mrs Griffin is said to have counselled Crees not to send their children because the priests and brothers mistreated the children.[135] In her history of the diocese of Moosonee, Olive Petersen, not surprisingly, presents Mrs Griffin in a different light, referring to her as her husband's able assistant and describing her as "looking sweet and demure."[136]

Elsewhere the Revillon Frères Company found reason to complain about the Catholic missions and their activities. At other posts, such as Attawapiskat, the Catholic mission was underselling the trading companies, causing the post manager to complain to the priests' superiors. Examples cited are a chestnut canoe, that cost the Crees $275 at the Revillon Frères store but could be bought for $200 at the Catholic mission, or women's footwear that was $6 less at the mission. Revillon

Frères pointed out that the mission received favourable transportation rates, did not give credit, and was not expecting to make a profit.[137] Whether this is what provoked Cotter into supporting the Anglicans over the Catholics or his proselytizing notions, contrary to company policy, is not known but is still a reasonable assumption.

Although the Oblates criticized certain Hudson's Bay Company traders for undermining their attempts to minister to the Crees, there are also references to company traders who were "good friends of the Mission." Such a one was Blackhall, who was in charge of Fort George until 1940 and also his successor, Ronald Duncan, there until 1945.[138] Despite the undercurrent of animosity, there was obviously some degree of cooperation. Thus in 1938 the Hudson's Bay Company manager asked a Catholic brother to repair the shaft propellor of one of its boats.[139]

Boisseau left in 1929, disheartened that he had made almost no converts, especially when compared to the successes the Catholics had achieved on the west side of James Bay. He did take solace in knowing that he had helped the sick. He died in Montreal the following year, according to Sister Paul-Emile the victim of seven years of "stupid espionage" and slander "invented by ultra-fanatic brains aimed at the impressionable minds of the Indians."[140]

The intense rivalry between the two denominations is also to be found in the writings of the Fort George Anglicans, in their reports to the bishop. Griffin urged Bishop Thorpe to build a school at Fort George, saying "if we build a School, then you will find the RC's will build a hospital." He also charged that the priest was trying to lure Cree children to school by providing the Thomas Rupert family of nine children with some food. Griffin countered by providing them food and clothing nearly every week. In another letter, Griffin said, sounding desperate, that food was being given to yet another family and that Chief Peter House, his wife and six children were living in the Priest's house.[141] In summing up the hostile relations between the two denominations, it may well be that the mix of personalities in those years accounted for it. Later, the two churches seemed to have settled into some sort of acceptance of each other's presence.

It seems reasonable to assume that the lack of success amongst the Catholics was because the Crees already had accepted and integrated Christianity into their religious beliefs.[xxvii] Why would one change? Yet, so convinced were the zealots of the two denominations that each held the truth that it was impossible for them to look at their version of Christianity from the perspective of the Crees. What substantial differences could they have seen that would encourage them to begin attending another church? What of extended family ties? Surely individual

Crees were not likely to separate themselves from the rest of their kin and attend separate services? There is also the question of loyalty. As one reconstructs the history of the fur trade in James Bay, it is striking that the Crees maintained a loyalty to the Hudson's Bay Company despite a series of serious competitors. It was not a blind loyalty, for the company was loyal to the Crees, retaining the fur trade even through difficult years and decades. Perhaps loyalty was part of the Cree strategy to withstand adverse circumstances, and that came into play also in religion. As long as the Anglicans served them well, why go over to the competition? So fierce was their attachment to Anglicanism at this time that it would have been impossible to presage that in the early 1970s the Crees would substantially weaken their ties to the Church of England and about half would embrace Pentecostalism.[142]

The Crees were certainly badgered by the officials of the Anglican Church and their allies at the trading companies, but it is not clear what price the Crees paid for this warring over their souls. One would have been monetary, for they might have been leery of trading at the Catholic store and might not have sought medical aid from the Catholics for fear of displeasing Renouf. One might also speculate on what effects such strong competitiveness between two Christian churches might have had on their acceptance of Christianity. The Crees at Fort George were not the only ones, it seems, to suffer the fallout from this church wrangling. In the early 1920s the fur trader at Rupert House was James Watt; his wife Maud was a Catholic. So strong was she in her Catholic beliefs that she accompanied her children to North Bay for their schooling, presumably Catholic schooling, rather than send them to the Anglican school at Rupert House. In doing so she said: "I spend everything my husband makes." She mentioned this in a letter to Bishop Belleau in the hopes that their promises for the last fifteen years of a Catholic Mission at Rupert House would finally come to fruition. If they would provide a teacher, then she would remain at Rupert House, much preferring "to pay a monthly salary to one of your teachers than to leave home every winter."[143] The Catholic clergy did not leave her totally without a Catholic presence. Beginning in 1929 when they had their own boat with which to supply their mission at Fort George, they did stop once a summer at Rupert House in order to enable Mrs Watt and her children to partake of Catholic rites.[144] Once Maud Watt and her children had the use of a two-way radio transmitter at Rupert House, they communicated with the priests at Moose Factory.[145] Maud Watt got her wish for a school at Rupert House in 1943 but too late for her own children. She obviously directed Crees towards Catholicism. Young George McDonald was the first and only pupil of the Catholic residential school at Fort George when it opened in 1930. The next year eighteen pupils attended, five of whom were from Rupert House and some may have been the children she is said to have foster-parented over the years.[146]

The discouragement that Father Boisseau felt did not dampen the spirits of the Catholic mission at Fort George. They established themselves in 1937 at Old Factory River, on the same island as both the Hudson's Bay Company[XXVIII] and the independent trader, Palmquist. The Hudson's Bay Company trader, Bill Anderson, granted them land for a settlement at one end of the island and loaned them a tent until their house was built. Fathers Lionel Labrèche and Aram Ethier, along with Brother Gérard Lavoie, were the ones who established the mission. According to Sister Paul-Emile, several hundred Crees were assembled there in the summer. At first surprised to see the priests, some of them soon decided to take advantage of their presence. Some of them traded with the priests, and others sought medical aid at their dispensary – a chest turned into a cupboard from which they dispensed medicines furnished by the federal government. The following summer they held school "en plein air," equipped with roughly hewn benches and tables, which Father Belleau dubbed the "Fresh Air University." That first year about forty students attended to learn the prayers and hymns and to read in syllabics. They had the field to themselves until the arrival of Louttit in 1940.[147]

The Catholic mission started at Eastmain in 1938 when the priests from Old Factory came there to claim some ground and erected a summer dwelling in 1939. The following year they built their permanent house and chapel with the help of some Crees and Inuit. The first resident priest was Father Gaston Grenon in 1941. Following his departure in 1944, Father Louis-Philippe Vaillancourt[XXIX] served Eastmain from Old Factory, running the school there in the summers, teaching about fifteen children of the families who camped on the island the Catholics shared with Palmquist. Still, the Anglicans continued to claim the most Christian souls, seventy taking Anglican communion in 1940.[148]

Rupert House had to wait until 1943 for the Oblates to set up a mission, the founders being Fathers Damase Couture and Hermann Fay along with Brother Alphonse Martin. However, the Oblates had visited each year and had recruited a number of children for its residential school in Fort George, so the Catholics were not complete aliens in the eyes of the Rupert House Crees; they called on the priests to provide medical care and some attended the services. Building began in 1943 but the house and chapel were not finished until the following year.[149]

Besides the medical services and schooling the Catholic missions provided, some enterprising priests sought other means to attract Crees to their church. Father Maurice Grenon, assigned to Rupert House in 1946, fashioned a wheel of fortune from a piece of linoleum. Instead of numbers he decorated it with drawings of fur animals such as beaver, otter, and hare, each assigned a price for the pelt. The game that he devised had as its object to see who was the best hunter, according to his score after five or six turns of the wheel. Grenon was also known for the spectacular, interesting crèches that he designed and made at Christmas. Once assigned to Eastmain in 1949, Father Grenon quickly installed a windcharger in order to have electricity, not only for his house but so that he could show slides, most of which were on Biblical themes.[150] The main object of this entertainment was not to convert so much as to enable the Crees to get to know the priests. Numbers did attend these shows but still very few converted. (See Appendix 5 for the number of Catholics in five communities as well as the number of resident religious personnel.)

Thus, eastern James Bay was well served by missionaries in the 1930s and 1940s. This helped secure for them some small amounts of relief, food, and clothing as well as publicity in congregations to the south, but these were not economic solutions.

BEAVER CONSERVATION

For the Crees, their rescue was not in government relief programs but in a privately conceived and implemented beaver conservation and regeneration program. The beaver had all but died out in James Bay.[xxx] Maud Watt made a telling comment in 1941: "the younger generation had never seen Beavers."[151] Or, as J. Kenneth Doutt, a mammalogist with the Carnegie Museum expedition in 1936, expressed it: "I was very much impressed with the scarcity of mammalian life. Never before have I seen so vast a region with so little animal life in it." He was also impressed with the Crees' plans to reintroduce and protect the beaver.[152] Since beaver do not suffer from cyclical highs and lows nor widespread disease, over-hunting is given as the major cause.[153] In fact, beaver reproduce quickly; leave a breeding pair alone for three years and five offspring will result, then four to seven annually. The decline of the caribou also put increased pressure on beaver as a major food source. The increased Cree population or at least the increased concentration of people in more restricted areas was a cause of over-hunting.[xxxi] So was the pressure put on the Crees by the competition from white trappers and from Indians of other bands encroaching on their hunting territories.[154] The Crees had had a conservation system, or perhaps more accurately, a system of husbanding beaver institutionalized in their family hunting territories.[xxxii]

Watt described them in 1929: "Up to about twenty years ago each Indian considered his hunting lands as his private property and handed them down to his family; this right was respected by all the Indians ... To take Ministokwatin as an example; this land used to be the hunting ground of old Katapaituk, who to all intents and purposes was a beaver farmer and when killing beaver on some particular lake on his estate, always tried if possible to leave sufficient breeders to restock the lake."¹⁵⁵

The right to long-term hunting of these territories[XXXIII] ensured that a hunter would know the land well and know where to find the beaver lodges in the winter. It also meant he could leave sections unharvested and be guaranteed that on his return in two to three years he would still find beaver in those lodges. These hunting territories were large, by our urban standards; for example, at Rupert House the Blackned brothers' hunting territory was given as three hundred square miles.¹⁵⁶ Another statistic to help us envisage the great size of these territories is provided by Rogers who informs us that in 1952 the Mistassini population of 646 individuals exploited a combined territory of 42,500 square miles or one person per sixty-six square miles. Some of those trapping grounds were located 320 air line miles from the post.¹⁵⁷

This knowledge of the Crees' method of harvesting beaver helped Watt formulate a plan for restoring beaver trapping. As seen previously, Watt, along with George Ray, was moved by the impoverished conditions of the Crees. He began to think in terms of farming beaver and set out to acquire as much information as he could.[XXXIV] He wrote a letter to the district manager on 16 August 1929 setting out his plan for farming, complete with predictions regarding the increase of beaver and a budget. The next day he had changed his proposal. It seems he came to believe that the most effective way to manage the beaver was to establish a system based on the hunter being able "to uphold his right to certain hunting lands," believing such a course would do more to conserve beaver than any close season.¹⁵⁸ Another source of inspiration for Watt was the old letterbook he found at the post from which he learned that the company, concerned with declining numbers of beaver, had set up a beaver preserve on Charlton Island in 1836 and another on Ministikwatin in 1842,[XXXV] in order "to maintain the Indian's right to his particular hunting ground and to limit the hunt of beaver in proportion to the number of beaver on the land."¹⁵⁹ Gradually the idea of a beaver sanctuary took shape in Watt's mind. He originally thought the Indians would be given the right to stake out one or more small lakes and creeks, much as a mining claim would be staked out, and registered with the Hudson's Bay Company post managers acting as the registrars. The controls for abstaining from beaver trapping would come from the Hudson's Bay Company's refusal to give advances and notification to the RCMP.¹⁶⁰

160   The White Man's Gonna Getcha

A beaver sanctuary was created in 1932 by provincial government decree. At the beginning, Watt thought he could establish a conservation program privately and to that end he began with several purchases of live beaver in the Pontax Creek area.[161] In 1929 Robert Stephens and Andrew Whiskeychan came to Rupert House hoping to borrow from Watt some traps or guns; they had found a beaver lodge on Pontax River and were without any hunting equipment. At that point Watt had no clear plan, but he knew he did not want the beaver killed. He told the men that if they left the pair alone, in ten years there would be 288 beaver on Pontax River. Evidently, Stephen burst out that his wife and children could not wait ten years and wanted to kill them right away so they could eat that night. Watt offered the men sixty dollars for the two beavers if they marked the lodge as his. Right away he credited their account and debited his own account. Soon after, another pair was sold to him in a lodge one hundred miles away.[162] What guaranteed the success of preserving the beaver in this way was the Crees' respect for "ownership" of the lodges. Once marked as belonging to someone, they were not trapped.

Watt recognized he could not finance the sanctuary himself and wrote to the company asking for help. This they refused, on the grounds they were not in the business of "doubtful zoological experiments." Watt then began looking to the provincial government for assistance and his wife insisted that she journey to Quebec to meet personally with the deputy minister of colonization, L.A. Richard. Her argument was that the government officials were more likely to listen to her than her husband as he was an employee of a private company with great vested interests. So, in the dead of winter, Maud and her two children travelled by sled[xxxvi] to Moose Factory and then by train to Quebec City, a trip that took a month. Her determination to see Richard helped convince him of the scheme, but so did the fact that Maud Watt was French Canadian.[xxxvii] On 17 March 1932 Richard announced that his government had created a beaver sanctuary of seven thousand square miles in the section between the Rupert and Eastmain rivers and inland twenty miles beyond Nemiskau post for a period of fifteen years. It was to be under the surveillance of James Watt, but the actual lease was granted in the name of Mrs J.S.C. Watt. The provincial government was not to assume any of the costs associated with it and, in fact, required an annual fee of $10 for the lease.[163] Watt spent the next year trying to finance this conservation scheme but to no avail, and in 1933 it was conceded that the Hudson's Bay Company would have to take on the lease with the Department of Colonization.[xxxviii] No beaver were to be killed until there were two thousand pairs. The Indian agent, Dr W.L. Tyrer, was not pleased, ad-

The Confiscation of the Land

vising the department to contest the lease on the basis that only eight families would benefit and the company could decide who eventually would have the right to kill beaver. The Hudson's Bay Company countered by announcing that twenty families were actually involved and each family would be paid $100 per year "for their cooperation." They could trap other fur-bearers.[164]

The logic of the Rupert House beaver sanctuary was instantly perceived by the Cree trappers, even though a century earlier their ancestors had registered an initial reluctance to participate. At that time the factor, Robert Miles, had requested some hunters to bring him several pairs of live beaver with which to restock Charlton Island. Their hesitancy resulted from their imagining "the Beaver would leave their lands altogether were they to bring them here alive."[165] There was no such wavering this time, though no one in James Bay was asked to trap and transport live beaver. However, live beaver were imported into the area and onto Charlton Island in 1934. Twenty pairs were purchased from a small beaver sanctuary in southern Ontario, which indicated just how scarce beaver were in James Bay.[166] Later, in 1948, some hunters on the Nottoway Preserve gave live beaver to those starting up the Mistassini Preserve.[167] On some occasions Watt even maintained the live beaver in the summer kitchen of the post.[168] It was the Crees themselves who had to make the sacrifices and alter their way of thinking about their relation to the land and to the beaver spirits. How did they view the drastic moratorium on beaver hunting? A fair way to evaluate their attitude is probably to look at their participation and cooperation. Within a year of the establishment of the Rupert House beaver sanctuary, the chief at Waswanipi, Alec Cooper, wrote to the Hudson's Bay Company, asking for a moratorium on hunting and buying of pelts for three years. By 1936, Chief Joseph Shaganash and Councillors Diom Blacksmith and Samuel Gull wrote, this time to the Department of Indian Affairs, requesting that beaver trapping be closed, arguing that a total of thirty-eight beaver had been harvested that year, not enough to "keep one family of Indians for the winter."[169] As for the Rupert House Crees, it is reported that "five or six prominent Indians" told an Indian Affairs official in 1936 that "they are very pleased with the results of the beaver preserve operated by the HBC and would like to see a similar preserve established south of the River ... The meat is as important as hide to an Indian and, as one Indian aptly stated, It is like putting money in the bank for our children."[170]

In the history of Indian-white relations few innovations or initiatives are attributed to Indians, history being usurped by those writing it. Therefore one approaches cautiously the attribution of an inspired idea. That the beaver sanctuary was Watt's initiative was made clear by several very prominent Cree men of Rupert House. John Blackned volunteered that it was Mr Watt's idea to try to preserve the beaver.[171] Similarly, Malcom Diamond,[xxxix] in talking of the terrible hardships of his people, noted "this was the time the company manager has closed down trapping of the beaver, for a few years. The manager said that if he did this then there would be more beaver in the future. He was right; today the people still trap beaver."[172] Watt did not launch the plan on his own, for Blackned tells how he consulted him and other Crees. Many disagreed evidently, but saw the wisdom of it and wanted to participate once the sanctuary was established.[173] Several old hunters in 1948 told A.J. Kerr that Watt had "come closer to understanding the way people think than any other white they knew of."[174]

By 1932 the initial two pairs of beaver Watt had purchased in 1929 had increased to twenty-five pairs.[175] A rough draft of Watt's speech to the Rupert House hunters announcing the sanctuary indicates that he welcomed suggestions from them.[176] However, his announcement indicated that the sanctuary was a fait accompli, telling them that the government owned the land and the government law had to be obeyed. This law was not completely restrictive – generous, as Watt phrased it – for it permitted them to hunt other fur-bearers. He ascribed the beaver depletion to them. "You have already killed off nearly all the Beaver so you cannot say the Government has taken anything away from you." He then offered to employ men to serve as game wardens. With so few beaver, only a few men would be employed, but as beaver increased so would the number of wardens. In the meantime, the wardens would be rotated. He called on the Crees to provide him with their opinions, but his approach was not as mollifying as the explanations of these provisions would seem, for Watt also told them if they did not agree the government would try the experiment elsewhere. Moreover, he announced that in future "all Beaver are going to be *the property of the Government* and when they think they are plentiful enough to kill the Government will tell you how many to kill, and will settle the price you will be paid."[177] Not surprisingly, the trappers began referring to "the government beaver."[178] Watt's justification for the ownership and settling of price was that the government had to be repaid for the monies spent on restocking the country and paying the wardens.

In the end, the success of the sanctuary helped ensure that the Crees looked upon the beaver preserve favourably. By 1937 there were 309 lodges, or 1,545 beaver, compared to 1933 when there were thirty-eight lodges with 162 beaver.[179] (See Appendix 3 for the yearly increases of beaver.) Limited trapping was finally permitted in 1940 and Mrs Watt excitedly wrote to Bishop Belleau that "Indians that had never made any hunt before had over $300 worth."[180] The

163   The Confiscation of the Land

Blackneds had reported only one beaver lodge of four beaver on their territory in 1932; by 1942 the number had increased to 415 beaver.[181] Another indicator of the revival of beaver hunting was the welfare rolls which were down to $2,092 in 1941 from $3,023 in 1940.[182] By 1943 the beaver population had grown to such a number that beaver trapping was set at two thousand pelts. The beaver population in 1952 was fifteen thousand and since 1940, twenty-nine thousand pelts had been harvested. By paying the men only half the value of the pelts, as agreed with the province, the Hudson's Bay Company recouped their expenses for the preserve four years after production recommenced.[183] Interestingly, in his speech, Watt represented the government as financing the scheme when, in fact, it was the Hudson's Bay Company; perhaps because the Department of Indian Affairs was concerned, the company could take advantage of its position.

The development of the beaver sanctuary sprang from Watt's great desire to find a solution to the poverty plaguing the Cree. However, as any other idea, it built on a number of others and he tailored it to the needs and conditions of the Rupert House people. We have seen that he was influenced by the 1836 successful experiment in restoring beaver numbers. What gave the particular hue to the Rupert House beaver sanctuary was, of course, the particular form of land organization the Crees had long ago developed to rationalize beaver trapping.[XL]

What was the role of the Crees in this beaver preserve? John Blackned gives an account of what he and others did to make it work.

Before they closed the area we had to count the beaver lodges. I was with Willie Weistchee's grandfather and we were able to find only three beaver lodges. I found two of the lodges, while Willie's grandfather found the other. We were out paddling for a whole month. We had to go every summer, counting beaver lodges. The more beaver lodges we found, the more men were asked to help in counting them. Finally, we were able to find more and more beaver lodges every summer. We could not kill the beaver, but we were able to kill other animals such as bear and Canada geese. The time we spent counting the lodges, we did not receive a payment; we were only given some food. Our wives also received food from the company. The company was unable to pay us, as they did not know whether the preservation will work. Finally, when the beaver started increasing, the company was able to obtain money. They started to pay us for the trips. We were not paid very much.[184]

John Blackned's details of the operation of the conservation program are mirrored in the post journal entries. For instance, on 18 August 1938 the Eastmain journal reports that "Alex Gilpin and Richard

Tammatuk came in to take up their rations to go on the beaver survey," while in the early winter David Moses is said to have come to the post to take "some of his beaver pay."¹⁸⁵ The records also tell us that come August when the Inlanders were ready to leave for their hunting territories, they did not know if they would be able to kill beaver that winter and had to await Watt's and D.E. Denmark's (of the company's fur trade department) inspection of the preserve. They could not trap beaver in 1940 but were provided with "beaver money" of $50 to each tallyman in 1941.¹⁸⁶

The beaver sanctuary was a success because the Crees recognized the wisdom of carrying out this plan. It must have been very difficult in tough times. The lure would have been the meat more so than the pelt, for beaver is one of the more delectable Cree meats and was the important mainstay of feasting. Some allowance was made for dire food shortages as the wording on this sign in the Eastmain post in 1940 explains: "To Whom It May Concern. Killing or attempting to kill beaver in any way is prohibited. In cases of dire necessity an Indian may kill a beaver to avoid starvation. In such cases the skin of the said beaver is to be brought to the H.B.Co. with full report on the killing."¹⁸⁷ˣˡⁱ

Starvation was still a very real concern in those years and people died, one of whom was an Inlander, Shanoush. He was near the mouth of the Opineka River about three days from the Eastmain post. Evidently the usual Cree system of reciprocity broke down in this case, for it appears that Shanoush was within a day's reach of two different Indian camps, well-stocked with food and one of them knew of his plight but refused to go to his assistance.¹⁸⁸ Keeping in mind that the Hudson's Bay Company was a profit-making company, one has to attribute to them not only the foresight in encouraging the conservation but also in the manner in which some of their managers conducted the trade in those lean years when beaver trapping was forbidden and food animals were scarce. Mr Foreman at Nemiskau penned this January entry in his journal: "On account of the scarcity of country foods we have not been pressing our hunters too hard for payment of debt. It is not our policy to handicap our hunters ... However, at the same time we are very firm with them and are Collecting debt where possible."¹⁸⁹

Soon after the launching of the Rupert House beaver sanctuary, other Cree communities asked for the same conservation measures. The government and the Hudson's Bay Company moved relatively slowly. As the 1952 report notes, "once the long term success of Rupert's House Preserve had been established beyond any possible doubt"¹⁹⁰ the Indian Affairs Branch of the federal government approached the provincial authorities for the lease of twelve thousand square miles lying to the south of the Rupert River. It became known as

165   The Confiscation of the Land

the Nottoway Beaver Preserve and was established on 16 June 1938, six years after the first. One of the reasons they had not acted earlier was the federal government's claim of lack of funds.¹⁹¹ Watt was consulted on the establishment of Nottoway and its design shows a continuity but also a refinement from the earlier one. Although this preserve was initiated by the Department of Indian Affairs, it was administered by the Hudson's Bay Company "in view of the Company's experience and proven success."¹⁹²

This preserve was divided into three sections to conform to the three trading posts at which the Cree hunters traded: Rupert House, Waswanipi, and La Sarre. The latter group, originally from Rupert House, evidently resented the management by the Hudson's Bay Company and caused a series of problems for them. This group's hunting lands were intermingled with Abitibi people hunting in Ontario which compounded the orderly management of the preserve. Furthermore, four of the families with the surname Trapper refused to be restricted by the regulations imposed over boundaries and closed seasons.ˣᴸᴵᴵ Banished from hunting in Ontario, they moved onto the lands of the La Sarre group of Abitibi Indians at a time when their lands were severely restricted because of colonization.¹⁹³ Eventually, with the consent "of the Company through their manager at Rupert House," five Trapper families agreed to return to Rupert House in 1943.¹⁹⁴ Many accusations followed before and after over boundary disputes with the government of Ontario, causing more problems for the Hudson's Bay Company than Quebec.¹⁹⁵ This section of the preserve was taken over by the Department of Indian Affairs and adjacent land was added to it, making the Abitibi preserve in 1941.¹⁹⁶ More importantly, it is worth noting that for the first time the Crees were subject to foreign control of their lands with the imposition of trapping territories, more circumscribed in terms of people and lands than the traditional ones, though not a radical restructuring of their old system.

Another land-based problem for the administration of the reserve was that hunting territories criss-crossed their administrative units. Thus, the Malcolm Diamond band hunted on both the Waswanipi and La Sarre section, this territory having been the hunting land of the family for at least three generations. Watt suggested that they be considered headquartered in one section but be granted special permission to also trap in another section and so in the summer of 1941 Malcolm Diamond and brothers are listed only under the Rupert House section.¹⁹⁷ The original Nottoway beaver preserve was then reorganized and divided into three sections: Rupert House, Waswanipi, and Nemaska.

As with the earlier beaver preserve and the subsequent ones in James Bay, the role of the provincial government was limited to passing orders-in-council directing that the lands be set aside. No monies were committed by the provincial government. This limited role of the provincial government in sustaining these preserves is highlighted in a 1947 confidential internal memo for Mr Riley of the Hudson's Bay Company informing him they would have to pay a toll to the Duplessis regime in order to get the Rupert House beaver preserve lease renewed. Cash was preferred; the sum was thought to be $10,000. The Hudson's Bay Company had encountered such pay-offs before; as the governor, P.A. Chester, wrote to the Hon. Charles Dunning of Montreal, "It seems fairly common gossip that there is a price for anything you want out of the Quebec Government[XLIII] … In the meantime I am all for democracy."[198] The work of the federal government and the Hudson's Bay Company did have the approval of L.A. Richard, Quebec's deputy minister of colonization, who wrote to his homologue in the federal government: "Like you I have been won over by sanctuaries. It is probably the best way we have of paying off our debt to the Indians for the harm we did them in the past."[199]

The Nottoway beaver sanctuary was a leased area rather than just an area on which beaver hunting was closed, because a lease implied management and restoration of beaver numbers rather than just a policing of the area, as Quebec had proposed. The Hudson's Bay Company was adamant about a lease and did obtain one from the province in 1938.

Hugh Conn, fur supervisor in the Department of Indian Affairs, believed that rudimentary organization was all that was needed in the Nottoway area, but events in 1945 proved him wrong. That year the men hunting in the preserve complained of poaching by the Reuben-Trapper group based at La Sarre. Accordingly, a provincial order-in-council was passed to establish a system of registered traplines not only on the Nottoway preserve but also on the earlier Rupert House one. Such a system had been instituted in 1945 for the Abitibi and Grand Lake Victoria preserves because of the numerous incidences of encroachment on each other's lands and the insecurity that resulted from their being located so close to settlement, lumbering, and mining industries. This management scheme had already been tried in British Columbia and Manitoba and proved to be efficient. It involved licensing to each trapper a certain definite area and giving him exclusive trapping rights on that area. Conn figured that "the resultant security enables the trapper to practice sound conservation and build up for himself a stock of beaver sufficient to assure him of a decent livelihood." He also acknowledged that although the plan was new, the basic principle was the "old Indian method of family trapping grounds."[200] This comment is explained in a letter from the deputy minister of Indian Affairs to RCMP headquarters in December 1942, in

The Confiscation of the Land

which he outlines the registered trapline system as it was being applied in the Nottoway preserve:

> When an area is set aside by the Province for the exclusive use of the Indians and marked by our Branch for development as a Fur Preserve, the first step is to divide the area into band or tribal areas generally called sections. These tribal areas are further divided into family hunting areas which we call districts and one Tallyman is placed in charge of each district ... When it is borne in mind that the Tallyman is the head of a family; that a district is a family trapping ground; that a section is the area trapped over by the whole tribe or band and that all boundaries are laid out by Indians themselves, it is apparent that we have not only adhered strictly to Indian custom but have actually improved on it since, through our Supervisor, we have maps of the districts and written records, which we can use to settle future disputes over trapping grounds.[201]

The registered trapline system applied in 1947 bore some additional restrictions and provisions not mentioned by Conn in his earlier report. Now the number of beaver that could be trapped would be authorized by zone by the province and each pelt was to carry a special seal bearing the name and address of the trapper. In the case of beaver trapped over the quota, these pelts were to be surrendered to the RCMP and shipped to Quebec for sale. The proceeds would be credited to the band rather than the hunter.[202] Once again the bureaucracy of the federal government had interfered with the Cree hunters' pursuit of their livelihood and it must have seemed puzzling to individuals caught up in competing jurisdictions. Thus, Charlie Weechie, George Gilpin, and Philip Small, who "had been trapping on Moose Indians grounds for some time but now on are barred ... they are Quebec Indians and according to the letter of the law cannot trap in Ontario."[203]

A third lease was negotiated between the province and Indian Affairs in 1941 but this one was to be administered by the department rather than the Hudson's Bay Company. This preserve was known as Old Factory. It comprised thirty-thousand square miles north of Rupert House between Eastmain and Factory River. The four hundred Crees located in this region had asked for such a sanctuary, as they had been practising conservation for some years and did not want to lose what ground they had gained.[204] Furthermore, in 1942 the Hudson's Bay Company applied for and was granted a lease on seventeen thousand square miles north of Old Factory, the Fort George preserve. The Fort George area had not been immune to the depletion of fur and food animals. With no furs there was no means by which to purchase cloth nor were there caribou by which the Cree men and women could produce their own clothing. The Oblates in the area made representation in

1937 to Richard in Quebec, at the request of Anderson, then James Bay district manager. The latter had written them to point out that Quebec had closed beaver trapping in all of the province to everyone, Indians included, and hoped that they could be granted the right to trap beaver for food and to trade their pelts for their livelihood, all the while presenting this as more in the Indians' interests than the company's. Marginal notes on Anderson's letter indicate that Father Belleau wrote to Richard asking him to permit the Indians of Eastmain and Fort George to kill some beaver, pointing out the success of the Rupert House reserve. Richard, according to the notes, indicated the government would change nothing in its edict.[205] Yet in 1941 there is conflicting evidence that indicates the Crees, as other Indians in Quebec, could sell their beaver if they declared they took them for food.[206] According to government documents, the "Old Factory Beaver and Fur Preserve" was organized in accordance with the Crees' traditional land tenure system. It included

> three band or tribal sections which by adhering to the traditional system of land tenure was subdivided into twenty-six family group areas. Each of these family group areas was placed in charge of the family head man who was appointed as a guardian or tallyman and placed on the department pay roll. The tribal areas are called for convenience "divisions" and the family areas "districts" … In cases where two or more brothers had equal claim to an area with no dividing line between the component parts and no acknowledged head of the family each was appointed as a tallyman and their lands are shown as one district.[207]

The Fort George division, covering 2,500 square miles, took in the trapping lands of six family groups with a total population of 116 men, women, and children, of whom sixteen were appointed tallymen. Old Factory Division, roughly seven thousand square miles with 250 people, had twenty-three tallymen looking after sixteen districts. Eastmain, the third division, had approximately 3,500 square miles with a population of sixty, four districts, and eleven tallymen. On the larger preserves the tallymen found it difficult to count all the lodges in any one year, something the Fur Preserve Section of Indian Affairs took into account when estimating the number of beaver. By contrast, the Rupert House sections were much smaller, the largest being three hundred square miles, while Eastmain and Nemaska had sections of three to five hundred square miles.[208]

The tallymen for the Fort George preserve were paid $30 each. Two invoices exist which indicate how this $30 was spent because the Hudson's Bay Company was required to file for each tallyman a list of the goods given him, amounting to $30. In October 1942 Geordie Sam and John Chiskamash were paid mainly in clothing, a very small amount in tools, and somewhat less than one-third in food, mainly flour. The lists of goods were not identical but the percentages of each category were close.[209] It is unknown whether this was by the choice of the Crees, the government, or the company.

Harvesting of beaver from the Old Factory reserve began in 1949 and yielded pelts that commanded prices higher than those from other reserves. Hunters were given quotas of about ten beaver each. There was even concern with over-crowding on some sections of the reserve, as an unusual number of pelts were found with teeth marks.[210]

Smaller preserves were set aside later at Great Whale River but administered through the Fort George preserve. One concern was to avoid Great Whale River hunters moving south and trapping on the grounds of the Kanaaupscow people.[211] At Great Whale River in 1950 and 1951 the Hudson's Bay Company purchased its first beaver from that preserve, just under two hundred pelts. It was said the Great Whale River people were catching more furs because of the increase on the Fort George preserve.[212]

Despite ongoing requests by people at Mistassini for similar protection for their beaver lands and despite its being considered extremely depleted, it was not until 1948 that fifty thousand square miles were leased to Indian Affairs for the Mistassini preserve.[213] The most recent request was in 1947, signed by Chief Isaiah Shecapio and David Neeposh representing the Neosweskau area, George Rabbitskin the Nichikun area, and William Bosum the Chibougamau area.[214] Set up similarly to the Old Factory preserve, it, too, had three subdivisions: Waswanipi, Obijuan, and Mistassini.[XLIV] Obijuan was the smallest with five family groups. Waswanipi had 350 people, sixty-eight of whom were trappers. The territory was subdivided into twenty-six family group areas with one or more tallymen. By far the largest subdivision was Mistassini, comprising three-quarters of the reserve. The population was six hundred of whom about 185 were active trappers. Accordingly seventy-one family trapping areas were registered, each of which contained two to five trappers. In total there were 108 family trapping areas, with 152 tallymen. Live beaver were brought in from the Nottoway and Abitibi preserves, which had by then a heavy concentration of beaver.

At the start of this preserve, Hugh Conn felt it had a very good chance to succeed. He wrote that "the natives throughout the Mistassini area are the better type of Indian and having learned for themselves of the advantages of beaver conservation were not only willing but anxious to undertake the rehabilitation of their area." While he praised the Crees, he had harsh words for the manager of the Hudson's Bay Company at Mistassini, who did not bother to attend any of the meetings held there with the hunters. On the other hand, the manager and owner of the Mistassini Trading Company, Emmet McLeod, did and served as interpreter.[215] For their part, the company was critical of McLeod being appointed the game guardian, in charge of collecting the beaver from the preserve, the issuance of the advances authorized by the Department of Indian Affairs, and the cheques in payment of the beaver taken. The report of 1952 reads: "if McLeod is to remain a competitor he can hardly at the same time act as a paid game guardian for the Province,"[216] though it is not clear how his duties differed much from the company's central role in the earlier preserves. The report is also critical of McLeod, noting that he was almost bankrupt and this appointment was made to assist him in his financial predicament.

As for the marketing of the furs, it depended on who held the leases. For Rupert House and Nottoway, the furs were sold directly through the Hudson's Bay Company and marketed in Montreal, London, or New York. Pelts taken from the other preserves, leased by Indian Affairs, were marketed through a provincial government outlet in Quebec City by sealed bid. In a Hudson's Bay Company report it is claimed that the furs sold through sealed bids realized prices consistently lower, as they were not sold through major auctions. The anonymous Hudson's Bay Company writer of this report in 1952 was at a loss to explain why Quebec would have gotten into the fur-buying business. It may have just been a trend, for Keighley describes how in 1944–5 the newly elected CCF party in Saskatchewan took over the fur (and fish) buying business through fur auction sales. The policy in Saskatchewan, as in Quebec, was probably aimed at the Hudson's Bay Company but the company was so much larger and more secure that it could wait out this new policy until the government tired of being in the fur-buying business. Keighley observed that the Hudson's Bay Company benefited; the Saskatchewan government got rid of all competition for them.[217] The Revillon Frères records also suggest that the Hudson's Bay Company benefited in the marketing of contraband furs – those furs not trapped under licence. Revillon had tried it but the fines became too high and one Revillon agent was even jailed in Ontario. The Hudson's Bay Company, on the other hand, it is suggested, went to great lengths to disguise the contraband furs. They were shipped and even invoiced as legal furs or disguised as trading goods.[218]

RESULTS

Due to its immense area and isolation and lacking a network of roads, most of James Bay escaped the destruction of the wildlife from settlement and clear-cut logging that occurred elsewhere in Canada's middle north. The harvesting of beaver in the 1940s also helped conserve and restore other animals, since the Crees could now rely, in part, on this important source of food and furs. In the early 1930s Watt had expressed a profound concern about the great impoverishment of the Cree people at Rupert House. In 1946 the reports were dramatically different; the Hudson's Bay Company reported that the large quota for beaver had netted exceptionally high prices. The income was spent by the Crees on food, clothing, canoes, and other much-needed equipment. For the Nottoway River, Rupert House section, the number of beaver trapped in 1945–6 was 884, yielding $42,754, or an average of $724 for each of the fifty-nine trappers.[219] This relative prosperity resulted from the high prices paid for furs in the postwar years. However these prices did not last. In 1945–6 a beaver pelt was worth $70 but fell to $30 the year after.[220] The drop in the economy was real and could be measured by the drop in bread sales that Maud Watt[XLV] experienced, commenting that the "Indians don't have half the money they did last year."[221] Nevertheless, in 1948, following his year's stay in Rupert House, A.J. Kerr reported that the prosperity of the Rupert House band was "unique" in James Bay; it was the one community not receiving government relief. Rupert House stands in contrast to Attawapiskat on western James Bay where that very year the anthropologist John Honigmann had reported finding malnourished teens who had never seen a beaver.[222]

Despite the conflicting interests of government, fur trade companies, independent traders, and southern industrial interests of mining and lumber, each with its own stake and reason for defining or redefining the beaver preserves, Watt's original vision came to fruition. It did so because the Crees saw its good sense and the necessity of making these conservation schemes work despite the enormous sacrifices they had to make in food and income. There is little about Cree thoughts on these beaver management schemes in the recorded accounts. The few comments represent a continuing approval twenty to forty or so years after the preserves were first established. It would be interesting to know what the Crees thought of the government involvement, whether, in fact, they saw the beaver preserves as impositions or as instruments of change. Undoubtedly, the Crees recognized that they were now subject to a new authority, different from the spiritual or consensual authority to which they had traditionally subscribed. They complied with the regulations, we must surmise, because the logic of them was instantly appealing to them. However, the Crees did surrender their decision-making to outsiders, to the company and government. For example, in Rolf Knight's field notes on Rupert House he reported that in 1959 Charlie Hester wanted to close down a section of his trapping territory for two years. However, the regulations required that a man continue to patrol his land "to count the beaver and see that none are poached." Hester was not prepared to do this and the Hudson's Bay Company manager sent Ronnie Salt to count the beaver and later assigned that section to him. The Nottoway preserve, although leased by the Department of Indian Affairs, was managed under the auspices of the Hudson's Bay Company traders at each post. Hence, the trader here was instituting government regulations. In his interview with Charlie Hester, Knight recorded that if a man wanted to live and trap out of Rupert House, he had to "see the [HBC manager] boss." Knight deduced from this that the Crees looked upon the Hudson's Bay Company as "their legitimate political system. There was no attempt or even consideration of the possibility of allotting areas or controlling access to land themselves."[223]

In 1961 Knight was unaware of the historical processes that had contributed to the decision-making powers of the post manager over land occupancy. For a hunting people to have abrogated such a right, it is reasonable to assume there was a dependence that had been forced upon them or that their independence had been wrested from them. On one level this is true, but on another it must be filtered through the knowledge that the Cree societies were on the brink of physical and cultural annihilation. With no favoured and marketable animals to hunt or trap, within a generation they would have surely lost their social and cultural cohesiveness as well as their numbers. It was their acceptance of an external authority that saved them. In order to maintain their economic order, they sacrificed control of their political order over specific issues and on specific terms. The overall effects of this decision were relatively benign in that their land tenure system and the social relations that defined it continued, albeit with modifications. A juxtaposition of John Cooper's map of Fort George hunting territories in 1932, made in the pre-beaver preserve era, with a 1977 map of registered trapping lines produced by the Crees[224] show similar boundaries of these lands despite the passage of forty years and layers of outside interference in their subsistence strategies. Similarly, Adrian Tanner, researching hunting territories in Mistassini in the 1960s, saw continuity and overlap with those charted by Speck in the 1920s.[225]

What changed was the formal nature of the family hunting territories. What had before been customary and flexible according to family circumstances was now rigid and subject to disposition by the trader or government official. It is this change, this formalization and rigidity, that suggested to the Crees that hunting territories began only with the registered trapline system instituted by the government. It is these types of comments that Knight heard in 1961, which led him to conclude in an influential paper on hunting territories that the genesis of the latter lay with the government and not the ancestors of the Crees. However, Knight's fieldnotes indicate the testimony he was hearing was not at all conclusive. His marginalia are particularly instructive. For example, Luke Mettaweskum told him that before beaver sections, "each man has his land and when he dies he leaves it to one of his sons." However he also told him that "we trapped wherever we wanted." Alongside his recording of these comments, Knight wrote: "Here is an example of a clear and straightforward contradiction I couldn't clear up or even show to be a contradiction." For those who have studied the land tenure system of the Crees, it is apparent that Mettaweskum was providing Knight with the principles of the territory being family owned but at the same time was expressing the flexibility of the traditional system before the lands were registered. One could choose where to trap on one's own territory or one could also choose to trap with someone else (provided permission was sought and granted). Knight also had difficulty in reconciling Matthew Cowboy's statement to him that the hunters "usually trapped in an area they knew." He could see the advantages of knowing the territory and conceded that this might have been effective in creating and maintaining family territory; he ended this discussion in his fieldnotes with the possibility that Cowboy's claim "might indicate the existence of some sort of territoriality." By the time Knight turned these data into his study in 1965, denying the existence of hunting territories, he had quite forgotten his earlier difficulty with the contradictions he had heard.[226] Furthermore, under the registered trapline regulations which the Crees now saw as a system, they did not have the freedom to alter it even if it conflicted with some other agenda of the company or government officials or perhaps even their judgment about how the land should be used or numbers of animals trapped. It is the formalization, the official status of the government system, that led some Crees to suggest it was a new system. What Richard Preston found in his analysis of the Cree concept of community is applicable here. He writes: "Previous notions relating to social grouping, by comparison with the contemporary concept, were little coloured by the ideas and values of non-Cree people."[227] As well, the confusion perceived by Knight might well be explained by Tanner's assessment of the registered trapline system. When he conducted fieldwork in the late 1960s at Nichikun he concluded that the Crees had not yet "internalized" registered traplines.[228] That the Crees supported the system indicates that, on the whole, it was consistent with their long-standing views on how to husband their beaver. In a final consideration, we return to the important 1987 article by Sarah Preston questioning the analyses of anthropologists who were only in the field for short periods. She discredits Knight's 1965 findings on hunting territories and hunting strategies by demonstrating that all the hunters he cites who indicated limited hunting and limited access to hunting territories had been company servants, not full-time hunters.

As for the Crees' views of the registered traplines and government involvement, perhaps the words of Joe Ottereyes as told to Harvey Feit in 1979 might serve as some indicator. Feit asked him several questions about whether the Crees were better off in the 1970s, with government involvement. In response to the question of whether people were less free now, Ottereyes said that "before we got help from the government – man was boss of himself – did what he thought was needed – not like that now since government – doesn't feel same." In response to being asked for other ways "a man is less his own boss," Ottereyes replied, "One who hunts and traps- he is still free, when someone works has to have someone tell or order him what to do." As for a question about game wardens restricting his freedom to hunt, Ottereyes said that they listen to what the game warden has to say. For instance, he might say that they were not to kill more than four moose. If a hunter decided to ignore this edict, then he would not give it to someone outside his hunting ground.[229] In other words, the rules were respected so long as they made sense. Joe Ottereyes may well have been referring to the game warden's visit to Cree communities in 1938; in the Mistassini records the game warden was said to have "laid down the law to the Indians regarding the killing of so many cow moose also of trapping out of season, especially mink."[230] My own reading of the company and government records suggests that the Crees may well have used their own judgment; who would have known in this vast territory, especially if they did not "give it to someone outside his hunting ground"?

The foregoing has demonstrated that into the 1940s the Crees continued hunting and seem to have been doing so along traditions and practices that reached back centuries. On one level, this may be an accurate statement. On another level, there was much change. The anthropologist Regina Flannery was in Rupert House in 1938 studying dreaming and hunting beliefs, as had her professor, Father John Cooper. The results of this research were published in an important article in which she counters this perspective we might have of ways that are not perceptible to those of us relying on written records. This article begins with a discussion of *powatakan*, the dream spirit that visits a hunter in his dreams, appearing as a person and talks to him. It emphasizes the centrality of *powatakan* in a hunter's life, for it gives the hunter foreknowledge about the animals and all else necessary to a successful hunt. However, by the 1960s the authors conclude that much had changed for the Crees so that the *powatakan* were no longer the organizing principle behind the seasonal round of hunting. They point out that with the availability of wage labour and government assistance, the Crees are no longer engaged in full-time subsistence hunting. With their use of aircraft, or serving as guides for sports hunters and fishermen, rather than preserving the animal resources and now harvesting a predicable quota of beaver, the *powatakan* concept has lost much of its function as an explanation for hunting success.[231] Perhaps also, as subsistence derived from the hunt decreased and other food resources opened up, this too weakened the sense of the forces that had guided their lives for millennia. Much had changed for the Crees behind the empirical level of observed behaviour, but the structures of their lives in the 1940s, their economy, their political organization, their social life continued to bear strong resemblance to life at the turn of the century.

That the Crees in the 1940s still had control over their daily subsistence is summed up in Ottereyes' comments, but the margins within which they could operate were continuously being narrowed by world markets, by white settler intrusion and by government interference and/or involvement. Most manipulative were the bureaucratic decisions, forged in Ottawa or Amos, which drew boundaries of beaver preserves, then registered traplines. The denial of access to some whose hunting lands long pre-dated the provincial boundaries, imposed to ensure beaver royalties to either Ontario or Quebec, must have seemed to the Crees totally irrational.

Even the Crees' belief system had been challenged by newcomers, and whatever blend of old and new they had forged was presumably being whittled away as the Anglicans constantly challenged them to take on more of their Christian perspective. "Whittled away" is probably an apt summation of what is to come in the following chapter as we look at the swelling of institutions whose seeds had been sown earlier, by the fur trade, the missions, and the government.

CHAPTER SIX

Pale Versions of Southern Institutions

Can any of us reading this know what it is like to be starving, to be so enfeebled that a hunter has not the strength or endurance to search for game or exert the energy to trap it, never mind the long trudge back to the camp to share it with his wife and children? This is just the physical state. What of the psychological state of people who have lost numbers of relatives to starvation and epidemics, people who gave them warmth and affection, provided them with valued cultural knowledge? Can we comprehend what it was like for people to have seen their prized game animals disappear at the same time as epidemics were decimating them and strangers appeared on their lands who, without consultation, began rearranging the landscape, mental and physical. With such a brutal existence in this century, is it any wonder that they took direction, permitted others to make decisions for them, especially since in return they were offered sustenance in the form of rations, or solace in the form of religion? Life could be easier; they saw it on their trips to the towns along the rail line or when in the interior of their lands they encountered Montagnais from Pointe Bleue who could set out one hundred traps to their twenty or thirty.[1] Perhaps they were feeling so impotent and demoralized that they granted there might be other ways to feed, clothe, and guide their children.

In the post Second World War era, still guided by the inspiration that the Indians had to be led to civilization, the Department of Indian Affairs simply grafted onto Cree life institutions from the south. It was a policy begun long before the tenure of the deputy superintendent of Indian Affairs, Duncan Campbell Scott, but continued by him, kept in place long after his retirement in 1932,[2] and continues to this day. However, these were not faithful imitations of southern institutions, for they were instituted and managed with niggardly funds[3] and, it seems, in complete ignorance of the dangers and requirements of social engineering.[1] The Crees of eastern James Bay encountered this rearrangement of their institutions later than Indians to the west partly perhaps because they were not treaty Indians and thus less visible bureaucratically, but probably because they were self-sufficient longer than other Indians. Given, for many Crees, the distance of their territories from the urban areas in southern Quebec, they did not suffer inroads of settlement or mining or lumbering. Unlike Indians living to the south, such as the Mi'kmaq or Abenakis, whose livelihood was destroyed by settlement, they were not forced into socially destructive and alien forms of work such as peddling baskets or taking on seasonal labour digging potatoes.[4] No roads were constructed in James Bay until the 1970s, except in its southern regions, and no reliable telephone system[11] was available until then. However, they were not isolated enough; they greatly felt the force of the great depression of the 1930s. The Crees' grinding poverty and deaths from starvation inexorably forced the government to take heed. As with other Native Peoples in Canada, this loss of their self-sufficiency brought on a loss of economic and political autonomy. Solutions were imposed with the intent of restructuring elements of the culture and the culture itself, rather than allowing the society to make its own decisions regarding change within its traditional cultural patterning.[5]

The effects of this imposed change reach beyond the economic impoverishment discussed in the last chapter. The federal government intervened in almost every institution that profoundly touched Cree society, but the intervention was a neglectful one. It was not even a question of government policy being misguided; we might forgive them for that. It was more malicious in outcome. Having undertaken to protect and provide for Indians, the government did the minimum and, in fact, abrogated its responsibilities. Bound within a colonial structure, the government demanded much in their expectations but gave very little to accomplish it. Positive results could never be seen.

This chapter outlines the imposition of pale configurations of southern know-how on the Crees of James Bay, begun at the turn of the century but reaching a more elaborate form in the 1950s and 1960s. We have already looked at the church and have yet to examine health, education, economic endeavours, and the role of government beyond the establishment of the beaver preserves. Along the way, we will try to present some glimpses of Cree daily life as seen through their own and outsiders' narratives.

THE FEDERAL AND QUEBEC GOVERNMENTS HAND-IN-HAND: THE CASE OF MISTASSINI

First, we must pick up the story of the Quebec government establishing itself as an authority in the James Bay region. Rather than make a treaty with the Indians in Quebec, Indian Affairs suggested that the provincial government should be willing "as claims are made by the outlying tribes" to set aside suitable reserves of land.[6] This the provincial government did, though "willing" would not be apt.

Most Indian reserves, in Quebec as in the rest of Canada, are set out on land to which the crown has title. The act setting aside this land gives the Indians the right to occupy and use it but ownership remains with the federal or provincial government, depending on which way the reserve was created. No matter which government has title to the land, while it is in the possession of the Indians only the federal government can legislate for it, by virtue of section 91 (24) of the British North America Act, which granted responsibility for Indians and lands reserved for Indians. There were a number of ways reserves could be created, but two acts are the most significant. In 1851 the Province of Canada Act set aside 250,000 acres in Lower Canada (Quebec). Eight reserves were created in this way but none in James Bay. The Quebec Lands and Forests Act of 1922 permitted the use of not more than 330,000 acres for use as reserves. Nine reserves, three in the James Bay territory, were created in this way through provincial orders-in-council. If the reserve becomes abandoned, the land reverts to the province. Additionally, until the 1970s there were twelve settlements in Quebec. These were not provincially constituted or recognized reserves but parcels of land varying in size from 18 to 127 acres, occupied by Indian peoples. Most of the James Bay Cree communities, until the James Bay and Northern Quebec Agreement in 1975 created new categories of lands, were designated as these settlements, having no official status. The five communities with no recognized claim to any of their ancestral lands were: Great Whale River, Fort George, Old Factory, Rupert House, and Nemiskau. Both Noeskweskau and Nichikun were noted as settlements, with the commentary that hunters visited there in the winter but there was no summer settlement.[7]

The three Cree reserves of Eastmain, Mistassini, and Waswanipi were all duly constituted in 1962. It is understandable why Mistassini and Waswanipi were legally registered since mining and other interests were impinging on their village lands. However, it is not clear why Eastmain was included when the other villages along the coast were not; no settlement or industries were moving that far north. It is even a wonder the provincial government or cabinet bothered, as they transferred all of 13.8 acres of land for the Eastmain reserve.[8] It was also a surprise to Chief Matthew Shanush who, in the course of his testimony during the injunction hearings in 1972 to stop the James Bay hydroelectric project, first heard from the government lawyer that Eastmain "had a reserve, just a few hundred yards from the settlement."[9] Waswanipi's land transfer from the provincial government to the federal government was 620 acres in 1962 when most of the people were living off the reserve.¹⁰

The case of the Mistassini reserve is an interesting example of the lack of goodwill by both governments. The deliberate stalling and foot-dragging as well as intergovernmental quarrelling must have left the Crees baffled and highly sceptical of governmental promises, not to mention downright discouraged.

[margin note: prov & fed stalling on reserves]

The Mistassini people began asking for reserve status in 1945 and again in 1952 in a letter to Indian Affairs signed by Chief Isaac Shecapio and sub-chiefs David Nepoush and George Rabbitskin, as well as thirty-two other signatories.¹¹ The Mistassini people were anxious to have a reserve finalized because outside interests were obtaining leases within their village from the provincial government. For example, Boreal Airways "have acquired a lease on the shore line for a certain parcel of land almost in front of our Nursing Station," and the region was drawing in tourists. Larivière, the Indian agent, also added in what surely was an understatement: "This is not well viewed by the Indians." He did add that he hoped "the Mistassini Indians won't be deprived of the ground. If we look back what took place elsewhere, Indians were pushed off from original natural holdings and that has caused difficulties which no one can practically solve."¹²

What was delaying the settling of the Mistassini reserve in the 1950s was not simply the bureaucracy of the federal government, but the provincial government's interests. According to the regional supervisor of Indian Affairs in Quebec City, J. D'Astous, it was the premier of Quebec, Maurice Duplessis, who "was not prepared to let go the land,"¹³ despite requests over several years by officials in Ottawa. D'Astous was even prepared to let the premier take the credit for the establishment of the reserve. The federal government had earlier also slowed down the process. In 1947 Larivière received a note from Ottawa that no funds were included in the estimates for the year for a survey of the reserve and therefore it was not possible to take any such action "at present."¹⁴

According to Indian Affairs documents, the branch in the region continued to campaign for a reserve. In 1953 D'Astous sounded a note of urgency when he wrote that "the makeshift organization of log schools, nursing stations, etc. which has lasted for some ten years now, will crumble within a short while."¹⁵ The long-drawn-out story of the establishment of the Mistassini reserve continued until 1962. Surveys got under way in 1959. A year later there was correspondence regarding the demands for land at Mistassini by the Hudson's Bay Company and the Oblates which Indian Affairs considered to be "more than their share." That year, as well, correspondence flowed on the location of the Anglican Church.[16] Eventually, on 13 February 1962, an order-in-council of Quebec transferred 5,281 acres of land to the federal government.[17] The file had been opened on 30 July 1945.

QUEBEC IN NOUVEAU QUÉBEC

The formation of the beaver preserves underscores the point that the provincial government had not taken an active interest either in the activities of the Crees or their welfare. There was no reason for them to do so: the Indians were wards of the federal government. Nevertheless, in 1960 a new provincial premier, Jean Lesage, who previously had served as minister of northern affairs in the federal government, and an energetic, nationalist-leaning minister of natural resources, René Lévesque, noticed that Quebec had scarcely any presence in its northern territories. They had campaigned on a platform of increased economic and social autonomy for Quebec and quickly moved to participate directly in the administration of its northern regions, mineral resources being the motivating factor.[18] In 1961 they established the Direction Général du Nouveau Québec (DGNQ) to administer the area of the province north of the Eastmain River, the northern territory that had been ceded to Quebec in 1912. Calling it Nouveau Québec was signalling only that it was "new" to the Quebec people, not the Crees and Inuit who had occupied it for millennia. Initially DGNQ concentrated its efforts in the Ungava or mainly Inuit territory, with regional headquarters at Great Whale River where they also posted a unit of the Quebec provincial police. At Fort George, where there was the largest concentration of Crees, DGNQ was scarcely visible until 1976. Then the solitary agent was joined by seven others, although the post never replaced Great Whale River as the headquarters. The goal of the agency was to aid communities, providing a range of services, from education to welfare to town zoning and policing.[19] The assessment of the anthropologists in Fort George in the mid-1970s was that as an organization "it was viewed favourably as one that enables native people to turn desires into more concrete realities," although the one accomplishment they credit to DGNQ was "informing the community about the existence and availability of unemployment insurance benefits which reduced the number of people on the provincial welfare rolls."[20] The Cree view might be subsumed in this comment of Billy Diamond, some years later: "DGNQ it was known as in those days, and we used to call it the 'Don't go near Quebec' Commission."[21] The provincial services were provided alongside federal ones so either the Native Peoples could play one against the other or, sadly, were at times caught up in the rivalry, reminiscent of the Anglican and Catholic contestants in their midst since the 1920s. Both the Indians of Quebec Association (IQA), then representing the Crees, and the Anglican Church became apprehensive in the early 1960s when the provincial government began establishing French-language schools at Fort George, Paint Hills, and Rupert House.[111] The schools were supposed to be secular but the IQA charged that parents were being bribed or coerced to send their children to French-language schools conducted by Oblate Fathers, while the Anglican bishop was alarmed by Cree children being taught in a second language other than English,[22] claiming that "it was bewildering and frightening to the Indians."[23] Present in Rupert House during this period, Richard Preston documented that the Crees were concerned their eighty-four students were divided among three schools (federal, provincial, and a private Oblate one, with two students).[24] In a striking demonstration of unity in 1967 under the leadership of Chief Malcolm Diamond, they had petitioned the federal government to remove from their school "the French Catholic teachers and textbooks."[25] The government complied but then reversed this stand a few months later.

These early beginnings of the Quebec presence in its unsettled northern territories provided the footing the province needed for the developments that sprang up in the early 1970s, in particular the James Bay hydroelectric project.

HEALTH

Next to food, the overriding concern of the Crees in the first half of the twentieth century must have been their physical state. Waves of epidemics had taken a huge toll. Even today, it is said the Cree notion of health is derived from their ability "to lead an active life in the forest and to follow the Cree way of life."[26] What was the nature of their own medical system in those years and why did the Crees turn to the medical expertise of the Euro-Canadians?

It would be foolhardy for me to attempt to discuss Cree traditional medicine in these few pages, especially given my lack of an in-depth knowledge of it. Nevertheless, the reader should be reminded that the Crees did cope for thousands of years with illness and accidents from which no society can be free. In coping with various afflictions they fashioned their own treatments based on a particular Cree psychology, supernatural powers, and a combination of plant and animal medicines. The old system may not have been as challenged prior to the late 1800s as it was to prove to be in the twentieth century when it gave way to Western medicine. A number of the epidemics proved to be beyond the reach of Cree medicines (and without Western ones to substitute, as for measles, chickenpox, influenza, scarlet fever, and so on). Nor could Cree medicines combat the widespread malnutrition they suffered in the early part of this century. Furthermore, the imposing presence of Christian missionaries whittled away at the faith a Cree held in his or her traditional healing methods. Nevertheless, despite this onslaught and prevailing misery, knowledge of Cree medicinal treatments did endure and were related in narratives collected in the last twenty or so years.[27] The narratives tell of the practical applications of medicines made of animal organs or plants, but unfortunately they do not transmit the considerable spiritual component that accompanied this form of healing.

A sampling of this traditional medicinal arsenal is found in the accounts of people from Wemindji and Fort George. Charlotte Visitor relates how various parts of the bear are used in different treatments. A man is treated by potions made from the female animal and the woman, by the male animal. For headaches, the brain is cooked and rolled up into a little ball, then swallowed whole, not chewed. For sore muscles, a liniment is made from *wiisuupii* from the bear. Another animal that provides healing properties is the skunk, its glands being used to treat people who have breathing problems.[28] At Fort George, Stephen Tabaituk recounted some of the medicines made from plants such as Labrador tea. An inland variety of this plant, but stronger, called *wuusciisibwuk*, was boiled and made into a poultice. The Crees used these and other plants and animals, such as the bear, beaver, caribou, and moose, when sick or injured.[29] For earaches, tobacco soaked in water was poured into the ear[30]; a cure for "craziness" was hot grease.[31] Unable to find someone to nurse an infant, the Crees would feed them baby "rabbit" brains.[32] Sam Masty related that "when he was a kid he heard there were people, healing people, who by singing songs ... put a spell on the person and the person was ok."[33] European diseases were new to the Crees but they would have had an age-old knowledge of accidents and how to treat them. Not surprisingly, we learn that Anderson Jolly recovered from the rifle bullet wound in his hand. The anonymous writer remarked that "the hand healed with hardly a scar, which says a great deal for the Indian method of dressing such a wound for it was several days after the accident before he received medical care."[34]

Sweat lodges are ancient and found throughout the Algonquian world. The Crees of eastern James Bay made great use of them for the curing of a variety of illnesses. The lodges were small tents, covered with lots of blankets with heated rocks inside and the sick people "would just sweat it out," and sometimes skunk medicine was combined with sweat lodges.³⁵ We do know that bleeding as a remedy was practised by the Crees in the mid-1700s,³⁶ but there is no indication when it was abandoned as a treatment. Doubtless, it was the elders who served as healers in the community. For example, they were called upon at Mistassini in 1926 to treat the epileptic fits of the daughter of Old Voyageur.³⁷

Much like religion, the Crees must have combined both systems of healing, for each must have worked in varying circumstances. In the early 1900s the Leith brothers remarked that every guide carries a bottle of pain killer with him³⁸ and we can assume that each man also carried with him the knowledge of how to draw on supernatural forces as well as an arsenal of plant and animal remedies.

Foreign pathogens required foreign remedies and these the Crees had pragmatically accepted almost from the start of their involvement in the fur trade in the early 1700s. If they were Coasters, or otherwise near the post, they sought medical assistance for conditions with which they could not cope – not that Western medicine had great healing powers until recent times. The practitioners they relied on were the post managers; thus the delivery of health care was dependent on each man's particular gift of healing and what medicines were in stock at the post. Perhaps they were aided by a medical manual prepared for the use of the post by Dr Robert Stewart in 1927, entitled "Post Manager's Medical Guide."³⁹ For example, in 1939 Elijah Blackboy came to the small outpost of Kanaaupscow for medicine for Samson Nahcapho's daughter who had "heart trouble." P.J. Soper, the post manager, recorded the people he treated and, in fact, once referred to himself as "Dr Soper."⁴⁰ He treated George Bearksin's frozen toe, offered care at the post for those recovering from accidents, and yanked out one of "Old Lady" Bearskin's upper teeth, with "nary a squawk though the procedure must have been painful as there's no anaesthetic."⁴¹ The efforts of the post manager's medical assistance were not always appreciated. Hurley dressed one man's foot but his sister-in-law objected, saying he "deserved to cut his foot as he chases after the girls too much" and the manager added in his journal: "seems to be quite a sinner though a married man."⁴²

A more systematic approach to healing became more urgent by the mid-1900s. The devastating illnesses were made more deadly by the poverty and malnourishment, and an improved medical delivery system in the south was becoming accessible to the north. The arrival of Father Boisseau in 1922 at Fort George brought additional medical expertise to the community. The Catholics soon recognized that the community and the coast very badly needed a hospital in order to offer a similar type of medical care that was provided to people in the rest of Canada.

Professional Western-style medical care had been available at Moose Factory since at least the 1770s when the Hudson's Bay Company had employed a so-called surgeon to oversee the medical needs of its employees at the post. If ever the surgeon attended to the needs of the Cree population, it was not a matter that made it into the annals. It was definitely not a service that was offered to either employees or Crees on the east coast of James Bay; the employment of a company doctor there ended in the 1890s.[43] The Moose Factory Crees were not recipients of professional medical care until the government began sending a doctor in 1905 (after Treaty 9 was signed) and then in 1929 when the first Indian agent and medical doctor, Dr B.H. Hamilton, was assigned there.[44] Back in the 1890s R.B. Borron, on a fact-finding mission for the government of Ontario in the Moose River basin, found the health and physical conditions of the Crees poor. He recommended a ten to twelve cot hospital. He believed that proper food and good nursing "would save many lives." As for the cost of erecting and furnishing it, which he estimated at about $10,000, the magistrate suggested that the Dominion government could draw on some of the $200,000 of import duties which it has "wrung out of the pockets of the poor people of this territory."[45] It took the government a good many years to accept this responsibility. Again, in 1921, the Reverend Walton recommended that the government provide a visiting doctor and also build and equip a hospital at a central post, with "subsidiary hospitals at outlying posts."[46] Until the government did establish a hospital in 1940 in Moose Factory, the Anglicans provided a small hospital in an "abandoned old log house"[47] which Letitia Newnham, the wife of the bishop, established about the turn of the century, complete with a trained nurse.[48] In 1937, with financial aid from the Missionary Society of the Church in Canada (MSCC), the Anglicans built a new, well-equipped hospital at the same time as they replaced the old boarding school.[49]

The government hospital at Moose Factory, built in 1940,[50] was for the use of the Crees but should not be confused with the thirty-bed one built at Moosonee in 1942 by the Catholics, licensed by the government of Ontario but with federal endorsement of Indian admissions. It was open to everyone but evidently built to serve the white Catholic population, stationary and transient, working in Moosonee, the new townsite built at the end of the rail line.[51] The government hospital at Moose Factory was rebuilt in 1949–50.[52] The impetus for it, Bishop Renison said,[53] was a meeting between the Moose Factory Crees and Paul Martin, minister of health in July 1947 who, it was said, was the first federal cabinet minister ever to meet with Indians. Plans for the 250-bed hospital began in 1948 and was officially opened in 1951, at a rumoured cost of $2 million.[IV] These were the years when tuberculosis was ravaging the Cree population and this facility seems to have been intended mainly as a sanitarium.

The hospital at Moose Factory did not play a significant role in the lives of the Crees on the east coast, because of the difficulty with transportation and communication. A rare example is a doctor's report of 1931 in which he recounted having removed a cancerous breast from a Cree woman in a house at Rupert House. He did so under local anaesthetic and the woman walked away herself from the table, requesting a "big meal."[54] Only a few references indicate an "eastern" clientele for the Moose Factory Hospital.

With air transport, even inland peoples could be flown out for medical attention. For example, from Waswanipi in 1938, Alec Cooper's wife was flown to the hospital in Amos, accompanied by Dr Bolduc, the Indian Affairs doctor for that region.[55] George Iserhoff was sent to the "Indian hospital"[V] at Cochrane.[56] Some patients were sent to hospitals as far away as Montreal; Willie Iserhoff was treated at the Royal Victoria Hospital in 1938.[57]

Health care prior to the Second World War was not a government priority, and eastern James Bay may have fallen outside of any semblance of priority. Schools which fell outside treaty areas in the late 1800s and into the early 1900s did not receive financing and this may well have been the approach to federal assistance in health care and other matters,[58] as the Crees on the Quebec side were without treaty. Certainly a reluctance to commit themselves to heavy expenditures for any native population is the explanation usually given for the government's paltry attempts at curbing the series of epidemics through which the Native Peoples suffered. The deputy superintendent, Duncan Campbell Scott, did not act upon the recommendations of his medical inspector, who had been primarily concerned with the high death rate in residential schools in the early 1900s; in fact, the position was abolished in 1918, the year of the Spanish flu.[59] However, to put his lack of attention or concern with Indian health in perspective, the federal Department of Health was only created in 1919. In the 1920s the tragic deterioration of the health of Indians was coming to the attention of socially conscious individuals[VI] and organizations and the Indian Affairs Bureau began a program of travelling nurses,[60] though not in James Bay. Not until 1927 was a full-time medical superintendent appointed for the Department of Indian Affairs.[VII] Only towards the end of the 1930s and after the war, with an improved budget for Indian health services, was medical care directed to improving their health rather than grudgingly offering only medical relief.[61]

A change in thinking after 1945 resulted in the government making an earnest effort to provide adequate health care to all Canadians by handing the responsibility to the Department of National Health and Welfare.[62] By that year, several nursing stations were built in Mistassini and Fort George, as well as at Waswanipi in the following year.[63] Great Whale River did not have such a facility until 1962[64]; no doubt the whites serving on the defence projects in the 1950s had their own medical services. The first nursing station in an Indian community had been established by the federal government in Manitoba in 1930.[65]

Until nurses were employed in the villages, the Crees were dependent for western medicine[VIII] on whomever had the knowledge and was willing to share it. However, the story of development of health care in eastern James Bay is dominated by the competition between Anglicans and Catholics. Father Boisseau had a medical knowledge superior to anyone else at Fort George in the 1920s and he recognized the great need for a hospital that would serve the Crees within reach of that community. Never far from his thoughts was that a hospital and a school could only benefit the Catholic cause.[66] To this end, in the cold of winter of 1929 he trekked down to Island Falls on the Temiskaming and Northern Ontario line to reach Haileybury, where he successfully petitioned his bishop for nuns to serve at Fort George. The hospital that was established in 1930 came about because of his efforts but he did not live to see it. The original building housed both the residential school and the hospital. Soon after, when the four Grey Nuns arrived, they found themselves in the midst of a flu epidemic and proceeded to provide nursing care despite the obstacles cast their way by the wife of the Anglican minister.[67] That first summer, Dr Benson H. Hamilton, the bureau's Indian agent stationed at Moose Factory, told the priest that he would not recommend the hospital for government subsidies but would use it for his medical examinations on his annual visits to Fort George. The complaints of Father Meilleur, now head of the mission, stem from a complex situation. Throughout the north of Canada, social services, education, and health and welfare were funded by overseas missionaries (Anglican and Catholic) with money raised in Europe. The missions were interested in remaining independent of government sponsorship to avoid attempts at intervening in what they considered their affairs, particularly in education.[68] So, although they grumbled, they were not willing to cede their jurisdiction. Accordingly, this was a national issue and in this case we need not think that the federal government was acting from an anti-Catholic position, as were the Anglicans.

In any case, government funding to mission hospitals was meagre, only sometimes making grants on a per diem basis. Evidently Hamilton's successor, Dr J.J. Wall, did obtain federal government recognition of the hospital in 1933, but Sister Paul-Emile claims that Mrs Griffin successfully prevented the Crees (except for five patients) from going to the hospital, threatening that Dr Hamilton would not see them if they were to do so. Thus, no funding was forthcoming even though the nuns treated the sick in their tents, travelling there by "ambulance-canoe." So strapped for funds was the mission at Fort George that the diocesan council at Haileybury considered abandoning Fort George to the Anglicans. In the end, they decided too much human effort, sacrifice, and devotion had been poured into it to take such a radical step. So they continued, and within several years their financial difficulties had improved. By 1934 they had thirty-one boarding pupils at the school-hospital and in 1935 Dr Wall obtained for them their first government subsidy. It was well deserved according to Sister Paul-Emile, who noted that for the year ending August 1935 the nurse, Sister Sainte-Rolande, and an assistant, had cared for forty-three patients in hospital and had tended to twelve hundred visits to the dispensary, not counting the tent calls. That summer the "southern chief," John Tchiskamash, and two concillors expressed their satisfaction with the school and hospital. They complimented the Catholics for their care of the Crees which, they pointed out, had not been a great concern of the Anglicans before the Catholics arrived in 1922.[69]

The Catholics received not only earthly rewards but heavenly ones as well, for occasionally some of the Crees they nursed accepted their sacraments. In 1936 George Matawaham was suffering from a "putrifying cancerous tumour, the size of a cauliflower, that disfigured him." The mission built a separate shelter for him and his family and cared for them until his death in 1939. Before his death he asked to be baptized, as did his wife after his death and before she died of tuberculosis. While in the hospital she asked that the priest take charge of their children, raising them as Catholics. They died in 1942 during the measles and pneumonia epidemic that devastated Fort George.[70] There are many other accounts of the devotion of Sister Sainte-Rolande until she left Fort George in 1945. There are no other reports, though, of other conversions.

Not to be outdone, the Anglicans were anxious to compete in medical services to the Crees in 1931,[71] a year after the Catholic hospital opened, despite the fact they had been in Fort George for seventy-seven years. They had requested from the Missionary Society an operating table, beds, etcetera for two wards of two beds each, but Archdeacon A. L. Fleming[IX] undertook further enquiries in the summer of 1931. He recommended that they open not a day school and a hospital but a residential school with a small hospital attached.[72] By 1940, and probably some years earlier, the Anglican hospital was established. An Anglican residential school, St Phillips, was opened in 1933,[73] which might well suggest the hospital was also operational by then. This "petit hôpital anglican" did close its doors in 1946 when the federal government's nursing station was built in Fort George at a cost of $60,000. This nursing station was part of the efforts of the new Department of National Health and Welfare but it did not measure up to the Catholic hospital, as Paul-Emile points out, lacking an operating room, a radiology service, and housing only four adults and three children.[74]

Within several years, Bishop Belleau managed to convince Albini Paquette, the minister of health in the Quebec government, to subsidize a new and larger Catholic hospital at Fort George. Belleau argued that the existing hospital was small and always filled with Indians, while it was the only Catholic hospital on the coast to serve the increasing number of prospectors, surveyors, pilots, scientists, and tourists. He must have been thinking of what had transpired when the federal nursing station was being built at Fort George in 1946. Then, there were in the crew eleven French Canadians. They were lodged with the others at the Anglican Mission, but on the first Sunday they discovered that the noon meal was at exactly the time as the mass, so they moved over to the Catholic mission.[75]

Construction began in July 1949, using, some of the materials from a mining operation located sixty miles south of Moosonee. The two-storey Hospital Sainte-Thérèse de l'Enfant-Jesus was completed in the fall of 1950 and its description in Sister Paul-Emile's history bursts with pride: able to house twenty patients, a well-lit operating room, a radiology room, nursery, two kitchenettes, running hot and cold water in each room, pharmacy. Her prose is also gloating when she points out that in the year, September 1950 to 1951, 113 patients were hospitalized there. On one day, 12 September 1951, nurse Sister Marie-Elmire had eleven patients in her care while her counterpart at the federal nursing station had one, prompting Paul-Emile to suggest that the preferences of the Crees had not changed since the early 1920s.[76] The Catholic Hospital was transferred to the charge of the Department of Indian Affairs in 1964[77] and in 1970 the province built a new hospital with the cooperation of the federal government.[78] Similarly, when the Catholics set up a mission at Rupert House in 1943, the Crees there frequently made use of their medical services, though the expertise there was no different to that found amongst other whites in the community, except that the senior priest was the only amateur dentist in the community.[79] The Catholics however, welcomed people at the mission for most of the day and children were provided with picture magazines and games.

A nursing station was not built at Rupert House until the early 1950s. People at the other posts, when they wanted to avail themselves of Western medicines, had to continue to rely on the services of the missionaries and the Hudson's Bay Company manager, as at Old Factory in 1956.[80] The kinds of ailments treated at the post were itemized for one day by the manager at Kanaaupscow: heart trouble, badly frozen arm and toe, worms, toothache.[81] Again, it cannot be said enough times that all the medical reports point to the fact that bad living conditions were at the root of the poor health of the Crees. Interviewed by Rolf Knight in 1961 at Rupert House, Nurse Lucas reported that the biggest problem was pulmonary diseases due to inadequate clothing and shelter.[82]

The federal government began delivering medical services to the Crees on the coast in the late 1920s by means of the Hudson's Bay Company's supply ship. The ship carried the Indian agent and doctor (same person) and sometimes an RCMP constable from the detachment at Moose Factory. The constable performed medical tasks in addition to his other obligations. For example, in 1931, the Moose Factory journal indicates that at Fort George, Dr Hamilton interviewed the Cree population while Constable E.S. Covell did the vaccinating.[83] That year they also visited the communities of Eastmain and Great Whale River. They may well have been responding to an outbreak of smallpox at Moose Factory earlier that year and perhaps the concern that the forthcoming rail line to Moose Factory would expose the James Bay people to more communicable diseases.[x] This health survey resulted in a report in 1931 which indicated that the people on the east side of James Bay had less incidences of tuberculosis than on the west side, probably due to the east side being higher, sandier, and hence drier. The greater "intermixture" of white blood on the east coast was also given as another factor.[84]

In the mid-1940s, nevertheless, tuberculosis was serious enough and the worse social-economic conditions became, the more widespread the disease. The government intervened, no doubt out of humanitarian reasons, but one cannot ignore the threat to the larger Canadian population posed by this highly contagious disease.[85] People with severe cases of TB were sent often to sanatoriums in the south. Richard Wills, in Great Whale River in 1969, learned that "roughly one-fifth of the Indian population have been hospitalized in the south with tuberculosis for an average of at least a year and a half."[86] Gathering data at Rupert House in 1961, Rolf Knight learned that Willie Wiestechee, at age eleven was sent to Hamilton in 1944 and stayed there for five years. Louis Whiskeychan was sent to the sanatorium in Windsor and he stayed there for twelve years, having been taken out when he was six years old. When Rolf Knight met him he was in the process of relearning Cree. Another member of the Whiskeychan family also was sent to the Toronto sanatorium for three years, and these three mini-anecdotes are but the tip of the iceberg.[87]

In the 1940s the annual visits in the summer included x-rays for tuberculosis, the equipment being carried on board ship. In the Arctic it was the supply ship, the *Nascopie*, that served this purpose, although the *Bayeskimo* and the *Bayrupert* also were used.[XI] After the wreck of the *Nascopie* in 1947 a new ship, the *C.D. Howe*, was commissioned to take its place.[88] For the James Bay coast, the boat used was the *Charles Stewart*, a much smaller boat referred to as the "doctor's boat."[89] These annual health trips along the coast also x-rayed the population until 1954, when the Department of National Health began using TB patch tests.[90] In 1947 another change in health delivery to the Crees was made. The role of Indian agent and medical doctor became separate positions, a function of the newly organized Department of National Health and Welfare which in the future would take responsibility for Indian and Inuit health services.[91]

For those Crees living closer to white settlement, health services were provided in the late 1930s via a flying doctor service. They carried out medical examinations at these posts, visiting camps by canoe[92] but in case of a medical emergency the doctors also flew in to take out the patient. For those who did not trade in the summer at any of the coastal posts or Waswanipi and Mistassini (such as Nichikun or Nemiskau people) they simply did not ever see a doctor but relied on their own healing remedies or those of the whites around them. The Crees living in the southern settlements began to receive treatment at Chibougamau when the hospital was established there in the early 1960s.

Tuberculosis became the illness on which the government health reports most focus[XII] but one can imagine that the communities suffered from the usual communicable diseases, some years being worse than others. Not only did German measles hit Waswanipi in 1935 but it spread through Mistassini in 1939 and was said to have been brought in by Peter Matoosh returning from Pointe Bleue.[93] A serious epidemic of measles, brought by a Cree man from Moose Factory, hit Great Whale River in the winter of 1956–7 and at least six died there and up the coast.[94] In 1946 the RCMP reports indicate an influenza epidemic swept the entire coastline of Quebec and a quarantine had to be set up at Old Factory in 1951 because of an outbreak of scarlet fever.[95] That year, also, the nurse at Waswanipi suggested the village be quarantined when a measles epidemic hit the community.[96] Furthermore, malnutrition was always a serious problem which made the diseases more deadly.

A 1949 study of the health of James Bay Indians, conducted for the eastern region only at Rupert House, commented on the high incidence of both pulmonary and extra-pulmonary tuberculosis as well as dental caries. By comparing Rupert House with Attawapiskat, a more economically depressed community on the west side of James Bay, the medical team concluded that raising the economic level alone would not necessarily improve the health conditions. It proposed health and nutrition programs to be organized through the new Indian services hospital at Moose Factory. Other remedies it proposed were the greater use of local foods and the installation at Rupert House of a deep-freeze unit to improve preservation of seasonal foods. Adding vitamins and minerals to the flour and powdered milk and the free distribution of cod liver oil and vitaminized biscuits to the children in the summer school were other solutions recommended.[97] Another health study, this one focusing primarily on tuberculosis, was conducted in the summer of 1950 and covered both coasts. On the east side of James Bay the survey team held clinics at Rupert House, Eastmain, Old Factory, Fort George, Great Whale River, and Nemiskau. Those found to be sick were evacuated to hospitals in the south. The Rupert House population was found to have the lowest incidence of tuberculosis, 3.4 percent compared to 6.3 percent at Eastmain and 4.5 percent and 4.7 percent respectively at Old Factory and Fort George. The white population in Ontario had a rate of 0.15 percent.[98] The incidence and severity of the disease was "staggering."[99] Inland was much the same. A geologist for the Geological Survey through Mistassini at the time remarked that tuberculosis was common.[100] Three years earlier only one person with a positive case of tuberculosis was left in the community; all others were sent out to be hospitalized. It was the serious problem of TB at Mistassini that motivated the government to build a log nursing station there in 1946, consisting of a nurse's residence, a dispensary, and a storage building.[101]

Another finding of the 1949 study based on a comparison carried out amongst 680 people at Fort George, was that the Inlanders were prosperous and healthy while the smaller group of Coasters staying near the post had a lower standard of health. All studies recommended that attention be paid to aiding people to hunt their own food. As Dr Bertram H. Harper, the superintendent of health services for the James Bay area, wrote in 1951, "those [people] living off country food are far healthier and less prone to disease, especially pulmonary and other forms of tuberculosis than those who live around the Posts on a diet of flour, sugar and tea."[102] One example, from the Mistassini region, of the variety of game on which the Crees subsisted was compiled in 1953–4 by Edward S. Rogers from his observation of the Alfie Matoush hunting group composed of thirteen individuals (see Appendix 7).

In addition to the medical neglect, Native Peoples were the victims of a striking lack of sensitivity to cultural differences. Such awareness was not a part of the approach to health care in the 1940s or 1950s or even much later. An example stems from the 1950s and without a doubt many more examples could be imagined, even today. The Inuit and Crees were historic enemies and yet the medical personnel at the hospital in Moose Factory did not consider the psychological trauma sick people would suffer when placed in the same hospital room as their arch enemies. While working in Great Whale River, the anthropologist Asen Balikci heard a number of searing complaints from Inuit that this was done. Johanassie Crow expressed it this way: "Being taken away from home is almost as bad as death ... At Moose Factory there are a great many Indians and they're not kind to the Eskimo. They tease the Eskimo and push them around. The nurses and doctors either don't know about it or they don't care."[103]

What was to be done in James Bay? The 1949 medical report recommended that the most immediate need for the James Bay communities was the "provision of adequate local health and medical services." Relying on the dispensary of the Hudson's Bay Company did not by any standards satisfy what was meant by "adequate local health and medical services." Clearly, the link between eating healthy food was understood to underlie good health. The curative side of medical services was initiated in the late 1940s and 1950s by providing minimal health services in the form of nursing stations or access to local hospitals. Surely, though, the preventive side of medicine was sorely lacking in not helping the Crees to maintain a bush life with greater access to country food. This resulted in inadequate diets and living conditions, both of which breed poor health. Large families also contributed to the impoverishment of the Indians. Compared to the southern Canadian population, the ratio of children to adults in an Indian community in Quebec was higher, with one adult supporting 1.31 dependants less than fifteen years of age compared to a factor of 1 for a southern Canadian male.[104] With insufficient resources, the Crees could not sustain adequately the physical needs of the population.

By the 1960s, health services to the communities had improved with the establishment of a nursing station in each community and improved communication. The company magazine reported in 1953 that their radio at Moose Factory was in contact with all the posts in James Bay twice a day and that "a great part of the traffic is messages to or from the Moose Factory Indian Hospital."[105] Each nursing station was manned by two nurses; in addition to providing normal medical services, it was the first stop for emergency cases whether they occurred in town or in the bush. The nurse would contact the doctor by radiophone and with a tentative diagnosis the medical personnel would decide whether the patient had to be flown out to the hospital or could be cared for at the nursing station. Salisbury points out that understandably the Cree patients would prefer to remain in the village close to family and friends. Cases were also referred to southern hospitals, where the hardship of loneliness and fear was greater. Medical care provided at the local clinic had to be short-term as the nursing stations were furnished only with one or two beds. The nurses, often French-speaking, did not speak Cree; therefore all nurse-patient or doctor-patient discussions had to pass through a bilingual Cree-English person. Alternatively, a unilingual Cree person could not understand when their case was being discussed. Even into the 1960s, there was no role for the Cree community in making decisions about its health. The organization and planning of the services were in the hands of the white personnel at the Department of National Health and Welfare. Although Salisbury describes a network of health services that seemed to be relatively well funded and ought to have provided reasonably good care, its efficacy was mitigated by the system of communication. The radiophone was an archaic system requiring, as this writer can attest, a switching from "transmit" to "receive" each time the party said "over," as well as frequent poor reception and difficulty in contacting the main exchange in Alma, Quebec, to make outside calls.[106] As poor as this system was, radio instructions from the doctor at Moose Factory was the only means of obtaining medical help. As for plane transportation, woe the individual who took ill or had a serious accident during the six weeks of freeze-up and the six weeks of thaw in the late spring. There were no runways into the coastal communities, nor were there roads.[XIII] The inadequate means of communication were decisions made in the south by government officials and one can see its effect on health care, as well-intentioned and funded as it was.

EMPLOYMENT

The Crees knew there was food in the bush but a host of factors drew them to live closer to the posts. The uncertainty of life in the bush, especially after the lean years of the 1930s, would weigh heavily in favour of remaining near the post on the chance that money could be earned or the missionary or trader might help out in desperate times. This uncertainty was also overcome if a hunter had access to wage employment. Thus, working for wages was preferred by many over a winter of hunting and trapping. Sometimes there was little employment. In the 1940s and 1950s, for example, the Hudson's Bay Company engaged few staff; otherwise there were only several pockets in which extraordinary employment could be found.^XIV Few whites resided at the posts, indicating there was little Canadian interest in Cree lands. Mistassini, one of the most southerly posts had a half-dozen whites living there in 1948 – the Hudson's Bay Company manager and a small staff at the Department of Transport's meteorological station located at Nichikun.[107] This population swelled for a brief period in the summer with the visit of the Indian agent, the doctor, the nurse, and the Anglican missionary. Over the next two decades wage opportunities would increase, creating tensions for the Crees between retaining their bush life or integrating into the industrial sector. This next section takes us through the Crees' options and some of the complications that accompanied them in the postwar years to 1970.

Great Whale River, located the farthest north of the posts serving Cree trappers, would be one of the last venues, one would think, where the southern interests would provide some form of employment. It was the Cold War that prompted the development of the Mid-Canada Defence Line,^XV a line of radar installations that Canada constructed throughout its mid-north in the 1950s.[108] In Quebec, this line ran from Great Whale River to Schefferville. Construction and services provided some few jobs for two years, from 1955 to 1957. Hunters at both Fort George and Great Whale River worked on an airstrip at Great Whale in 1955 and also at Cape Jones on a radar installation.[109] People who had been trapping out of the post at Richmond Gulf moved down to Great Whale River to take advantage of the wage labour. According to one company report, few Coasters were trapping in 1958, as they "were still living on the proceeds of last year's defence work and are reluctant to trap while they are still solvent."[110] These comments mask the difficulty the Crees had in obtaining this defence work. The anthropologist Richard Wills, while conducting a study there in 1964 on Cree economic perceptions, reported that initially Inuit workers were favoured over Cree ones but eventually the Crees, too, were hired. According to one of his informants, Samson G., "everyone was working then; some for three years, some for only one." The hunters did go back to the land but in 1961 ten men of the approximately fifty-two Cree hunters at Great Whale River were hired to build the nursing stations which opened in 1962.[111]

With radar stations on their hunting lands, Great Whale River hunters had an advantage over Crees from other bands in plotting a winter's hunting and trapping strategy. Store food was left at each of the radar sites for use of the crews. These sites were never locked. For the most part, the white crews, when on site, shared their food with passing hunters. At unmanned sites, Crees helped themselves and were reported to "take only enough food at a time for a meal." Furthermore, the crews knew when Cree hunters had used their food supplies; they left the plates on the table.[112]

195 Pale Versions of Southern Institutions

If gross disparity in income and lifestyle is one of the defining characteristics of colonialism and breeds discontent and paralysis, the disparity the Native Peoples encountered at Great Whale River surely qualifies as this type of colonialism or the enclave economy Norman Chance described for the region.[113] Once the Mid-Canada line was completed, more than two hundred Euro-Canadians moved into the Great Whale River area. Prior to 1955 there were only a half-dozen or so whites in the community: the company manager, a clerk, the radio operator, and the Anglican missionary, with or without wives.[114] A larger percentage of the Inuit population (15 percent compared to 6 percent Crees) were living in frame houses built by the Department of Northern Affairs, whereas the Crees were living in wood-frame tents. Although the Cree population was half the size of the Inuit one in 1964, one would not think of that when looking out over the sixty-six Inuit houses compared to the Crees' sixteen houses. At the same time the Crees were receiving $10 for a beaver pelt while prices for sealskins (the pelts traded by the Inuit) were soaring from $15 to $28 in 1964. There was disparity in the amount of relief payments as well, because of the differences in policies between Northern Affairs and Indian Affairs. Inuit were given not only food but ammunition, fuel, and clothing; relief for the Crees was only food.[115] Interestingly, data gathered in 1949–50 found the Inuit to be poorer than the Crees. This economic disparity was reinforced by the company as the Inuit received in credit $25 or $40 to the Crees' receipt of $300 and $400 in debts.[116]

The Euro-Canadian population at the base all held jobs, mostly high-paying, and all lived in comfortable, well-furnished quarters supplied with running water and electricity. By contrast the Indian and Inuit homes had none of these services and the houses were very simple. Furthermore, the base was off-limits to the Native Peoples; only five Cree men worked there.[117] Contact was possible with the fifty or so other Euro-Canadians working in Great Whale River,[XVI] but one assumes that the caste system Walker described for the 1950s in the community continued into the 1960s, as Preston found at Rupert House in those years.[118]

It is one of the themes of this study that the Crees fell into the grip of colonialism more through government intransigence, short-sightedness, or ineptness than because of their involvement in the eighteenth- and nineteenth-century fur trade. Great Whale River offers several illustrations of this ineptness. When the defence operation began there in 1955, presumably after several years of discussion and planning, no thought was given to the Native Peoples there. A public school was opened only in 1958.[119]

Another classic example was played out in Great Whale River in the 1960s. The Department of Indians Affairs, perhaps in compensation for the Crees' lost trapping incomes because of the disturbance to the wildlife caused by the construction of the Mid-Canada Line and the noise and oil pollution of the increased use of airplanes and motor boats,[120] decided to provide the people of Great Whale with an alternate source of revenue. They initiated a handicraft program in Great Whale River. Begun in 1961, it expanded slowly, reaching a peak in the summer of 1963, but was terminated in early 1964. The short period of success centred around the carving of wooden animals such as beaver, otter, and mink that were given a natural finish on wood with pronounced grain. The carvings were marketed through a cooperative[XVII] run by the Department of Northern Affairs and the project was subsidized by Indian Affairs to the amount of $32,000. The carvings were exhibited in the south at shows and fairs. Many individuals worked on carving, some combining it with trapping, others abandoned trapping to carve. The highest price paid by the cooperative for a carving was $2.50. When they sold their carvings to the cooperative, some individuals could accumulate enough money to purchase outboard motors or guns. Soon, however, businessmen in the south began manufacturing similar animal carvings on a tracer lathe and flooded the market with these goods at half the price. The Great Whale carvings ended up in a warehouse in the south.[121]

If this had been an isolated incident of Indian Affairs officials misjudging the market, they could be forgiven for drawing the Crees away from trapping and raising their hopes about their future prospects; the growing success in the south of Inuit soapstone carvings must have given Indian Affairs officials some encouragement. Unfortunately this carving program did not receive sufficient financial support from the department to establish a unique place in the market, as was done for the Inuit carvings.

This was not an isolated make-work project; in fact Indian Affairs went on to establish in the north many more such futile projects of their own or sponsored others through the federal departments of Manpower and Regional Economic Expansion (DREE). As Buckley caustically charges, "The projects were short term and labour intensive ... But benefits of a more lasting nature did not flow despite the millions that were spent, while individuals and communities experienced damage of various kinds: for example, the fostering of a short-term outlook and the belief that the people would be taken care of ... But the greatest harm lay in the high levels of frustration imposed on a people which, like anybody else, wanted jobs that lasted and paid a decent wage."[122] None of this activity addressed the basic need to improve employability and put pressure on private companies to train and hire Indian people.[XVIII]

The south only became really interested in Cree lands with the recognition of the potential for the discovery of gold and other minerals in the southern portion of the territory. By 1906 mining was taking place in the Chibougamau Lake region. Prospectors Joseph Obalski (formerly inspector of mines) and Peter Mackenzie (formerly fur trader) teamed up to begin drilling operations but not before they had transported fifty-two tons of material and provisions, with a team of twenty-eight men and thirty-two dogs, using the old Indian route. By 1909 the government had built a winter road from St Felicien to Chibougamau, shortening the old route by nearly twenty miles. The government rejected the idea of building a railway to Chibougamau, so mining activity waned.[123]

Once the CNR rail line pushed through to Senneterre in 1914 and to St Felicien in 1917, geologists, prospectors, and surveyors began to arrive in the Waswanipi area; by the late 1920s the Obalski mine at Cache Lake was opened.[124] In 1934 the discovery of gold south of Amos and east of Noranda gave rise to the towns of Val d'Or and Amos.[125] The Hudson's Bay Company records, naturally, do not give full details of Cree involvement in activities other than the fur trade, but from them we do learn that Crees were involved in a number of aspects of the mineral exploration. In the earlier Chibougamau Lake mining, William Couchees, on whose hunting lands the iron ore was mined, had discovered a rock with the ore and shown it to a white man who promised him a good job in return, which his daughter, Mary-Ann Bosum, said he never got.[126] In 1932 some unnamed Cree hunters found some minerals which were to be looked over by others, including T. Dickson, a Cree, flown out from Waswanipi for that purpose, and in 1936 R. Cooper brought in some samples.[127] Like the gold finds in the Yukon,[128] many of the gold and iron finds in this region were undoubtedly made by the Crees. According to the journals, 1933 was a particularly active year of exploration; many Crees were hired by prospectors, presumably as guides. Private companies such as the Engineers Exploration Company were in the area, as well as parties of the Geological Survey of Canada.[129]

Mining activity returned to the Chibougamau Lake area in the mid-1930s, and the Mistassini and Lake Chibougamau Crees were hired by the prospectors. Presumably some Crees were also hired when RCAF planes landed and stayed about a month to photograph the countryside between Mistassini and Chibougamau.[130] In addition to guiding, Cree hunters could also earn money by supplying the mining camps with meat in the winter. Just how many were employed in the summer months is impossible to determine, but at least the Crees living in the Mistassini-Waswanipi region had alternatives to trapping and could supplement their income from the sale of furs. Some chose to leave trapping altogether, as Jefferys at Mistassini wrote in his journal. "One of the best hands John Mark is going to try and get a job at Dons Lake ... made a poor hunt last winter and is sort of fed up with trapping."[131]

John Mark was the exception. Most Cree hunters managed a trapping economy in the winter and wage labour in the summer months. Reading the Mistassini and Waswanipi records for the 1930s is quite unlike the reading of the journals of other posts. These were busy, relatively prosperous times for these Crees. Not only did they have ways of supplementing their income but they also had the good fortune to have moose and bear on their lands. No doubt it is telling that in 1937 the manager at Waswanipi could report that he only had $175 of debt out.[132] As another indication of prosperity, Waswanipi Chief Shaganash had organized a number of men to cut logs, his intention being to make board floors for all the Indian camps.[133] This increased economic life also attracted a number of free traders to the area and one can imagine the Crees benefiting from this keen competition, even though they preferred the Hudson's Bay Company because the independent traders "gave no credit and had only limited supplies."[134]

With the influx of prospectors, fire rangers, and others, life at the post took on enhanced social activity. Some of the outsiders hosted dances while the Geological Survey party, at Waswanipi for a week in 1935, held a dance practically every night. Their cook, George Best, served as caller and evidently kept fun at a high level.[135] Success in hunting moose and bear also enhanced the Crees' social and religious life. Thus, a feast involving speeches and a dance was held on 20 June 1932 to mark the killing of a bear and ten days later the killing of a moose resulted in another feast.[136]

The mining activities in the Lake Chibougamau area strengthened the unity of the hunters whose lands were in the region. In 1929 the Hudson's Bay Company transformed the supply post it had maintained at Lake Chibougamau into a fur-trade post, enabling the hunters to congregate there instead of travelling to several of the other posts. However, the Second World War brought a decline in mining activity, so the company closed the post in 1942.[137] Indian Affairs officials encouraged the Chibougamau band to take their trade to Mistassini and summer there, just as they had encouraged the Crees at Neoskweskau and Nichikun when those posts were closed in 1940 and 1943.[xix] "Encouragement" is the term used by the Reverend Scanlon but does not really convey how Indian Affairs tried to influence the Crees to use Mistassini as their base.[138] After the closure of the post, the Chibougamau Crees settled at Doré Lake.

This region came to life again between 1947 and 1950 when the Quebec government constructed a road from St Felicien through the bush to Chibougamau. For the Mistassini people the road reduced the cost of transportation of imported goods, road transport being cheaper than air. Additional stimulus was given in 1955 when a railway was built to connect this region to the smelter at Noranda.[139]

When copper was discovered on the Lake Doré site in 1951, the Cree settlement moved across the lake to a low swampy point. In 1966 there were about a dozen houses in the village as well as a community hall called Beaver House, built by an international group of young people with $1,700 coming from Canada's Centennial Commission. However, in 1970 officials from Indian Affairs told the Crees that with reduced numbers (about 128 people) they could not have their own reserve and would only receive financial assistance and housing if living in Mistassini. They were also told the water was unfit to drink. Finally, they were told the Campbell mine had discovered ore on their hunting lands and had staked out the land. The housing and Beaver Hall were destroyed in 1974, and the Doré Lake people dispersed. Those who went to Mistassini found the promises hollow and a number left.[140]

Despite the government's attempt to destroy their sense of themselves as the Chibougamau band, they preserved their identity and fought for recognition by the Department of Indian Affairs, which was only granted in 1992.[141] Their newly constructed village is situated on Lake Opemiska; in 1999 it was home to 650 individuals.[142] This recognition is a limited one; so far the Ouje-Bougoumou people have not been granted the same land entitlements as the other Cree bands. Registered as members of the Mistassini band in the 1975 signing of the James Bay Agreement, lands were granted to them then. Thus, it is awaiting an internal Cree settlement before Quebec recognizes the lands of the Ouje-Bougoumou band.[143]

The decision not to summer at Mistassini was a costly one for the Crees of Chibougamau, as those who wished to hunt were forced to take taxis to Mistassini some sixty miles away to outfit themselves. The stores in the town of Chibougamau did not stock trapping equipment or provide trappers with credit.[144] The road from Chibougamau to Mistassini was partially completed in 1963; the company then began moving freight in by truck to Perche River and from there took it by canoe the remaining thirteen miles to the Mistassini store. The road was being pushed through to tap the mineral reserves at Lake Albanel, north of Mistassini.[145]

It was only in 1948 that the beaver lands of the Mistassini and Waswanipi became protected as the Mistassini Preserve. The viability of the post was obviously affected. In 1955 the company proposed to

Indian Affairs that they would rebuild the Waswanipi post closer to the highway and railway line as they considered it to have always been an inaccessible post to which it was difficult and expensive to deliver freight.[146] Larivière, the Indian agent, objected to the relocation of the post, arguing that if the store was moved, the Indians would follow and settle nearby "which will destroy these Indians, which means over a period of a few years, the burden will be on the Department."[147] A new store was erected at the same site in 1959,[148] but by the winter of 1964 the company manager, Bob McLeish, declared that the future of the store was not very promising; many of the Indians had moved to Matagami, Miquelon, or other places where work was available. In their summer 1965 magazine the company proclaimed that "the history of Waswanipi as an Indian settlement and trading post appears to be coming to an end ... Now only two or three families are left at Waswanipi and we will have to close up this summer."[149] The McGill Cree Project gave a different version, saying it was the closing of the post by the company in 1963 that forced the entire population of four hundred to move off their reserve.[150] The people attached themselves to three towns along the Amos-Chibougamau Road – Matagami, Waswanipi River, and Miquelon – where the men moved around looking for casual labour and the women and children stayed in squatter settlements devoid of any amenities and services.[151]

Despite Crees living on the outskirts of new mining towns, Scanlon, the Anglican minister in Chapais from 1957 to 1965, reports that not much attention was paid them and "hardly ever were they given jobs at the mines ... they could only find work in the bush camps or on road gangs."[152] Even in the summer period, unemployment rates in the 1960s for Mistassini and Waswanipi Crees were estimated at about 50 percent.[153] The minister's overall assessment was that "the Indian's lot was a poor one when he came into contact with white society."[154] This contact also enabled the Crees to discover that whites, doing the same work as they were, received higher wages. For pulp-cutting, a white cutter could earn $20 to $30 per day, while a Cree cutter earned about $10, including the labour of his family. This was due partly because the Crees missed more days of work, but it was mainly the result of the swampy and sparsely wooded areas they were assigned. In all, the Crees provided the mines and forestry companies with a cheap labour force.[155] In addition to their impoverished condition, the southern-based Crees suffered another great blow to their sense of well-being. Even on their hunting lands they found themselves in enclaves, surrounded by rapidly growing industrial towns. The disparity in their lifestyles must have been very discouraging, especially since the riches were being drawn from *their* land and many Crees had to vacate their

Pale Versions of Southern Institutions

campsites and abandon cemeteries which were located in the midst of the blast area.[156] "The Indian became a trespasser on his own land," Scanlon commented.[157]

The mining activity that started up again after the war was facilitated by the gravel road and railway from St Felicien to Chibougamau. Base metals were mined at Matagami, creating a town of two thousand.[158] In the Chibougamau area, to provide services for the mine employees, the Quebec government laid out a townsite on the west side of Gilman Lake in 1950 and sold commercial lots for over $4,000. By 1970 the population of Chibougamau had grown to ten thousand and continued to increase.[159] However, the Crees were left out of the prosperity that came from the mining of their land, which had been simply appropriated. Although living either in or near the town of Chibougamau, the Mistassini Crees were excluded from the social services offered there and, in fact, had to work through the distant Indian Affairs offices either in Amos or Pointe Bleue.[160] Without recounting all the forms of discrimination they endured in the towns, perhaps one will suffice: they were required to sit on one side of the tavern.[161]

Despite the limited opportunities and the decline in wage labour as the mines became developed, the Crees from Waswanipi and Mistassini always had greater wage-earning opportunities than Crees in the coastal settlements. Although the industrial work in which they engaged in the 1950s and 1960s – pulp cutting, staking, freighting – was generally carried out in all-Cree work groups, ultimately the work was directed by a white boss. The jobs the Crees did were all unskilled and they were not offered training for anything else.[162] Furthermore, this casual work lasted from only a few days to a few weeks and involved long periods waiting around in or near white urban centres. This was in sharp contrast to the hunting and trapping which required "preparation and commitment, usually for a whole season and, at least on the part of the leader of a hunting group, a large degree of entrepreneurship and control over work organization and pace."[163] Nevertheless, the ready cash from wage work attracted the men, so that in 1967 Glen Speers, the post manager making the rounds to the Crees' camps by air between January and March, reported that he visited a reduced number of camps. Furthermore, "with the school now in operation on the Reserve and the construction of several more houses, a substantial number of Indians will be staying out this winter rather than trapping inland."[164]

Their proximity to the south also drew the Crees into the commercial fishery that had begun in the early 1920s, first at Bell River, then at Lake Waswanipi, and later at Gull Lake. All these enterprises had collapsed by October 1931 when the Commercial Fisheries Company went bankrupt.¹⁶⁵ Commercial fishing was reintroduced in 1958–9 by Indian Affairs, including a fish-processing plant at Matagami. It was not a great success, employing very few men despite the large sums of money invested by the government. Ignatius LaRusic found in 1966 that there were more supervisory personnel than teams of fishermen operating, and wages were extremely low, usually less than $5 per day. By contrast, Cree men working on line-cutting were paid $20 per day for staking mining claims and had their food supplied. Seeing figures such as this prompted LaRusic to query whether, given the shortage of protein in the summer diet and its high cost, it was not foolhardy to export the fish protein to the south to provide money to buy back high-priced protein in cans, especially when the former is good bush food.¹⁶⁶ This dilemma was moot: in September 1970 the fish plant at Matagami closed suddenly in the midst of the fishing season. Unacceptably high levels of mercury were found in the fish of Lakes Matagami, Waswanipi, and Gull.¹⁶⁷

This development of towns and industry, along with the infrastructure of roads and rail lines in the midst of the hunting lands of the Crees, drew large numbers from the hunting communities of Mistassini and Waswanipi. However, despite its low monetary returns, a high percentage of Crees from these two regions maintained a hand in hunting and trapping (see Appendix 6, table 3). This prompted the company district manager to comment: "In spite of all this modernization, the Mistassini Indians' main occupation is still trapping."¹⁶⁸ It was their way of life. Bally Husky talked of how the Crees were needed to cut lines and stake.ˣˣ "I went to work for them and earned a bit of money. In winter, I stopped following them. I went back into the bush to hunt."¹⁶⁹ The Waswanipi band managed to maintain its integrity despite ten years or more of being scattered, impoverished, and denied any government social services. In addition, they were treated like a political football. The federal government refused to provide services unless the Crees were living on federal land and Quebec was reluctant to transfer the lands for a new reserve close to the highway.¹⁷⁰ That the Waswanipi Crees did not have to wait as long as the Mistassini Crees for an officially designated reserve was due to the requirements spelled out in the James Bay and Northern Agreement. Building began on their new town site in 1976, located twenty miles upstream from their old post.¹⁷¹

A preferred form of work was guiding, drawing as it did on bush skills. It was less disruptive to family life and provided the families with country food. However, the rate of participation of Crees in guiding was only half as high as Indian guides in Ontario.¹⁷² Only in Mistassini were many men employed in the tourist industry. In the summer of

1967 thirty-one men or (20 percent) were guides while at Waswanipi the number was only four.[173] A number of the tourist camps were owned by the Quebec government or the Department of Indian Affairs, which sold each camp to individual Crees in the 1970s and provided grant money to improve the facilities. The guides hired by the camp owners were paid $10 to $15 per day in 1968.[174] Although such money-earning activities complemented the Crees' lifestyle, important issues were raised in the early 1960s. Half of all the moose killed in the Waswanipi area were killed by white sportsmen. Thus, although small numbers of Crees were earning money as guides, they were contributing to the risk of depleting the moose numbers. Similarly, Cree fishermen were encouraged to stop fishing to permit the white fishermen to catch trophies, leading to the question whether the income from guiding compensated for loss of subsistence food.

The purchase of food imported from the south was expensive, much of it as a result of freighting charges. Fifty pounds of flour at Fort George cost $7 while ten pounds cost $1.19 in Montreal in 1972; a dozen fresh eggs at Fort George were $1.15 and 58 cents at Montreal in 1968, while two pounds of chicken legs were $2.30 in the north and 69 cents a pound in the south.[175] Depending on location and type of transport, prices varied within James Bay at the Hudson's Bay Company stores and some commodities such as flour, were subsidized by the company.[176] Nevertheless they were always higher than consumers in the south paid while Cree incomes were considerably lower.

Work was different in the coastal settlements, except for the military installation at Great Whale River and some mining activity there in the early 1960s. The employment opportunities were limited to more traditionally-based work. Thus the canoe factory, established in 1923 by Watt at Rupert House as a Hudson's Bay Company enterprise, continued to be a source of revenue for about a half-dozen skilled canoe-builders in the summer months in the 1940s. The canoes were made of local cedar and by 1950 were being built to hold motors.[177] Despite the fact that in 1947 not one of these freight canoes was built due to the inability to obtain the necessary materials, it was still a source of "semi-permanent" work there in 1967.[178] In 1946 twenty canoes were built, but previously as many as seventy-five canoes had been constructed in one year. Since its inception the canoe factory had produced about nine hundred canoes. The salary paid in 1923 was $30 per month and had increased to about $20 per week in the 1940s.[179] Evidently in the late 1950s the company still considered it a success; its magazine mentioned a sizable order for 23-foot canoes, though five sizes were built and the factory only operated in the summer as the shed was not heated. The foreman at the time was Walter Blackned. Working with two gangs, they could turn out two canoes a week, selling from $138 to $375 and shipped as far away as to British Columbia.[180] By 1967 the Hudson's Bay Company was hoping to convince the Department of Indian Affairs or the provincial government to take over the operation. It was losing money[XXI] but it had also dawned on company officials that they were not paying minimum wages, workmen's compensation, unemployment insurance, and so on. They worried they could find themselves in trouble for contravening the Quebec laws despite the fact that "We recognize that we are morally right, we are doing a good thing for the Indians."[181]

Other minor economic activities were based on services to the white population, such as the supply of firewood, or the domestic work of a few young women, or occasional guiding.[182] In 1948 C.S. MacLean of Kentucky was inspired by the beauty of the Rupert House region and its size of fish to build a camp on Little Middleboro Island at the mouth of the Nottoway River, employing four Crees "who were very good carpenters."[183] It remained a small source of employment thereafter, as did several other goose camps. At each of the posts, hunters provided the resident population with geese and fish; the Anglican Mission at Fort George in 1948 spent about $7,900 on country provisions.[184] In 1959 Indian Affairs decided to test the waters regarding the feasibility of commercial fishing along the coast and rivers of James Bay. A project at Seal River focused on char fishing but failed because the "equipment supplied was inadequate." Nevertheless, the dossier ends with the federal government seeking permission of the Quebec government for a commercial char fishery north of Cape Jones.[185]

EXPANSION OF FACILITIES AT RUPERT HOUSE

The 1940s saw a surge in construction as the government began building schools, houses, and nursing stations in all the communities and a freezer facility in Rupert House in 1948.[XXII] The best information for this construction boom comes from Rupert House because the anthropologist A.J. Kerr was commissioned by the federal government in 1947 to conduct an economic study there. He reported that a handful of men who had gained experience in frame construction were employed more or less regularly and were assisted periodically by other less experienced men. The demand for the skilled workers produced an increase in their wages, from two to three dollars per day. The building of public facilities such as schools and clinics in each of the communities also opened up permanent, government-paid positions as caretakers.

Not only was the government spending money in Rupert House after the war, but so were the Anglicans; they began building a new church in 1948, which Kerr saw as the last new structure to be built there for some time. The community hall project still being built in 1948 was also said to be providing a significant amount of employment for Rupert House men.[186]

The building of this hall has a story associated with it that evokes James Watt's vision for Rupert House. Before he died in 1944 he had spoken of building a community centre in Rupert House when the beaver harvest had reached a specific level, which it did about the time he died. Maud Watt returned to Rupert House in 1945 to build this centre as a memorial to her husband. The community hall was completed in 1947 at a cost of $15,000 to $20,000 which Mrs Watt had financed personally, seemingly with some material help from the Catholic Mission.[187] Once the building was nearly completed, Maud Watt asked the Crees to begin paying for it and by June 1948 well over $12,000 had been subscribed. With one or two exceptions, every hunter made an annual contribution (on average $50, usually the price of one or two beaver pelts), including hunters from Nemiskau whose hunting lands adjoined Rupert House's. The Quebec government also contributed by permitting hunters to take an extra one hundred beaver from the Rupert House sanctuary, the proceeds of which were used to purchase a billiard table. The federal government paid for a projector for the hall and the Hudson's Bay Company contributed a gas-powered generator.[188] The enthusiastic support for the hall might, in part, be attributed to the original plans for it, whereby the basement was to be made into a bunkhouse for the trappers to use on their winter trips to the post. The Crees thought of it as a fitting tribute to James Watt as he had always travelled in the bush with them "Indian style." Maud Watt reneged on this promise, which the Crees considered an ungenerous and disingenous act on her part.[189]

An undercurrent in Kerr's 1950 report on Rupert House is the subordination of the Crees to white interests in the community. It is not surprising, then, that he wonders why the Crees so wholeheartedly supported a memorial to Watt, a white man. He gives three reasons which give us some insights into his view of Cree thinking in the 1940s. First, Mrs Watt was the widow of a man who had helped them bring prosperity to Rupert House and now she needed help. Then, the community hall was perceived as something they saw as necessary and not imposed on them and which they could financially underwrite as their incomes had risen faster than their material needs. Finally, after support of the community hall had become accepted in Rupert House, the amount of each hunter's contribution became a matter of prestige and contributing less than the expected amount[XXIII] was a cause for some form of public censure.[190] For our purposes, in addition to measuring the gratitude the Crees had for James Watt, their substantial contribution to the building of the community hall is also a measure of what Kerr referred to as their prosperity in the late 1940s.

PAINT HILLS AT THE END OF THE 1950S

The Crees at Paint Hills also saw something of a construction boom. Beginning in 1953, Indian Affairs officials began a file on the community of Old Factory. They had been receiving complaints that the island on which the community was located was entirely denuded of wood and lacked drinkable water.[191] The Hudson's Bay Company had launched Old Factory as a trading camp only in 1935, with Thomas Mark in charge, and it gradually developed into a settlement, complete with a log church.[192] As the trade was provisioned from Eastmain, government officials hoped the Crees would agree to move to Eastmain, enticing them with the promise of a possible nursing station there. The Crees rejected this proposal[193] and chose instead the site of Paint Hills.[XXIV] In 1958, when one child had died of typhoid due to the unsanitary conditions, the Crees pressed for this move as soon as possible.[194] In this way, employment came to Paint Hills at the end of the 1950s when initially eleven houses were built compared to the eight permanent houses that had existed at Old Factory.[195] Later, in 1971 and 1972, new housing and a school provided construction jobs.[196]

If the posts along the coast could yield some industrial-type wage employment for the Crees, generally in construction, no such employment was available for the Crees at the inland posts of Nemiskau, Nichikun, and Neoskweskau. These posts experienced no construction boom and in fact were closed before the federal government began spending money in the communities.[XXV] Whatever wages they could earn came from the old-style employment for the Hudson's Bay Company – that is, cutting and hauling wood and summer transport.[197] The community of 160 people at Nemiskau continued, though with minimal services. In 1964 it still did not have a nursing station, although log cabins were built providing some wages for a few men; in the mid-1960s they were asked to participate in the doomed commercial fishery.[198] In 1970 the Hudson's Bay Company had closed its post there in a cost-cutting measure, although the Nemaska band had also previously heard from the provincial government that the land was to be flooded. Half the band members attached themselves to Mistassini and half to Rupert House, summering at these posts in enclaves at the outskirts[199] (for further details on wages see Appendix 6, table 1). Salisbury estimated that for these smaller communities farther away from industry or government services, roughly 80 percent of the families depended on the resources of the bush for their support.[200]

FOCUS ON GOVERNMENT IMPEDIMENTS

The Crees experienced their own Catch-22 situation long before such a predicament became popularized. Being poor and needing cash with which to buy essentials, the Crees seized whatever opportunities they could for wage employment. However, now that the government was playing an active role in the lives of the Crees, it erected obstacles and sent mixed messages to them concerning wages. Seemingly, there were two different philosophies operating in the Department of Indian Affairs and they collided with each other, to the great disadvantage of the Indians. At first, Indian Affairs appeared concerned that wage employment would take the Indians away from their hunting skills and they would lose their self sufficiency. They proposed limiting native employment in the industrial sector to three years.[xxvi] On the other hand, some eight years later the department personnel favoured assimilation, as is seen in this 1951 correspondence between H.M. Jones, superintendent of welfare service in Ottawa, and J.S. Allan, superintendent at Moose Factory. A Moose Factory Cree man and Second World War veteran by the name of Peter Wynne had been employed by the Canadian National Railways for two years but decided to quit in 1951 to return to trapping. This was disturbing to Jones for he wrote: "It is considered by the Branch to be a recessive step if any Indian well established in a permanent employment should return to the traplines as a means of livelihood."[201]

That was one half of the government's 1950s schizophrenic approach to the Indian economy. The other half had to do with denying those Indians who were employed the right to hunt, particularly ducks and geese. The game laws of Ontario in 1957 stipulated that "if an Indian has a permanent job, he is classed as a white hunter." Much of the correspondence in government circles that year had been devoted to defining what "permanent employment" meant. Finally, at a meeting at Moose Factory of representatives of Indian Affairs, Game and Fisheries, and the RCMP, by a vote of six to five, it was decided that "an Indian who is employed more than three and a half months of the year is not an Indian living off the land and is 'gainfully employed'" and hence ineligible to be classed as an Indian hunter. Like Ontario, Quebec required Indians in the province wishing to hunt ducks and geese for food to obtain a certificate attesting to their not being gainfully employed.[202]

Goose hunting in spring and fall provides a considerable amount of food for a Cree family. One of the reasons the government built a freezing plant at Rupert House in 1948 was to preserve fresh food without having to salt or dry it. Geese and ducks, along with fish and beaver meat, were the fresh foods for which the plant was built. In his report, Kerr points out that the fall goose hunt was particularly welcomed for it provided meat to eat after a summer's diet of fish. He goes further in his description of the significance of goose hunting to the Crees of Rupert House. It was not just the promise of large rewards of food that made it so attractive to the Crees and filled the air with excitement. Goose hunting season was an event that was eagerly anticipated and provided a great deal of excitement in the village. Kerr warned that "wavy [goose] hunting fever in communities such as Rupert House is a condition which a community organizer [the government] must accept."[203] Ten years later his advice was not heeded. Government officials, many of whom had had long experience in the north and should have known better, assumed that such fundamental Cree traditional activities as goose hunting could be easily abandoned in favour of living like a white man. Yet others knew that if they had to choose, many Crees would quit their jobs.[204] Such a definition of who is an Indian would have repercussions for hunting other than shooting wildfowl. In 1942 the Quebec government decided that hunting licences would be issued to any Indian, but whites or halfbreeds who applied should be refused and referred to the local provincial game warden.[205]

Finally, in providing summary comments for the 1960s about economic opportunities in the coastal communities, Richard Salisbury has noted that no longer did the Hudson's Bay Company "manage" the entire village economy. They had switched to the fur-buying business and operating village stores, food, and dry goods. Nevertheless, it still played a considerable role as one of the larger employers in the village and it controlled the variety of goods that came in on its freight barges.[206]

TRANSFER PAYMENTS

Next to income from beaver, at Rupert House the most important cash source for purchasing goods was the family allowance payments. In some other communities where income from beaver hunting was half that of Rupert House, family allowance payments probably exceeded revenue from trapping. Called "children's money" by the Crees, it was a monthly grant made by the federal government to all Canadian mothers beginning in 1944 for each child sixteen years and under. The Crees began receiving it in July 1945. All other mothers received these grants in the form of a cheque mailed to them without restrictions on their use but not the Crees or other Indians or Inuit.[XXVII] They received this monthly payment (an average of $163 a year for a family), in the form of credit at the Hudson's Bay Company, to be used against a list of approved food and clothing drawn up by Indian Affairs. Those families who were in the bush during the winter more often than not returned to the post in late spring with a large accumulation of credit only to find that the dwindling stock at the Hudson's Bay Company severely limited their choice and forced them to take goods of little value to them. The requirement that they take this accumulated credit all at once,[XXVIII] of course, was for the convenience of the post manager and to the benefit of the company; it sold goods it might not otherwise have sold.[207] Moreover, across the country, family allowance payments were used as a weapon by the government to force children into schools. As Joe Ottereyes tells us, "if parents didn't let kids go to school, then the family allowance was taken away."[208] It is unlikely the Crees would have thought to complain or demand better services, for the family allowance payment must have been very welcome to many of the Crees, particularly those not living in the vicinity of Rupert House.

Another transfer program, old age pensions, had considerable benefits for the Crees. These payments enabled the old people to stay at the post in the winter months rather than being a drain on the energies and resources of the winter hunting group.[209]

Welfare, or social assistance, became the most significant transfer payment, especially as it increased in coverage and amount beginning in the 1940s. The Crees benefited in the short term from the new outlook on social services which developed after the war. Joe Ottereyes remembers how the doctor and the Indian agent would visit the Waswanipi camps and the Indian agent would go into a tent asking what the family needed to go into the bush. The agent was told and he would present the hunter with a piece of paper for the store. A large family would get about four to five hundred pounds of flour. In a similar vein, Stewart Ottereyes commented that not many people had enough when they went hunting "before Indian Affairs came and all those things ... there was no flour then." In a later interview, Joe Ottereyes told how in 1945, the year he and Eva were married, there was nothing to eat. He was sure everyone was going to starve so he wrote a letter to the Indian agent in Amos and told him about the children having nothing to eat. The agent sent a plane "with flour and everything."[210] Rolf Knight's judgment that "welfare was a major event" seems correct.[211] Indeed, a welfare subsidy made it possible for families[XXIX] to maintain a bush lifestyle; it took the edge off what had become a precarious existence. "If Indian Affairs told the Indians to go trapping without relief and loans, they wouldn't go," Elijah V. declared at Great Whale River in the mid-1960s.[212]

As for Joe Ottereyes' attitude to welfare, being the recipient of monthly rations was not his only objective in life. Tragically he had lost an arm when the rifle he was carrying had gone off; he was hospitalized in Amos for two months and then in Montreal for another six. He was fitted with an artificial arm but did not like wearing it because it got in the way when he worked, and the upper part of his arm got cold from the metal braces. Initially, he received a monthly ration for two years. This disability pension would have continued had he worn the arm.[213]

Except for the annual visit of the Indian agent, the relief was distributed by the company manager, so it was he who decided need and the amount to be given to hunters who fell on bad times. A caring post manager would be called into question should his relief expenditures be considered excessive. One such post manager, D.G. Boyd at Nemiskau in 1938–9, was constantly tormented by this balancing act of meeting the needs of the hunters in a very poor year for food and furs. He anguished over the amount of S&D rations he was distributing and his compassion for the suffering of the hunters and their families. One also has to understand the perception the managers had of their jobs. Boyd was there as a fur trader, yet he wondered "whether we are fur trading here or running a 'bread line' for the Department of Indian Affairs."[214] Accordingly, another constraint on the manager's distribution of S&D rations or, later, welfare, was the disparaging reputation he would earn if he dispensed it too freely.[215]

In addition to the hardship cases among active hunters when hunting was poor, there were the "local rationers" – people who lived in the vicinity of the post and depended on these rations, such as widows or the disabled. Occasionally an Indian agent became keen about relief projects. Thus, a "wee house" was ordered for Rupert House in 1938 and twenty "young fellows were set to work on a drainage ditch behind the house."[216] Knight pointed out that such projects, such as the village road, constructed in 1960, were initiated "primarily to pump money into a community that needs help and are calculated to inculcate an ethic of having to work for what you get."[217]

Writing in the 1950s, the Indian Affairs Branch did not seem overly disturbed by the amount being paid out for welfare. At Eastmain, as one example, the regional supervisor, Fred Matters, wrote that "welfare is not a large problem at Eastmain but it could become one overnight if some disaster or disease struck the beaver population. The outlook for work of any kind is nil ... four families are presently receiving, being cripples and those not being able to fend for themselves."[218] Control seems more likely to have been levied at the Hudson's Bay Company. This is not to say that the Crees received vast amounts of welfare, but that the government was concerned the company might be taking advantage of their position in its distribution. This provoked the ire of the company in 1940 when Dr Tyrer, Indian agent, decided to divide the issuing of the weekly rations between the Hudson's Bay Company and a private trader at Moose Factory, as Cargill had evidently submitted a lower tender for the S&D rations. As Cargill's establishment was farther away, the writer of this company report hoped "the Indian Agent will have trouble with the Indians over this new arrangement."[219] The government was concerned, though, about the efficacy of this program; in 1957 we find a federal welfare officer making the rounds of the communities to assess the situation, but there is no report in the records indicating his findings.[220]

Without access to wages, with declining animal resources, and with rising needs and wants, social assistance in Cree communities kept rising over the years. For those Cree populations in the far reaches of James Bay, the percentage of their people on social assistance was the highest (see Appendix 6, table 5). Fort George, Eastmain, and Old Factory all had rates of 50 to 63 percent dependent on welfare. Rupert House and Waswanipi, closer to the south, were down to 29 percent, though Mistassini, only sixty miles from the mining town of Chibougamau, had 55 percent of its population on welfare in 1972.[xxx] Without existing data on per capita income for James Bay, it is not possible to estimate what percentage of the household income came from social assistance. One obvious fact that leaps from the statistical tables the Department of Indian Affairs maintained was that the real dollar value the federal government turned over as welfare was low. Despite high percentages of people on welfare in the James Bay region, the per capita amount of welfare expended by the government was $140 (always in the form of rations) in 1972.[xxxi] LaRusic, in his study of the Waswanipi economy in the mid-1960s, pointed to the scale of Indian Affairs rations allocated to those in need, which he deemed merely to enable a family "to maintain itself only at a level of hidden hunger."[221] This minimal welfare allowance was matched by the difficult conditions for people living in the villages. Almost all were living in tents without any of the basic services such as electricity, running water, indoor toilets, telephone. The few houses were woefully overcrowded, with eleven people per house at Eastmain and ten at Mistassini. When Indian Affairs did help with housing subsidies, it was to a maximum of $8,500, far from adequate to cover the cost of a basic house in 1970 and requiring all the materials to be shipped a great distance. Désy points out at Fort George that the housing, much of it makeshift, had neither water nor electricity, in contrast to that of the Euro-Canadians.[222]

Yet another of the government's contradictory policies was in the realm of social assistance. Until 1 September 1971, all recipients of social aid had their food allowances deducted on the basis of their abilities as hunters. Those who were considered by the welfare administrator to be good hunters had half the total amount deducted. Those who were fair hunters lost one-quarter the amount. There was no way of objectively evaluating a man's ability or even predicting how much he could hunt in the next month. However, this policy was abandoned, not because of its highly arbitrary nature or because it hindered subsistence hunting but because of the publicity that followed two deaths in Arctic Quebec from what was thought to be mercury poisoning. The Crees continued to live on country food but they no longer had their food allowances deducted.[223]

In hindsight we can see the barriers to opportunities that welfare across Canada erected for Indians and whites alike. It created a dependency at a time when technology, education, and the need for access to capital made it more difficult to create new revenue-producing ventures for themselves.[xxxii] Indians had less opportunities than whites to borrow money since they had no access to capital; their land was communally owned; in fact, in James Bay they did not even have communal lands or reserves. Education on reserves, as we know, was a dismal failure, further hindering individuals from seizing opportunities. These obstacles weighed more heavily on the Indian communities than others. In addition, their dependency was forced on them by a bureaucracy that became preoccupied with "providing services ... obscuring the more sensible course of helping people to become self-supporting and able to pay for services in the ordinary way."[224] In other words, the government provided welfare rather than viable economic opportunities.

SCHOOLING

School was another institution from the south imposed on the Crees, as on other Indians across the land. We must distinguish between education and schooling. Education for the Crees was as old as their culture; schooling, though, was a new and foreign institution. Whatever schooling Indian children might have had, it was in missionary-run schools at the post, most often in the summer. As we have seen, the Anglicans were forced into expanding their schools at the posts when the Oblates arrived in eastern James Bay in 1922. The level of financial support from the government is not discussed but we may assume that it was minimal, if it existed at all. Sister Paul-Emile,[225] writing of the Catholic mission on the east coast, remarked that the Anglican schools at Rupert House and Fort George did receive subsidies while the Catholic one did not. Missionaries, for their part, were reluctant to permit the government to intervene in education, fearing interference. The Oblates were particularly concerned that the government might impose the English language and curriculum on them. An additional factor was the government's reluctance to fund schools not in treaty areas, the reasoning presumably being that only under the treaty requirements were they responsible for schools. However, the largest school outside treaty limits, funded with government monies, was the Bishop Horden Memorial Residential School at Moose Factory, which had forty-one students in 1901.[226] Originally installed in the former home of Bishop Newnham, in 1937 a new residential school was built with a capacity for one hundred pupils. In 1906, with the Anglican see moved to Chapleau, Ontario, the Anglicans raised funds in England for the building of a residential school there which opened in 1907.[227]

In the 1940s the federal government made several attempts to improve social services for Indians and Inuit; schools were built or improved to facilitate the government's desire to assimilate and/or modernize its northern Native Peoples.[228] Although attendance at school became compulsory for Indian children in 1920,[229] the Crees were not pressured to comply until after the war years. The government began building and staffing secular schools and family allowance was linked with attendance. This move away from mission schools and to government ones was stepped up in the 1950s, particularly since the requirement for school attendance was strengthened in the revised Indian Act of 1951. For example, the Bishop Horden Memorial School at Moose Factory, in a new structure built in 1955–6, became the Moose Fort Indian Residential School, housing 233 boys and girls. At the same time, a day school was built there.[230] The historian Richard Diubaldo links this awakening of interest in Indian and Inuit welfare to the trauma of the Second World War and the advent of the Cold War, both of which resulted in redressing the earlier government neglect.[231]

Prior to village schools, some children were sent away, generally in the face of parental opposition, to attend boarding schools for two to four years and then return to bush life. In 1946 a group of twenty-six Mistassini children left the village to go to the school at Chapleau.[232] Earlier three Waswanipi children attended the same school in 1939, and the year before Sam Gull's daughter died there.[233] As early as 1934, Sam Iserhoff, retired post manager and lay catechist, ran a school each summer at Waswanipi for the few children,[234] and there were similar summer schools wherever there were Anglican preachers. Other Crees, such as Thomas Mark at Old Factory, might have gone as far as grade eight in the late 1930s or 1940s in a school that would have been outside the James Bay territory.[235]

214 The White Man's Gonna Getcha

In 1948 Rupert House had a secular school,^xxxiii while at Mistassini that year a school was under construction. One was built at Waswanipi, together with the nursing station, in 1947.²³⁶ These were all elementary schools; the first local high school was not opened until 1972, at Fort George.²³⁷ Some Cree children were schooled away from home as a result of being sent south to tuberculosis sanitariums. Willie Wiestechee (born 1933) completed grades one to seven in Hamilton, Ontario, in the five years he was there and years later served as the interpreter for the anthropologists Rolf Knight and Richard Preston.²³⁸ Children of the Nemaska band were exposed to book learning in the summer months when a teacher was sent there beginning in 1947.²³⁹

Little is said about the teachers at the schools, but one expects that for the first number of years the missionaries continued to teach, as did the minister at Rupert House in 1948. Mrs Greene, who taught at Fort George, was the wife of the Anglican missionary.²⁴⁰ The teaching materials and curriculum were supplied by the government. Nevertheless, at Old Factory, Sister Paul-Emile wrote of the Catholic school, held outdoors initially in 1937; the dozen children attending were taught prayers, reading, syllabics, and have "erected a cement statue of the Notre Dame des Lourdes."²⁴¹ Undoubtedly the instruction at the Anglican schools was similar, especially since the same teachers continued to teach after the federal government commandeered the schools. At Moose Factory, it was said "the supervision of the School [1950] was still under the Anglican Church though the administrative body was the Indian School Administration in Ottawa."²⁴² The Anglican Church's supervision of schools and their operation of the hostels was not ended in James Bay until 1969, leaving the church the right to appoint administrators and supply religious services when requested.²⁴³ It is worth recalling that the federal government does not have its own Ministry of Education, so the development of teaching programs was carried out within the Department of Indian Affairs. With the passing of the revised Indian Act in 1951, the federal government began making arrangements with the various provincial governments to integrate Indian children from reserves accessible to neighbouring white communities – a program that could not be implemented in James Bay.²⁴⁴ It is difficult to know how committed the Department of Indian Affairs was to improving its pedagogical policies in the isolated communities where schools remained a federal responsibility. Its schools, most often located in isolated regions and catering to non-English or French-speaking children, received a per capita grant in 1940–1 of $40.94, compared to the national average for general public schooling of $58.26.²⁴⁵

These were elementary schools; if children wanted to continue their studies beyond grade six they had to leave the villages. In 1963 they were sent to Brantford Residential School, but it was deemed too far, so high school students were sent to La Tuque, Sault Ste-Marie, and Moose Factory residential schools or to schools in North Bay, Ottawa, and Noranda, where they boarded with families. By the 1960s most students were sent out of the village, but by 1972 a high school was built in Fort George and the children from other communities either boarded or lived with a family.[246] There were also cases where a child was sent off because the family could not manage, for various reasons. Beatrice Fairies was sent in the 1930s[xxxiv] to the Chapleau Residential School because her mother was in hospital. She stayed there two years without returning home in the summer. Besides the schooling, the children were expected to work in the gardens picking potatoes, doing kitchen work, and cleaning the buildings. As with so many other Indian children, Beatrice said she had almost to relearn her language; she would have been strapped if she was heard speaking Cree. Her half-sister did forget Cree because she was kept at school for ten years, having been taken at age six. She ended up learning her husband's Abitibi dialect rather than her own Rupert House one. Marion Wesley gave a similar account of being sent to the Catholic Fort George Residential School. Priests has come around asking if parents would send their children. They did. Three girls were sent to school on the boat from Moose Factory. However, three years went by without the children coming back. The mothers asked that their daughters be sent home; once there, they would not let them return to the school.[247]

The drive to ensure schooling for every Cree child was not stimulated by a need to deal with the problem of illiteracy. Neilson remarked that "all read and write syllabics," while only three or four speak English or French. Undoubtedly the schooling of Indians was intended to provide the means by which Crees could be employable and/or assimilate to Canadian ways. The hope Neilson had for the Mistassini children was that they "would be taught woodworking and mechanical skills, the value of conservation and the domestic cares."[248] Although in other provinces Indian parents could sometimes choose between the federal Indian day school and a nearby provincial school, for some Cree villages the decision required the weighing of political and pedagogical considerations when, in the 1960s, the provincial government established day schools in several of the villages.[xxxv] The choice the Cree parents had to make was largely over language. Did they wish to have their children learning English or French as a second language? The reader can decide whether the provincial school system in Nouveau Québec was motivated by a concern for educating the ten thousand Indians and Inuit in this new region or establishing a French presence there, as the *Thunder Bay Times* suggested in 1987.[249] As with the competition in the fur trade, a number of Cree parents were pragmatic and chose to send some of their children to each of the schools, thereby ensuring that the family would have speakers of both second languages. The Fort George provincial school had 215 students enrolled in 1971–2, though included in this number may have been non-Cree students, given the large number of non-Crees living there. In a community of 1,120 Crees, 175 were said to be non-Crees.[250] The number of Cree students in the Rupert House provincial school in 1972 in grades one to seven was forty-three.[251]

Needless to say, the Cree chiefs or councils were never consulted about their community's schooling needs, even when the officials were present in the community.[252] Besides two schools in Fort George, Richardson noted other overlapping services to this community of twelve hundred people. The federal government maintained a large student residence and a health centre while the province administered the big new hospital,[xxxvi] an adult-education centre, the water supply, garbage collection, and some municipal services. Duplication of services also brought in a large influx of outsiders to oversee the operations of the institutions. Désy counted fifty-seven Euro-Canadians divided almost equally between the Indian Affairs and Catholic residential schools.[253] The bill for the provincial services would have been charged to the federal government, the Department of Indian Affairs.

None of these schools had any local control over the curriculum; the running of the school was by outsiders, often transients. In the 1960s, educators in North America began stressing the importance of starting a young child's schooling in his mother tongue to avoid inhibiting the child's thought processes,[254] but this was not done in the federal schools. By contrast, in Arctic Quebec in the provincial schools Inuktitut was made the language of instruction from kindergarten through to grade two.[255]

Undoubtedly the education system was one of the most destructive southern institutions imposed on the Crees. It tore the children away from the cultural context in which their parents had been raised, provoking what must have been a heart-breaking generation gap. At the same time, it did nothing to prepare them for another world that would enable them to acculturate, should they have so wished. Furthermore, it added to an already beleaguered people a colossal social and economic cost.

Whatever the government thinking might have been, the school curriculum was nothing more than a policy of social engineering. The quality of the teaching given to children of minority groups became an area of focus in education only in the 1970s. Teachers in the schools knew very well what the problems were, but it took several decades for the governmental institutions to look for approaches to education that were more accommodating to children raised in non-western traditions. This lesson was quickly learned by a non-educator, A.J. Kerr, when he was in Rupert House from 1947 to 1948 as a young anthropology student. His report to the government is damning of the kind of schooling to which the Cree children were subjected. In brief, he told the government that much of what was being taught "is practically meaningless" to them. It had no bearing on equipping them to live in the bush and to feed themselves. In addition, children were required to go through routines that had no meaning to them or their parents. Frequent hand-washing was the example he used in a society that had not embraced the concept of germ theory. If the educators in Ottawa considered the children would be the agents of social change and once back in their homes advise their parents of the wisdom of what they had learned, Kerr reminded them that Cree children "would never think of attempting to advise their elders." He also queried how children returning from boarding school could ever expect to continue the practices forced on them at school, such as using a fork at a table. For the Crees with whom Kerr interacted, he judged that the only value parents might see in sending their children to school was to learn English, an ability which provided status in the community. Kerr was also critical of the language of instruction, which was in English only since the teacher knew no Cree. He even provided the government administrators with the answer to the question that everyone asked in those days: if immigrant children can learn and become acculturated, why not Indian children? His concluded that, unlike European immigrants who feel the necessity to conform to the practices and values of the dominant group, the Crees simply do not take for granted the correctness of the white man's ways.[256] Fourteen years later, at Rupert House, Knight found that few of the children at Rupert House went beyond grade six.[257] Psychologists studying the effects of schooling on young Mistassini children in the 1960s found that school radically disrupts the traditional processes of enculturation and "severe conflicts in identity arise" with the alternating of school and bush life in the summer.[258]

Little in the recorded oral histories inform us about Cree attitudes to schooling thirty and forty years ago. What there is confirms Kerr's criticisms. One comment was that before children went to school they would listen to their parents.[259] Despite the artificial environment and its dissonance with Cree life, it is evident that many Cree parents found schooling a necessity and sent their children to school, even to residential school. One mother told Rolf Knight in 1961 that she missed her children, away at residential school "but maybe my son can get a job outside; hunting is a hard life."²⁶⁰ He did. Eddie Diamond became director general of the Cree Regional Authority in 2000.

Schooling also played havoc with Cree social solidarity and economic well-being. There was no attempt by the government to tailor the school year to the requirements of bush life, preferring to keep to its farming agenda of breaking in the summer. Schooling had an effect opposite to what the Department of Indian Affairs intended. For a hunter to send his children to school was expensive unless he chose to live at the post. Yet living at the post was contrary to the objectives of the department; they wanted the Crees to be self-sufficient. This dilemma was articulated in 1958 by W.J. Harvey, the superintendent for James Bay, to Fred Matters, the regional Indian Affairs supervisor in North Bay. He was discussing Rupert House but obviously it applied to all posts. "Owing to two classrooms operating, with approximately 60 children attending, more women have stayed at the Post which means that the family do without the country food and have to exist on Family Allowance ... The crux of the matter is that trapping is poor and the Indian cannot afford to keep two homes going on $500 which is the average money earned by the trapper during the winter months. The children seem to be the big factor on account of the school."²⁶¹

In addition to the pressure on already precarious household subsistence, children in school also meant that the solidarity of the nuclear and extended families was undermined by long absences with no communication, either with the children away in residential schools or mothers and children separated from their husbands and fathers.ˣˣˣᵛⁱⁱ

The schools were alien places, unrelated to their lives when they returned home. The curriculum, grades, and recruitment of teachers were all decided by outsiders following a system used in southern Canada.²⁶² The lessons the children sat through were meaningless. No doubt Cree children were expected to tackle arithmetic problems like the rest of us, using the speed of a train or comparing apples and oranges. The difference is we knew what these items were and how they looked. How any Cree person learned to read using the Dick and Jane books complete with a pet dog, a neat white house surrounded by a picket fence, and Sunday excursions in the family car, is remarkable.

It was not a wilful destruction of culture and psyche that the government practised by imposing schooling on them. They saw no alternative. As Fred Matters wrote to his superiors in Ottawa: "I think we all agree that some education is essential in even the most primitive areas. Rupert's House is getting to be comparatively close to the area affected by development of industry in north western Quebec, therefore education is of greater importance than it used to be ... I feel quite certain that within the next generation or so, opportunities for other types of employment will be available to this band, therefore, education should be vigorously pursued so that the children at school now may be better qualified to take advantage of the opportunity if and when it is available. To this end, a certain amount of welfare assistance will be necessary in most cases."[263]

The government imposed schooling without having any real plan. It is a pity Fred Matters did not indicate what industry would come into the area which would employ many Crees. Undeniably schooling was important, but as with the other institutions that were thrust upon them, the programs were glued onto the communities as cheaply as the government could manage. They were imitations of southern institutions. No one asked the Crees. It is also a pity that Kerr's cogent analysis of the schooling system did not spark any interest within the Department of Indian Affairs to meet some of those challenges.

The highly effective challenge a group of young Crees mounted against the Quebec government's unilateral decision in the early 1970s to erect a massive hydroelectric dam on their territory indicates that for these exceptional people residential school held some benefits. They could meet southern society on its own terms. This group – Billy Diamond, Ted Moses, Walter Hughboy, Steven Bearskin – had all attended the Moose Factory school in the late 1950s and later the school at Sault Ste Marie where they met other young Cree leaders from inland communities – Philip Awashish, for example, and Henry Mianscum. Another of the young leaders was Abel Kitchen who also had been out to school.[264] Thus, the residential schools[xxxviii] benefited these budding leaders from different Cree communities by providing them with networks and contacts which were well used in the 1970s. This is not to mitigate the suffering they and all the other Cree students must have endured in such harsh, alien institutions. The Crees, as other Native Peoples across the country, are now beginning to grasp the extent of psychological injury done to them, a subject that only recently have people begun to articulate and analyse, much like the notion of women's equality that only came to the fore in the 1960s. Without studies of the residential school experience in eastern James Bay, one might still be permitted to suggest that the residential schools were less brutal for the Crees, for three reasons. The Crees of eastern James Bay were not sent to residential schools until well after Indian children in western Canada. By the time they began attending, the running of the schools was more in line with the schools in the south. As well, most of the schools they attended were in Indian communities, so the discordance between home and school was not as great. Finally, they all came from Cree communities that were continuing to maintain a traditional lifestyle, again unlike many other communities.

Cree was their mother tongue, hunting was their parents' occupation. They knew who they were. A fourth observation is derived from J.R. Miller's suggestion that in the residential schools in this region of northern Quebec and Ontario, the children came from a number of cultural backgrounds, so using English as a lingua franca was viewed positively.[265] That a number of young people were able to build successfully on their school experience does not, however, mitigate the criticisms. These particular young people seized opportunities to generate their leadership. For most other Indians, in James Bay and elsewhere, there were no such opportunities. Only in the last several years are other James Bay students of these residential schools making known some of the psychological traumas they experienced. That the political leadership have looked, with hindsight, on the positive side of their experience should not mask the pain other Cree children suffered in coping with the loneliness, the strangeness, and above all the assault on their identity and self-esteem.

THE NATURE OF THE GOVERNANCE

The requirement that the Crees adhere to a politico-legal system fashioned in Ottawa must have created for them social and psychological effects, similar to what was encountered in schooling. The description that follows of the displacement of Cree political functions by federally imposed ones is less detailed than the previous discussions of health, education, and economics because in the archival records, including the oral accounts, much less is disclosed on this subject. This is a reflection of how little the Crees were involved in policies and decisions that affected them and, on the other hand, how relatively little attention was paid them by Ottawa or Quebec. Perhaps it is also a reflection of the interests of the anthropologists conducting research in this region.

Nationally, the federal government began exerting its dominance vis-à-vis Indians as a consequence of the 1885 North West Rebellion in its Northwest Territories (today Saskatchewan). According to historian Olive Dickason, the consequence of this conflict was the increasingly centralizing tendencies of the Department of Indian Affairs. Undoubtedly to the benefit of the Crees of James Bay, the department seemed preoccupied with the Indians in the West with whom it made treaties. More accurately, the federal government involved itself in regions of economic benefit to it. As seen, the two levels of government never expected to sign a treaty in Quebec until the events in the 1970s forced them to do so.

Not until the Quebec Boundaries Extensions Act of 1912 did the Crees, Naskapis, and Inuit come within the jurisdiction of Quebec. Quebec did not appoint a game warden for James Bay until 1942, when René Lévesque[XXXIX] was named.[266] However, he quickly became caught up in the problems of Ontario Indians hunting in Quebec which kept him in the more southern portions of the territory. The role that Quebec played in its so-called unsettled territories was basically as policy-maker regarding game and fish conservation and only sporadically as enforcer of these regulations. Their role in the beaver preserves followed along these lines: the government passed orders-in-council designating the territories but provided no funding or management. It was federal government personnel in the fur supervisor division of Indian Affairs that oversaw the running of the beaver sanctuaries and the sale of fur – individuals such as Hugh Conn,[XL] a looming figure in the north, judging by the correspondence.[267] Not until the early 1960s, under the Lesage administration, did the Quebec government begin demonstrating an interest in its northern territories and asserting its presence.[XLI]

Until the 1960s the jurisdiction of the federal government in James Bay, through its Department of Indian Affairs, went unchallenged, even by the Crees. Theirs was not an active challenge, although petitions for matters such as establishing recognized reserves abound. One can imagine many instances when the Crees simply turned their backs on government directives. Since distribution of the S&D rations was allocated by the federal government to the company manager, it is unlikely the Crees would have had a sense of the government. In fact, Joe Ottereyes mentioned that he did not know of the government until told about it by the company trader.[268] Even the Indian agents were ambiguous; until the late 1940s they were mostly doctors, based at Moose Factory, who on their annual visit took care of other non-medical matters such as authorizing payments. The two most recent doctor-Indian agents for the James Bay coast and interior were Dr W. Lorne Tyrer who began in 1931 and died suddenly in 1940,[269] and then Dr T.J. Orford, who served until 1947 when the position was split into two[270] and medical services were transferred to the new Department of National Health. Taking up the duties as the new non-medical Indian agent was J. Allen, who worked at Moose Factory and was in charge of the James Bay Agency, east and west. In the 1960s this office was moved to Val d'Or. To the south, the Indian agent and doctor were always two individuals. Hervé G. Larivière was the Indian agent of the Abitibi Agency, which included Mistassini and Waswanipi, with the office located first in Senneterre, then in Amos, Quebec. In 1941, for example, Dr Bolduc was providing the medical care and the two would visit communities together.[271] In 1962 this agency was subdivided, with one half, including Mistassini, being assigned to the Lake St Jean (Pointe Bleue) Agency.[272]

222   The White Man's Gonna Getcha

At the time of transition from doctor-Indian agent to a separation of the two, Kerr judged that the Crees had no sense of what the government was or their relationship to the "boss," whereas it had always been clear what the role of the doctor was.²⁷³ Yet the Crees at Great Whale River did have a special name for the agent – "money man"ˣˡⁱⁱ – as he authorized relief payments.²⁷⁴

The full story is yet to be told about the kind of control Indian agents could exercise over the Indian communities. Given that the agents were the gate-keepers to Indian reserves, it is interesting that so few studies have been made about their roles and influences. R.W. Dunning initiated the discussion in 1959 in his "marginal man" study. More recently several works, by Noel Dyck and Victor Satzewich, have debated how we should characterize these agents. My reading of Indian Affairs correspondence in this regard has not been systematic, but it suggests that Dunning's work of forty years ago seems consistent with what I could see in the records and what has been reported in Kerr and Walker. Preston has provided a highly useful analogy to help those of us lacking experience with living under the direction of Indian agents by drawing a comparison with the absentee landlord who controls the property but does not live there and has little motivation to understand his tenant's viewpoint. Rather, his rewards proceed from his management performance.²⁷⁵

Dunning had been a teacher and anthropologist amongst the Pekangekum Ojibwa in southwest Ontario, close to the Manitoba border. He says the Indian agents, as well as other whites in the community, were "often not representative of or compatible with the social ethics of the national society" and possessed "a fairly general attitude of superiority," dispensing an authority that was "capricious and discriminatory."²⁷⁶ His forty-year-old study is also very instructive in his general analysis of the white contact persons in the Indian communities: teacher, nurse, trader, missionary, policeman, and Indian agent. Each of these white individuals represented a specialized knowledge from the external culture, but there was no degree of integration of this leadership and cooperation was not always forthcoming. We have already seen in James Bay the conflicts between traders and missionaries, which one assumes were compounded when the other contact individuals joined the community. Until such time, of all the whites in the community it was the trader who wielded by far the greatest powers. As government services – that is, cash subsidies – were slowly extended to the James Bay people, they were funnelled through the company bestowing upon the trader the possibility of directing almost every aspect of an individual's life. Dunning gives an example of one trader who used a widow's family allowance cheques and rations to move her and her family by chartered plane to trapping grounds where they would be stuck for the winter. The trader wished to recover old debts, and at the same time he could demonstrate to the government he was not permitting "his" Indians to live off relief.[277] In James Bay, Honigmann's notes from his fieldwork in Great Whale River include a letter written to him in 1952 by a student who reported that "George Mastee and Joseph Maste [sic] have not received any family allowance since they left Richmond Gulf as Allen [Indian agent] say they shouldn't be at Great Whale River."[278] There are doubtless countless similar stories of the patronizing behaviour of the agents, but the traders did not leave such explicit accounts. For the most part, they would not have been critical of such posturing by the agents. An example of a trader acting in a similar paternalisitic fashion comes from the Nichikun trader's entry in which he, George Dunn, writes that he would not perform the marriage ceremony for a young man until he was self-sufficient.[279] It does not seem necessary to belabour the point about the paternalism of the traders, but is worth commenting that it formed the essence of the company's dealings with the Native Peoples, in James Bay and elsewhere.[280] A graphic example is an illustrated 1940 flyer[281] found by the archaeologist James Chism in the mid-1970s in the abandoned post of Kanauupscow. It is entitled "Handling Natives" and subtitled "Frankly we are Disappointed." The gist of this notice is the lack of interest by the post managers in the competition the company launched in 1939 to solicit "notes on the care, treatment and handling of Natives." As encouragement there were four categories of prizes for winning suggestions from $10 to $50.

In looking at the Indian agent, one must bear in mind that he was also part of a network of decision-makers thrust upon Cree society, particularly after the Second World War. Inasmuch as the Indian agent visited the communities generally only once a year, one might relegate them to the nether parts of this network of white authority. It is not so simple. The agents were, after all, the conduit between the Indian community and Ottawa; decisions or petitions had to pass through them. Indian leaders could not petition directly to Ottawa.[282] It did not matter that most Indian agents, when first starting out, were totally ignorant of Indian life. There would have been little point in learning the way of life or catering to it, as their mandate was to assimilate and integrate the Indians into Canadian society. They were the employees of the Department of Indian Affairs, not of the Indian communities.[XLIII] The template they would have imposed on each community was a southern one in terms of practices and values. Moreover, they made decisions, filed reports, made recommendations, all far from the direct supervision of Ottawa.

Although there is a correspondence between Hervé Larivière and the department in Ottawa, mainly over the land issues, it is hard to read what kind of agent he was as compared to Armand Tessier, agent at Pointe Bleue in the early 1900s. Tessier wrote sympathetic letters to newspapers supporting Indian rights to hunt at a time when Quebec was treating them as any other inhabitant of Quebec.[283] The Reverend Scanlon, serving at Mistassini in the 1950s, "had built up a healthy respect" for Larivière, who by that time had had a forty-year career as an Indian agent, beginning in the early 1900s as a Hudson's Bay Company manager[284] in the Abitibi region.[XLIV] Nevertheless, it is telling that Scanlon referred to him as "a contemporary Count Frontenac. He would have been very much at home in the seventeenth century. In the Department of Indian Affairs, his was an age of paternalism with all power and authority vested in the Indian Agent. He knew so much about his immense region and its people, that he, in effect, controlled his superiors and their policy. They never questioned him ... He was feared and respected by the Indians ... It was a case of control from the bottom up."[285] One of the reasons Larivière was able to exercise such control in James Bay was because he "enjoys the close cooperation of our post managers in the work of improving the lot of the Indian," as it was stated in the company magazine.[286]

A predecessor of Scanlon's at Mistassini, Norman Burgomaster, held a less respectful view of Larivière, writing in 1945 that "I am convinced that he is [a] demoralising influence to the Indians. He is a simple case of unethically disposed inflated ego, and his tendencies will become a nuisance to us all concerned unless active steps are taken to check the trouble now."[287] Then, in a study attempting to characterize Indian agents, to determine if, although occupying positions within a racist structure (Indian Affairs), they always incorporated that racism into their own definition of the situation, Victor Satzewich studied agents' responses to a 1946 request by the minister of mines and resources for their views on what they conceived as the "Indian problem." Satzewich found that while some "did articulate racist and paternalisitic attitudes towards Indian peoples," others "offered fairly sophisticated ... analyses of the nature and scope of the problem." In providing examples of one type of racist statement – what he termed blaming the victim – Satzewich pointed to Larivière's response, in which he stated that he "was not particularly impressed with 'his' eastern Indians," claiming they "are all more or less the primitive types."[288]

Whether benevolent or autocratic, the Indian agents made most of the decisions for the Crees and undermined their traditional leadership, which was based on supernatural powers, wisdom, and age. It could not have been encouraging to young Crees to see judgments made for them by strangers, thereby thoroughly undermining the traditional leadership and the wisdom of their elders. Many Canadians bristle because the publishers of our newspapers or CEOs of our national airline are Americans, yet Indian agents were much further removed culturally from the peoples over whom they had such enormous power. Dickason reminds us, that as the Department of Indian Affairs assumed more and more control over the lives of the Indians, the power of the agents became more arbitrary.[289] On the ground, in Rupert House in the late 1940s, Kerr reported there were no government officials there but indirectly their role was "constantly increasing."[290]

Perception is an important consideration in governance. As interfering as the Indian agent was, his non-appearance in a community could also have been devastating to the morale of the community. As a young anthropology student, Willard Walker was at Great Whale River in 1952. He found it surprising that although the agent at Moose had told him that "Great Whale River was the most poverty stricken and most disease ridden" of Cree communities, the agent did not visit there that year.[291] No doubt had he been asked, the agent would have said that the Department of Indian Affairs restricted his travel on budgetary grounds. That may well have been so, but people in Great Whale River, including the anthropologist, would not have known of the constraints he was under and would have interpreted his absence otherwise. Equally, an obvious perception that the Indian agent disliked visiting remote communities could easily be a fair one to explain his absence. When the Indian agent did visit Great Whale River, it could only be termed a fleeting visit. Balikci, there in 1957, noted that W.J. Harvey visited there for a day, to arrange the problem of relief, leaving the matter in the hands of the company manager. Then he was gone, not to return for a year.[292]

Armed with these ultimate powers far from the watchful eye of Indian Affairs in Ottawa and with no means of appeal by the Indians, the agents became one of the supreme rulers over their Indian charges. Furthermore, the position the agent played in the community was always a paternalistic one, as is clear from this entry in the Waswanipi journal of 8 August 1940: "Dr Bolduc and Nurse Cere and Mr Thibault of the Indian Department arrived. Mr Thibault took a walk around the tents and greeted all the Indians and inspected their tents."[293] Even so, the Indian agent was probably much less visible and was regarded less importantly than the Indian Affairs officials who made annual inspection tours of the beaver preserves.

Another of the Indian agent's tasks was to organize the elections of the band chief and councillors. As of 1899, the Department of Indian Affairs directed that all bands in Ontario and Quebec should hold elections every three years.[294] The terms of the 1951 Indian Act stipulated that there be one chief and one councillor for every one hundred members of the band, where previously large bands had elected one chief and two second chiefs for every two hundred people.²⁹⁵ Only men voted in the elections, but in the 1950s the Mistassini Crees thought that, "since a woman is now the British queen ... women should also vote."²⁹⁶

In 1934 there were new elections for chief at Waswanipi[XLV] at the request of the Crees, and Joseph Shaganash was elected, with Deom Blacksmith as second chief.²⁹⁷ Both the chiefs addressed the band. Their speeches were recorded and presumably translated by the post manager, Fred McLeod.

Speech of Deom Blacksmith, Second Chief of the Band:

As you all know that the former Chief Alec Cooper did not rely on us, his councillors, for much help. Now I want to tell you all that we, who have been chosen to lead you, want you to come to us with your troubles and any time that we can help you and make the conditions better than they are now we will do so as best we can. At present the conditions of the band is in a bad state and we will take some time to better it. I also want to tell you than any Indian who has any complaint to make against the Indian Dept. or the Hudson's Bay Company to come to us with it and if we see fit we will take the matter up.²⁹⁸

A meeting was held today by the Chief and councillors and after a short prayer by S.R. Iserhoff the council was opened with the speech given by the newly elected Chief Shaganash. The speech was as follows.

The first thing that I want to tell you of the Waswanipi Band is concerning the Indian Department. We do not want to become a bother to them by asking to [sic] much from them. They have been very good to us and we appreciate all that has been done for us in the past. I am now asking you all to try and do your best and pay your debts and you will find that in the end that both the Hudson's Bay Company and the Indian Department, when they see that we are trying to do our best will help us more. But if any of you lay around in your camps, you are going to find it very hard for yourself when you come in again next summer. Our employers the Hudson's Bay Company wants fur and it is up to us to get that fur for them. By us supplying them with fur we are making it better for ourselves in every way ... this is important ... I want you all to think of what the Hudson's Bay Company does for us and the freighting we do in the summer for them which helps us so much ... I do not want you to trade your furs any other place but with the Company at Waswonaby. I will be here in the spring to see that you do ... I want you to come to us with advice and for advice ...

A loud cheer from all the Indians greeted the Chief as he finished.²⁹⁹

227 Pale Versions of Southern Institutions

Although these speeches were reported and translated by the company manager, we might still presume that most Waswanipi men were in agreement with the policies set by the Hudson's Bay Company, always mindful, of course, that they had few options.[XLVI] Little is said in the speeches of the government, as opposed to the Indian Department, because in 1934 there were few federal policies imposed on them. A new election in 1939 switched the positions of Shaganash and Blacksmith with John Gull as councillor.[300]

The Indian Affairs chiefs were not necessarily the traditional chiefs; they served different functions. The traditional chiefs or leaders were usually elders, wise and in possession of supernatural powers, rendering them skilled hunters. Mary Sheshamush at Great Whale River looked back on the role of chiefs, using her brother, Joseph Ennish, as an example. She commented that chiefs in the past were generous; they did not use welfare but, on their own, fed a lot of people.[301] Also at Great Whale River, Honigmann inferred from the leadership of Sam Masty that ideally a band chief is a "good" man, good referring to one who is familiar with the Bible.[302] The traditional leader would not have claimed a following the size of the Fort George or Rupert House bands, for these were conglomerates of hunting groups formed by the changing demands of the fur trade, summer missionization, and the beginnings of government services. A more accurate portrayal of the traditional leader's sphere of influence is found in the words of Stephen Tabaituk of Fort George who, in speaking of his father-in-law, Jimmy Bearskin, described him as "a leading figure amongst those who went furthest inland."[303] As the traditional leader legitimated his influence by his proven skills in hunting and feeding a large camp of people, what effect on the Crees' view of leadership would there have been when their subsistence practices changed and they were now feeding themselves from the store? Dunning raises this question[304] and of course the same question can be applied to our understanding of why the traditional religion dimmed when Christianity was being preached at the turn of the century.

The Indian Affairs chiefs required different qualities. They had to intercede on behalf of the band with government officials. They probably combined a deferential manner while at the same time trying to control the situation. Preston has made an interesting comparison between Indian Affairs chiefs and the eighteenth-century trading captains who were valued for their oratorical talents and ability to bargain with the Hudson's Bay Company manager.[305] Certainly the Crees were quick to elect young men who had been to school, knew something of the white man's ways, and could speak English. In 1964 Chief Isaac Shecapio resigned to make way for Smally Petewabano, a young man who knew

English,[306] and young Robert Kanatewat was elected chief at Fort George in 1967.[307] It may have been more stressful to be an Indian Affairs chief than a traditional leader, as the former served as the complaint department for situations and policies quite beyond his control. The traditional leader would have called on the supernatural in times of sickness or scarcity of game; such an appeal would have been useless in trying to cajole government or company officials. Despite their inability to control the variables, chiefs were not necessarily acquiescent. In 1937 Chief Shaganash and McLeod, the Waswanipi post manager, had words over an issue and Shaganash threatened to quit his job as chief.[308]

The band chief need not necessarily have been recognized as the spiritual and economic leader, though he could have been. A more recent example of this division is Billy Diamond, only twenty-five when he was elected chief of the Rupert House band while his father, Malcolm Diamond, continued as the real leader. Prior to the son's election, at the time of the Quebec hydroelectric project that would flood a vast portion of their hunting territories, Malcolm Diamond had been both types of leaders, having also been an elected chief in the 1950s.[309] Likewise, at Great Whale River, Honigmann singled out "especially highly esteemed men," naming the catechist James Mamiamiskam and Charlie Dick as well as several others considered to be especially wise. His list of esteemed men also included the band's first and second chiefs.[310]

Eventually all the bands in James Bay chose chiefs. Mistassini had a chief in 1937, probably Matthew Shecapio, who, as we have seen, took the train to Quebec City to see a minister about conditions in Mistassini hoping he could send a message to Ottawa asking for aid. The company manager sneeringly complained he was put up to it by the free trader Olav Brièvre, and on Shecapio's return three weeks later, he reported that he came back with nothing "except a good time."[311] At Eastmain there was Chief Walter Tammatuk in 1938, while John Georgekish was chief at Old Factory then.[312] Fort George had a chief by 1920 at least, for Chief Peter Waskigan's arrival at the post was announced that August.[313] However, in 1931 the Indian agent, Dr Wall, replaced Waskigan and Joseph Naposh[XLVII] was said to have been "reappointed" in his place.[314] In Wall's 1932 report of the James Bay agency he conjoins two notions: that the Crees were taught to believe the government was duty bound to support them, and that the chief was deposed and the new one put on "probation for one year."[315] In today's parlance, we might consider that Wall thought the chief to have an attitude problem and thus used his legislative powers under the Indian Act to discharge him from this elected office.

229 Pale Versions of Southern Institutions

One can only speculate if Waskigan were removed as chief also because he may have been a Catholic or sympathetic to the religion. He was living in the priests' house in 1929 and two years later, Griffin reported that his two children were enrolled in the Catholic school.[316] Despite a reference to the Fort George chief in the 1938 journal of Great Whale River and detailed reporting about the activities of individuals in the 1938–40 journals, no chief for Great Whale River is designated until 1949–50 when Honigmann named Sam Masty the chief for the Great Whale River and Richmond Gulf bands and John Kawapit the assistant chief.[317]

Surprisingly, Rupert House did not have its first election for band chief and council until 1946. It was arranged by the Indian agent. There was no ballot; instead, each adult male lined up behind the nominated candidate whom he favoured.[318] Frank Moar was elected the first chief, along with two councillors. His father had been a company servant and he spoke Cree, English, and French. Knight tells us that Indian Affairs "demanded" a band chief, but the people of Rupert House were opposed to the idea and the new status was considered a joke. It is perhaps telling that the next chief elected spoke no English.[319] Interestingly, Regina Flannery said that all the time she was in James Bay communities in the 1930s, she "never heard of anyone called a chief," and the records bear her out.[320]

It is clear that the government imposed on Indian bands a political office that had no precedent in their social organization. It made the Crees go through the motions of a political process to produce a chief and councillors but it did not ascribe to them any particular social or political duties that would give meaning to their position. As the speech-making and feasting presided over by the chief and councillors at Waswanipi in the late 1930s indicated, it was largely a ceremonial office and that is the way Indian Affairs kept it for decades. The agents, not the chiefs, had the real power and had taken over many of the significant traditional duties of chiefs, such as helping people in difficulty. The chiefs and councillors helped maintain the status quo. They had no choice; to do otherwise would have meant dismissal. A 1960s study was forthright: "In point of fact, Indians have had little opportunity to engage in meaningful policy questions. Instead they have been given the task of implementing previously set government policy."[321] Yet, despite appearing to be only a ceremonial position, the chief did hold status as the most important person in the community, or so a study at Mistassini in the 1960s showed. When questioned, the people most frequently named the chief as this most important person, then the Hudson's Bay Company manager, thirdly the Anglican minister, fourthly the Indian agent, then the teacher, a member of the band council, and so on.[322]

As time went on, the chiefs increasingly pressed the government on behalf of the band. At Great Whale River, the chief in the 1950s recommended to the Indian agent those who required relief. In the mid-1960s Jimmy Mianscum, chief of the Chibougamau band, travelled to Ottawa and made numerous representations regarding financial aid and the establishment of a reserve.[323] The chiefs may have become more active, but the government was not any more responsive. Other chiefs, in other communities, also made appeals to the government, as at Great Whale River in the mid-1960s. When they were not successful, the chiefs and councillors were criticized by the community.[324] In his important article in 1968, Preston expressed his concern that the lack of effectiveness of Cree chiefs in the face of the government's unwillingness to recognize their leadership could result in a denial of the authority of the chief by community members. Preston described the government's denial of a community request to terminate French-language schooling in Rupert House, claiming that the government's handling of the situation was a serious threat to the unity of a community that "is only beginning to reach any real degree of solidarity."[325]

At the end of the 1960s the political and societal organization of the Crees looked very different from what it had been a hundred years earlier. However, the differences were more striking in the villages than in the bush. There the constraints of winter hunting and trapping maintained a cooperating group of three to five nuclear families. Whereas in the previous centuries whole families lived in the bush with only the elderly and maimed left behind at the post, now it was more likely that only some members of families went into the bush, with children being away at school or a wife left behind to mind the children. Previously the bond that formed the nucleus of the hunting group was patrilocal, fathers and their sons, but now non-relatives were likely to be found in these groups. In the towns, extended families rather than several families formed the household. Chance reminds us the overcrowded urban setting differed from the living conditions in the bush, where territorial controls had long ago been worked out. In some communities where the division between Inlanders and Coasters had been pronounced, as at Rupert House and Fort George, the residential arrangement in the village respected these divisions. At Fort George the Coasters lived on the north shore of the island while the Inlanders resided to the southeast, but still grouped themselves in family units, as to whether they were from the north, south, or interior.[326] The housing structures were also different. In the bush, conical or dome or sometimes log cabins were constructed, using a variety of coverings, hides, canvas, and mud;

in town people lived in log cabins, Indians Affairs housing, or canvas tents, some with raised wooden floorings and half walls.[327]

The most significant change was to the band structure. Prior to extended village dwelling and the imposition of band elections by Indian Affairs, the important grouping beyond the crucial winter hunting group was the local band, the network of hunting groups who cooperated economically during the winter months. Their hunting lands were contiguous, making communication and cooperation sometimes possible in winter and definitely so in summer at good fishing spots. Most of the men making up this band of about five to eight families were patrilocally related with a recognized leader. Modern living altered this band structure; now the village members, from several regions, became the band, with one elected chief and councillors. With the village as the focal point rather than the region where a number of families hunted, peoples' social ties turned inward to the village rather than outward to other contiguous bands who might have frequented different fur trade posts. This village band has been designated as the government band, a direct outcome of government control that resulted from the regulations of the Indian Act which prescribed the elected leadership.[328] When Neoskweskau, Nichikun, Nemiskau,[XLVIII] and Chibougamau posts were all closed, the Crees were encouraged to trade at Mistassini. Today, except for Nemiskau and Chibougamau which are separate bands, the others have fused with the Mistassini band.

By the 1960s the Crees had learned more about the functioning of Indian Affairs and had fine-tuned their political manoeuvring. Salisbury points out that communities favoured long-term chiefs[XLIX] who had learned how to relate to the Indian agents and knew the issues that were dear to their hearts. They also had to be speak English. The chiefs could perhaps persuade the agent of specific needs in the community but, of course, they had no control over the budget. The councillors had even less input into decision-making and were changed more frequently. However, in the 1960s, with movements in western countries towards increased democratization, there were developments within the Department of Indian Affairs towards more involvement of Crees in the administration of their communities. In the 1960s the department imposed a regional structure in James Bay, creating three regional chiefs, located in Mistassini (Smally Petawabano), Fort George (Robert Kanatewat), and Rupert House (Billy Diamond). The intention was to facilitate greater communication with the Indian Affairs district offices in Val d'Or and Pointe Bleue; the majority of Cree villages were located in the Abitibi region, administered from Val d'Or.[329]

The more activist role that developed amongst the elected chiefs in the 1960s was a reflection of the anger that was now coursing through the communities. More contact with the southern community, schooling, and improved communication helped the Crees to better understand the responsibilities of the Department of Indian Affairs, and to see their situation in the Canadian context. Indian Affairs, presumably unwittingly, contributed to this greater Cree scrutiny with its policy in the late 1960s of training and paying band managers.[330] From Great Whale River there is a report of a community meeting that had been called by one of their young men. He had been sent in the mid-1960s by the Quebec Department of Natural Resources to a conference on cooperatives in Montreal. Thirty-three men gathered to discuss with him what he had learned; he recorded their comments, voicing their complaints about the paltry amount of expenditures by Indian Affairs, their inferior school compared to the one at Fort George, the Hudson's Bay Company profit, the services of the nurses, and so on.[331] Thus, everything in the community was coming under scrutiny as people were developing a more global knowledge of the government operations.

When the Crees realized they had to take notice of the operations of the Department of Indian and Northern Affairs, they found that these operations were dictated by the district offices of Abitibi, in Great Whale River, and Pointe Bleue. Over these offices was the regional office in Quebec and, finally, Ottawa, where a number of administrative divisions within the department were housed.[332] These divisions managed all aspects of Cree life. The chiefs had some latitude in deciding who got housing or welfare but decisions on budgetary constraints were always made elsewhere. As for the bureaucracy that administered the Crees, Salisbury estimates that in 1971 there were perhaps a total of fifteen Crees serving as chiefs or band managers (a full-time manager of the band office), while the number of Indian Affairs administrators in Val d'Or alone was an astounding eighty persons, half of whom he estimates were involved in Cree administration. In 1971 the Cree population living on their territory numbered 5,500.[333]

The Department of Indian Affairs changed gradually. Politically and bureaucratically it was influenced by the values and attitudes sweeping through the larger society, mainly a recognition of minority rights and a feeling of the injustices that had been suffered by the Native People.[334] Accordingly, the federal government reached into its deep pockets and produced subsidies for provincial associations of Indian Peoples. Thus was formed the Indians of Quebec Association (IQA) in 1960, spearheaded by strong leaders of the Mohawks, Hurons, and Montagnais.[335] It was this organization that the Crees first worked through to confront the issue of the James Bay hydroelectric project in 1971 that was to harness the La Grande River. The project was located for the most part on the hunting grounds of the Fort George Crees and

JUSTICE

Justice used to be in the hands of the elders of the community and probably still was, to a large degree, well into the 1950s and 1960s. With the informal system of family hunting territories used to govern access to beaver, trespass was an on-going problem for the Crees. The overlay of registered traplines onto the traditional system did not eliminate this source of conflict for the Crees, although Knight said it was rare. Nevertheless, John Blackned told him that usually if a hunter took a beaver from a lodge he would tell the owner and then recompense him later. It did not always work that easily and Blackned told Knight of a dispute he had with one man over beaver for which he felt magic was inappropriate. It ended with the two men not talking to each other for many years. He also commented that it was inappropriate to ask the band chief or Hudson's Bay Company manager to intervene.[336]

There were some extraordinary offences that the government imposed on the Crees and on other Native Peoples, such as hunting out of season and trespassing onto provincial lands. For example, by continuing to hunt on their usual lands in Ontario, Quebec-based Crees were considered to be trafficking in illegal furs. The government solution was to require the Crees to stay on one side of the provincial border.[337] No thought was given as to how the Crees would find vacant hunting lands or how disruptive this would be to family ties.

Additionally, because the Crees did not have treaty rights, those living in the southern portions of the territory were not only subject to Quebec game laws but were also harassed because the game wardens there regularly patrolled the region by airplane. Here is what happened to Jimmy Mianscum, the chief of the Chibougamau band, when he was hunting moose. Boyce Richardson, in presenting this account, also draws our attention to the fact that moose-hunting season in Quebec is in the fall, so designated for the convenience of sports hunters and tourists. A moose is useless to a Cree hunter in the fall when there are other food resources; but he does need it in the winter, in the bush, to feed his family. These are Jimmy Mianscum's words:

I did not know why the game wardens came and landed at my hunting ground by aircraft while I was hunting in the bush. I did not know who sent them to come at my camp. They ask for my meat. They took all my moose meat and when I come out from my trapping ground, when I come by aircraft they have also waited for me at Cache Lake, Fecteau Transport [at Chibougamau]. And of course they took all my moose meat again, when I had left.

I was 40 miles out in the bush, that is where I brought my meat along for me to keep going while I am at Doré Lake. I also told them that I was a sick man, not in good health. This is the reason why I brought my food along with me, because I had to go to the hospital and my family needed that food to eat. They told me their boss or manager want that meat.

And so I am short of food to eat. The food they took from me, it would keep me going for at least one month. I did not understand any of this, why they took my meat. They did not even tell me what's the reason they took my food.[338]

Richardson termed this systematic harassing of the Crees by the Quebec game wardens "a cruel practice."

Cree society did not have much problem with violent crimes. There are only a few recordings of murder over three centuries, and thus there is very little recorded on the apportioning of justice. The Crees did respond, it seems, when necessary. A Cree father killed a company man from Scotland when he raped his daughter, and the company officers turned a blind eye. As for murders within the Cree community, the company, other than expressing disdain, had a hands-off policy and allowed the Crees to govern themselves. A typical response was this report from Donald Gillies, manager at Fort George in 1906: "One of our good inland hunters was beaten to death this spring by his family who was under the impression that he was devil-possessed. Would the Indians only kill off a few of the useless weeds in sight one could bear thereof with resignation, but this was a good man energetic and half civilized from contact with whites. He had been with Low a whole summer years ago and went across country with Tasker in 1906."[339]

Alcohol, often the mechanism that unleashed anger, was not a factor in James Bay up to the end of the 1960s, as it was not for sale at the post. Sam Masty, at Great Whale River, recounted that the only person who possessed alcohol when he was small was the Hudson's Bay Company manager who would give a drink to a man when he had paid off his debt.[340]

How might the Crees of the 1940s view a system of justice that was gradually being imposed on them? Writing about northerners, Inuit, and Indians, Keith Crowe judged that for a people accustomed to settling things themselves, "it seemed wrong and childish to refer matters to outsiders."[341] On the other hand, living as they did in small communities, the Crees may well have been relieved when non-community members would take decisive measures for them for particular wrongdoings that might be contentious. Doing so on their own could lead to

235 Pale Versions of Southern Institutions

further internal dissension or, given the face-to-face nature of small-scale societies, they might have been incapable of punishing a wrongdoing. In 1832 an outpost manager at Hannah Bay and seven Cree members of his family were massacred by a party of six Crees. They were either looking for hand-outs of food or were guided by the need to fulfill certain spiritual requirements, depending on whether one reads the company's version or the oral history recorded in the 1960s.[342] The company managers at Moose Factory and Rupert House took justice into their own hands and, with a posse of company men, executed the six men. The oral account does not judge these punitive actions.[343] Similarly, Knight, in his field notes, commented that he thought the people of Rupert House looked upon the Hudson's Bay Company as their legitimate political system. He sensed that they referred all extra-family matters to the company managers for a decision.

The RCMP first visited the James Bay coast in 1920 when an inspector and sergeant came through in a boat on their way to the Belcher Islands to investigate some murders there in the winter.[344] In 1926 the RCMP opened the Moose Factory detachment with the posting there of one constable. This detachment covered the east side of James Bay as far north as Richmond Gulf.[345] With no early RCMP records extant for this detachment, we find in 1931 only the name of the constable, E.S. Covell,[L] who became actively involved in trying to control the influx of white trappers.[346]

The annual reports of the RCMP, discontinued in 1957, clearly indicate their mission was to oversee the Inuit communities. They seem to have spent very little time in the Indian villages, no doubt because the Indian agent came through once a year. The year 1944 was when the RCMP patrol first went north of Fort George and the report reads that it was "the first time the Indians and Eskimos there encountered a police patrol pass though their hunting domains."[347] The constables were also called upon to settle disputes between Crees; Constable Jim Davies did so when he passed through Old Factory River in 1947.[348]

It is not clear what the RCMP mandate was in James Bay,[LI] for they were a federal authority and could not interfere in matters involving more than Indians and Inuit.[LII] According to Zaslow, the RCMP detachments in the Northwest Territories and in the vicinities of Indian reserves, where the people were still living by hunting and fishing, was to "supervise the native inhabitants ... and watch their relations with their white neighbours." They were to patrol the enormous districts, and show the flag,[349] but there were limitations to their authority. Constable Covell complained that his hands were tied in the matter of whites poaching on Indian lands. Although there was no Quebec game warden for the region, he still had no authority to apprehend anyone under the Quebec Game Act except for "two Finns" for illegal trapping. Nevertheless, the RCMP were called in to investigate when individual Cree hunters were accused of killing beaver on the preserves, as at Fort George, Rupert House, and Eastmain in 1939. In one instance eleven beaver pelts had been confiscated by the chief at Fort George and turned over to the company, and in another the company manager received seven pelts from Albert Cheeso who said they had been caught in his otter traps. In the latter case, these pelts were forwarded to the Department of Indian Affairs with the instructions that since the skins did not seem to have been taken illegally, the department might want to reimburse the trapper. As for the Eastmain preserve case, Watt informed Constable Kupkee that rumour had it the Sam Shacapot family were eating beaver, which explained why they had not visited the post that winter. Kupkee made a surprise visit to the winter camp thirty-five miles along the coast to the north of Rupert House. There he discovered the family had a large supply of moose meat, which explained their not having visited the post. Kupkee, finding no traces of beaver meat, was satisfied they had not been illegally trapping beaver.[350]

Problems concerning the administration of justice were discussed in a provincial government report of 1971. It was said that the Crees and the Inuit were receiving none of the judicial protections found in the south. In most cases the accused were told to plead guilty, which they often did even when innocent. A number of factors accounted for this, including the most basic unfamiliarity with the court system, the use only of English or French, lack of legal advice except in the most serious of cases, and the lack of standardization of the sentences handed down. Additionally, the Crees found the presence of RCMP or QPP officers intimidating at any time, yet they performed a variety of tasks in the courtroom. None of the administrators, judges, police, or lawyers was trained to deal with native peoples. All these factors added up to the Crees being overwhelmed by the system; so they chose to prevent the unnerving situation being drawn out by pleading guilty. Sentenced to prison, an Indian offender found himself or herself in a prison far from home and deprived of contact with the family. Anthropologists in the communities regarded the trials evidence of blatant discrimination, pointing out that when there was a case between an Indian and a white, "it is almost always the Indian who loses."[351]

The Crees were faced with legal and financial problems because their settlements were not deemed legal entities known as reserves. Quebec expected them to pay taxes on goods they purchased, yet the Indian Act provided that Indians did not pay taxes on goods they owned or used on Indian land.[352] The Quebec sales tax was imposed in 1940. P.J. Soper, the company manager, presents its introduction to the hunters at

237 Pale Versions of Southern Institutions

Kanaaupscow in this way: "Mail in. Much grief from now on with the new Quebec sales tax. All sales must be taxed and the Indians docked for it. I expect this is going to lead to a few arguments at first until they get used to it."[353]

Whatever additional protests the Crees must have made were not recorded and it is not apparent that the company took a position on this tax. The sales tax continued until 1972 when Quebec exempted on-reserve Indians via an order-in-council.[354] To illustrate how this issue became mired in bureaucratic stalling we can look at the case of Mistassini. It was officially a settlement and thus the residents were considered subject to paying taxes on their purchases only outside the community. In 1957 the Hudson's Bay Company sent a letter to the Department of Indian Affairs asking if Mistassini was constituted as a reserve and therefore would not be paying sales tax. The regional supervisor for Indian Affairs, R.L. Boulanger, located in Quebec City, was asked to reply as Ottawa was "not too familiar with the statute on taxation by the Province." Boulanger replied that no reserve had been created at Lake Mistassini yet. He also added his own personal remarks that in Quebec there is "a tax of 2% on all articles, except food and children's wear, which I believe should be paid by Indians. In a City like Quebec and Montreal we have an additional Municipal tax of 3%."[355]

That the Crees, other Indians, and Inuit in Quebec had to pay sales tax is analogous to the charges made by Borron in the 1890s at Moose Factory when he found that they were paying duties to the Canadian government on goods coming from England but were not recipients of any government services. Now in the 1940s the Crees were paying sales tax and receiving not one service from the Quebec government. In the same vein, one might also question the royalties the Quebec government received for each beaver taken from the preserves and sold through the Department of Indian Affairs. Their role in the beaver preserves was only symbolic, for they granted the right to create the preserve and ever so often passed orders-in-council decreeing the number of beaver that could be hunted on each preserve. Quebec had made no financial commitment to the preserves; this was left to the Department of Indian Affairs and the Hudson's Bay Company.[356] It would be impossible to reconstruct what the Crees paid to the Quebec government from 1940 to 1960 in fur royalties and sales tax,[LIII] but it could be described as considerable, especially when taken from a people that were impoverished. The Crees paid these sums to a government that did not even permit them to vote. The same charge could be levied at the federal government and the duties they took in from the sales of pelts; their services to the people of James Bay were minimal and here, too, the vote was denied them until 1960.[357]

SUMMARY

Towards the end of the 1950s the Crees still thought of themselves as subsistence hunters living in a hunting-trapping society,[358] even though the government was drawing an ever-increasing number of families away from bush life. Practices were being lost or transformed to the extent that one post manager was prompted to write: "David Loutit's grandsons were initiated to hunters by the old style,"[359] referring to the walking-out ceremony held for young toddlers. New practices were added. At Christmastime in 1938 at Waswanipi the post children, seeing nine caribou running along the shore, became convinced "they are Santa Claus' reindeer."[360] In July 1940 the Inlanders visiting Fort George participated in a sports day organized by the Anglican Church.[361] Some practices remained the same. On Christmas Day 1940 the usual handshaking and visiting was underway at Fort George,[362] while at Mistassini "women and children returned to the habit of beating drums" to mark a successful moose hunt.[363] The practice of witchcraft, or at least the belief in it, continued. A marriage at Nichikun was called off in 1941 because of the fear of witchcraft.[364] However, the old religious rituals were disappearing. Billy Jolly of Nemiskau told Knight that drumming and other forms of "hunting magic" were now done only by a few, as people have a great deal more food from the post and do not need to trap as much.[365]

Moving ahead to the 1960s, anthropologists of the McGill Cree Project fanned out into several Cree communities to study "the processes of economic, social and political change and development."[366] They focused on the southern communities most affected by industrial development, Mistassini and Waswanipi. Notwithstanding what are referred to as significant changes to traditional life ways, Norman Chance, the project head, reported that "for many of these Indians, the traditional stresses and adaptive responses are still very much in evidence. The seasonal pursuit of fur, fish and game determine the tenor of their life."[367] Even at Great Whale River, where defence work engaged the Crees in employment in the late 1950s, about 40 percent of the Cree population spent the winter in the bush in the mid-1960s.[368] Life for the Crees had changed, yet the continuity with their past life was still very evident, poorer that it was.

This chapter chronicles the encroachment of southern institutions on Cree society after the Second World War which, like cancerous cells, insidiously supplanted the existing ones. There are few native narratives. Again, much like a cancer, one does not see the growth, only the tumour once it wreaks havoc.

239 Pale Versions of Southern Institutions

Undoubtedly, the Crees were spared a great deal of misery and death due through sickness and starvation, although the causes of each can often be connected to events set in motion by Canadians, not Crees. Nevertheless those who unleashed those afflictions were more likely to be seen as saviours; they brought in relief, health measures, and food.

The turning point in the post-1945 period was the more assertive role of the federal government. It seized control over almost every aspect of their lives. The Crees were helpless to oppose the government, given their very limited resources. They were not totally blind to what was befalling them. Knight tells us that "in the eyes of the local people the establishment of government controlled beaver quotas and territories along with the introduction of welfare payments, defines the demarcation point for present conditions."[369] What is not expressed here is how the government did it. The expression that best conveys this treatment is that the Crees were jerked around. Programs were started and stopped; those that continued were doled out on a budget far less than other Canadians were given; administrators served the government, not the people. To this litany of problems with feeble government attempts at maintaining a basic standard of living must be added schooling – the government's real assault on Cree culture and society. This section in the chapter only touched on the psychological distresses to the children. Without a literature providing the authority, I can only suggest what open wounds and lost souls were created in the culture and society because of the extreme generation gap produced by schooling in a society that highly valued old age and the wisdom that flowed therein.

Whatever efforts the government made in enculturating the children to southern society, the Crees could not have been receiving clear messages. The church, the most venerable of the institutions, visibly aired its internal divisions between Catholics and Protestants in Fort George, less so elsewhere. That each vied energetically and shamelessly for the Cree soul could only have diluted the sanctimonious exhortations to imitate white society with which no doubt the minister, Indian Affairs agent, and Hudson's Bay Company officials were bombarding the Crees. It is not hindsight that provides this observation. In 1944, Richard Finnie attributed the "palpable weaknesses in the school and hospital system" to the enmity and competition between the two denominations which he described as a "savage game in which the natives are bewildered pawns."[370] Twenty years later it was basically the French-speaking Quebec government officials versus the English-speaking federal officials who continued this factionalism in the Cree communities, not only on an institutional level but a personal one as well.[371]

The Crees were affected in other ways. With the safety-valve offered by the federal government, the Crees understandably thought it unwise to venture and camp hundreds of miles away from the post. Additionally, as Noah B. and others told Wills, the Crees could no longer live the way they did a hundred years ago; they were too sick to carry loads of three- to five-hundred pounds or withstand the physical strain it took to hunt and trap.[372] By circumstances, by changing perceptions of the world, by need, by the demands of the school calendar, they were drawn to village life, with bush life becoming secondary.

This replacement of Cree institutions with southern ones was imposed in a manner which must have shattered the sense of integrity and dignity due to any society. An Inuk, Johanassie Crow, expressed it cogently: "The white people move us around as if we weren't human. We have no say. The Eskimo used to go where they wished and the great men (the old and the good hunters) were bosses. If they didn't want to go somewhere they didn't ... we are nothing."[373]

CHAPTER SEVEN

Despite Government Domination, the Crees Weave Their Own Tapestry

This book could have been several others. It could have been one with a distinctly Cree perspective, but then I could not have been the author. It could have focused more on what Natalie Davis terms "exchange and hybridity,"[1] looking at the cultural exchange and adaptation that resulted, in this case, from mixed Cree-British families; but then it would move the focus from the Crees and might be misconstrued by government bureaucrats as testimony to the cultural disappearance of the Crees. With the Crees and Quebec in almost continuous confrontation over hydroelectric development, use of forestry resources, rights to the offshore islands, nationalism and independence, it did not seem smart to remind government officials that Crees, as every other people, were not "pure laine." It could have been a book about the powerlessness of the Crees in face of the encroachment of the larger Canadian society, but then it would be more a study of the larger society and its coercive powers than of Cree society. I might have oriented this book towards the dependency within a wardship system or as a representation of Indian-government relations based on Dyck's concept of coercive tutelage, "a form of arbitrary restraint or guardianship exercised by one party over another"[2] but it would be a stretch to incorporate in this thinking people who were on the margins of Canadian society and whose lands and resources were not yet expropriated.

Instead, I have chosen to write a book that is less categorical in its accusation of exploitation and less harsh in its assessment of the role of government in the James Bay territory. Nevertheless, the federal government and southern society were imposed on the Crees and their various agents did tinker and experiment with Cree institutions. Capitalism did, in several eras, exact harsh, cruel tributes from the Crees. However, for a variety of reasons, the full force of the colonial administration was not brought to bear on the Crees and the colonialism they endured was less blunt than for other Indian societies, those living on valuable lands or close to Canadian settlement, rural and urban. Needless to say, the Crees were catching up to other Indian bands in the 1960s when the two levels of government noticed them and began exercising greater controls. As this history's main thrust focuses mainly on the inter-war years, what they endured has to be differentiated from other regions in Canada. This is also a reminder that as more attention is devoted to defining the nature of Canadian colonialism, this country will yield up a multiplicity of examples, the James Bay case being representative of a less virulent variety[1] in contrast, say, to the history of the Indian and Metis peoples on the prairies. Though less dramatic in its unfolding and less provocative in its results, nevertheless it was colonialism: the usurpation by foreigners of the Crees' political, economic, and cultural autonomy. The particular hue of this state colonialism I call bureaucratic for the reason the Crees were most affected, not by settlers or capitalists but by the infusion of low-quality versions of Canadian services: education, welfare, health, government management.[II] Nonetheless, they were also the beneficiaries of an enlightened bureaucratic project – the beaver preserves and registered traplines – that drew its inspiration not from the southern society but the Crees themselves.

As we review the contours of Cree-white relations in James Bay we must recall another of the themes of this study: survival. The main focus for the hunter and his family was survival in the face of powerlessness or unpredictability in terms of what the land would yield for food. By contrast, any thoughts of powerlessness they might have harboured vis-à-vis the Canadian government were of much less consequence, particularly at a time when no one in Canadian society would have considered government the source of sustenance. Recall the several remarks the Crees made to the effect that the government was distant and scarcely recognized. Compare this to the many haunting accounts of their inability to find food.

As the Crees began the twentieth century they suffered greatly through devastating foreign epidemics which came at a disastrous time when their food resources were in severe decline. Technological advances aggravated this situation as telegraphic communication between the continents enabled the Hudson's Bay Company to alter, usually downward, prices paid for pelts. Without competition in James Bay, the company could squeeze its hunters on the prices it paid for furs and imported goods. Inevitably, over the two hundred years of the fur trade, the Crees had come to rely exclusively on many imported items. The First World War brought a near-curtailment of fur markets at the same time as the caribou, one of their most important foods, disappeared. Some perished; yet the culture survived. Their life on the land was modified but not drastically. The genius of their social organization had long been their ability to split up in times of scarce resources and amalgamate in larger numbers when food supplies increased. This flexibility has been demonstrated for the eighteenth century and far earlier via the archaeological record and was still a functioning principle two hundred years later. At the turn of the twentieth century, the Crees were also confronting missionary zeal and perhaps their own recognition of the value of Christianity. Rather than being disruptive, Christianity seems to have been welcomed throughout James Bay. Perhaps the syncretism that was adopted made this transition possible, whatever the reasons they had for accepting Christian practices. The Crees' conviction, as Anglicans, was steadfast despite the Catholics' considerable attempts to convert them. Unlike the fur trade rivalries, the Crees viewed this competition differently. Their solid, meaningful Anglican conversion easily took its place alongside the traditional Cree spirituality.

A presumed disadvantage to Christianity may have been the foreign-born priests for whom cultural relativism was an unfathomable concept. As Christians and as Englishmen (as most were, though they could just as easily have been Canadians) they would have seen themselves duty-bound to assimilate the Crees to Christian and English values, the two being synonymous. The tone of the writings and correspondence of the Church Missionary Society is generally respectful of the Crees but every once in a while there is a reference to a moral lapse. What the priests have not recorded is their scolding which surely they must have delivered to Crees in and out of church. As such, they undoubtedly would have contributed to a certain degree of undermining of the integrity of Cree culture and the self-esteem of the people, possibly hastening other aspects of acculturation. On the other hand, this may well have been countered by the Crees who may not have been swayed by Anglican ministers' claims of superiority and knowledge. In James Bay at beginning of the twentieth century it was still very much a Cree world and Cree skills would have prevailed. Some modifications in seasonal patterns did occur for the Inlanders. The Anglicans did their best to encourage longer stays at the post in the summer to provide Christian instruction but the duration of the visits was tempered by availability of food resources in the vicinity of the post.

It was actually the decade of affluence, the 1920s, that introduced the most significant changes The Crees benefited materially from the presence of the Revillon Frères and, of course, they were in James Bay because fur prices were soaring in the 1920s. Several situations followed from this intersection of prices and competition. First, the highly favourable markets were for fox furs, a non-preferential food animal. With the high prices paid, the Crees could afford to purchase more store food particularly since the new modes of transport reduced the cost of store-bought food, especially staple items such as flour. It is in this period that we can begin to look at Cree hunters as trappers in the sense that they trapped pelts in exchange for food. That is, trapping became a means to gain subsistence, not the subsistence activity itself, as it previously had been. Leacock's and Knight's studies have linked hunting territories to the rise of individualized trapping. Leacock held it was a turning to store food that enabled this trapping, not the dependence on other sources of income suggested by Knight. However both erred in concluding that the development of family hunting territories followed; such a system of land tenure was well set centuries earlier. More likely, the Crees' perception of themselves changed from full-time hunters to part-time trappers engaged in exchange of skins for food. Correspondingly, as foxes, muskrats, and mink were not part of the Cree spiritual pantheon, their approach to trapping, at least of these non-food animals, might have become more secular. With food now also coming from the store, the traditional religion might well have lost much of its function; the dream-spirits seemed to fade away and Cree culture lost much of its cognitive underpinnings. Perhaps there was also less of a commitment to communal living, although the family winter hunting groups endured into the 1960s and beyond, when food stocks permitted. Perhaps, also, such modifications facilitated a transition to a more permanent village life and single family living in the 1950s and 1960s, when the government began pressuring them to settle.

At the same time as the Crees' fortunes were climbing, the Hudson's Bay Company's were declining; a more restricted business climate was less tolerant of excesses in management and labour. In the 1920s they were also embroiled in a vigorous competition with the Revillon Frères Company. They restructured, reduced personnel, and developed new modes of transportation, thus making large voyaging and work crews redundant. Restricted limits on credit were also imposed. The effects of this restructuring hit the Crees the hardest when the animals also failed them. They suffered badly and the searing memory of those times has provided us with moving accounts of their terrible hardships.

There was one favourable outcome to these desperate times. In the long run, the cost-cutting measures of the company may have benefited a number of Crees. Coasters and company families, no longer employed by the company, were forced to draw their subsistence from hunting and fishing and thus returned to the land, to what would be considered an Indian lifestyle. When the Department of Indian Affairs began compiling lists of registered Indians in the 1940s in eastern

James Bay, all those leading an Indian life were duly registered as Indian. At each of the posts only one or two men were listed as company family and not counted as Indians.[III] By contrast, on the west coast of James Bay when Treaty Nine was signed in 1905, all those listed as company families were kept off the treaty lists.[3] In those days Moose Factory had a considerable labour force, as it provisioned all the posts on both coasts of James Bay. There, the government was particularly vigilant as to numbers of Indians as it was paying four dollars annuity to each of the signatories. The government officials made arbitrary decisions that were divorced from the identity and social statuses of the individuals, and numbers of Crees on the west coast today continue to press their claims for recognition of Indian status.

The effects of the starvation period had a profound effect on the Crees. Testimony to this is found in the numerous stories the Crees, from every region of James Bay, told when anthropologists asked them in the late 1960s and 1970s to record their oral history. They are haunting stories, conveying sentiments of vulnerability and powerlessness. They stand in contrast to their history, over centuries, which has been one of remarkable adaptability. In times of scarcity they managed to extend the range of their resources or claim new lands. They incorporated the European fur trade and turned it to their advantage, particularly during times of fur trade competition. Even in the nineteenth century, when the company held a monopoly and there were few checks and balances on their profits, the Crees were able to hold their own; they accumulated debt or worked as labourers.

This time, though, in 1929, there were no new resources to mobilize; world markets and animal cycles had crashed almost simultaneously. Even so, there was a sense of pragmatism issuing from the Crees' strong sense of survival. When one benevolent Hudson's Bay Company manager, James Watt, introduced a scheme that seemed to make sense to them, they adopted it and incorporated it into their daily subsistence strategies. By embracing these conservation schemes, the Crees loosened their grip on their political and economic autonomy – a small matter at the time, compared to the alternatives.

This acquiescence produced the transformation of the Crees into a subjugated people, clients of the government. Other Indian bands, on the prairies or in the Maritimes, met their declining economic fortunes in the 1920s and 1930s by turning to itinerant wage labour. They somehow managed to eke out an existence on their own without the benefit of welfare programs, yet the federal government still actively imposed itself in their daily affairs.[4] In these regions, the lands were of great interest to the settler society while racist attitudes dictated that the Indian population needed to be kept at a distance. Armed with the

1876 Indian Act, the federal government took a prominent role in the running of the reserves and the coming and goings of its people.⁵ In James Bay the consequences of the successes Watt and the Rupert House Crees produced within six years drew in the federal government, initially an unwilling player. As the number of beaver preserves multiplied, government bureaucrats began setting the rules for preserves across the country. The Crees were now firmly in the bureaucratic system. The difference for the James Bay Crees, in contrast to other Crees and Indians on the prairies, was that the federal government involvement was directed to their traditional life in the bush. With some few exceptions in the southern portions of James Bay, the Crees were being encouraged to live off the land and maintain their way of life. As erratic, authoritarian, and stupid as some of the government edicts must have seemed to the Crees, they must have viewed the new developments as some sort of partnership – the Crees, the company, and the hazy presence of the federal government, only to be invoked as the final arbitrator when issues were contentious. Such a prewar partnership with a postwar economic fur-trade boom could not have prepared the Crees for what was to follow.

This partnership was to end, of course, as the postwar years saw increased involvement by the government in social matters: education, health, and welfare. These were genuine concerns pushed along by an awakening liberal, social conscience in southern Canada. Although assimilation was for long the hallmark of the federal government's involvement in Indian affairs, it was only in the 1950s that it began instituting this policy in James Bay. Prior to this state intervention of the 1950s, except for the beaver preserves where they were reluctantly drawn in, the federal government had no need to go into James Bay; there was nothing to bring them there – no conflict over land, no treaty obligations to meet. The lack of infrastructure made it a difficult region to open up to government bureaucracy. Although the hunting territories of the Crees at Great Whale River and at Waswanipi were being usurped for defence establishments or mining operations, it was not an extensive seizure of lands. The Crees did not oppose these for the simple reasons it was just not done. It was not an idea entertained in those years by either the Crees or by southern liberals. Instead it was viewed by the larger Canadian society as perfectly normal that the Crees, as other Indians, would want to join Canadian society as full-fledged members, participating in it as did other Canadians.

To achieve this end, the government imported to James Bay its full range of educational and social programs though not its commitment or finances. Along with these programs came southerners to run them – teachers, nurses, and administrators so the Cree communities' outsider population burgeoned. As agents of the south and thus as individuals with considerable influence in the community, the personalities of the whites assumed an important factor in how these programs were presented to and received by the Crees. Although Dunning presented the outsiders as marginal in terms of their ability to fit in their own society, it is likely their views of Indians were no different from those of southern Canadians. Working in Moose Factory and Great Whale River in 1952, Walker found amongst the "anglos" two camps of opinions; both conceded, though, the Indians to be "good men in the bush."[6] Some held that Indians "are thought to be dirty, lousy, lazy and cruel to animals," and others thought of them "as innocent children, deserving the spiritual and material patronage of whites." Both, of course, we would consider to be racist ideas today. In whichever camp the white agents fell, the delivery of the programs to the Crees could not have been implemented in such a manner as to interest or endear them to the Crees.

Additionally, there was no meeting ground built into the programs. Government administrators had not yet been introduced to the concept of cultural relativism. Astoundingly, almost fifty years later, the understanding of cultural differences and working with them rather than ignoring them still seems not to have become commonplace. The *New York Times* of 22 August 1999 presented a front-page story of the elusiveness of reconciliation of the two Germanies and quoted the mayor of Bonn as saying: "Our mistake was to underestimate the thousand differences in mentality." This was a country, a people with the same language and culture and a nationalism forged by war who were separated only for twenty-eight years. The mayor was not speaking of two distinct peoples, a traditional, family-based hunting one and a modern, individualistic, industrial one.

In Canada, when one speaks of social engineering, the primary institution the reader is steered to is education. The serious pedagogical mistakes, the poor funding, the elitist assumptions, and above all the vigorous efforts to erase the native values and thinking to be replaced with the dominant society's are all legendary. However, none of this really worked. As Dickason points out, "the vast majority remained distinctly Indian."[7] The terrible legacy, though, of the Indian residential schools has been one of violence, alcoholism, and child abuse. The Crees of James Bay were, comparatively speaking, spared these tragic consequences. If the correlation is only with the residential schools, perhaps this escape is explained by the young Crees from James Bay having attended these schools later, generally in the 1960s. The schools they were sent to were usually in native communities and they frequently boarded with families in those communities. Their attendance at the schools was voluntary; they had been sent there by their parents who wished their children to be educated while they themselves wanted to continue hunting and trapping in the winter rather than take up residence in one of the villages. Additionally, the Cree leaders who graduated from these same schools today recognize that they did gain an education, probably due more to their motivation than any new pedagogical approaches. It is this education which has stood them in good stead in their opposition to the hydroelectric projects. It was also an education that helped prepare them to take their place as negotiators, as band managers and chiefs, as heads of airlines and construction companies, to sit with United Nations committees on human rights, and to wage public relations campaigns on an international scale.

Other governmental programs were not so successful. The adult education and make-work projects took people away from the land where they could, at least, find sufficient food; it left them with inadequate wages, a discredited sense of the value of their hunting life – the core of their cultural system – and few marketable skills. Not so much malicious as short-sighted, poorly funded, and not attuned to local problems,[8] this drawing people away from their subsistence practices without having a viable alternative to offer also occurred in Newfoundland. In the 1960s scores of small outports were closed and its inhabitants relocated to larger towns where it was more efficient for the provincial government to deliver its services.[9] Although the federal government relocated Inuit from northern Quebec in the 1950s, the Crees were spared that kind of upheaval.

When there were thousands of jobs in James Bay throughout the 1970s, constructing the giant hydroelectric project, the federal government neglected to institute an accelerated job-training program to enable Crees to qualify for many of the skilled and semi-skilled jobs that opened up for a number years.[10] Instead southerners were brought to James Bay, at high wages, to fill these positions. Is this not another cogent example of bureaucratic colonialism?

The Canadian government's economic policy of permitting the concentration of industrial development in central Canada was also to blame for not encouraging economic development in the hinterland regions other than resource extraction. For the Maritimes and many rural regions of Canada, such an economic policy forced people to move to these industrial centres. Across Canada, many Indians left their reserves as well, in search of better living conditions.[11] This is one economic consequence that did not happen in James Bay; the Crees did not migrate to the cities.[IV] Perhaps the isolation and difficulty of travel is one explanation, perhaps because French was the language of work, perhaps because the Crees preferred remaining at home on their territory where life was reasonable and hopeful. Not having lost their land base to treaty-making or settlement, perhaps the Crees saw a future in their homeland. Whatever the explanation, the Crees were not confronted with a sector of their population encountering situations of powerlessness and hopelessness in the cities of Quebec.

The Crees also did not have to confront a new class of people in their midst – entrepreneurs. Those in James Bay who might have thought about opening a business would have been thwarted by their inability to raise capital, not having any collateral; under the Indian Act they could not own reserve land individually and therefore could not mortgage it. Loans became available from the federal government after 1969.[12] Thus any business development in James Bay was in the more limited service sector, such as guiding, and not in production or commerce. Whatever development occurred, such as the Great Whale River carving project, was provided by Indian Affairs. Not only were the meagre economic development initiatives in James Bay unsuccessful, but Indian Affairs has been bitterly criticized for its failure to accomplish economic development overall despite the large amounts expended. Economically, the federal government had taken charge in the 1950s and 1960s. So, too, had the market forces that brought down the price of pelts and the technological advances that reduced labouring opportunities. The federal government had stepped in but their solutions were inadequate and, at times, counter-productive. It left the Crees with few, if any, resources, bringing them into a state of economic dependency and tutelage.

Concomitantly with its policies, the Department of Indian Affairs in James Bay neutered the leadership. Away from their life associated with subsistence pursuits, the other important issues of modern life, such as education, health, welfare, housing, economic development, were settled by the bureaucrats. As a consequence of needing to cajole the bureaucracy, the Crees modified their requirements for leadership and leaders came to be elected who had the skills to deal with the government: the ability to speak English and understand southern ways. It would take a change in the political climate in the rest of Canada before these leaders were heard by the government.

As for a Cree nation, there was little unity until its opposition to the hydroelectric project in the early 1970s. Had the Crees wished to confer about common issues, they would have had difficulty meeting because of distances, isolation, and lack of funds to use for travel. Thus the communication from the Indian Affairs district office in Val d'Or provided a link between bands and in the 1960s the government created regional chiefs, all of whom would later contribute to assisting the Crees in organizing against the James Bay hydroelectric project.

Additionally, the system of residential schools assisted in creating networks between future leaders of the different villages.

The Crees were not demoralized. Although materially very poor, they managed to maintain the important traditional aspects of their culture – spirituality, a sense of extended family that shared in their economic well-being, and a resource base that gave meaning and purpose to the first two features of their society.[v] This spirituality at the heart of their identity as a people is seen by Preston as having survived in the east when it had not for Crees to the west, who had experienced more radical changes to their society. Preston uses the continued significance of the bear, a symbol that is central to the east Cree way of thinking, to illustrate this, saying that such a core symbol expresses their continued spiritual connection to a hunting way of life.[13] Perhaps the inner dynamics of their culture would have always shielded them from the forces that tore apart aboriginal societies, but perhaps also they were fortunate in encountering a milder form of bureaucratic colonialism. Mixed in with government interference in James Bay was also a good deal of government indifference and neglect, less intervention than elsewhere, all of which ensured that Cree society was not dismantled before the people were able to seize the opportunities presented by the hydroelectric project in the early 1970s and construct a new society whose elements were continuous with their past. Except for their relations with government. This is the subject of the Epilogue.

This study began with an explanation of the common Cree expression "the white man will come and get you," which is embodied by the pwaat figure, one said to represent a contradictory image of positive and negative qualities whereby the white man is represented both as a partner and as an exploiter. After this long meander through a century of historic events in James Bay, has this Cree view not been proven to be most appropriate?

CHAPTER EIGHT

Epilogue: A New Order

They were a strange group, in their great, plain working boots, the laces tied with no concern for appearance, their wind jackets weatherbeaten and torn, their shirts hanging below their jackets, their faces curiously open beneath their rude, home-fashioned haircuts. But they looked no stranger than they they felt, for they were Cree and Inuit (Eskimo) hunters from the huge Ungava Peninsula of northern Quebec, come to the city for the first time to undertake the audacious and apparently hopeless task of asserting their rights as occupants of their hunting lands from time immemorial, and bringing to a halt a hydroelectric project on which the provincial government had staked the entire economic future of Quebec. The older men regarded the building with dignified incomprehension, for they had never seen such huge enclosed spaces before, and they waited patiently to be told what to do, whether to go into the strange room which moves up and down and which was causing them much trouble at their hotel, or whether to go to the other side of the lobby and try to mount that moving staircase as many other people were doing, and so be carried upstairs in the strange manner of the white man, without having to bother to walk a step.[1]

The hydroelectric project was announced by Premier Robert Bourassa on 29 April 1971 at a Liberal party rally in Quebec City, saying "James Bay is the key to the economic and social progress of Quebec, the key to the political stability of Quebec."[2] The feasibility studies for such a project, ordered the year before, had not been completed, neither had the government consulted or even informed the Crees, on whose lands this monumental project was to be built. It was this announcement that brought Cree hunters into the strange land of downtown Montreal in December 1972. Despite their unfamiliarity with the terrain, and even more with the law and structure of the courtroom, the Crees, still very much a hunting culture with a firm sense of their connection to the animals and the land, held fast.

In November 1973 Justice Albert Malouf of the Quebec Superior Court rendered his decision on the Crees' request for an interlocutory order of injunction to halt the work in progress on the dams and the flooding in James Bay. The plans announced for this mega-project were to involve the construction of four powerhouses, four main dams, eighteen spillways and control structures, 128 kilometres of dikes, the creation of several reservoirs, and the flooding of 10,500 square kilometres on once-productive hunting land.[3] Needless to say, the project would result in enormous changes to the environment and the Cree way of life. The lawyers for the James Bay Development Corporation (in other words, the Quebec government) alleged crown immunity and, moreover, argued that the petitioners had no Indian title or any rights whatsoever. As Philip Awashish later commented, "We are among the original inhabitants of Northern Quebec, yet we were considered squatters on our lands."[4] Justice Malouf's judgment found that the Crees did indeed have substantial rights in the territory and granted them the opportunity to present their case to the court.

His decision came after deliberating over testimony presented over seventy-one days of hearing in a four-month period (during which time construction work proceeded in James Bay). The proceedings involved 167 witnesses,[5] a good number of whom were the Cree hunters themselves who testified to the on-going use of their lands and described their hunting and trapping way of life. They were unyielding in their insistence that any threat to this way of life constituted a "ferocious onslaught"[6] on their religious and spiritual well-being, the beliefs and values of which governed their traditional way of living. Within a week of Malouf's judgment, the provincial government had appeared before the Quebec Appeal Court and had the interlocutory injunction lifted, the court deciding that the public interest of six million Quebeckers took precedence over those of six thousand Indians and Inuit.[7] With the Malouf decision, with initially favourable soundings from the Supreme Court of Canada, and with most of the editorialists urging them to negotiate, Quebec finally undertook to do so and appointed John Ciaccia, former deputy minister of Indian Affairs, to represent them. Although the federal government constitutionally held fiduciary trust over Indians, it was unwilling to force the Quebec government to recognize their rights[8]; it limited its support to subsidizing the legal wrangling and the negotiations as a loan, to be paid back by the Crees after settlement of the claim.[9] Awashish characterized the federal government's position as "alert neutrality."[1]

Despite the wardship principles inherent in the federal government's role to safeguard the constitutional rights of the Indians, the federal government pressured them to accept the first proposal Quebec submitted in November 1973. However the Crees held steadfast and refused. They found the arrangements for remedial and compensatory measures for destruction to the land inadequate and were dissatisfied with the provisions for local and regional autonomy. Their wishes, as enunciated by Awashish, included: modifications to the existing project to minimize its damages to the land and resources; environmental protection; land and territorial (aboriginal) rights and community development; programs and assistance for Cree hunters; local self-government to include economic and social development, and control over health and education; and monetary compensation. In sum, the Crees reluctantly agreed to the construction of the project, as they recognized they would have to balance their interests as against those of non-native society.[10] They had established a deadline to complete the negotiations which, if not met, would have sent the Crees back to the courts. Within a year of the Malouf decision, in November 1974, the two parties signed an agreement in principle. On the 11 November of the following year, with the precise terms and details worked out, the James Bay and Northern Quebec Agreement was signed.[11] Before this, in August 1974, the Crees had withdrawn from the Indians of Quebec Association on the grounds that this organization was making demands of the Quebec and federal governments that would serve the greater Quebec Indian population and they felt it was hindering the progress they were making on their proposals. The Crees continued to negotiate under the auspices of the newly formed Grand Council of the Crees which took each clause back to the villages for discussion and approval by the people.[11]

The Crees gained recognition of their aboriginal rights and modifications to the project as well as remedial measures to protect the lands. The two levels of government also granted them quasi self-government, whereby each village was constituted as a municipal corporation and an overall regional government, to be run politically by the Grand Council of the Crees and administratively by the Cree Regional Authority. As for control over education, health, and social services, in each of the villages these were coordinated by boards: a Cree school board and a board of health and social services, each placed under the jurisdiction of the appropriate Quebec ministry but with on-going funding from the Department of Indian Affairs.[12] All these gains were, of course, on paper and ten years after the signing of the agreement the Crees were bitterly complaining[III] that "the proper implementation of some important provisions has been a serious problem."[13]

Land rights were recognized and compensated for ($232.5 million over twenty-one years), but the degree of Cree control over them were allocated over three categories with diminishing rights by the Crees as one moved from Category 1 lands (5,543 square kilometres), the smallest allocation wholly reserved for Cree use, to Category 2 lands (62,160 square kilometres), with exclusive hunting and fishing rights over most of it though some portions are shared with Quebec, and Category 3 lands (the largest expanse) where the Crees have the right to hunting only on unalienated crown land.[14]

The James Bay and Northern Quebec Agreement, signed in 1975, is considered the first modern treaty since Treaty 11 of 1921. However, close examination reveals that rather than initiating an entirely new way of settling jurisdiction and hunting rights, it clearly establishes the rights and duties of each of the co-signers and is devoid of the ambiguous and vague allegorical language so fondly held by the treaty commissioners of yore. Similarly, although innovative in its design, the Income Security Program for Hunters and Trappers, which guarantees full-time hunters a minimum cash income for each day spent in hunting[15] is not unlike the treaties of a century earlier. Those promised the Indian hunters rights to hunting and fishing over the lands they were surrendering "as long as the sun shines and the water flows."[16]

Rather than belittling the James Bay and Northern Quebec Agreement, my comments are meant to direct the reader to considering what the Crees achieved in their negotiated agreement. Like the earlier treaties, the intent was not to change the aboriginal life. In the 1970s, though, the Crees insisted on measures to reinforce the traditional life. Moreover, they recognized the importance of advancing those societal changes necessary for their participation in the modern technological society. To this end, they gained a good measure of control over government, education, and health services. They clearly rejected the alternative future recommended in a federal government commission report of 1966, which advocated that Indians be provided with job training so they could leave the reserves.[17] In fact, by 1981 the number of hunters out on the land had increased by 22 percent over the previous decade.[18] In 1981 Salisbury reported that their economy had quadrupled and the standard of living, housing and fittings "would not appear out of place anywhere in a southern Canadian town."[19]

Within a few years, though, it became clear that the Crees could not rely only on a hunting and trapping economy; their rapidly increasing population was dependent on a fixed territory. Neither did this subsistence economy provide for subsequent generations' desire to participate in the greater industrial economy. Although the Canadian economy is not particularly supportive of development in its hinterland regions, the Crees have had some success in promoting such industries as forestry and tourism.

Despite Kerr's claim half a century ago that the Crees "did not venerate their past," they certainly knew who they were, were proud of their achievements, and wished to continue to build on this traditional base. It is doubtful if anyone would have predicted in the late 1960s that the Crees could have produced such a clear definition of who they were and the routes they wished to follow, not to mention the internal organization so necessary to maintaining such sustained intensive negotiations and mounting a highly successful public relations campaign. Norman Chance, who headed the 1960s McGill Cree Project, declared that "the small size of the population, fragmented into hunting groups is not a sufficient 'critical mass' to allow for the emergence of social and political infrastructures necessary for internal growth."[20] The Crees proved him so wrong, not only in the 1970s when they were a David to Quebec's Goliath, but again in the late 1980s when they ran a highly visible and lauded international campaign against "James Bay II," Hydro-Québec's project to dam the waters of Great Whale River. The ease with which the young Cree leaders, such as Billy Diamond, Matthew Coon Come, and Ted Moses, born and raised on traplines, could confer with political leaders throughout North America and Europe and persuade them of the folly of flooding even more rich hunting land is a study in itself of ethnopolitics.[21] The Crees have, in fact, defined the notion of ethnopolitics in Canada.

The idea of the Great Whale River Project, floated in 1988,[IV] was a project closely tied with the Quebec economy and nationalism. It took the Crees six years of lobbying, first aimed at the federal government on the grounds that no environmental impact studies were undertaken, thereby violating federal law, then on the international stage, targeting politicians, environmentalists, and the media. The Crees, with the Inuit, even staged a dramatic public relations event. Starting in Ottawa, they paddled down into the Hudson River, via Albany, in a specially constructed combination canoe and kayak, arriving in New York City on Easter weekend of 1991. There, with local supporters, they held demonstrations, making world-wide headlines.[V] Eventually, the project was halted in 1994 by the premier of Quebec, Jacques Parizeau, shortly after the Grand Chief of the Crees, Matthew Coon Come, denounced the Quebec government as racist in a speech in Washington. So tied to nationalist aspirations was this project and so threatening were the Crees to the government's goals that headlines in the Quebec nationalist press read that "Coon Come has injured all of Quebec."[22] As it happened, the Crees had provided the Quebec government a politically saleable context for cancellation of the project at a time when American electric companies had become unwilling to sign such mega contracts.

The Crees who, a generation earlier, were considered a fragmented, isolated, bush people, in the 1980s were making things happen on the international stage. In Canada they were financially sponsoring other Indian protests and claims, such as the Teme-agama Anishnabay and the Lubicon Crees in their long-standing territorial claims against the federal government. Their own referendum, held at the time of the Quebec referendum on independence in 1995, clearly indicated the Crees' preference for remaining within Canada. Quebec and Canadian federalists continue to hope that the Crees will be able to thwart any attempts by Quebec to separate unilaterally. The political clout of the Crees today extends well beyond their numbers or resources.

A very recent agreement signed between the Grand Council of the Crees and the Quebec government on 7 February 2002 suggests that both governments are attempting to establish a new relationship of cooperation. In this extension to the original 1975 agreement, as reported in the national newspapers, the Crees have addressed some of their key concerns omitted previously. In exchange for permitting further hydroelectric development on the Rupert and Eastmain rivers, the Crees are ensuring for themselves management of their natural resources and greater environmental protection, substantially increased training and employment opportunities, and a measure of full political autonomy.

Richardson's description of the Cree hunters' awkwardness at negotiating in the modern setting of Montreal is now a relic of the past. Although hesitant in their steps in the big city in 1973, the Crees today are very much in step with Canadian society and globalism and still very much in control of who they are.

Their story of survival and revitalization, whether we end it in the 1970s or the 1990s, is testimony to what Raymond Fogelson has termed the internal strengths of Indian society.[23] The Crees of east James Bay manifest that in abundance.

APPENDICES

APPENDIX I

Quantity and Price of Furs Paid by Hudson's Bay Company, James Bay District, 1923–24*

Fur	Quantity	Total	Average
Bear, black	212	$ 1,586.23	$ 7.48
Bear, white	19	211.68	11.13
Beaver	6,762	74,479.28	11.01
Castorum 16	204.75	277.78	1.35
Ermine	1,164	633.32	.54
Fisher	70	3,634.39	51.91
Fox, silver	71	8,931.13	125.79
Fox, cross	378	12,240.97	32.38
Fox, red	1,021	12,558.97	12.30
Fox, white	738	13,216.53	17.90
Fox, blue	10	234.67	23.46
Lynx	427	6,135.10	14.36
Marten	2,400	46,107.19	19.21
Mink	3,878	22,999.18	5.93
Musquash	26,385	22,789.27	.86
Otter	1,551	37,365.02	24.09
Skunk	118	183.86	1.55
Wolf, timber	33	435.54	13.19
Total		$264,020.11	

Source: HBCA A.74/33, fo. 25, 1923–1924, Annual Fur Trade Report, James Bay District.

* The James Bay District included posts on the west side, including Moose Factory, Albany, and Attawapiskat.

APPENDIX 2

Table 2:1
Census, 1911

	White	Mixed	Eskimo	Indian	Total
Rupert House	11	46		388	445
East Main	5	11		144	160
Charlton	0	7	20	0	27
Stretton	2	0		1	3
Nichikun	0	6		57	63
Mistassini	0	22		169	191
Nemaska	1	8		34	43
Waswanipi	1	15		138	154*
Totals	20	115	20	931	1086
Fort George					429
Great Whale River					151
Total					1,511

Source: Anglican Records, Diocese of Moosonee Records, Correspondence and Papers of Bishops, I-1, microfilm 81-4, reel 1, Rupert's House Mission Report, 14 May–28 Aug., 1911, 14 Nov. 1929.

Note: This census does not record the numbers for Fort George or Great Whale River; it does record the number of widowers and widows for each post (14 vs. 33) which have been omitted here. The census figures for Fort George and Whale River were found in a 1929 report by Reverend Griffin of Fort George and are believed to be his recording of the figures for those two posts from the 1911 census which he found in the Preacher's book of 1911. He refers to them to compare to the 1929 census which he says is appended to his report but is not in the archives.

* There are 43 Protestants at Waswanipi.

Table 2:2
Census 1924-1969

Posts	1924	1934	1939	1944	1949	1954	1959	1969
Eastmain	251	319	345	156	180	175	182	246
Fort George	479	736	729	662	684	784	900	1,171
Great Whale River	100	175	197	187	181	182	216	293
Mistassini	159	275	270	543	599	669	864	1,004
Nemaska	152	150	140	100	113	118	137	165
Old Factory (Paint Hills)	140	100	148	287	266	319	364	440
Rupert House	262	340	361	383	416	535	621	645
Waswanipi	177	172	216	312	313	333	416	572
Total	1,720	2,267	2,406	2,630	2,752	3,115	3,700	4,536

Sources: Désy 1968:144; for Mistassini and Waswanipi Posts: Annual Reports of the deputy superintendent general of Indian Affairs, Canada: departmental database, Department of Indian Affairs and Northern Development, Canada; for the year 1969, Ornstein and Marchant 1973:277–80 on reserve/settlement population.

APPENDIX 3
Increase of Beaver in the Rupert House Beaver Sanctuary, 1933–37

	No. of lodges	No. of beaver	Beaver per lodge	% increase
1937	309	1545	5.00	48
1936	209	1045	5.00	105
1935	115	509	4.42	28
1934	93	368	3.95	128
1933	38	162	4.26	–

Source: NA RG10, vol. 6754, file 420–10–4–1, pt. 1, 16 Sept. 1937.

APPENDIX 4:
EXAMPLES OF DEPARTMENT OF INDIAN AFFAIRS REPORTING OF BEAVER PRESERVES

Table 4:1
Statement showing Number of Beaver Trapped and Amount Paid Each Trapper on Nottoway Beaver Preserve, Nottoway River, 1946

No. of beaver trapped	Name of trapper	Amount pd. to Native $	Amount pd. to Dept of Indian Affairs $	Royalty $	Total cost of beaver $
10	Capasisit, Sandy	511	40	20	571
20	Capasisit, Bertie	994	80	40	1,114
10	Capasisit, Oliver	556	40	20	616
10	Capasisit, David	452.50	40	20	512.50
10	Capasisit, Philip	512	40	20	572
10	Capasisit, George	459	40	20	519
15	Cowboy, James	697	60	30	787
20	Diamin, Walter Sr.	1,141	80	40	1,261
20	Diamin, Walter Jr.	953	80	40	1,073
20	Diamin, George Jr.	1,090	80	40	1,210
20	Diamin, Malcolm	1,146	80	40	1,266
10	Diamin, Philip	480	40	20	540
20	Diamin, Bertie	1,164	80	40	1,284
15	Esau, Abraham	694.50	60	30	784.50
20	Esau, Solomon	891	80	40	1,011
10	Esau, Rupert	503.50	40	20	563
10	Esau, Eddy	469.50	40	20	529.5
20	Frank, David	1,180	80	40	1,300
10	Frank, James	586	40	20	646
20	Georgekish, Sam	941	80	40	1,061
10	Georgekish, George	490	40	20	550
10	Georgekish, Sidney	437	40	20	497
10	Hester, Chas. Sr.	512	40	20	572
4	Hester, Angus	169	16	8	193
20	Hester, George	868	80	40	988
20	Hester, Joseph	1,077	80	40	1,197

Table 4:1 Continued

No. of beaver trapped	Name of trapper	Amount pd. to Native $	Amount pd. to Dept of Indian Affairs $	Royalty $	Total cost of beaver $
20	Katapatuk, Abraham	767.50	80	40	887
10	Katapatuk, Simon	440	40	20	500
10	Katapatuk, Alex	963	80	40	1,083
20	Katapatuk, Edward	1,000	80	40	1,120
15	Katapatuk, David	807	60	30	897
10	Katapatuk, Malcolm	427	40	20	487
10	Katapatuk, Walter	550	40	20	610
18	Kitchen, Peter	845	72	36	953
13	Namagoose, Sidney	766	52	26	844
15	Shacapot, Sam	631	60	30	721
10	Shacapot, Abram	373	40	20	433
20	Shacapot, George	1,133	80	40	1,253
20	Wapachee, Andrew	1,016	80	40	1,136
20	Weechee, Philip	1,040	80	40	1,160
5	Diamin, Widow Geo.	279	20	10	309
10	Georgekish, Widow Geo.	401	40	20	461
5	Katapatuk, Widow	270	20	10	300
5	Minister, Widow Sally	171	20	10	201
5	Moar, Jane	279	20	10	309
Total 625		$ 31,133.5	$ 2,500	$ 1,250	$ 34,883.5

Source: NA RG10, vol. 6755, file 420–10–4–1, pt. 4.

Table 4:2
Statement of Nottoway Beaver Preserve Showing Number of Beaver Trapped and Amount to Each Trapper, Nemaska Post, 1946

No. of beaver trapped	Name of trapper	Amount pd. to Native $	Amount pd. to Dept. of Indian Affairs $	Royalty $	Total amount $
20	Cheezo, Joseph	916	80	40	1,036
10	Chief, Joseph	876	80	40	996
20	Jimmikin, David	981	80	40	1,101
12	Jimmikin, Louisa	593	48	24	665
20	Jolly, Anderson	906	80	40	1,026
20	Moar, James	812	60	40	932
20	Ottereyes, Edward	1,108	80	40	1,228
20	Ottereyes, Matthew	1,001	80	40	1,121
20	Ottereyes, Sydney	708	80	40	828
12	Tanoosh, Mary	450	48	24	522
20	Tent, John	924	80	40	1,044
20	Wapachee, Billy	945	80	40	1,065
20	Wapachee, Daniel	857	80	40	977
15	Wapachee, Simeon	544	60	30	634
Total 259		$ 11,621	$ 1,036	$ 518	$ 13,175

Source: See Table 4:1.

Table 4:3
Beaver Count: A Composite of the Old Factory Beaver
and Fur Preserve Annual Reports, 1944 and 1947

District No.	Tallymen	1942	1943	1945	1947	Increase 1942–7/ 1945–7
	Fort George Division					
1	Geo. & Ronnie Sam	2	7	12	28	26
2	Wm.. & Malcolm Sam	3	6	9	19	16
3*	Joseph Cox	–	–	5	16	11
4*	Peter Cox	–	–	11	19	8
5	Ernest & Sam House	4	5	14	23	19
6	David Cox	–	–	18	31	13
7*	John Chiskamash	–	–	11	23	19*
8*	David Chiskamash	–	–	16	31	15
9	Chas. & Simon Kanatiwat	6	8	19	35	29
	Old Factory Division					
10	David Swallow	2	3	10	26	24
11	Albert Ichinaya	–	5	15	32	27
12	William Visitor	3	5	17	36	33
13	Sam Visitor, Jr.	2	5	2	18	16
14*	Bosun Kakabat	–	–	10	26	16
15*	Rupert Kakabat	–	–	13	31	18
16	John Ashquabaneskum	4	6	20	39	35
17	Richard Houghboy	–	4	17	35	31
18	John Visitor	–	1	11	28	27
19	William Matchee	5	16	28	46	41
20*	John Mistochesik	–	–	14	31	17
21*	Joseph Mistochesik	–	–	9	23	14
22	David Minicouagan	–	1	11	26	25
23*	Jacob Georgekish	–	–	22	38	16
24*	John Georgekish	–	–	22	42	20
25	Geordie Georgekish	3	7	16	33	30
26	Edward Stewart	2	10	12	28	26
27	Thomas Stewart	3	6	11	26	23

Table 4:3 Continued

District No.	Tallymen	1942	1943	1945	1947	Increase 1942-7/ 1945-7
28*	Henry Gilpin	–	–	13	30	17
29*	Luke Gilpin	–	–	14	33	19
30	Wm. D. Visitor	–	–	28	52	24
	Eastmain Division[†]					
31	William Gilpin	6	11	32	126	120[‡]
32*	David Weshinicappo	–	–	60	136	76
33*	Bob Cheezo	–	–	15	38	23
34*	Geo. Mayappo	–	–	71	89	18
35*	Allan Mayappo	–	–	79	140	61

Sources: NA RG10, vol. 6752, file 420-10-1-3, Old Factory Beaver and Fur Preserve, Third Annual Report, 1944; Vieux Comptoir Preserve, 1947.

Notes:

* indicates which sections in 1944 listed two or more tallymen and then only one in 1945-7 due to a reorganization of territory.

[†] The 1944 report explains why the better beaver concentration is in the Eastmain Division. It is due to better seed stock, a more favourable topography, and the fact that trapping had already started in the adjacent Rubert House sanctuary, causing a migration of beaver across the river to the Eastmain Division.

[‡] Exceptional increase in section 31 was due to reorganization and exchange of territory.

Table 4:4
Recapitulation of Beaver Increase* between the Years 1942–47, by Division

	1947
Fort George	1,125[†]
Old Factory	3,395
Eastmain	2,645
Total	7,165

Source: See Table 4:3, Vieux Comptoir Preserve, 1947.
Notes:
* The "usual converting factor" of five beaver per house was applied.
[†] Fifty-six live beaver were purchased from Rupert House hunters and transferred to the coastal strip north of Comb Hills because it was lagging behind the remainder of the preserve in beaver increase.

Table 4:5
Beaver Lodges Counted and Marked on the Waswanipi Division, 1943 and 1944

District	Tallymen	1943	1944
1	James Happyjack	2	18
2	Tommy Gull	5	7
3	Joseph Ottereyes	1	5
4	Joseph Saganush	4	5
5	Abraham Gull	0	0
6	Edward Gull	4	7
7	George Diamond	6	13
8	Dion Blacksmith	5	7
9	Charlie Gull	10	20
Total		37	72*

Source: See Table 4:3, Nottaway Preserve, 1944.
Note:
* The correct addition is 82.

APPENDIX 5

Catholic Presence in Five Cree Communities, 1968

Village	Religious personnel	Catholic Indians	Non-Catholic Indians*	Total Indian population	Whites	Total population
Nemaska		0	230	230	5	235
Rupert House	1 priest	2	600	602	17	619
Eastmain	1 priest 3 religious	0	255	255	7	262
Paint Hills		0	400	400	2	402
Fort George	3 priests, 3 religious, 8 religious women	20	1,100	1,120	175	1,295

Source: Gauthier 1973:3
Notes:
* The author does not break down this figure but it is presumed the vast majority are Anglicans.

APPENDIX 6

ECONOMIC PROFILES OF CREE COMMUNITIES, 1968-72

Table 6:1
Earned Income Living on Reserves/Settlements, 1969

	Number of Persons with Income					Reserve Population Ages 15-64		
	Under $1,000	$1000–1999	$2000–2999	$3000–3999	$4000+	Total	Male	Female	Total

	Under $1,000	$1000–1999	$2000–2999	$3000–3999	$4000+	Total	Male	Female	Total
Abitibi District									
Eastmain	26	1	2	3		32	73	58	131
Fort George	68	2	23	23	34	150	290	282	572
Great Whale River	16		4	11	7	38	69	72	141
Mistassini	66	70	32	21	16	205	239	248	487
Nemaska	28				1	29	42	41	83
Old Factory	52	8	3	2	2	67	121	118	239
Rupert House	52	21		6	9	88	151	133	284
Pointe-Bleue District									
Waswanipi	143		10	2	6	161	117	120	237

Source: Ornstein and Marchant 1973:III:5.
Note: The value of the food and fuel derived from the land are not included in these income totals.

Table 6:2
Estimated Man Years of Employment, by Type of Employment for Males, Living on Reserve/Settlement, 1969

	Abitibi District							Pointe Bleue District
	Eastmain	Fort George	Great Whale River	Nemaska	Old Factory	Rupert House	Waswanipi	Mistassini
Trapping/hunting	2.4	5.7	1.3	9.3	6	4.8	13.3	70.9
Transportation		6.6			1.6			1
Steelworker								
Soldier								
Services	2	6	8.8		1			
Professional	1.8	4	3				1	1
Production		1						
Painter		1						
Miner etc.		2				5	10.8	
Mechanic		5.8			1			11.3
Machinist		1.0						1
Logger							5.8	
Labourer		7.5	5.7	0.8	1.3	8.8	8.3	
Handicrafts							4.7	
Guide							1.7	9.8
Fisherman							8.3	0.7
Farmer								
Electrician	0.6					1.0	0.8	
Domestic Work	0.1							2
Clerical/sales		6	1		1	1	1	2
Construction		11.3	1					9.6

Source: Ornstein and Marchant 1973:II:16–17.

Table 6:3
Per Capita Income from Beaver Trapping, 1971–72

	No. of trappers	No. of pelts	Value of pelts $	Per capita income $	Males age 15–64
ABITIBI DISTRICT					
Eastmain	28	420	13,393	478	81
Fort George	72	649	22,930	318	342
Great Whale River	13	130	3,640	280	71
Nemaska	(now trapping with Waswanipi and Mistassini band)				
Old Factory (Paint Hills)	32	405	15,592	487	151
Rupert House	69	457	39,574	574	222
Waswanipi	75	1,918	49,669	662	141
POINTE-BLEUE DISTRICT					
Mistassini	292	6,472	182,159	624	346

Source: Ornstein and Marchant 1973:II:40.

Table 6:4
Band Population Living off Reserve/Settlement, 1971

	Band total	Off-reserve/ settlement	% off
ABITIBI DISTRICT			
Eastmain	268	32	12
Fort George	1,309	47	4
Grand Lac Victoria	201	30	15
Great Whale River	326	3	1
Nemaska	135	1	0.9
Old Factory (Paint Hills)	557	86	15
Rupert House	878	228	26
Waswanipi	650	198	30
POINTE-BLEUE DISTRICT			
Mistassini	1,511	219	14

Source: Ornstein and Marchant 1973:II:57-8.

Table 6:5
Social Assistance for June 1972, Number Assisted, by Band

	No. of family units	Total No. in families	No. single persons	Total single and family persons	Band population	% on social asst.
ABITIBI DISTRICT						
Eastmain	27	115	19	134	275	49
Fort George	159	777	47	824	1,345	61
Great Whale River						
Nemaska						
Old Factory	68	310	53	363	572	63
Rupert House	57	239	23	262	902	29
Waswanipi	44	174	14	188	668	28
POINTE-BLEUE DISTRICT						
Mistassini	168	778	75	853	1,553	55

Source: Ornstein and Marchant 1973:II:101–2.

Table 6:6
Enrolment in Schools by Place of Residence, 1969

	Total enrolment	Student residence	Boarding home	At home
ABITIBI DISTRICT				
Eastmain	56	29	7	20
Fort George	386	109	66	211
Great Whale River	55	4		51
Nemaska	42	35	7	
Old Factory (Paint Hills)	143	13	28	102
Rupert House	260	46	68	146
Waswanipi	165	121	9	35
POINTE BLEUE DISTRICT				
Mistassini	302	182	10	110

Source: Ornstein and Marchant 1973:II:157–8.

APPENDIX 7
QUANTITIES OF GAME TAKEN BY ALFIE MATOUSH GROUP, AUGUST 1953 TO EARLY JUNE 1954

Game	No. taken	Weight edible, appr. (lb.)	Weight by group (lb.)
Fish	1582	3,165	3,165
Moose	10	4,000	
Caribou	12	1,500	
Bear	1	210	
Beaver	55	2,120	7,830
Hare	76	114	
Muskrat	120	240	
Porcupine	6	60	
Mink	132	33	
Squirrel	33	8	
Marten	5	5	
Otter	11	138	598
Loon	11	44	
Geese	12	67	
Ducks	132	231	
Ptarmigan	301	150	
Spruce grouse	75	38	
Ruffed grouse	2	1	
Owl	2	1	532
Total			12,125

Source: Rogers 1963:35.

Substantive Notes

CHAPTER ONE

I This threat I first saw in print in Kerr (1950: 58) and have heard of its continued use. Truman Michelson, a linguist who conducted research in 1935 along the eastern James Bay coast, learned at Fort George that when a child is naughty, they sometimes are told "a Husky [Inuk] will take you" or "a white man ..." (NAA, Michelson Papers, # 3399, fo. 81). J.J. Honigmann first heard of this expression at Great Whale River in the 1940s under the name of *otsibwewah*; he saw it as a focus for the anxieties aroused through contact with intrusive Euro-Canadians and he suggested such feelings were more intense at Rupert House than at Great Whale River (Honigmann 1964: 365). Brian Craik (pers. comm., 13 December 2000) comments that at Chisasibi the word used, *pwachigee*, is similar and at Waskaganish it sounds more like *gotchiibweo*. A psychologist working in Mistassini in the 1960s discovered that parents there threaten children who misbehave by telling them "the *wabinkiyu* is going to take them away." He described it as kind of bogeyman, thought of as white (Sindell 1968:83). Similarly, at Waswanipi this bogeyman is termed *wabinkish* (Caroline Diamond Oblin, pers. comm., 6 December 2000).

II See two excellent works which amply demonstrate this: Olive Dickason (1997) and J.R. Miller (1989).

III Richard Preston (pers. comm. 24 September 2000) reminded me that not all whites the Crees encountered were high on the hierarchy of authority. Many were "more proletarian than bourgeoisie."

IV These stories were collected mainly by anthropologists in the 1970s and 1980s (see Feit 1968–70, 1982; Scott 1977–81; Sun 1979; Turner 1974) under the auspices of the Urgent Ethnology Program within the Ethnology Service of the National Museum of Man. These collections are on deposit at the Museum of Civilization.

v An offshoot of state colonialism would be Howard Adams's (1995:145) "constitutional colonialism" which also "develops a bureaucracy and judicial system of oppression."

vi This is perhaps akin to what Noel Dyck (1997:333) refers to as "state tutelage" or the "internal colonialism" of Satzewich and Wotherspoon (1993: 6). It is not, though, the "welfare colonialism" described by Paine, a 1960s development in the Arctic.

vii The arguments set out here are more fully developed in a recent paper. See Morantz (2001).

viii The practice of distinguishing between these kinds of narratives is found all over the world. One example of a culture observing this dichotomy is that of the Waura of Brazil who distinguish between myths as "real stories" and stories about "mere facts" (Hill 1988:4).

ix An example demonstrating identical accounts, one a *tipachiman* story, the other from the Mistassini Post journal is the account of the drowning of three people in 1917. Here is the oral account which is really a storytelling about the canoe brigades from Mistassini: "Another time the Mistassini manager was on the trip, as they came closer to Nemaska their canoe turned over. Two men and one girl drowned ... The girl was buried at the same place where the men were buried. The girl that drowned was Mr Anderson's daughter, and he was the manager at Mistassini at that time" (Cree Way 1975, Willie Jacob and Charlie Blackned). The entry in the Mistassini Post journal, kept by manager J.W. Anderson reads: "August 16, 1917. Had a sea accident ... 26th July, Nemaska Lake, daughter Chrissie, aged three years and two of the crew were drowned" (HBCA B.133/a/66). Richard Preston (pers. comm, 24 September 2000) identifies one of the men as Robert Petawabino. He was said to be an excellent swimmer but he drowned while trying to save Anderson's daughter in a tickanagun (cradle board).

x The longer story of the canoe brigades involves the Rupert House transporters being pursued by an *atoosh* (an evil spirit), "a curse from someone in Mistassini" (Cree Way 1975, Willie Jacob and Charlie Blackned).

xi See, for example, the work of Preston 1975a; Tanner 1979, Feit 1978, and Scott 1983.

xii The Dunne-za are the Dene-speaking people of Northern British Columbia who were labelled by outsiders the "Beavers" (Ridington 1988).

xiii See for example, Regina Flannery's (1985) important study of "dream visitors and Frank Speck's (1935) comprehensive study of the religion.

xiv "Cree Way" refers to a curriculum development project initiated at school in Rupert House in the mid-1970s under the guidance of, amongst others, John Murdoch and Annie Whiskeychan. For much of its source material it used a copy of the stories Richard Preston had recorded with John Blackned and gave to the project.

xv The exceptions are those few anthropologists who have spent many years with the people whose history they are studying and speak the language. In addition to the works of Julie Cruikshank, I direct the reader to Richard Price's fascinating 1983 history of the Saramaka people, entitled *First-Time. The Historical Vision of an Afro-American People*. However, I add a cautionary note to the reader that this history, merging oral and documentary sources, revolves around a single confrontational issue which lends itself to greater correspondence with the conventions of Western history. Price's history focuses on the Saramaka at a time when they were runaway slaves. Similarly, Joanne Rappaport's 1994 history of the Cumbe of Columbia pit them against the interests of the larger society, specifically over land issues.

xvi Under pressure from the intense competition faced by the rival companies a trading system arose whereby Cree men, with the ability to influence a number of other hunters, were encouraged to head a gang of men to trade their furs at the posts. These men of influence, called trading captains by the English, received special uniforms and presents of brandy and tobacco to redistribute amongst the gang. The trading captain gang was sometimes identical to existing winter hunting groups or the small local bands, but most often it was an ad hoc arrangement with the gang composed of men from several local bands.

xvii Rogers had not undertaken any historical studies, but knowing the issues in the literature, hunting group size, and the probability of hunting territories, he was able to provide some educated guesses about the possibilities, given specific situations (see Rogers 1963).

xviii Richard Preston (pers. comm. 24 September 2000) rightly points out that in the 1950s there were sometimes summer camps of fifty people. As Leacock was a summer sojourner in Cree and Montagnais-Innu territories, she might have erred in assuming these large camps existed in the winter as well. In the archaeological and written records there is no reference to such large winter camps.

xix I am grateful to Adrian Tanner for pointing out the distinction between egalitarianism as applied to material differences and as applied to status differences. He is of the opinion that the Crees "recognize differential status between the same kinds of people," such as superior status recognized for old people in general, for shamans, and for chiefs.

xx Richard Preston suggests that this ethos of egalitarianism prevented non-egalitarian processes, such as the trading captain system, from assuming extreme proportions; it was also the basis for criticizing those who set themselves above their "followers."

xxi Typical of the many comments which indicate this Cree view of their needs and willingness to participate in the trade are the following: "Nothing will induse Long Shore Indians to catch many furs more that what will trade them a kettle, hatchet or ice chisel" (HBCA B.59/a/14, 16 Mar.1747). In 1814 the company managers were still complaining of the Crees' refusal to hunt more than what they perceived necessary to provision themselves (ibid, B.59/e/1, fo.5). Again in 1872 the manager is exasperated at their carrying on a bear feast rather than hunting furs (ibid, B.186/a/97, 27 Nov.).

XXII Preserving the pelt for trade required extra labour for the women, who spent many hours scraping and tanning the skins. Perhaps one might consider this back-breaking work offset by the women's access to steel needles, iron knives and axes, copper kettles, and cloth, which lessened the time and labour they spent in sewing, gathering firewood, and food preparation.

CHAPTER TWO

I The reference to "unprecedented decline in food resources" may be an artifact of the shortcomings of both the oral and documentary records. "Widespread starvation" was first reported from Albany to Eastmain in 1703 (Davies 1965:8), and thereafter there are regularly reports of food deprivation in different regions of the James Bay territory. However, beginning in the 1860s the records permit us to chart a decline in food resources.

II This confrontation only occurred then in the southern portions of James Bay, regions opened up by the railways in the 1930s.

III In the 1970s the Quebec Regie de Topynymy began francisizing place names so that Richmond Gulf, named by the British in the eighteenth century, became Lac Guillaume Delisle. Note that the Regie also declared the gulf a lake, as under the Canadian constitution the federal government has jurisdiction over navigable waters and the provincial government over inland waterways. Since the 1980s the Quebec government has been using the long-standing Cree and Inuit names in this part of the Quebec-Labrador peninsula.

IV For a fuller discussion of the debt system, when it began and how it functioned, see Morantz (1990).

V Until 1927 J.W. Anderson managed different posts in east and west James Bay, moving to head office in Winnipeg in the 1930s. He died in 1962 and was buried at Nemiskau alongside his infant daughter who drowned nearby and was buried there in 1917 (Rogers 1965; Moccasin Telegraph 1962, Fall: 31). He lived to see his highly informative book about early twentieth- century life in James Bay, *Fur Trader's Story*, published in 1961.

VI This is similar to university students today boasting of the amount of their student loans; the higher they are, the greater the status amongst other students.

VII Although under dispute, some biologists distinguish between the barren ground variety and the woodland caribou. Others see them as one species. Nevertheless, the barren ground caribou, located on the tundra, migrated in herds of thousands, whereas the woodland, in much smaller troops of several dozen individuals, occupied a restricted migration range. For each, however, the movements were difficult to predict and caribou, particularly the woodland variety, were never a reliable resource (Audet 1979).

VIII The task of haying at Rupert House is amply recounted by Willie Jacob, whose father cut and dried the hay for the cows to eat. The grass was harvested across the river from the post and hauled by a special boat manned by six men whose foreman was the late Edward Namagoose. The grass was spread on the ground to dry and turned and turned over days and finally stacked. His father employed "a lot of helpers." Once the haying was done the manager distributed pilot biscuits, jam, butter, sugar and tea. "It was a big treat eating and drinking tea with sugar at those times" (Cree Way 1975). A by-product of the cattle kept at the post was the manure which people would gather to burn in the tents to drive the mosquitoes away.

IX This (MB) was the company's longtime standard for valuing both furs and trade goods. One made beaver referred to a flensed, dried, and stretched prime winter male beaver pelt. This standard was gradually phased out in favour of cash after the First World War (Ray 1990b:82).

X In the year 1869-70, 304 individuals (presumably some coming in several times) received 320 pounds of flour from the Fort George post and 395 individuals received 371 pounds of oatmeal (HBCA B.77/d/16, fo. 25-27, 1869-70).

XI The price differential also seems to have annoyed a sportsman in 1914. In his article in *Rod and Gun* he mentions that at Abitibi Post (south of James Bay) he and his companions were surprised to find that the company was still selling old muzzle-loading rifles and more surprised to see them priced at $12 there when in a department store in the south they would sell for $2.50 (Miller 1914:118).

XII The posts on the east coast of Hudson Bay were administratively located in a different district from Fort Chimo; so, although the same company, there was an air of rivalry between the posts. In 1879 Mr McDonald wrote that two of his hunters visited Fort Chimo and he hoped they received a "cool reception" (HBCA B.77/b/5, 23 Aug. 1879). This competition is understandable when one considers that the officers of the company were recompensed through a profit-sharing system (Ray 1990b:8).

XIII According to Titley (1986: 63), Frank Pedley, the deputy superintendent, suggested this in 1903, in the context of the estimates of the cost of the treaty-making. Thus, Treaty No. 9 applied only to Ontario Indians and excluded all Quebec-based ones. As an aside, but a telling one for purposes of understanding the great injustices suffered by Indians in Canada, the treaty cost the Dominion government $40,000 ($15,000 of which was the administrative costs and $24,000 payments to the Cree and Ojibwa). At the time Treaty No. 9 was being "negotiated" with the Indians, silver mining began at Cobalt that for the next eighteen years would produce in excess of $206 million (Titley 1986:63,73). Although Titley erred in implying that Cobalt lay in the treaty watershed (John Long, pers. comm., 1 Mar. 2000) these figures are still telling.

XIV Rousseau's botanical studies "handsomely complemented" Low's geological surveys. In addition, with his wife Madeleine, Rousseau made significant contributions to studies of the Mistassini Crees (Cooke 1964:166–7).

XV "Long ago there were whitemen who were paddling near Mistassini. One of them asked the Indians, what does an Indian eat when he has no food?" So begins a story told by John Blackned at Rupert House. It is about a surveying party who got stranded when freeze-up began; they ran out of food and were without winter gear such as snowshoes. The manager (a "half-breed") at Mistassini had been expecting them and asked a conjuror to help locate them, which he did, and also assured the manager they were alive, living on boiled wood, and white moss (Cree Way 1975). Regrettably, there is no parallel story in the incomplete Mistassini journals, but in the winter of 1885 it was reported that Bignell's party were down the lake without provisions (HBCA B.133/a/52, 8 Jan. 1885) while in April Isaac and Nebowish were dispatched to carry provisions to Low and his men said to be "starving about 2 days from here" (ibid., 26 Apr.).

XVI A number of Inuit were principal guides on the Leith geological expedition and the book gives some profiles of them as well as comments about some of the Crees, such as Natawhum, Salt, Tom Snowboy, William Snowboy, among others (Leiths 1912).

XVII It was not unusual, beginning in the late 1800s, for the Hudson's Bay Company post managers to refer to the Inuit as "huskies." John Long (pers. comm., 1 Mar. 2000) identifies Husky as the Cree word for Inuit.

XVIII The region east of James Bay missed out on hosting the likes of two men who appeared at Moose Factory in the early 1900s. They were insurance men from New York who "came to escape investigation" (Leiths 1912:25).

XIX Alanson Skinner made two expeditions to the James Bay region. In 1908 he travelled along the east coast, spending two weeks at Rupert House and then briefly at Eastmain. In 1909 he travelled to the Ojibwa communities of Fort Hope, Lac Seul, and the Cree community at Albany. The purpose of these expeditions was to collect artifacts for the American

Museum of Natural History in New York. At Rupert House he purchased an old beaver-tooth knife as well as a number of other items such as snowshoes. He commented that painting was considered the aboriginal form of decoration but beadwork and silkwork were now common and thought to be "very recent" with the flower design post-European. He added that the painted tents were gone but he collected a list of the old designs and took photographs of face and body painting, tattooing, and scarification. He also wrote to Charles Iserhoff, clerk at Nichikun, asking him to collect specimens of "old Indian tools, clothing, etc." up to $150 to $200 as they had discussed the year before at Rupert House and to identify if they were made by "Cree or Nascopi" (AMNH Skinner Papers, fos 1–2, 24 Aug., 1908; 18 May 1909). He published his ethnographic findings in 1911.

XX Virgin soil refers to the first encounter populations have with specific pathogens and assumes that all ages are affected (like dropping "lighted matches into tinder") rather than just the young in a population that has for some time been exposed to the disease (see Crosby 1976:289–90).

XXI Preston (pers. comm. 24 Sept. 2000) suggests Turner mis-identified this part of the bear and probably it was the bear's chin, which certainly is a Cree token.

XXII It may be that Ellen Smallboy, her mother, and sisters caught fish the way it was described in a Waswanipi account: "In the days when women were wearing long dresses they would use their dresses to catch fish in the rapids of small creeks. They would go down on their knees below the rapids to catch the fish which were coming down from above. Some would jump out of her dress and right onto the shore" (Marshall 1987:34).

XXIII This is also the concern in a life history recorded by Frank Sun at Wemindji in the 1970s. In this account, "some men" were said to keep meat in scarce times rather than share with the women or children (MC Sun 1980:C2).

XXIV About 1917 a thousand caribou were killed by spearing on the George River of Ungava Bay (Leacock and Rothschild 1994: 116).

XXV Hare might not have been a food source for the Crees north of Eastmain in the late 1800s. In the early 1960s Preston was told that there are "no rabbits north of Eastmain" and fewer as you go north (Preston Fieldnotes fo. 299). Hare were also said to be scarce earlier in the vicinity of Fort George (HBCA B.186/b/1:21).

XXVI John Blackned, born about 1894, lived into the 1970s. He was a highly respected historian and philosopher in the community who relayed to Richard Preston much of the wisdom of his people.

XXVII The botanist Jacques Rousseau (1949: 36) explained that the yellow water lily is a vital food for moose and its northern limit then (1949) was at Lake Mistassini, hence the reason for moose being rare.

XXVIII As an aside, in 1909 it is said the Inlanders were still doing beadwork on items such as garters and shot and cap pouches. Some were very elaborate and the Leiths expected this craft work would soon disappear. If the Coasters were doing any beadwork, it is said they copied designs rather than originating them (Leiths 1912:164).

XXIX John Kawapit remembered a humorous occasion when on a trip to Fort Chimo they encountered a camp of people who were working for one of the two trading companies. In an attempt to influence Kawapit's group to trade with their company (unnamed) they offered them some bannock which was to be cooked on a stove, located outside the tent. "In those days, people were not used to the mechanics of stoves" and one of the women put her pan of bannock on top of the stove pipe causing smoke to surge out of the mouth of the stove (MC Turner Collection 1974, tape 33-A). Another observation about the smoke in the lodges was made by Father Maurice Grenon who described his stay in a goose camp located between Eastmain and Old Factory. He was told by his host that in entering the wigwam one should not remain standing "like a white man" as the smoke would bother his eyes. Close to the ground, he was told, there is no smoke (Paul-Emile 1952:213).

XXX Boots figure into a fire on 20 October 1902 that burned down the officers' house at Great Whale River. It was during the terrible measles epidemic and an Indian lad who was tending the sick Louttit family (David Louttit was manager there) struck a match to look for his boots. It is supposed that match caused the fire. No one died in it, though David Louttit did die a week later possibly from his exertions on the night of the fire (HBCA B.372/a/16, 20 Oct. 20, 1902; James 1985:19).

XXXI In the discussion of country foods no mention is made of beluga whales. It was first noted in 1744 that they had been the summer mainstay of Crees in the vicinity of Great and Little Whale rivers. The commercial whaling run by the company had depleted the resources and the fishery had ended in 1870 (Francis and Morantz 1983:72, 147). John Mukash tells us the Crees continued to hunt and eat whales until the 1920s when the whales stopped coming into the Great Whale River (AR Trudel Collection 1978, fo. 7.1).

XXXII One such resident at Fort George was Waskihagan (HBCA B.77/a/47, 1 Apr. 1899). Not surprisingly, *waskihagan* means "house."

XXXIII Ross also served in the capacity as a lay reader for the Anglicans at Great Whale River (HBCA B.372/a/22, 11 Feb. 1939).

XXXIV This is the list of dances Anderson mentions for Moose Factory in 1911 and one can only assume these same dances were held up and down the James Bay coast but not inland, where Anderson says there was "little of what could be called social life" at Mistassini (Anderson 1961:29, 96).

XXXV Anderson was describing a time before the wireless when the price of furs was stable throughout the year and was announced in summer (Anderson 1961:106).

XXXVI *Wemstukshiokan* literally signifies "made into white man," the ending *kan* signifying surrogate or manufactured (Brian Craik, pers. comm. July 1999). It is a term employed today to refer to Crees of mixed ancestry (Long 1985:56). The word for whites, *wemistikushiiu* derives from the words for "shaped-wooden-people," which the Reverend Cartlidge at Waswanipi explained arose because everything seemed to come in wooden boxes (Marshall 1987:24) while Long (1991:81) suggests the word likely refers to people with wooden boats. This term applies to English-speaking whites; the French speakers are referred to as *opiishtigoyao*. Slight dialect differences and a non-standardized transcription account for the differences in the writing of the core words.

XXXVII Band lists commenced in the mid-nineteenth century; they were made more systematic in 1913 (Titley 1986:38, 57) although the more northern, scattered peoples were more difficult to keep track of. More contemporary lists with birthdates and religion of each individual date back to 1951. Following the revised Indian Act of 1951, the Indian Register, different from the band list, was initiated which provided all formally reported information about each individual such as dates of birth, marriage, death, children, etc. (McCardle 1982:139–41).

XXXVIII In over two hundred years, perhaps no post manager came to eastern James Bay with a non-native wife until James Watt arrived at Rupert House in 1920 with Maud Watt, born of a French-Canadian mother and Irish father in the Gaspé and raised at Mingan on the lower north shore, where the Watts met (W.A.Anderson 1961:3–6, 99).

XXXIX Harold Udgarten was born at Moose Factory in the late 1860s of a Norwegian sailor father and a mixed-ancestry mother (Harriet, daughter of Joseph Turnor). The company sent him to Great Whale River when he about fifteen years old, where he worked as a labourer and interpreter even after his official retirement in the 1930s. He died there on 3 April 1950 (NAA Honigmann Papers, box 29, "Udgarten"). The Crees called him *wamsteegoashish* (MC Turner Collection 1974, tape 23, Rupert George).

XL The Inuit men at Charlton in the late 1890s were Fleming, Mananck (Minarick?), Houdlat, and Tudlakudluk.

XLI Miles Spencer, James L. Cotter, and William Broughton were other managers at Rupert House before him.

XLII This servant, Erland Vincent, from Fort Hope, was a nephew of archdeacon Thomas Vincent (John Long, pers. comm. 1 Mar. 2000).

XLIII Wife of James Watt, Rupert House Hudson's Bay Company post manager in the 1920s until his death in 1944. Watt played a pivotal role in the establishment of the beaver preserves.

XLIV The Leiths point out that it was not unusual for the post manager to keep a hunter waiting long hours to transact the trade; the way a Cree was treated depended on the amount of his debt (Leiths 1912:40).

XLV In 1900, 193 men and their immediate families were the employees of Moose Factory and thus dependants (Ray 1990:209). Rupert House, though smaller, was still large by James Bay standards and had a permanent native staff and their families of about sixty while in 1912 there were two white employees and their families at the post (Anderson 1961:49 and see Appendix 2, 1911 census).

XLVI David Cooter suggested that he took the position with the company because he could not find suitable employment in England in the 1930s and thought this would be adventurous. After thirty-seven years of service, Cooter, who had been managing the post at Pointe Bleue, decided to take early retirement to teach first high school then university (pers. comm. Sept. 1985).

XLVII Not surprisingly, J.W. Anderson was married to a McLeod woman of mixed ancestry from Moose Factory (John Long, pers. comm. 1 Mar. 2000).

CHAPTER THREE

I The zeal and anti-Catholic hostility displayed by Ernest Renouf in his Fort George journal in the years from 1922 to 1925 most likely was particular to him; other journals seem to ignore the subject.

II The baptismal and marriage registers of the Oblates begin in 1851 for Waswanipi at which time twenty-one were baptized. In 1887, the last year for which the registers contain information about Waswanipi, there were eleven baptized. (OMI Registre des Missions Indiennes, 1843–1878, c–16).

III The Iserhoff family started with the marriage at Waswanipi of Shabookwhy and a Hudson's Bay Company employee who formerly had been in charge of the Northwest Company post there. It is said he was a Russian sailor shipwrecked from one of the Hudson's Bay Company ships and he remained in James Bay. He died at Waswanipi in 1823, leaving his widow and some children (B.227/e/2, 6d, 1823; Anderson 1961:118). On 10 August 1847 the Nichikun Post journal entry reads:"Joseph Iserhoff married my Caroline. I [John Spencer] read the matrimony of England to them so that I am thinking that they are almost lawfully married until they get married by a minister hereafter" (HBCA B.147/a/14). The four Iserhoff brothers were sent to work at a number of posts: Joseph was manager at Mistassini and presumably the father of Charles, clerk and catechist at Mistassini (Scanlon 1975:9) as well as of William, a canoe-builder there. This Joseph died at Rupert House on a business trip there in 1913 (Anderson 1961:70). There were also John, manager at Waswanipi and Samuel (born 1862), who retired as manager at Ogoki on the Albany River (Anderson 1961:118; Petersen 1974:78). It is difficult to keep track of them as they generally are named in the journals only as "Iserhoff." It is known that Canon Samuel Iserhoff is a fourth-generation Iserhoff and was the son of John. He was born in 1885 and raised at Waswanipi, early becoming an employee of the Hudson's Bay Company, serving first as a cook on the summer transport to Rupert House, then as clerk at a number of interior posts until he took up full-time work in the Anglican missions, eventually rising to canon (Petersen 1974:51, 78).

IV William Wapachee had two sons who were also catechists. Johnny Wapachee is described in the Nichikun journals as "the clerical gentleman who was supposed to arrive at Nitchequon and give services" (HBCA B.147/a/40, 25 Mar. 1940). He also served at Mistassini and died there in 1970. Billy Wapachee became catechist at Nemiskau. Their father and mother were married at Rupert House in 1902 by Bishop Newnham (Scanlon 1975:4).

V Guinard, in his memoirs, writes something of Father Jean-Pierre Guégen, missionary in the Upper St Maurice region from 1865 to 1899. Although considered a great missionary, one who "loved very much the Indians," he was subject to slights by the Hudson's Bay Company clerks and Rupert House Crees (Protestants) who were on the brigades to Waswanipi and would ridicule him. Evidently "divine vengeance" intervened, for on the way back those insulting him died (Guinard 1951:33).

VI In 1915 Father Guinard, with the help of four Obedjiwan men, – Louis Wéjina, son Mathias, Pian Sateihaw, and William Awacic – reconstructed the chapel. Originally the company had promised him two thousand feet of lumber but instead gave it to the Protestants. Cartlidge built the Anglican chapel there (Guinard 1951:68, 62).

VII Several comments in the post journal also bear witness to the interest the Crees developed in church attendance, as: "Indians having quite a churchy time of it, two services with old Edward [Loutit] for parson" (HBCA B.77/a/50, 12 July 1902).

VIII In Long's discussion of Wapachee he points to what may be interpreted as the waning influence of this catechist. Wapachee was described as a "real Bush-Indian" (Long 1991:85) but from a story collected by Preston we learn that Wapachee had four wives but only two church marriages (Preston 1975c:248).

IX Symbols derived from shorthand, Greek, and Hebrew are the consonants; the positioning of them in one of four directions determines the vowel sounds (Rhodes and Todd 1981:63).

x John Horden was said to be a linguist with an amazing gift for languages (Petersen 1974:10, 14) so we can assume it was he who translated the religious tracts. In the case of the Reverend E.A. Watkins at Fort George in the 1850s, he seems to have done so in conjunction with his wife, for in his annual letter he writes: "I have translated several of the psalms ... which are now distributed amongst the Indians in the syllabic character in small books written chiefly by Mrs Watkins" (NA CMS, microfilm, 78-13, reel 24 (A-97), 14 Jan 1855).

XI Renison states that Vincent walked on snowshoes all the way to Winnipeg to be ordained there in 1883 as an archdeacon, a journey of sixteen hundred miles there and back (Renison 1957:32; Petersen 1974:25).

XII Except for a few committed missionaries such as Horden, Peck, and Walton who learned the language well, the others were itinerant missionaries reliant on interpreters or their own imperfect rendering of the language. This reminds me of the remark one Inuk made to the anthropologist Asen Balikci in the 1950s at Great Whale River when asked to comment on a certain missionary. His reply was that he was a very nice man "but he talked baby talk" (Balikci fieldnotes 1957). Scanlon (1975:54), writing about Waswanipi, commented that Iserhoff's Cree language abilities "would continue to strengthen the mission greatly."

XIII John Gull was raised at Waswanipi by Maria Blacksmith, described as a very religious old lady who taught him to pray and sing in Cree. He was made a deacon in 1953 (Scanlon 1975:54). Edwards, a graduate of the Moose Factory school, was made a deacon in 1887, a priest in 1881, and was sent to Rupert House from where he also served other communities such as Fort George in 1896. His last ministry was at Fort Hope (HBCA B.77/a/46, 24 Feb. 1896; Petersen 1974:16, 118). Second Bearskin was the catechist at the inland post of Kanaaupscow in the late 1930s, holding services there. He ran into conflict with P.J. Soper, manager of the post, when he told him that the minister at Fort George, the Reverend Greene, had ordered him to remain at the post for the winter. Soper thought he ought to be out on the land, but he remained (HBCA B.496/a/1, 10 Sept. 1938). Second Bearskin was an Inlander and one of a number of sons of a prominent hunter, Bearskin. He was the father of Job, also a catechist, known outside of Fort George for the 1975 film, *Job's Garden*, in which he expressed his fears as to what would befall their lands as a result of the James Bay hydroelectric project. Second Bearskin first appeared in the Fort George journals on July 1894, arriving with his father and older brother (HBCA B.77/a/45, 26 June, 9 July 1894).

XIV In 1905 Walton wrote despairingly that "they do not hate 'sin' – but only hate 'being found out', hence the reason why there is so much lying and deceit among the Indians and half breeds" (NA Walton Letterbook, 4 Jan. 1905).

xv A sample of Walton's teachings is passed down in the oral tradition. When George Kakabat of Wemindji was asked why *matuu* (sorcery) is not much in use in present-day, he attributed the falling away from the practice to Walton, saying "he was the one that talked about what would happen to a person who did that kind of thing ("matuu"). He could truly state what would be the consequences of the person who was a matuu. This is the reason why it has slowed down somewhat. He said a person couldn't go to Heaven if he was a matuu. And this is what scared the people from doing it" (MC Scott Collection 1982: tape 20IT, 19 Nov. 1981).

xvi The reader is cautioned that Speck's (1977 [1935]:16, 17) writings about Cree acceptance of Christianity are disparaging of Catholicism. As his study of the Cree-Montagnais-Naskapi peoples took place to the south of the James Bay territory (in Pointe Bleue), he encountered mainly those who had been converted to Roman Catholicism. One does not find, then, references to Protestant ministers; we do not know if he would be equally disparaging of them.

xvii J.A. of Eastmain told Sun that when the Crees first heard about religion they believed a variety of things, including one old man who believed that if he and the young men went to heaven they would all go caribou hunting (MC Sun Collection 1979:C-26).

xviii For instance, the Reverend Harry Cartlidge told of his visit to Mistassini in 1924 when he was advised by the manager, F. Macleod, of the great deal of conjuring there. Cartlidge recounts that he called a meeting of the men at which he told them the story of the early Britons and the worship of the Druids and of witchcraft on into medieval times, all through which the "white men were growing up from being children to fuller manhood." According to Cartlidge, Solomon Voyageur, guide and chief, was quite impressed with his explanation and replied: "No one ever told me that the white people were once children like we are. But if the Church filled the mind of the white man with good things to make him fearless, then the Church with the Gospel of Jesus will do it for us. There will be no more conjuring in my band" (Scanlon 1975:7).

xix Charles Iserhoff, in the employ of the Hudson's Bay Company (HBCA B.133/a/66, 10 July 1918), served, from 1903 to 1930 as catechist at Mistassini Post (Peterson 1974:78,198). He was ordained a priest by Bishop J.R. Anderson in 1929 but died the following year, in his seventies. He was succeeded at Mistassini by Matthew Shecapio, first as a lay reader, then as a deacon. The first church was built in 1910 and only replaced in 1950 (Scanlon 1975:9).

xx Although the combined recorded oral accounts for the Crees of eastern James Bay are quite extensive, their discussions of the Christian religion are generally only elaborated in Sun's report. His interviewing of people at Wemindji was aimed at learning about their syncretic

religious views whereas others anthropologists looked to traditional beliefs or to life histories.
XXI Linguistic code switching was not unique to the East Crees. (see Valentine 1995:76).
XXII Bragdon (1993:26, 30), writing of eighteenth-century Massachusetts Algonquians, describes a similar attraction to literacy.
XXIII The little we learn from the records about the participation of women in the church as distinguished from men tells us that in church the women and men sat on different sides. The men came out first, followed by the women, although the chief and councillors normally exited first (Scanlon 1975:13). John Long rightly notes that in the *miichwaap* the sexes also sat on opposite sides (pers. comm., 1 Mar. 2000) and Désy (1968:173) found at Fort George that this separate seating also applied to the cinema and community centre.
XXIV The Crees converted to Christianity many years before any of their children were sent to residential schools, contrary to the explanation of conversion often given for Indian communities out west (Miller 1991:332).

CHAPTER FOUR

I J.W. Anderson left Rupert House in 1919 for Attawapiskat on the west coast of James Bay. Here he confessed that competition was also good for the trader. He argued that holding a monopoly was a serious responsibility, having to take blame for all. Furthermore, no one trader could satisfy everyone and it was also an opportunity to steer difficult customers to the rival traders (Anderson 1961:137).
II The Hudson's Bay Company was not free from competition in areas close to the US border, or in the former King's Posts, a series of old French posts in Quebec, south of the height of land in the territory drained by rivers flowing into the St Lawrence. For the Cree hunters who traded at Mistassini, Waswanipi, and their various outposts, these former Kings Posts were accessible to them. The company finally gained control of them in 1831 but by the 1860s much of the region had opened to settlement, particularly in the Lake St Jean region.
III This more authoritarian relationship between the monopolistic company and the Crees did not translate into their general acceptance of policy or directives. Hudson's Bay Company traders in James Bay often complained of the Crees' intransigence and separate agendas (see Morantz 1988).
IV A.A. Chesterfield's usual post was at Great Whale River. He served there from 1901 to 1904 but is known today for his legacy of the photographs he made there (see James 1985).

v Gaston Herodier, whose descendants today can be found at Chisasibi, was born in France in 1880. He left there to join the Revillon Frères Company in 1903 and was posted to Fort George. In 1909 he was sent to establish a post at Churchill, Manitoba, taking young David Louttit (a cooper for the Hudson's Bay Company at Fort George) with him. When the war broke out in Europe he returned to France to fight and was decorated for his bravery. He returned to Canada after the war, working for the Hudson's Bay Company in several places in the Mackenzie Valley as district and post manager. He died in 1930 in a fire at the post of Fort Good Hope while trying to salvage the company's records (Louis A. Romanet in Robertson 1984:140; HBCA B.77/a/54, 10 Feb. 1910).

vi Foxes were said to dominate conversations in James Bay because of the extremely high prices they commanded, especially silver foxes. As the Leiths write, "whether the signs point to a good season or a bad one is the topic of conversation ... waking they are talked about and sleeping they are dreamed about." We also learn that a Cree hunter could, on seeing fox tracks, distinguish whether the animals was white, cross, red, or silver (Leiths 1912:169).

vii The Revillon Frères Company's store at Rupert House had a fire on 9 February 1919 at which time they lost $8,000 of stock (HBCA A.92/19/1).

viii A Revillon Frères post (or operation) is first mentioned at Mistassini in 1905 (HBCA A.74/14, fo. 26, 1905) but was not in the 1915 listing (ibid., DFTR/3/1915, fo. 107) and by 1923 Mistassini is said to have one (independent) resident trader, Mr Fleury, though Revillon Frères were running a post on the other side of the height of land at Chamouchouane, halfway between Lakes Mistassini and St Jean (ibid., A.74/34, fo. 355, 1923).

ix In 1932 Matthew Esquinamow recounted what he knew about the company's "beaver farm" on Charlton Island of one hundred years earlier. His testimony was witnessed and part of a file showing the company's long-standing involvement at Charlton. On this deposition it is stated that he was ninety-two years old and had completed sixty-six years of service with the company (HBCA, unclassified, Fort George, 13 Apr. 1932).

x Ernest Renouf was a Jersey man who began as an apprentice with the Hudson's Bay Company at Moose Factory in 1910, and was employed at Great Whale River and Moose Factory before he enlisted in the First World War in 1917. On his return two years later, he was posted to Fort George, becoming manager in 1921. Five years later he was transferred to the Lake Superior region. In 1922 he married Edith Johnstone, daughter of John Johnstone, an employee of mixed ancestry of the Hudson's Bay Company at Fort George (HBCA B.77/a/57, 7 Sept. 1922).

xi The James Bay District at this time also included posts on the west side, including Moose Factory, Albany, and Attawapiskat (HBCA A.74/34, fo. 356, 1924).

XII The prices paid the Cree hunter for each species varied according to the post. Thus in 1924 the high price for beaver was $11.40 paid at Waswanipi while the lowest price was $9.62 at Mistassini. A silver fox pelt brought a high of $130 at Nemiskau and a low of $99.57 at Rupert House. The price differential was a result of both competition and the quality of the fur. In this chart of prices the company also listed what price they expected to get on the April 1924 market. For beaver, this was $21.05, but for silver fox, it was $71.67 – obviously a loss leader (HBCA DFTR/21, fo. 5, 1925). During the Depression the average price for a silver fox pelt was $81 in 1930 and $29 in 1932 (Harris 1976:144).

XIII Canvas (for canoe and tent covers) figured into the competition between the two companies in the early 1900s. Revillon Frères used the modern canvas-covered canoes, built at a small factory at Lake St Jean. It was said to be stronger and more durable than the birchbark canoe and took less time to make. The Hudson's Bay Company followed suit and also began importing these canoes (Harris 1976:140).

XIV Neacappo was nicknamed "Ubumiscow Ucimaaw," i.e. "Ubumiscow [Opemiska] boss" and was succeeded by Eddie Pash (Tanner Collection 1977, 18 July, Emma Neacappo; 6 July, Mina and Stephen Tabaituk). Opemiska or Upimskaau Lake is also known as Lake Vincelotte and is located in the Grande River drainage area (David Denton, pers. comm., July 2001).

XV The Revillon Frères posts on the western side of James Bay in the early 1920s were at Moose Factory, Albany, and Attawapiskat (Sexé 1923:58).

XVI Regarding the Revillon Frères store at Rupert House burned down on 9 February 1919, losing approximately $8,000 in stock (HBCA A.92/19/1, 20 Feb. 1919), ordinarily, the Hudson's Bay Company's post journal would have given a graphic description of this event but journals do not exist for the years 1911–29. In their account, Willie Jacob and Charlie Blackned noted that the store burned down when Mr Dufour was manager. After he left, a new store was built and Thomas Bell managed it for many years until he committed suicide (Anderson 1961:231). This must be the same Thomas Bell who had been manager at Mistassini; in the Mistassini journal of December 1927, somebody has written at the bottom of the page: "The Journal kept by Mr Bell seems a badly written conglomeration of inaccurate information supplemented by much of his own invention" (HBCA B.133/a/67, fo. 22d).

XVII Two of the freighters are mentioned on their return to Fort George by Richard Matenwensum and Jimmy Sam (HBCA B.77/a/57, 14 July 1921).

XVIII Richard Matthew (Richard Esquinamow) was discharged from his duties in 1925 for what the district manager, George Ray, considered reckless advances (HBCA DFTR/21, fo. 8, 1925). He was replaced by R.M. Duncan who had served as clerk at Fort George the preceding year (ibid., B.77/a/58, 6 Aug. 1925). In 1922 Richard Esquinamow had married Hannah Cox (ibid., B.77/a/58, 26 Sept. 1922). David Rat explained that one branch of the Matthew family is called "Skwenumo" (i.e. Esquinamow) because one of the ancestors used his nickname as a family name (CRA Tanner Collection 1977, 17 July).

XIX David Pashagumskum told Adrian Tanner in 1977 that he remembered that fire fifty-six years earlier. Prior to it, he said, the area around Kanaaupscow was covered with low bushes "making it a good place to chase girls." However, after the fire burned the bushes "they used to hide behind the canoes near the shore, and jump out on the girls when they came down to fetch water" (CRA Tanner Collection 1977, 27 July).

XX Some of the Inlander families who traded at Kanaaupscow in the 1920s were: Fireman, Cox, Blackboy, Bearskin, Pashagumiscum, Crow, Wostapuno (Quartermaster), Head, English Shoes, Nine O'Clock, Rat, Pipabano, Nahacapao, Benjamin, Mukash, Dick. John English Shoes, being childless, offered his hunting territory to John Pachano who was originally a Coaster. One possibility as to why he made this offer was because they were "something like brothers," both having the same name of John (CRA Tanner Collection 1977, 23 July George Pachano). English Shoes' Cree name was Kowochepetuskquait (HBCA B.77/d/159, 1890–99). He died in a flu epidemic in 1957 (HBCA RG7 NSD Correspondence File 6–9-9(4), 4 Nov. 1957). John Nine O'Clock's father was Mamcinikaabuu (Big Tall Man), brother to Nahaabinaawskum whose English name was John Blackboy and father to Elijah Blackboy (CRA Tanner Collection 1977, 22 July).

Most Cree men trading in the late 1800s were known by their Cree names, variously spelled. Some became surnames and others were translated but not always correctly. Job Bearskin explained that the original version of "Bearskin" was "Kaawumskwiiyaan," meaning "he has a beaver skin" and somehow the species got changed in translation (CRA Tanner Collection 1978). One Bearskin chose his nickname "wecsw," meaning muskrat, as his surname because he felt there were already too many Bearskins. He was immortalized in the company records as David Rat (ibid., 1977, 17 July). These names highlight the Cree practice of assigning nicknames to individuals by which they became commonly known. There was even a man called Fat Bearskin who died in 1917 (HBCA B.77/a/55, 21 June 1917). Rather than considering such a label derogatory, it must indicate high regard for this inland hunter who could be fat during lean years (see Spielmann 1998:30).

XXI It is difficult to know how to read the reports of George Ray in terms of whether he was speaking for himself or the company. Unlike any other district manager for the James Bay region, his reports are full of compassion, yet a number of his policies, such as raising rates paid for Indian labour at Fort George, seem rare (HBCA DFTR/1922, fo. 4, 1922). He served in the capacity of district manager for five years from 1921 to 1926, seemingly longer than his predecessors. An anonymous assessment of him in the annual fur trade report in 1924 suggests he was unable to "exact obedience" from his post managers, but even so allowed that he had "done better than many of his predecessors" (ibid., A.74/33, fo. 25, 1924). In his memoirs R.H.G. Bonnycastle mentions him in 1928 as the new Northern Traders' manager, noting that this position is "quite a comedown for him" (Robertson 1984:29).

XXII Originally Jack Palmquist and George Papp were partners but in 1931 they dissolved their partnership (HBCA DFTR/23, fo. 8, 1931) and divided up the north, Palmquist trading in the Fort George vicinity and Papp at Great Whale River and Richmond Gulf (ibid., DFTR/27, fo. 12, 1934). According to the Hudson's Bay Company reports these traders, along with Louis Martineau at Cape Jones, "got more than they should have," with Palmquist securing $5,000 worth of furs in 1932 and Papp only $400 to $500 (ibid., DFTR/25, fo. 8, 1933). When the Kanaaupscow post journals end in 1941, Palmquist was still trading with the Fort George Cree hunters (ibid., B.496/a/2, 23 June. 1941) as he was with Old Factory and Eastmain. Willie Georgekish of this last-named post was one of his assistants (ibid., B.59/a/132, fo. 24; 20 Oct. 1940). In 1932 Reverend J.S. Griffin, writing from Fort George, reported he had married Jack Palmquist, age forty-one (and "a Lutheran and a Swede") to Winnie Lameboy, age nineteen (AA Diocese of Moosonee, microfilm 81-4, reel 1, 18 Jan. 1932). He died in 1943 and his wife, along with his assistant, Frank Dupuis, continued to operate at both Fort George and Old Factory (Paul-Emile 1952:201, 206).

XXIII Papp either fired his assistants or they quit. Some of these men were: Ernest Herodier, Mathew Pisteswayan and John Mukash (HBCA B.372/a/22, 1938).

XXIV The 1918 Fort George journal shows D. Pachano as the mail courier for Revillon Frères (ibid., B.77/a/56, 30 Jan. 1918).

XXV Evidently the Hudson's Bay Company traders and post managers were also loyal to the company as Revillon Frères in 1906 was unsuccessful in luring them away despite offers of higher wages (ibid., A.74/15, fo. 28, 1906).

XXVI Cree loyalty to the company could not have come easily. The comments about John Sealhunter in the 1921 Fort George journal illustrate this: "the Belcher Fur Company is apparently causing him much attraction and unsettling him generally by their high priced fur and low cost of goods" (ibid., B.77/a/57, 19 Jan. 1921).

XXVII One such story is also told by John Kawapit. One winter his brother and a party travelled to the post at Fort Chimo to trade furs with the Hudson's Bay Company. At the post they were lodged in a building for the night before they traded their furs and were given food by the post manager. That night a "man who worked for the French Company came to visit us. He was a Wapnodaweeyeou [person from the east]. His name was Shishgoonyagan. We had not given our furs to anyone yet. He came to see us in the hopes that we would give our furs to the French traders. We gave him tea to drink and something to eat. While he was eating the HBC manager came in. Right away, he told our visitor to get out ... But the manager would not even let him finish his tea. He put down his cup, got a hold of him on the shoulder and led him out the door, literally throwing our visitor out." That summer when John Kawapit travelled with his brother to trade at Fort Chimo, he found the Hudson's Bay Company manager seemed happy to report that Shishgoonyagan was dead. "That was the first thing that the manager uttered, 'Shishgoonyagan is dead'"(MC Turner Collection 1974, tape 33-A).

XXVIII Presumably Jefferys and Hurley at Mistassini were grateful for the accommodation between the two companies; on 19 June 1927 they enjoyed "a very good dinner" with the opposition, Mr Bowen. "He proves to be a better cook than we deserve," the entry reads (HBCA B.133/a/67).

XXIX Olav Brieve, a Norwegian independent trader, established in 1933 a winter trading camp one hundred miles north of Neoskweskau at Alkanow Lake (Cat Lake), first employing sixteen-year-old Sam Blacksmith. Having set out one hundred traps, Brieve was illegally trapping. Some Cree hunters reported him to the RCMP. No action was taken as the report stated that what he was trapping was insufficient to warrant the cost of a patrol (NA RG10, vol. 6751, file 420-10X, report of Cpl. E.S. Covell, 13 Aug. 1934). Other independent traders in the Nichikun-Mistassini-Chibougamu area were Gabriel Fleury, Eddy Malone, Ed Litalien, Johnny Mark, and the Robertsons from Pointe-Bleue (Frenette 1985:32).

XXX In 1923 Revillon Frères operated forty-two posts compared to the Hudson's Bay Company's two hundred and fifty posts (Zaslow 1988:135).

XXXI Morris Zaslow notes that in the early 1930s the Hudson's Bay Company experienced heavy losses, with profits resuming only in 1933. New personnel took advantage of radio communication and air transport, which enabled the company to consolidate districts and reduce their posts from 334 in 1931 to 230 in 1937 (ibid., 137).

XXXII So desperate was the situation at Fort George that an Oblate priest wrote to Quebec Premier Taschereau on 6 February 1932, informing him that the Indians of northern Quebec were far worse off than the Indians in northern Ontario. He sent him a graphic account of their distressing condition: "Many in the Fort George area were so poorly clothed that they dared not venture far from their tents for fear of freezing to death. They had no covers to sleep in outdoors in winter and as a result could not attend to their traplines, the hunting was poor and if it were not for fish the greater part of these people would have died of starvation" (Harris 1976:152).

XXXIII The Hudson's Bay Company seemed to respect free traders such as Fleury but complained about the "whisky pedlars and petty traders" who visit the post in the spring (HBCA B.133/a/67, 14 Mar. 1927).

XXXIV The journal entry of Jeffery for 27 June 1929 tells of his offering William Couchees work "but that would be against Couchees principle. He spent a nice winter supplying the mining camp with meat and guiding prospectors" (ibid., B.133/a/68).

XXXV A graphic example of falling prices is given in R.H.G. Bonnycastle's memoirs (Robertson 1984). He cited a lot of white foxes that a free trader, Captain Pedersen, successfully bid for at $40 a skin against the Hudson's Bay Company's bid of $39.50, doing so while they were still on Herschel Island (NWT). When they got back on ship, word came over the wireless that the price of white fox had dropped to $22.50 and by the time Pedersen returned to Seattle the price was down to $12 per pelt. He sold the whole lot of fifteen hundred skins at that price to the Hudson's Bay Company.

XXXVI Prices also would have fallen because of the ranched or farmed fox. The average price for silver fox in 1934 was $24.34 (NA RG10, vol. 6756, file 420-10-4-4M); ten years earlier it had been $125.79 (HBCA A.74/33, fo. 25, 1924).

XXXVII Watt wrote to Ray at Moose Factory that he thought in future the company servants could do their own cutting and hauling of firewood as they did at other posts. He said it took over two months' work with three animals to haul wood for the servants at Rupert House (OA Watt Papers, 20 Jan. 1923).

XXXVIII Although foxes were plentiful in some years, they were not considered food but were only eaten to avoid starvation (Leiths 1912:169).

XXXIX It was not until 1942 that Charles Elton established the existence of animal cycles. However, in 1912 the Leiths wrote of six-year fox cycles, with every sixth year a "great hunt year" followed by a poor year but each year following would improve to the sixth. A sign of a good fox year was when the mice appeared unusually fat (Leiths 1912:169). Presumably they learned this from the Cree and Inuit hunters. Not everyone did, as Ray commented in 1924: "It is believed by many people that increases in the number of certain fur-bearing animals occur in cycles. I do not, of course, speak authoritatively, but it seems to me that there are too many alien forces, too many potent interferences with the scheme of the wild animal life for any set law to maintain, as to increase numbers" (HBCA DFTR/19/1923-24, fo. 358).

XL In a report based on interviews with Crees from the northern communities, Adrian Tanner writes that families were able to move into areas such as the Lake Caniapiscau–Bienville region because Fort McKenzie was opened in 1916 as a resupply post and Kanaaupscow in 1921. From the traders' viewpoint, the posts were located inland to give them a competitive advantage over other traders, but from the Crees' perspective their function was their own security (CRA Tanner Collection, 1978, fo. 42).

XLI Matthew Cowboy told Knight that as a young man he worked at Rupert House as the cow herder, then he freighted from Rupert House to Nemiskau for the Revillon Frères Company; from the age of twenty-one until he was seventy he trapped inland (MC Knight Fieldnotes 1961, 11–12 July). At one time, Charlie Weistechee also hunted with Charles and Thomas Blackned. Their arrival at the Rupert House post in mid-March of 1930 indicated they were not hunting far inland (HBCA B.135/a/203, 13 Mar. 1930).

XLII As the statistics on the prices of imported goods at the James Bay posts are missing, it is possible to get only some sense of the differential in price between the south and a fur trade post from the article published in 1914. As previously noted, at the Abitibi post the author found a muzzle-loading rifle to be $12.00 compared to the $2.50 he claimed they would be selling for in an American department store (R. Miller 1914:118).

XLIII In 1929 the post managers' salaries were cut. Watt's decreased from $2,000 to $1,500 (OA Watt Papers, to Parsons, 12 July 1929; W.A. Anderson 1961:124). In contrast, Keighley said that post managers' salaries in 1929 had been cut to $50 or $60 per month while he was being paid $100 per month (Keighley 1989:184), making Watt's salary still higher. On Watt's unexpected death in 1944 of pneumonia, Mrs Watt carried on a long-running dispute with the Hudson's Bay Company over his pension and her rights (OMI Deschâtelets, LCR 3434.R82W, 1935–1947).

XLIV A new threat for the company was voiced in an unsigned memo about 1926: "the Indians have been advised, as they are wards of the Government they are not responsible for their debts" (HBCA A.93/45, fo. 45).

XLV In his biography of Maud Watt, W.A. Anderson commented that the post was showing an annual book loss of $20,000. As well, there was talk of the post being abandoned but it was kept open because of the "symbolic significance attached to it as a pioneer post" (1961:104).

XLVI In this letter Watt also suggests that the efficiency of the company is reduced by conflicting perspectives coming from the London and Winnipeg offices and, more specifically, by poor communication in the James Bay District, where the head of transport was located at Charlton, another head at Moose Factory, and the inspector travelling along the coast much of the time (HBCA A.93/46, 1 Sept. 27).

XLVII Not only did the restructuring of the Hudson's Bay Company affect the well-being of the Crees, but company employees as well. When the Watts arrived to manage Rupert House in 1920 there were six or seven domestic servants employed; by 1927 this number was drastically reduced. The company also eliminated the dairy herd of four cows, replacing their supply of fresh milk and meat with canned goods (Knight 1968:23).

XLVIII In 1938 Watt remarked that "work for the natives is very scarce and things are getting a bit tough for them" (HBCA B.186/a/112, 20 July 1938).

XLIX There were six cows at Rupert House in 1923 requiring hay feed. Watt found all but the fur trade not worth it, writing: "After all is said and done, the Company's sawmills, boat and canoe factories, farms and piggeries are a damn nuisance and the straight fur trade is a better proposition every time" (OA Watt Papers, 20 Jan. 1923).

L This is the same rate Crees were paid for their labour in 1912 at Waswanipi; the engaged servants' pay was $2.00 per day (HBCA B.186/b/73, 17 Aug. 1912).

LI Donald Gillies of Fort George post made a similar comment about the Coasters: "they seem to have utterly lost the energy and self-reliance so characteristic of the upland hunters" (ibid., B.77/b/8, fo. 158, 1903).

LII Voyageur (b. about 1860, d. 1930) was the great-great grandson of Joseph Beioley, Hudson's Bay Company chief of the Rupert House district in 1824 and later head of Moose Factory district. It is said that, when excited, Solomon Voyageur would throw off his cap and shout "in Indian," "See my head is a white man's head." It is also said he led a revolt against the post in 1880 but this is not explained (Nanuwan 1929:162-3).There were many stories about Voyageur's strength, how he carried seven hundred pounds over a half-mile portage and he probably never weighed more than one hundred and fifty pounds (Nanuwan 1929:162). A force on the river but perhaps a kitten in other matters, the post manager at Mistassini commented that "Old Voyageur was supposed to come in to have a tooth extracted today but I think his nerve failed him" (ibid., B.133 /a/68, 25 Nov. 1928).

LIII According to Anderson, Solomon Voyageur's father-in-law was the hereditary chief but because of his outstanding qualities, Voyageur was for all practical purposes the chief (Anderson 1961:123).

LIV The departure of the canoe brigade was attended with ritual. The day of the departure was a gala one at the post with flags hoisted and rounds of farewells in the village. As the brigade left the post, and a few miles before the first rapid on the Rupert River, the head guide distributed half a plug of tobacco to each man. Without speaking, there was a ceremonial smoking and the dropping by the chief guide of a plug of tobacco into the river as an offering to the "spirit of the waters." On the return home, on the last day, the men donned "their finery" and the factor hoisted the flag (Anderson 1935:16-18). Sometimes the wives and families of the men on the canoe brigades from the inland posts accompanied the men to the coastal post where they visited for the summer while the men worked, as George Pachano said his family did at Fort George (CRA Tanner Collection 1977, 24 July). When the Waswanipi women and children travelled with the brigade to Rupert House, it was a canoe trip of 270 miles (HBCA B.227/a/56, 22 Aug. 1911; Marshall 1987:20). For those already on the coast, as at Rupert House, the women and children remained in the vicinity of the post. Harriet Whiskeychan (born 1879) said that while the men freighted, the women were left to fish at Boatswain Bay (MC Knight Fieldnotes 1961, 30 June). A few wives accompanied the canoe brigade to help with the work of the camp and the cooking. Those from Mistassini travelled down river with the canoe brigade but on the return trip they took smaller canoes from Rupert House, often travelling ahead of the men so they could ready the camps (Anderson 1961:114).

LV The Revillon Frères Company, after deciding not to use them in 1915, eventually did. Ronnie Cowboy describes the company's using teams of twelve horses to supply Nemiskau and Neoskweskau (CRA Denton Collection 1983, tape 2).

LVI A household or family was made up of parents, children, and additional members, such as unmarried brothers or sisters, elderly parents, orphaned children, etc. Some anthropologists refer to this social unit as the commensal unit (see Morantz 1983a:89-91).

LVII The Eastmain manager, C. Jobson, said in the early 1900s that tea was now a necessity but when he had entered the service fifty years earlier, "hardly a pound was sold to them [Cree]" (Leiths 1912:52).

LVIII Back in 1745 the Eastmain postmaster explained that the Indians had to go one hundred miles inland to find adequate food, but that he needed them near the coast for the spring goose hunt (Francis and Morantz 1983:93).

LIX In fact, in the 1840s Trapper and Namagoose were brothers, sons of a Cree Coaster named Governor. As was the case when the Methodists and Anglicans first began baptising Crees, each man's Cree name (either in Cree or in translation) became his family name, so that brothers gave rise to families with separate names as in this case (see NA MMS Moose Factory Mission Church Records, 1843).

LX Reynolds expanded the Hannah Bay goose camp, making Beatrice Fairies' father one of the head guides (S. Preston Collection, 1984).

LXI Alice Butterly, née Esau, before her marriage worked as housemaid for Mrs Watt at Rupert House; Mary Dick (originally from Eastmain) was the wife of a Moose Factory trapper. Once a year-round resident at Moose Factory, she worked in the hospital laundry beginning in the 1950s (S. Preston Collection 1984, 18 July, 14 June).

LXII Alec Louttit was manager at Eastmain for sixteen years from 1916 to 1932 (HBCA DFTR/24, fo. 13, 1932).

LXIII The James Bay and Northern Quebec Agreement does not distinguish categories of people. All with Cree ancestry were included in the agreement, reconfirmed several years later in the Cree-Naskapi Act.

LXIV Presumably this is an error in transcription as there was no Catholic mission at Rupert House but there was one in 1922 at Fort George, hence "moved to Rupert House" is in quotation marks.

LXV Preston (pers. comm., 28 Sept. 2000) reports that for a very brief period, "old Hester" (likely Matthew, born 1868) was the first elected chief.

CHAPTER FIVE

I Already in 1910 Robert Flaherty was commissioned by the president of the Canadian Northern Railway to undertake an exploration of the Nastapoka Islands (Belcher) "for the purpose of examining and reporting upon the commercial value of the iron-ore deposits" (Flaherty 1918:433).

II Alan Penn estimates that in the post Second World War period the Crees of this region were outnumbered by nearly ten to one by non-aboriginal residents within their territory (pers. comm., 29 Feb. 2000).

III These soldiers are: Alfred Cheechoo, Samuel Ice, William Luke, and Daniel Quachigan (Gaffen 1985: Appendix B). Of course, the information on which this list was based could be incomplete or Anderson could have been referring to the larger James Bay area, on both sides of the provincial border. Although Anderson was at Mistassini during the war, from 1919 to 1927 he did work at Attawapiskat and Albany, both in "James Bay" (Anderson 1961:127) and some of those names, such as Cheechoo, are from the west coast. Jane Chum, daughter of George Fairies at Moose Factory, said her three sons went to war (S. Preston Collection 1984, June 18), (presumably the Second World War) though their names are not on the Gaffen list. John Long adds to the list of First World War servicemen the names of Bertie, Philip, and Lawrence Morrison, Andrew Wapachee, and five of the Mark family (pers. comm., 1 Mar. 2000).

IV For example, Anderson heard about the start of the war at Mistassini Post on 27 February 1915, when the packet arrived from Pointe Bleue (HBCA B.133/a/66).

V Louis Romanet signed on with the Revillon Frères Company from the beginning of its Canadian operation and he began his long career as a fur trader at Fort Chimo in 1903. In 1916 he joined the Hudson's Bay Company because Revillon Frères refused to transfer him to the North West River post. He returned from the war to James Bay in 1919 but left the region in 1923 for an assignment in the Athabasca district (Harris 1976:22, 29, 37).

VI The first steamer to arrive in James Bay, at Rupert House, was in 1902 (HBCA B.186/a/109, 15 July 1902). The earliest record of a gasoline-powered boat being used for travel along the west coast of James Bay to Moose Factory is 1918 (Harris 1976:163). Watt recounted an episode when he was manager at the Hudson' Bay Company post at Fort Chimo in 1915-16. Fearing that no supply ship would come, with the instrumental help of "an old crippled Indian," they repaired and refitted an old yawl, the *Fox*, which they towed out with the motorboat *Saint Ann*, called by the Inuit 'Satan' (OA Watt Papers, MV 1385, Report on Burwell section transport, circa 1916).
VII This was suggested by David Cooter who was employed as post manager at Nichikun in the late 1930s (pers. comm., 1985).
VIII One such hiring was of Noah Cheechoo, "who has consented to take me [D.G.Boyd] to Rupert House in his 'kicker'" (HBCA B.59/a/132, 4 June 1940).
IX The Hudson's Bay Company's first use of radio was at Norway House in 1921-2, using the *Free Press* station in Winnipeg. Fort George was receiving radio broadcasts via KDKA in Pittsburgh in 1925 (HBCA B.77/a/58, 7 Nov. 1925). Needless to say, the messages about ships and prices were transmitted in code. The first radio at Fort George was owned by the Anglican mission (NA Diocese of Moosonee, film 81-4, reel 1, Rev. J.S. Griffin to Bishop Thorpe, 3 Feb. 1929). By 1931, all the missionaries and traders were listening in to the arctic and sub-arctic radio broadcasts from KDKA (Anonymous 1931:187).
X These windchargers converted wind into electricity through a propellor-driven generator and batteries, providing current for electric lights, radio, and an electric motor for the water pump at the company facilities as described in 1951 for Great Whale River (Moccasin Telegraph 1951, Summer:20).
XI There is no explanation why only "Eskimos" are mentioned as listening to the broadcast as both Crees and Inuit were at the post. It is possible Eskimos refers to the employees of the company.
XII On 23 August 1920 the first seaplane landed in front of the Revillon post at Moosonee with "moving picture men to take moving pictures of the place." Evidently for a period of time they flew in and out of Moosonee, delivering two-day old newspapers. A number of the fur trade men, even the clerk from Rupert House and Reverend Walton of Fort George, all had short flights in the seaplane (Harris 1976:108-9). The advent of air travel, although not seen for a few years, was known to Hudson's Bay Company men such as Anderson, who wrote in 1914 that he had read about "the aeroplane" (Anderson 1961:89). In August 1931 Colonel Charles Lindbergh and his wife landed in Moose Factory on their way to Fort Churchill and the Orient. Both of them

stayed overnight in the district manager's house (HBCA RG3/3B/3, fo. 4, Aug. 1931).

XIII The Revillon Frères records indicate it was not until after the Second World War that flying was used much as a means of transport. In the early years the cold air played havoc with the aircraft as the oil had to be drained and kept on the stove overnight (Harris 1976:136).

XIV In the spring of 1931 six hundred men were working on the rail line close to Moose Factory (HBCA RG3/3B/1, 31 May 1931). One can only speculate how disruptive to Cree life such working gangs would have been. The clearing of the townsite of Moose Harbour (soon changed to Moosonee) employed some ninety Indians (ibid., RG3B/3, 5 Sept. 1931).

XV The report prepared by Father John M. Cooper was for Dr Harold McGill of Indian Affairs but was read by Anderson to a Hudson's Bay Company fur trade conference in 1933. Its title was "Aboriginal Land Holding Systems" (ibid., Unclassified fur trade conference Minutes 1933, Appendix E).

XVI One of Louis Martineau's children, Madeleine, attended the Catholic School at Fort George from 1931 to 1935. She entered a convent in Ottawa in 1936, taking her final vows as a Grey Nun in July 1941 in the Fort George church. This ceremony was the first ever held in James Bay. She was considered fluent in English, French, and Cree and was appointed to the Catholic mission at Fort George. She took on the name of Sister Louis-Martin (Paul-Emile 1952:269).

XVII One can only assume that these unfavourable reports of beaver numbers came from areas to the south of James Bay. For example, the Mistassini annual reports for the last five years of the nineteenth century indicated that beaver and other fur returns were up and favourable (HBCA A.74/6 – 9).

XVIII This was the era that gave rise to Grey Owl, the acclaimed defender of wildlife and promoter of conservation (Smith 1990).

XIX The first relief payment noted was in 1894 when Commissioner Chipman of the Hudson's Bay Company asked Hayter Reed, deputy superintendant general of Indian Affairs, for financial assistance for Rupert House Coasters, as twelve had starved to death that year and others had been forced to eat their furs. Reed authorized the expenditure of $400 but counselled the greatest care in its expenditure "so that the Indians will not be inclined to call for aid again too readily" (Ray 1990b:209). In the district report for that year, mention is made of the Dominion government having provided some relief in Ungava (HBCA A.74/3). It is not likely that the Crees themselves would have called on the government in 1894; it would have been an unknown entity to them.

XX The recipients of the "sick and destitute rations" were clearly spelled out by the Indian Affairs inspector of the James Bay district in a reply to Watt at Rupert House; these rations were intended for those "of actual necessity and are not meant to be issued for the maintenance of Natives who during the Winter have made no efforts to provide for themselves." This was V.W. West's position despite the fact that Watt had emphasized that fish were practically unobtainable, while hare appeared to be extinct, and thirty or so Coasters were unable to undertake the strenuous freighting work which would bring them some wages (HBCA A.93/46, 2 July 1927; 18 June 1927).

XXI This decree was in terms of the BNA Act of 1867 which gave the federal government authority over Indians; with this decree Inuit, living within provinces, other than the Northwest Territories, became a federal responsibility. At the time, this affected only the Inuit in Quebec and Manitoba. Newfoundland with its Inuit population in Labrador did not join confederation until 1949.

XXII Governor George Simpson's practice of permitting only one religious denomination to take root at a Hudson's Bay Company post was initiated because he believed that if Catholic and Protestant missionaries were permitted to reside at the same post their conflicting doctrines would simply confuse the Indian people (HBCA B.186/b/53:51). More than a century later, when in James Bay, Adrian Tanner (pers. comm. 10 Oct. 1999) learned of a gentleman's agreement among the major religions not to poach on each other's territory. As to why this agreement broke down, I can only speculate that the strong presence of the Revillon Frères at Fort George and Catholic missions on western James Bay persuaded the latter to open missions on the east coast.

XXIII This information is from Father John Cooper's field notes. He derived his information from Renouf, the Hudson's Bay Company trader (CUA Cooper, "List of Fort George Coast Indians," 1932).

XXIV The Church Missionary Society evidently withdrew to consolidate its missionary efforts in India and China where the populations were more concentrated (Harris 1976:163).

XXV John Long (pers.comm. 1 Mar. 2000) points out that Fred Mark was chosen chief at Moose Factory in 1905. He was also a teacher and church leader there before his work in east James Bay.

XXVI Redfern Louttit, son of William, became one of the graduates of the Indian Residential School at Chapleau, Ontario, established in 1907. He also studied at Wycliffe, where he was known for his athletic abilities. After serving at Old Factory River for eleven years, in 1951 he was transferred south to the Western Mission of Lansdowne House on Lake Attawapiskat (Petersen 1974:128, 107, 166).

XXVII The Crees were not the only Native Peoples to resist strong Catholic attempts to convert them. In discussing the Inuit of Nunavik (Arctic Quebec), Dorais wrote: "the Nunavimmiut did not feel the need to become Catholics because they were already Christian" (1997:74).

xxviii In 1943 the Hudson's Bay Company, finding its buildings too exposed to the winds and the island to small to house everyone, moved to another island to the south. Palmquist and the Catholic Mission remained in their original location (Paul-Emile 1952:206). The Anglicans chose to move and to relocate their beautifully adorned church. Louttit and the Crees sawed each wall of the church into three sections which they rafted on canoes to the new location (Renison 1957:237).

xxix Father Louis-Philippe Vaillancourt served in eastern James Bay from 1943 until recent years, then worked as a government translator. Beginning in the 1970s, he was an active participant at the annual meetings of the Algonquianists and published a number of articles on the Cree language at Eastmain (see, for e.g., Vaillancourt 1984).

xxx Watt reported that "at one time this post [Rupert House] exported 10,000 skins annually, while this year's returns amount to only eight skins (OA Watt Papers, MU 1385, 5 July 1932).

xxxi Although no one disputes that the Crees were conservationists, they were also pragmatic and when hungry they killed beaver to eat (HBCA B.186/b/47, fo. 33, 1839).

xxxii The subject of family hunting territories, for many years a contentious issue, has an extensive literature dating back to the early 1900s (see Bishop and Morantz 1986).

xxxiii If in need, a man and his family could hunt on another's hunting territory, if permission were sought. If not, the hunter would still be allowed to hunt for food. J.A. Burgesse, a trader at Pointe Bleue, noted that the traveller must "leave everything as he finds it," and "He may not hunt the territory for personal profit but only for food enroute" (Burgesse 1942:19). Fishing spots were considered neutral ground (Morantz 1986a:80). The way the Department of Indian Affairs viewed these hunting grounds is expressed in a memo regarding the Crees at New Post Band on the west side of the Bay. It reads: "John Marten has no hunting ground in this area but goes on other Indians ground and takes everything he can get ... I do not see that there is anything we can do about it as the Indians have no legal claim in their hunting grounds, it is just an understood fact that the Indian will keep to his own ground" (NA RG10 vol. 6747, file 420-8 10, 29 Aug. 1939).

xxxiv Anderson commented that beaver farming turned out to be impractical as "it takes one acre of land to support one beaver ... a relatively small beaver colony will destroy a tremendous amount of timber and willows in the process of procuring food" (Anderson 1961:185).

xxxv In the 1836 beaver preserve scheme, the company paid Cree hunters to bring in live beaver in order to restock Charlton Island (Francis and Morantz 1983:129).

xxxvi The drivers of her two dog teams were Philip Diamin and Katapatiuk (W.A. Anderson 1961:127-30).

XXXVII Maud Watt's father was Charles Maloney; her mother was Elizabeth Poirier. Their home was in Mingan on the lower North Shore of the St Lawrence (W.A. Anderson 1961:3–4).
XXXVIII Evidently neither the Watts nor anyone in the company would speak openly that the Hudson's Bay Company now held the lease because it would look as though the government was favouring them over the Revillon Frères Company (OMI Deschâtelets, LCB 3431 .R82H 13, fo. 3, "Rupert's House History" by Maud H. Watt, 30 Oct. 1941).
XXXIX Malcolm Diamond, born about the turn of the century, died in 1984. He was a highly respected leader of the Rupert House people and chief for fourteen years. He retired in 1975 from hunting and his son Charlie took over his hunting grounds. Another son, Billy, succeeded him as chief of the Rupert House people in 1971 and became grand chief of the Crees, leading the Crees through the difficult years of negotiating the James Bay Agreement in 1975 and its implementation (MacGregor 1989:223, 47–8, 125; CRA Denton Collection 1985, tape 6, side 2).
XL This was recognized in a report to the Special Joint Committee of the House of Commons on the Indian Act, where the anonymous person testifying on beaver preserves noted "our organization is based on Indian tradition and custom ... once the white man's practices of written leases and agreements are disposed of we revert to Indian custom, pattern our organization after their sound, well-established practice and divide our preserves according to the original plan of land tenure that from time immemorial has served the Indian population" (HBCA RG7 14-1-2(4), 25 July 1947: Special Joint Committee, fo. 689).
XLI Needless to say, differences arose in interpretation as to how legitimate some of the beaver pelts traded were. One such altercation was between the independent trader, Jack Palmquist, and D.G. Boyd, the Eastmain manager (HBCA B.59/a/132, July 1, 1940).
XLII The Trapper family was descended from one of the sons (Wanihikai) of Governor, a prominent Rupert House Coaster in the mid-1800s (Morantz and Chaikin 1985:70–2). The Trapper families left Rupert House in 1924 with Joe Trapper and family being the first, followed in 1928 by Obadiah, James, Ronald, and Harriet Trapper as well as the families of Sinclair and George Reubens, Matthew Frank, and David Frank. In 1929 the families of James Echum and Andrew Wapachee also followed, making a total of 112 of the Rupert House band in La Sarre. They moved in search of better trapping grounds which "has been one of continual trouble and difficulty"(NA RG10, vol. 6748, file 420-8-2 2, 7 Oct. 1944). They were not allowed to register for trapping lands in either Ontario or Quebec and were not welcomed by the Abitibi band of Algonquins, who complained of their poaching. The Indian agent attributed the cause of the conflict over land to a religious division: the Trapper families were Protestant and

the Abitibi Algonquins were Catholic (ibid., vol. 6755, file 420-10-4-1, pt. 3, 13 July 1942). In 1944 the Indian agent ordered them back, as Bishop Renison says, "300 miles to a country their children have never seen." A number in the Rupert House band were not pleased with the return of these families, saying "this group left when trapping was poor and now returning when fur is plentiful" (ibid., vol. 6748, file 420-8-2 2, 7, 12, Oct. 1944). They were settled in the Hannah Bay division.

XLIII John De B. Payne, who joined the public relations office of the Hudson's Bay Company in 1949, confirmed that political figures in Ontario also expected pay-offs but it was not as open as in Quebec (pers. comm., 7 Sept. 1995).

XLIV The provincial government seems to have had more involvement in the administration of this preserve than previous ones. At about the same time the province established other preserves: Grand Lake Victoria (1948), Bersimis, Roberval, and Manouane all in 1951 (HBCA RG 3, series 67-68).

XLV After the death of her husband in 1944, Maud Watt returned to live in Rupert House and, complaining of problems regarding her pension from the company, opened up a bakery to support herself there (OMI Deschâtelets LCB 34334 R82W, 23 Nov. 1944).

CHAPTER SIX

I See the controversy surrounding the relocation of Inuit by the federal government to the high Arctic in the 1950s (Tester and Kulchyski 1994).

II Dial phones were installed by Bell Telephone and Ontario Northland in 1964 for use only within the settlements of Rupert House, Paint Hills, Fort George, and Great Whale River. Otherwise radio telephones were still in use for long-distance connections. It was a mode of communication which was quickly accepted, as this anonymous quote suggests: "Indians were not shy to use the phone ... now use it frequently" (Moccasin Telegraph 1964, Summer:28).

III Actually, Rupert House lay south of the jurisdiction of DGNQ whose boundary was north at the Eastmain River.

IV Bishop Renison stoutly defended this expenditure, saying "It is a great source of satisfaction to me to know that these original Canadians are cared for now at a fine hospital" (1957:261).

V The "Indian hospital" was identified as the Lady Minto Hospital by John Long (pers. comm., 1 Mar. 2000).

VI Similar social pressures were demanding adequate health services for Canadians in rural or fringe areas (Zaslow 1988:66).

VII Statistics from 1930 demonstrate the low priority in which the government held Indians. The health budget, per capita, for their care was only half that of the Canadian population and totally inadequate to meet the problem of the rampant tuberculosis that was afflicting them (Zaslow 1988:172).

VIII John Long reminds us (pers. comm., 1 Mar 2000) the Crees did provide their own medical services, such as midwives or help in tending to accidents, or dealing with psychological problems.

IX During this period and until 1959, the mission at Fort George was administratively in the diocese of the Arctic (Petersen 1974:194).

X According to the health inspection report for the Abitibi Agency, all Indians since 1941 were innoculated against smallpox, diptheria, typhoid, and pertussin (DTP); see NA RG10, Mistassini Records, file 27074-3, 19 Nov. 1945.

XI The *Bayrupert* had been built in 1926, complete with hospital facilities and a dispensary, but was shipwrecked in 1927. In 1922 the governor and committee of the Hudson's Bay Company had decided that a doctor should accompany each of the vessels supplying the posts in Labrador, the Eastern Arctic, and Hudson Bay to look after the health of the crew, the post staff, and the Native Peoples. From 1922 to 1928 Dr Robert Boyd Stewart was the attending physician (HBCA information sheet on Dr Stewart, Dec. 1986).

XII Tuberculosis was a tragic, virulent disease that devastated families. For example, Willie Iserhoff's twelve-year-old daughter was dying of tuberculosis of the spine in 1938 and at the same time his fourteen-year-old son was suffering from consumption of the lungs (HBCA B.133/a/74, 1 Feb. 1938). Several years later his wife's lungs were said to be in bad shape and she also had tuberculosis in the hip joint (ibid., B.133/a/76, 1 May 1940).

XIII Only when helicopters began being used in James Bay in 1951 (as for a search and rescue operation) was there sometimes an alternative. During a particularly bad outbreak of measles and whooping cough at Fort George and Great Whale River in 1957 the ice was not sufficiently thick for a ski-equipped aircraft to land. Eventually the RCAF sent a helicopter from the Maritimes to take in Dr Harvey and nurses from Moose Factory (Moccasin Telegraph 1951 December 7; 1957, Breakup:28).

XIV There are records of three recruits from Rupert House in the Second World War: Bert Hester, Clarence Hester and Alan Trapper (NA RG10, vol. 10,829, file 44/-3, Rupert House Band List, circa 1962). More documentation exists for Alan Trapper because, as an Indian veteran, he felt he was the victim of discrimination and he complained. Alan Trapper, then age nineteen, was stationed at Timmins. In 1947 he requested that Indian Affairs grant him his "re-establishment benefits," something to which Indians, as others, were entitled if they had spent a minimum of eighteen months in the army. Alan Trapper had intended to use this money to purchase a new trapping outfit. Not surprisingly, he was caught up in one of the relatively common Indian bureaucratic "black holes." As a veteran, he was eligible to a grant of $2,320 for settling on crown land. As an Indian, this land was to come from his reserve. The records clearly point out the extraordinary complications of being Indian. They read: "... however, that Trapper belongs to the Band at Rupert House, and, as they have no reserve, it is not possible for us to provide the land for him, consequently he cannot obtain a grant under Section 35A" (ibid., vol. 6806, file 452–953, pt. 1, 5, 8 July 1947). Trapper may not have pursued this claim, for his file is marked "dormant." or he may have been transferred, along with his father, to the "Abitibi Indian Agency" sometime after the war (ibid., vol. 10,829, file 44/–3, Rupert House Band List, circa 1962).

xv In 1941 the Americans built a small airfield at Fort Chimo that served first as a simple radio and weather station. After the United States entered the war, it was substantially enlarged. Fort Chimo was one of a number of airfields built as part of a northeast staging route that would permit the Americans to refuel enroute to Europe. A 1944 report indicated that this route was little used, as a more southerly one through Goose Bay, Newfoundland, was found to be more practical (Grant 1988:62–3, 276).

xvi Socialization between the Crees and the Inuit was discouraged in the 1950s; the missionary and company trader did their best to keep the two communities separate, although the men worked together unloading the boats and sometimes played soccer together (Walker 1953:10). Dances were attended by both Crees and Inuit but there was little intermarriage. A language barrier and lack of the necessary skills for the Inuit or Cree women to fit into the subsistence economy of the other group are the explanations offered by the anthropologist John Honigmann (1962:65, 18). At Fort George, Pierrette Désy (1968:135) found more of an openness to intermarriage, perhaps because the number of Inuit was much smaller and more assimilated to Cree life.

xvii Cooperatives were initiated in Ungava in 1959 and quickly spread throughout the Arctic and Northwest Territories. They were endorsed as an economic policy by the Department of Northern Affairs (Dickason 1997:377). A cooperative was started in Great Whale River for the Crees in the early 1960s, most likely because of the presence of the Department of Northern Affairs there and a large Inuit population.

xviii Even schemes that would provide no benefit to the Crees were proposed for the territory, without more than a cursory regard for their safety or well-being. Indian Affairs correspondence in 1957 indicates that a bombing and gunnery range was being considered for the James Bay area, to be located on Akimiski Island. Its northern boundary was to be about sixteen miles south of Cape Jones. How Crees would be affected was quickly reviewed by the Indian Affairs regional supervisor who proclaimed "there is little or no Indian traffic in this area" (NA RG10, vol. 10,850, file 44/30-1, 17 May 1957). Although the return letter indicated the RCAF were interested in using this bombing range, there is no indication the island served such a purpose. This proposal preceded by thirty or so years NATO taking over the hunting lands of the Sheshashit Innu for testing flights of their low-range bombers (Armitage and Kennedy 1989).

XIX In 1950 Neosweskau was said to be used in winter for outpost trading supplies and Nichikun was a "small trading shack." A new store was built there in 1961 (HBCA RG 7/7A/233). In 1965 Glen Speers, the manager at Mistassini, had two caches erected for the storage of food supplies in the Nichikun area (Moccasin Telegraph 1965, Summer:21).

XX One exploration company official remarked that "if we employ whites to do staking we have to pay them twice as much and they do a worse job" (Tanner 1968:56).

XXI The company report indicates that the major reason the canoe factory operated at a loss was because almost all of the materials had to be imported except for local spruce used for the ribs and stems. Thus distance plus "inefficient work habits" made the canoe factory an unprofitable venture even with the low rates paid the workers. The writer of the report suggested that "the development of handicrafts is best left to the government" (HBCA RG7, general correspondence 2-12-20, 6 Apr. 1967).

XXII A freezer plant was erected at Rupert House in 1949 from a prefabricated structure powered by a gas motor. It had a capacity of sixteen thousand pounds of meat or two hundred pounds per family. Its purpose was to eliminate wastage of the meat in the summer. The Hudsons's Bay Company's staff magazine reported that this facility "will put an end to the old beaver feasts where the natives had to gorge themselves on fresh meat before it spoiled in the summer heat." The plant was also to used for the storage of fish and game thereby improving the diet of the Rupert House people (Moccasin Telegraph 1949, Summer:2). Eastmain had a freezer plant erected in 1957 which was built by Indian Affairs with money subscribed by the hunters from the sale of their beaver (ibid., 1957, Break-up:28). A charge was made for this storage at Rupert House – 6 cents a bird for geese and 4 cents a pound for meat (ibid., 1959, Summer:3).

XXIII The amount to be contributed was suggested by the community leaders in the spring after they knew the price they would be receiving for their furs (Kerr 1950:73).

XXIV It was a surprise to discover that Indian Affairs had not imposed its wishes on the Crees and had acquiesced to their choice of location for the new village. More surprising is W.J. Harvey's discussion of how Indian Affairs might attempt to convince the Crees. He writes: "The Indians at Old Factory may decide to amalgamate with the Eastmain Band and move to Eastmain ... If the move could be nurtured it would be better have it come from the Indians themselves, rather than the Hudson's Bay Company or our Department. I believe that this would not give the Indians any excuse that they were transferred somewhere against their wishes" (NA RG10 vol. 10,858, file 44/30-1, 1 Mar. 1957). The Old Factory people unanimously rejected the suggestion of moving to Eastmain. So this line of thinking was abandoned. The area proposed by the Crees is in the centre of their trapping area looking inland from the coast and not too far from the water route (i.e. Paint Hills), (ibid., 16 July 1957). The notion that the Old Factory band chose the new site themselves was reiterated in the company staff magazine in the winter of 1960. Harvey's superior, Fred Matters, regional supervisor in the North Bay Agency, wrote a month later that "Woods Harbour will be the new location. To try to have it changed now would only embarrass the new Minister and it is our job to see that does not happen." The Crees moved to Paint Hills.

Indian Affairs' new interest in a consultation process (a meeting in the community was held on 14 August 1957 attended by all males over sixteen) can perhaps be explained by the short-lived community development program it instituted in the mid-1950s, borrowed from India and Greenland. It sought to mobilize the Indian population, to create conditions of economic and social progress for the whole community by encouraging the maximum amount of community participation. It was a community self-help program with an animator and funds coming from the outside. The program called for a change from people administration to people development. Indian Affairs sent out sixty-two community development officers to work as resource persons and coordinators in the native communities (Buckley 1992:102–30). According to Ponting (1986:29), despite its early successes, the program quickly disintegrated in a welter of bureaucratic infighting and conflicts among the community development staff, Indian agents, senior bureaucrats, and factions in the native communities.

xxv There was a short-lived flurry of activity in the early 1960s when the Canadian Nickel Company was surveying (Moccasin Telegraph 1963, Spring:38).

xxvi This was also the policy in the Northwest Territories. Inuit were limited to two or three years of wage employment so they would "return to their traditional lifestyle" (Grant 1988:88).

xxvii Although family allowance payments began for the Crees in November 1945 (NA RG18 AC 85–86/048, vol. 56, file TA-500-8-1-30-34), the Inuit of northern Quebec had to wait until 1947 until the government had registered them (Davies 1948:361).

xxviii This was a company practice that reached back into the previous century (see Morantz 1990). One RCMP officer, commenting on the people living off family allowance payments instead of hunting, suggested that rather than the payments be made in cloth and food they ought to be paid in ammunition to encourage them to hunt (ibid., vol. 83-83/068, box 23 file 567-60, 5 Apr. 1946).

xxix Even with a subsidy, it was not always possible for families to go into the bush, depending on what arrangements could be made for childrens' schooling and care for the sick.

xxx Preston (pers. comm., 23 Oct. 2000) attributes the high rate of social assistance at Mistassini to the Nichikun and Neosweskau bands living there and on whose hunting territories animals were scarce in these years.

xxxi This per capita figure is for the Abitibi administrative district. Only Mistassini was not included in this Indian Affairs district, though seven other bands of Algonquins also form part of this global statistic (Ornstein and Marchant 1973:11:105).

xxxii In connection with economic development, no doubt this is a very minor consideration, but one Cree man at Great Whale River told Richard Wills in the mid-1960s that entrepreneurial activities were frowned upon in the Bible. Mr Walton had told them "if someone wants to start a business or tries to become rich, he can't go to heaven" (Wills 1984:76).

xxxiii In 1892 Parliament granted $200 to the Rupert House day school, as it did to other schools in non-treaty areas. In 1908 the day school was held at Reverend Woodall's home (Long 1978:85, 80).

xxxiv Determining that Beatrice Fairies' sojourn at the residential school was in the 1930s is based on her saying "it must have been during the depression because we used to work in the kitchen and men came asking for food" (S. Preston Collection 1984).

xxxv Provincial agreements for educational facilities were made in 1963 for Waswanipi and Mistassini and in 1961 for the James Bay/Noranda region. Along the coast, only Fort George is listed as having a provincial school in 1972 (Ornstein and Marchant 1973:11:179).

xxxvi The provincial hospital at Fort George was to replace the use of the federal one at Moosonee in providing services to the Indians and Inuit of Nouveau-Québec (Désy 1968:134).

xxxvii The entry in the Kanaaupscow post journal of 13 September 1938 reads: "Gave Walter Pachanos $5 debt today. He is going with his father after being in school for four years and had no clothes fit for winter" (HBCA B.496/a/1).

xxxviii The Cree leaders of the 1960s and 1970s seem to have had different experiences in the residential schools from Crees who in the 1940s attended Chapleau Residential School in Ontario (Milloy 1999:263).

xxxix This was not the future premier of Quebec. In 1945 the provincial and federal governments agreed to share the game warden's $1,800 annual salary because of their joint interests (NA RG10, vol. 6751, file 420-10X 6, 16 June, 1945).

XL Hugh Conn began his lengthy tour of duty among the Crees in the early 1920s as a fur-trade inspector for the company (HBCA B.227/a/57, 20 Feb. 1925). Presumably a river was named after him as Richard Tomatuck said he hunted with his father "on Conn River and south side of Eastmain River, 20 miles inland" (MC Knight Fieldnotes 1961, n.d.).

XLI In the southern portions of the territory, as at Waswanipi and Mistassini, Quebec played a much more active role, for this area held valuable minerals. In 1939 the Hudson's Bay Company trader reported that a dozen or so Quebec land surveyors were working in the area (HBCA B.227/a/69, 18 Mar. 1939).

XLII John Long (pers. comm. 1 Mar. 2000) is certain Honigmann meant to write "money boss."

XLIII Keith Crowe, who began working for the Indian Affairs Branch in 1958, has commented that the general atmosphere within the branch in the 1950s and 1960s was one of ignorance of cultural differences. He termed it a "colonial mentality"(Crowe, pers. comm., 19 Dec. 2000).

XLIV Larivière retired on 1 Apr. 1966 (Moccasin Telegraph 1966, Summer:41).

XLV In 1927 Noah Diamond was band chief at Waswanipi, followed by Peter Nayassit in 1928 (Marshall 1987:131), and then Alec Cooper in 1932 (HBCA B.227/a/60:22 Mar. 1932).

XLVI John Long (pers. comm.,1 Mar. 2000) is struck by the reference to "our employers." This may have been an error in McLeod's translation, but it nevertheless reinforces the notion of the Crees being bound to the company.

XLVII By 1935, John Chishkamush (or Tchiskamash) was referred to as Chief (Paul-Emile 1952:170; HBCA B.59/a/131, 27 Feb. 1939) and was replaced again by Chief Joe Naposh in 1938 (ibid., B.372/a/22, 13 Aug. 1938; NA RG10, vol. 303 3, file 235, 225, pt. 1, 1939, fo. 20).

XLVIII Nemiskau post was closed in 1970. The company said they had given the Crees two years' warning but the Crees remember arriving there from their traplines one year to find the food stocks low (Richardson 1975:112).

XLIX The chiefs were considered half-time employees and received a salary. By accepting this position they could not be full-time hunters (Salisbury 1986:28).

L Regina Flannery, who conducted research at Moose Factory in the 1930s, stated that people were attracted to Covell because he did magic tricks for them (pers. comm. 16 Mar. 1994).

LI One RCMP constable at Moose Factory taught Jimmy Echum how to play the violin (S. Preston Collection 1984, Alice Butterfly).

LII A function of the RCMP during wartime was the inspection of gas caches at the posts to make certain there were not surpluses that could be commandeered by the Germans (HBCA B.59/a/132, 28 July 1940).

LIII In 1950, the Quebec Ministère de la chasse et de la pêche was receiving $2 royalties per beaver pelt, $1 per otter skin and so on (NA RG10, vol. 10,819, file 44/20-10-16, pt. 1, circa 1950).

CHAPTER SEVEN

1 Both a Dene history of the Mackenzie drainage system (Abel 1993) and that of the Yukon Territory (Coates 1991) seem similar in their having remained isolated from much of the developments to the south until the Second World War and similar in governmental approaches. Nevertheless, there were important differences, such as settlement in the Yukon and significant mineral extraction in the Mackenzie that, had these authors chosen to frame their histories within a colonial framework, they would not have arrived at the same conclusions as I did for James Bay. The title of this chapter borrows from Oknuki-Tierney (1990:12) who notes that the interconnection between historical changes in different parts of the world is not unilinear development but that "all cultures weave their own tapestries."

II Similarly, and in an earlier work, Coates had concluded that government frugality which did not provide the Yukon Indians with any other economic options lay behind their ability to sustain themselves on the land, and it was cost effective for the government (Coates 1988:248, 251).

III This information is derived from undated band lists in the author's possession. Most of the information on them dates to the 1940s and additions were made until 1956.

IV Désy (1968:148;152-3) documents cases of Fort George people leaving for larger centres such as Toronto, Ottawa, and some of the mining towns but she says they are "la grande minorité."

V It has been the vogue for the past decade or so to speak of resistance (Satzewich and Wotherspoon 1993:11). Did the Crees resist? Certainly it is not intended to portray them as hapless victims, for they were not. Their rich oral tradition is testimony to their active participation in their lives on the land. Since passive resistance is by definition invisible, it is difficult to discuss Cree resistance. What is certain is that they did not always follow the instructions of the officials, thus distancing themselves from the priorities established by government.

CHAPTER EIGHT

1 To put this dramatic change on the part of federal government in terms of funding and support of its "wards" into context, Dyck (1991:108,111) points out that after the 1969 White Paper which tabled the federal government's intention to abolish all the specific constitutional, legislative, and

administrative statuses of registered Indians, there was a great outcry throughout the country. In its aftermath, the then minister of Indian Affairs, Jean Chrétien, urged Indian leaders to discuss alternatives to improve the existing system of Indian administration and offered considerable financial support. It is in this Canadian political climate that developments surrounding the James Bay settlement were played out, and it is doubtful if ten years earlier the Crees would have had the public and government support they did. Earlier immense hydroelectric projects were constructed in the Quebec-Labrador peninsula without any opposition: Manicouagan was completed in 1968 and Churchill Falls in 1971. Moreover, the Montagnais/Innu aboriginal rights to these territories were never recognized and no compensation was ever paid.

II The terms for the Inuit on land rights and jurisdiction are different, hence reference to "Northern Quebec" in the title of the agreement. As well, three Inuit villages – Povungnituk, Ivujivik, and half of Salluit – refused to sign the agreement (Sivuaq 1988:57). Only the issues affecting the Crees are discussed here. Later, in 1984, the Cree-Naskapi Act recognized Naskapi claims to portions of the James Bay territory. It was primarily this legislation that replaced the Indian Act, providing a measure of self-government for the Cree and Naskapi peoples (Dickason 1997:389).

III One serious example of the failure to follow through on the provisions of the agreement was shown in the gastro-enteritis epidemic that hit the Cree communities in 1980. The outbreak was the result of no running water and inadequate sewage systems that under the terms of the James Bay agreement should have been in place. Over one hundred children in two villages were very ill, and one died. Grand Chief Billy Diamond's son's life was in peril. Furious and despairing, he went to the media when the government continued to drag its feet and he even took his complaint to the first United Nations Conference on Indigenous Peoples in Geneva (MacGregor 1988:180).

IV Damning the Great Whale River was Hydro-Québec's original plan in the early 1960s and their basic design concept had been drafted in 1966. It emerged as a major issue during the negotiations of the James Bay Agreement in the 1970s and was raised again in the early 1980s. Finally, Hydro-Québec launched it again in 1988 at a time of rapid evolution of the North American energy market (Alan Penn, pers. comm. 29 Feb. 2000).

V The Crees quickly learned to master what Dyck (1991:111) has termed the politics of embarrassment, based on a set of moral claims against the Canadian state.

References Notes

CHAPTER ONE

1. Scott 1992:53.
2. Trudel 1992:70.
3. Scott 1992:47, 59.
4. Quoted in Eberstadt 1993:110
5. Hickerson 1973:39.
6. See Frideres 1993:8; Satzewich and Wotherspoon 1993:11; and Ponting 1997:8.
7. See Coates 1991.
8. See Abel 1993.
9. Thomas 1994:192; Comaroffs 1992:183.
10. Warren 1989:14.
11. Comaroffs 1992:198–9.
12. Ibid., 200.
13. NA, CMS reel A–97, 18 July 1853.
14. Comaroffs 1992:198
15. Ibid., 211.
16. Ibid., 183.
17. See *Globe and Mail*, 11 December 1997.
18. Tester and Kulchyski 1994.
19. Frenette 1985:93, 87.
20. Morantz 1995.
21. Comaroffs 1992:211.
22. Leach 1989:37.
23. Kerr 1950:123.
24. See Terence Turner 1988.
25. Tough 1996:9 fn 11.
26. Appleby et al. 1994:53.
27. Tonkin 1992:3.
28. Preston 1975a:292; and see Vincent 1982:1; Scott 1983:21.
29. Vincent 1992:20.
30. Preston 1986a:4.
31. Drapeau 1996:174.
32. Preston 1986a:4, and 1964 Fieldnotes, fo. 79.
33. Preston 1975a:290.
34. Hastrup 1992:9.
35. Vansina 1985:8, 12–13.
36. Ridington 1988:71, 74.
37. Flannery and Chambers 1985:3, 4.
38. Chance 1970:19.
39. Ridington 1988:70.
40. Preston 1986a:8.
41. Cruikshank 1991:19.
42. Tonkin 1992:2.
43. S. Preston 1986:158.
44. Thwaites 1896:47:151–3.
45. Erickson 1983.
46. Cruikshank 1990:339.
47. Sylvie Vincent, pers. comm. May 1977.

48 Francis and Morantz 1983:158.
49 Tonkin 1992:8.
50 Hill 1988:2–3, 7.
51 Ibid., 6, 10.
52 Turner 1988:241.
53 See Bauer 1973.
54 Appleby et al. 1994:218.
55 Preston 1986a:4–7.
56 Vincent 1982:14.
57 Cruikshank 1996:443.
58 Cruikshank 1990:346.
59 Ignace 1991:119–21.
60 Vincent 1996:10–11.
61 Bhabha 1997:14.
62 Morantz 1984:171–2.
63 Tonkin 1992:6.
64 Biggar 1922:1:124.
65 See Morantz 1992a.
66 See Ray 1974, Bishop 1974, and Fisher 1979.
67 See Morantz 1982:491.
68 Leacock 1954, 1969.
69 Rogers 1963, 1969.
70 Leacock 1969:8.
71 Morantz 1983:106.
72 Laliberté 1981:62.
73 Denton 1981:3–4.
74 Morantz 1983:90–1.
75 Speck 1915:289.
76 Feit 1991.
77 Morantz 1986a:79–80.
78 Leacock 1954:6.
79 Low 1896:49.
80 Leacock 1978:249.
81 Rogers 1969:40.
82 See Ray 1980; Morantz 1983:18.
83 Cooke 1979:100.
84 HBCA B.186/b/70, fo. 48d, 1865; also see Morantz 1988.
85 Tough 1996:9, fn 11.
86 Thwaites 1896:45:227, 1659–60.
87 Ibid., 6:297–9.
88 Canadian Encyclopedia 1985:1:154.
89 Wolf 1982:4.
90 Warren 1989:6.
91 Hugh-Jones 1989:53.
92 Wallerstein 1974.
93 Asad 1986:158.
94 Hastrup 1992:2.
95 Ray 1990a:201–2.
96 Anderson 1961:56–7.

CHAPTER TWO

1 Bourassa 1973:33.
2 Ducruc et al. 1976:382.
3 Bider 1976:394.
4 Dunbar 1968:92.
5 Denton 1998:21.
6 Martijn and Rogers 1969:62; Denton 1998:21.
7 Laliberté 1978:96.
8 HBCA B.373/d/9, fo. 49, 9 June 1869.
9 Morantz 1990:213; HBCA B.186/b/70, fo. 47d, 1870.
10 Anderson 1961:56.
11 Morantz 1990:221; Ray 1990a:85.
12 Kerr 1950:42.
13 Ibid., 41–3.
14 Adrian Tanner, pers. comm. 10 October 1999.
15 HBCA A.74/5, n.p.
16 Ray 1990b:28–9, 51–5.
17 HBCA RG7, General Correspondence 2-4-95, fos. 6,–7, 15 Aug. 1892.
18 Low 1896:70.
19 HBCA B.186/d/6a, fo. 4, 39.
20 Marshall 1987:47.
21 Anderson 1961:58.
22 HBCA B.373/a/13, 7 June 1894, 4 Apr. 1900.

23 Ibid., B.77/a/43, 19 July 1888.
24 Ibid., B.77/z/1, fo. 81, 1863.
25 Ibid., DFTR 15, fo. 4, 1922; B.186/a/109, 10 Aug. 1901.
26 See Morantz 1990:209.
27 MC Knight Fieldnotes 1961, fo. 9, 12 July.
28 HBCA B.133/a/50, 2 July 1881.
29 Bouchard 1980:115.
30 Tough 1996:222, 281.
31 Ray 1990b:28–9.
32 Tough 1996:7–9, 281.
33 HBCA B.77/d/21, fo. 101d, 1869.
34 David Cooter, pers. comm., Sept. 1985.
35 Borron 1890:84–5, 78.
36 Ommer 1990:15.
37 HBCA B.77/a/41, 4 Apr. 1880; B.77/b/5, 23 Apr. 1881, 22 June 1889.
38 Ibid., B.186/b/70, fo. 65d, 1870; B.59/a/123, 1893.
39 Ibid., RG7 2-4-95, fo. 6, "Report," 15 Aug. 1892.
40 Francis and Morantz 1983:121.
41 HBCA RG 7 2-4-95, fo. 3 "Report" 15 Aug. 1892.
42 Mattox 1964:13.
43 HBCA B.186/a/106, 1 June 1896; B.186/a/94, 17, 21 July 1884; B.186/a/109, 10 Aug. 1901.
44 Anderson 1961:53; Tanner 1978:154.
45 Scanlon 1975:8.
46 HBCA B.186/a/103, 11 July 1891; B.186/a/109, 24 Feb., 31 Mar. 1902.
47 Linteau et al. 1989:1:112.
48 HBCA A/74/1, fo. 378, 1891–93; B.133/a/51, 11 June 1883; RG 7 2-4-95, fo. 2, "Report," 15 Aug. 1892.
49 Ibid., B.227/a/46, 29 May 1870; B.133/a/55, 16 Mar. 1892.
50 Ibid., B.133/a/54, 30 Aug. 1892.
51 Ibid., B.186/a/97, 30 June 1871.
52 Ibid., B.186/a/99, 1877.
53 Zaslow 1971:10, 81.
54 HBCA B.77/a/40, 13 Sept. l877; B.77/a/44, 22 July 1887.
55 Zaslow 1971:84–5.
56 HBCA B.133/a/51, 23 Dec. 1884; B.133/a/52, 13 May 1885.
57 Ibid., 133/a/52, 8 Jan., 2, 15, 18 Feb. 1885.
58 Ibid., B.77/a/44, 3 July, 27 Aug. 1888.
59 Low 1896:45.
60 HBCA B.186/a/107, 24, 25 June 1899.
61 AMNH Skinner Papers, 28 May, 1 June 1908.
62 Hubbard 1908.
63 HBCA B.133/a/50, 1881.
64 Ibid., B.133/a/57, 27 Aug. l897.
65 Ibid., B.133/a/58, 13 Feb. 1899.
66 Loring 1987:168–9.
67 HBCA B.133/a/63, 10 Aug. 1907.
68 Anderson 1961:86.
69 NA CMS Reel A–88, Horden, 11 Oct.
70 HBCA B.77/b/5, 18 Jan. 1884; 17 Jan. 1885.
71 Ibid., RG 7 2-4-95, fo. 1, 15 Aug. 1891.
72 Ibid., B.186/a/106.
73 Ibid., B.186/a/107, 15, 27 June.
74 Ibid., B.77/b/7, fo. 40, fos. 87–91, 1901.
75 Ibid., B.77/b/8, fo. 157, 1902; NA Walton Papers, 1903, fo. 10; 1904, fo. 19.
76 HBCA A/74/12, fo. 47, 1904 fo. 47; B.77/a/52, 13 Feb. 1906.
77 Leiths 1912:60.
78 AMNH Skinner Papers, fo. 5, 12 Aug. 1908.
79 HBCA B.373/d/5, fo. 9d, 1869–70.

80 Leiths 1912:59.
81 HBCA B.77/b/8, fo. 91, 1901; B.59/a/125, 10 Oct. 1902.
82 Ibid., A/74/12, 1903.
83 MC Turner Collection 1974, tape 32–B.
84 HBCA RG 7 2-4-95, fo. 6, "Report," 15 Aug. 1892.
85 NA Walton Letterbook,1903?, fo. 16.
86 Turner 1979:20.
87 Cooke 1979:100.
88 Turner 1979:17–19.
89 Ibid., 79:103–4.
90 Thwaites 1896:45:21.
91 Francis and Morantz 1983:139.
92 Mackenzie 1977; Pentland 1978; Rhodes and Todd 1981:55.
93 NAA Michelson Papers #3399, fo. 1, Aug. 1935; #3396, fo. 78; #3397, fo. 17, 10 Sept. 1935.
94 Turner 1979:138.
95 Ibid., 158–9, 111.
96 Tanner, pers. comm. 10 October 1999.
97 Flannery 1995:7–13, 22.
98 Ibid., 15.
99 Ibid., 44, 17.
100 Ibid., 37, 45.
101 Ibid., 1935:82–6.
102 Knight 1968:56.
103 Petersen 1974:43.
104 Crowe 1991:116.
105 Walton 1921; Low 1896:319; Flaherty 1918:454.
106 Leacock and Rothschild 1994:116.
107 Stephen Loring in Leacock and Rothschild 1994:193.
108 MC Turner Collection 1974, tape 33–B.
109 Ibid., tape III–D–16T.
110 Walton 1921:21; Cooke 1976:58.
111 MC Turner Collection 1974, tape 33–A.
112 MC Knight Fieldnotes 1961, 15 July.
113 HBCA B.186/a/100, 25–26 June 1880; B.186/b/71, 16 July 1880.
114 Ibid., B.186/a/108, 16 Feb., 30 Mar. 1900; 8 Jan. 1901.
115 See Smith 1976:18; Brightman 1988:337, 351; Flannery et al. 1982:59.
116 Preston 1980b:124.
117 Flannery et al. 1982:58–9.
118 Ibid., 59.
119 HBCA B.186/a/101, 2 Aug. 1883.
120 Ibid., B.186/e/11, fo. 9d.
121 Marshall 1987:32, 47.
122 Thwaites 1896:56:183.
123 Low 1896:70.
124 HBCA B.133/a/63, 20 Mar.
125 MC Feit Collection 1968, 28, 29 Oct.
126 HBCA B.142/a/11, 11 Mar. 1939.
127 NA RG10, vol. 6754, file 420–10-4-NO-1 1, 22 Feb. 1949.
128 Leiths 1912:63.
129 MC Feit Collection 1970, 24 Sept.; Marshall 1987:32.
130 Knight 1968:8.
131 AR Trudel Collection, 1978, fo. 16.12, Dec.
132 Low 1896:50, 101; see also Marshall 1987:32.
133 MC Knight Fieldnotes 1961, fos. 1–8, 20 June, Matthew Cowboy; Kerr 1950:137.
134 MC Feit Collection 1970, 24 Sept.
135 Anderson 1961:104.
136 Knight 1968:19.
137 HBCA B.409/a/1, 25 Oct. 1940; ibid., B.142/a/11, 1 May 1939.

Notes to pages 55–64

138 Low 1896:98, and MC Feit Collection 1969, 18 Oct.
139 Leiths 1912:61, 64.
140 Low 1896:44–7; Turner 1979:121; Leiths 1912:166–7.
141 Taylor 1994:356.
142 MC Sun Collection 1979, C–10.
143 MC Turner Collection 1974, tape 33.
144 MC Knight Fieldnotes 1961, 20 June, fo. 6.
145 Leiths 1912:172, 187–8.
146 Low 1896:49.
147 Harris 1976:106.
148 HBCA B.77/a/46, 11 June 1986; B.133/a/61, 22 Aug. 1901.
149 Bouchard 1980:115–16.
150 HBCA B.77a/58, 23 July 1924; B.77/a/57, 2 July 1920.
151 Rogers 1963.
152 Long 1985:144.
153 Marshall 1987:36.
154 AR Trudel Collection 1978, fo. 17.5.
155 HBCA B.77/a/54, 8 July, 2 Aug. 1910.
156 Ibid., B.77/a/53.
157 Ibid., B.372/a/22, fo. 12, 15 July 1938.
158 Iserhoff 1925:9.
159 HBCA B.147/a/40, fo. 19, 10 Oct. 1939.
160 Ibid., B.186/a/97.
161 Anderson 1961:105–6.
162 HBCA B.186/a/98.
163 Ibid., B.373/a/13, 1 Jan. 1896; B.186/a/98, 1 Jan. 1875.
164 Ibid., B.186/a/106:1 Jan. 1897.
165 Ibid., B.186/a/107, 13 Nov. 1898.
166 AA Diocese of Moosonee Records, 1–1, 12.
167 HBCA B.77/a/43, 3 July 1887.
168 Ibid., B.77/c/2, fo. 114; B.133/a/49, 19 Mar.
169 Ibid., B.186/a/98, 1 June 1874.
170 John Long, pers. comm., 1 Mar. 2000.
171 AA Diocese of Moosonee Records, 1–1, Rupert's House Mission Report, 14 May– 28 Aug. 1911.
172 Kerr 1950:16.
173 Long 1986:149; Long 1994a:1061.
174 Long 1985:146–8.
175 Ibid., 148.
176 John Long, pers. comm. 1 Mar. 2000.
177 Ray 1990b:183.
178 John Long, pers. comm. 1 Mar. 2000.
179 HBCA B.77/c/2, fo. 143, 11 Feb., 1875.
180 Ibid., B.186/a/98, 18 Mar., 1878.
181 See Francis and Morantz 1983:156.
182 Van Kirk 1980:205.
183 Long 1985.
184 HBCA B.77/a/40, 20 Sept. 1876.
185 Peterson 1974:45.
186 Curran and Calkins 1917:101; Peterson 1974:20.
187 HBCA B.77/a/55, July 27, 1915.
188 Anderson 1961:122.
189 Turner 1979:20.
190 Harris 1976:191.
191 S. Preston Collection 1984, 14 June.
192 Leiths 1912:151.
193 HBCA B.186/a/103, 2 Mar. 1880; B.77/a/41, 1881.
194 Honigmann 1962:18–19.
195 NAA Michelson Papers, #3396, fo. 78.

196 HBCA B.186/b/53, fo. 38; B.59/a/124, 20 Jan. 1898.
197 Ibid., B.186/a/97, 6 May 1871.
198 Ibid.; 19 Feb. 1872.
199 NA RG18 AC 85–86/048, vol. 56, file TA-500-8-1-34, fo. 39, undated.
200 Moccasin Telegraph 1960, Winter:28.
201 HBCA B.186/b/40, fo. 31, 1836.
202 Leiths 1912:180.
203 Francis and Morantz 1983:141, 74, 117.
204 HBCA B.186/a/104, 1892; B.186/a/109, 19 July, 19 Sept. 1901.
205 Ibid., B.186/a/104, 10 Apr. 1892.
206 Ibid., B.186/a/106, 15 Dec. 1896; B.186/a/108, 23 July 1900.
207 Ibid., B.186/b/71, 18 Feb.
208 Ibid., B.186/a/106, 20 June, 21 May 1896.
209 Ibid., B.186/a/106, 30 Nov. 1895.
210 NA CMS Walton Letterbook, 4 Jan. 1905.
211 HBCA B.77/a/53, 27 June 1909.
212 Buckley 1992:44.
213 Anderson 1961:129.
214 Ibid., 101.
215 Cree Way 1975.
216 NA Diocese of Moose Records, Archdeacon A.L. Fleming to Bishop Anderson, 30 July 1931.
217 Leiths 1912:33-4.
218 Ibid.; Anderson 1961:56.
219 Godsell 1932:65, 31.
220 Anderson 1961:47.
221 HBCA B.142/a/11, 11 July 1938; B.142/a/12, 26 Oct. 1940.
222 Harris 1976:36.
223 HBCA B.142/a/11, 5 Jan. 1939.
224 Ibid., B.142/a/10, 2 Oct. 1929.
225 Ibid., B.142/a/10, 28 Oct. 1929, 19 Oct. 1935, 11 Dec. 1929, 22 May 1930.
226 Ibid., B.372/a/22, fos. 29, 39, 10 Mar., 13 May 1939.
227 Ibid., B.133/a/67, 23 Nov. 1926; B.133/a/68, 30 Jan. 1929.
228 Anderson 1961:96, 97.
229 Kerr 1950:30.
230 Nanuwan 1929:162.
231 Kerr 1950:49.
232 Anderson 1961:60.
233 Harris 1976:110.
234 Walker 1953:15–16.

CHAPTER THREE

1 Kidwell 1996:723.
2 HBCA B.77/a/58, 21 Nov. 1925; Paul-Emile 1959:209–11.
3 Cooper 1933; 1934.
4 Tanner 1979:211.
5 Rousseau 1952:89.
6 Long 1986; HBCA B.186/a/62, 7 Sept. 1840.
7 Petersen 1974:23, 32.
8 Francis and Morantz 1983:162.
9 Brown 1987.
10 Nock 1988:3, 36.
11 Francis and Morantz 1983:164.
12 Carrière 1957:46–7, 191.
13 Carrière 1969:155; Carrière 1957:117; AA St Barnabas Parish Register 1916–46, n.d.; HBCA B.227/a/45, 4 June 1866.
14 AA St Barnabas Parish Register 1916–1946, n.d.
15 HBCA B.186/a/94, 27 Aug. 1865.

16 Scanlon 1975:66.
17 Ibid., 66. 47.
18 NA CMS Diocese of Moosonee, microfilm 81-4, reel 1, 28 Aug. 1911.
19 Bouchard 1980:111.
20 Guinard 1951:61.
21 Ibid., 61, 62, 32; Bouchard 1980:111.
22 Scanlon 1975:47.
23 Ibid., 47; HBCA B.227/a/56, 30 June 1913.
24 Scanlon 1975:52; Guinard 1951:62.
25 Bouchard 1980:114.
26 HBCA B.227/a/57:10 July 1922.
27 Bouchard 1980:117.
28 Ibid., 112-13.
29 Speck 1977:16.
30 Scanlon 1975:6, 19.
31 NA CMS Diocese of Moosonee, reel 81-1, St Philip's Parish.
32 Guinard 1951:65; Low 1896:46.
33 Turner 1979:18-19.
34 Speck 1977:21.
35 Low 1896:46.
36 Leiths 1912:46.
37 Guinard 1951:156.
38 HBCA B.147/a/40, 22 Nov. 1939.
39 Leiths 1912:51.
40 Anderson 1961:101.
41 See Flannery and Chambers 1985.
42 Preston 1975:25-90.
43 Harvey Feit, pers. comm., Nov. 1998.
44 NA RG 10, vol. 6755, file 420-10-4-1, pt. 3, report of H. Larivière, 5 July 1942.
45 MC Knight fieldnotes 1961, 22 Aug., 24 Aug.
46 HBCA B.147/a/41, 4 May 1941.
47 NA CMS Diocese of Moosonee, 1-1, 28 Aug. 1911.
48 Low 1896:46, 102.
49 Walker 1953:71.
50 Ibid., 48-9; HBCA B.77/a/24, 23 June 1850.
51 Leiths 1912:52.
52 Long 1986:149.
53 Petersen 1974:14.
54 Renison 1957:32-3.
55 Long 1986:143.
56 Petersen 1974:16, 118; HBCA B.186/a/107, 7 June 1898.
57 NA CMS Diocese of Moosonee, 1-1, 28 Aug. 1911.
58 Zaslow 1979:102-3.
59 MC Turner Collection 1974, tape 23-A.
60 Ibid., tape 20-B.
61 Preston, pers. comm. 24 Sept. 2000.
62 Berkes 1986:24.
63 Leiths 1912:47.
64 MC Sun Collection 1979:C-15.
65 NA CMS Diocese of Moosonee, Rupert House Mission Book, 27 Feb. 1906.
66 NA Walton Letterbook [1900?], fo. 3.
67 Petersen 1974:44.
68 Ibid.
69 Walton 1920:19.
70 HBCA B.77/a/58, 5-6 July 1908.
71 NA Walton Papers MG 30, D133, 4 Jan. 1905, fo. 2.
72 MC Sun Collection 1980:38; HBCA B.77/a/46, 26 Nov. 1897; B.372/a/13, 8 Aug. 1895.
73 HBCA B.77/a/44, 9 Nov.
74 Ibid., B.77/a/50, 5 Oct. 1902; James 1985:12-13.
75 Sun 1980:45, 46.
76 Long 1986:144.
77 HBCA B.77/a/54, 1909.
78 NA Walton Letterbook, 4 Jan. 1905.

79 NA CMS, Diocese of Moosonee, microfilm 81-4, reel 1, 12 Jan. 1914.
80 Tanner 1979:114.
81 Grant 1984:261.
82 Preston 1975:105.
83 Long 1987:13.
84 NA Walton Letterbook, Jan. 1902.
85 See Axtell 1985:121-2, and Comaroffs 1992:251.
86 NA Walton Letterbook, 4 Jan. 1905.
87 Klass 1995:15.
88 Speck 1977:7.
89 See ibid.; also Tanner 1979 and Sun 1980.
90 Comaroffs 1992:193-4.
91 See Conn 1986:2.
92 NA Walton Letterbook, 4 Jan. 1905.
93 Speck 1977:22.
94 Long 1987:21, 22.
95 MC Turner Collection 1974, tape 20 B, fos. 1-3.
96 Ibid., tape 23 B, fos. 8, 20.
97 Sun 1980:44.
98 Flannery and Chamber 1985:21; Preston 1975a:27ff.
99 See Tanner 1979:113-16.
100 Sun 1980:60, 58, and Berkes 1986.
101 Sun 1980:51, 54.
102 Preston 1988:150.
103 Sun 1980:53, 54.
104 Leiths 1912:47.
105 Preston 1988:153-4; pers. comm., 24 Sept. 2000.
106 Sun 1980:56.
107 Preston 1988:153.
108 NA CMS, Diocese of Moosonee Records, microfilm 81-4, reel 1, 11 June 1912; 1 Aug. 1913.
109 MC Sun Collection 1979:C-14, C-8.
110 NA Walton Letterbook, 4 Jan. 1905, 6 Jan. 1902.
111 Sun 1980:46.
112 NA CMS, Diocese of Moosonee, microfilm 81-4, reel 1, 6 Jan. 1904.
113 Ibid., 12 Jan. 1914.
114 NA Walton Letterbook, 1901.
115 Ibid., 6 Jan. 1904.
116 Goody 1986:3, 5-6.
117 Ibid., 17-18.
118 Harkin and Kan 1996.
119 White 1991:103.
120 Preston 1988:151.
121 Long 1986:225.
122 MC Feit Collection 1970, 26 Sept.
123 Niezen 1997:466.

CHAPTER FOUR

1 Keighley 1989:96.
2 Rich 1967:109.
3 HBCA B.186/a/109, 7 June 1903.
4 Ibid., B.77/a/50, 17, 29 July 1903.
5 Ibid., B.186/a/109, 2 Sept. 1903.
6 Ibid., B.186/a/110, 30 Sept. 1907.
7 Ibid., B.77/a/50, 24 Aug.-15 Sept. 1903; NA Walton Letterbook, 6 Jan. 1904.
8 Sexé 1923:59-79.
9 NA Walton Letterbook, 6 Jan. 1904.
10 Ibid., B.77/b/8, fo. 219, 1904; fo. 47, 1905.
11 Ibid., B.77/a/52, 15 June 1906.

12 Ibid., 22 June 1906; B.77/b/8, fo. 47, 1905.
13 Ibid., B.77/a/54, 19–21 Jan. 1910.
14 Leiths 1912:165.
15 HBCA DFTR/3, fo. 107, 1915; A.74/14, fo. 76, 1915.
16 Ibid., A.74/18; A.6/17, fo. 301; RG 7/7A365.
17 Cree Way 1975, W. Jacob, C. Blackned.
18 MC Knight Fieldnotes 1961.
19 HBCA B.77/b/8, fo. 79, 1906.
20 Anonymous 1935:64.
21 HBCA B.77/a/52, 13 Sept. 1906.
22 Ibid., B.77/a/52, 21 Feb. 1907; B.77/a/57, 4 Nov. 1920.
23 Ibid., A.74/43, fo. 12, 1929.
24 Ibid., DFTR/3, fo. 107, 1915.
25 Ibid., B.77/a/57, 26 Jan. 1921.
26 Ibid., A.74/33, 1924.
27 Linteau et al. 1989:1:67.
28 HBCA B.77/a/57, 26 Jan, 6 May 1921.
29 Ibid., B.227/a/69, 9 June 1940.
30 Ibid., B.77/a/58, 8 Oct. 1925.
31 Ibid., B.227/a/67, 17 Jan. 1939, 31 Dec.1938.
32 Ibid., DFTR/13, fo. 6, 1921.
33 Sexé 1923:58.
34 Harris 1976:123.
35 HBCA B.77/a/54, 10 Feb. 1910.
36 Ibid., B.77/a/57, 24 Feb. 1921; 11 July 1921; DFTR/13, fo. 6, 1921.
37 AR Trudel Collection 1978, fo. 16.13, Andrew Kawapit.
38 HBCA B. 77/b/9, fo. 472, 1910.
39 Ibid., B.77/a57, 29–30 June 1921.
40 Ibid., B.77/a/57, 15 Sept. 1921.
41 Ibid., DFTR/24, fo. 12, 1932.
42 Ibid., DFTR/21, fo. 14, 1925; A.93/46, fo. 18 Report, James Bay District, 1927.
43 CRA Tanner Collection 1978, fo. 72; HBCA RG7, NSD Correspondence File 6–9–9(4), 30 July 1958.
44 HBCA DFTR/21, fos. 13–14, 1925.
45 Ibid., B.496/a/1, 10 Sept., 1938; CRA Tanner Collection 1977, 19 July.
46 Ibid., B.135/a/196, 21 June 1929; Paul-Emile 1952:202.
47 HBCA DFTR/27, fo. 12, 1934.
48 CRA Tanner Collection 1977, 22 July.
49 Ibid., 1977 22 July.
50 Paul-Emile 1952:202, 205.
51 HBCA B.409/a/1, 25 Feb. 1939; B.59/a/131, 26 Feb. 1939.
52 Ibid., DFTR 19, fo. 14 1924.
53 Cree Way 1975; HBCA B.77/a/55, 14 Dec.1915.
54 HBCA B.142/a/11,1 Oct. 1938, 12 Apr. 1939.
55 Ibid., DFTR/19, fo. 341, 1924.
56 Leiths 1912:41.
57 Anderson 1961:57.
58 Leiths 1912:58.
59 Robertson 1984:15; HBCA RG3/28/1, fo. 31, June 1918.
60 MC Turner Collection 1974, tape 33–A.
61 HBCA B.77/a/53, 4 Oct. 1909; B.77/a/56, 14 June 1919.
62 Ibid., DFTR/9, fo. 105, 1919.
63 Ibid., B.77/a/58, 21 Sept; 15 Nov.; 6, 25 Dec. 1924; Anderson 1961:129.
64 Leiths 1912:58.
65 Anderson 1961:28–9, 34.
66 Tanner 1978:20.
67 HBCA B.147/a/40, 3 Dec. 1939.
68 Frenette 1985:32.
69 HBCA B.147/a/40, 29 Dec. 1939.

70 Ibid., A.93/45, fo. 20, 9 Oct. 1929.
71 Ibid., DFTR/9, fo. 106, 1919.
72 Ibid., DFTR 13, fo. 180, 1921.
73 Ibid., B.77/a/57, 28 Dec. 1920.
74 Sexé 1923:78.
75 Ray 1990b:93; Harris 1976:144.
76 HBCA A.93/46, fo. 17, 1927.
77 Harris 1976:68; Ray 1990b:160.
78 Anderson 1961:195.
79 Keighley 1989:138.
80 Keighley 1989:129.
81 W.A. Anderson 1961:120–1.
82 HBCA DFTR/24, fo. 9, 1932.
83 Ibid., A.93/46, fo. 17, 1927.
84 MC Knight Fieldnotes 1961, 15 July.
85 See HBCA B.133/a/68, 8 July 1929.
86 Ibid., B.133/a/67, 18 June 1928.
87 Ibid., B.133/a/67, 12 June 1929; B.133/a/68, 15 June 1929.
88 Ibid., B.133/a/74, 6 June 1937.
89 Anderson 1961:56.
90 HBCA DFTR/3, fo. 101, 1915.
91 Ibid., A.93/46, 17 Aug. 1927.
92 CRA Denton Collection 1983, tape 3.
93 OA Watt Papers, 17 Aug. 1929.
94 NA RG 10, locator X310, file 480/23-17, June–Oct.1931.
95 Low 1896:101.
96 HBCA DFTR/19, fo. 341, 1924.
97 Ibid., A.93/46, fos. 40, 43, 1927.
98 Anderson 1961:57.
99 MC Knight Fieldnotes 1961, 20, 30 June.
100 Ibid., 4 July 1961.
101 HBCA DFTR/13, fo. 182, 1921.
102 Morantz 1990:213.
103 HBCA B.227/a/57, 8 July 1923.
104 Copland 1985:145.
105 Ray 1990b:85.
106 HBCA B.133/a/67.
107 Ibid., DFTR/19, fo. 341, 1924.
108 Ibid., A.93/46, 1 Sept. 1927.
109 Ibid., 18 June 1927.
110 Ibid., 1 Sept. 1927.
111 Ibid., 1 Sept. 1927.
112 Ibid., DFTR/27, fo. 10, 1934; B.227/a/65, 13 June 1936; B.227/a/68, 23 May 1940.
113 Ibid., A.74/43, fo. 22, 1929.
114 Ibid., DFTR/15, fo. 4, 1922.
115 Knight 1968:23.
116 HBCA DFTR/13, fo. 182, 1921.
117 Cree Way 1975.
118 Copland 1985:156; and see Leiths 1912:90–1.
119 CRA Denton Collection 1983, tape 6.
120 Nicholson 1924:49.
121 Anderson 1961:123.
122 Ibid., 117.
123 HBCA DFTR/5, fo. 92, 1915.
124 Ibid., DFTR/15, fo. 154, 1922.
125 Ibid., RG3 series 2/2, fo. 140, 1926.
126 Frenette 1985:20.
127 Anderson 1961:99.
128 Ibid., 117; HBCA B.142/a/12, 27 Feb. 1941.
129 Matthew Wapachee in Frenette 1985:30.
130 HBCA B.77/a/57, 26 Sept. 1922.
131 Keighley 1989:114, 138.
132 Ray 1990b:190; HBCA B.135/a/203, 31 Dec. 1929.
133 HBCA RG3/3B/3, 19 Feb. 1932; CRA Denton Collection 1983, tape 2, Ronnie Cowboy interview.
134 Cree Way 1975.
135 CRA Tanner Collection 1977, 7 July.

136 MC Sun Collection 1979, fo. C-17.
137 HBCA B.77/a/54, 10 Sept. 1909.
138 CRA Tanner Collection 1977, 7 July.
139 AA Mission Journal, Rupert House 1939-1958.
140 HBCA B.186/e/26, 1880; B.186/e/27, 1881; B.186/e/28, 1882.
141 McFeat 1974:35.
142 Preston 1996:3.
143 Rogers 1963:55.
144 HBCA B.186/e/28, 1882.
145 MC Sun Collection 1979, fo. C-18.
146 HBCA A.74/33, fo. 25, 1924.
147 MC Feit Collection 1982, 31 Aug., Alan Saganash.
148 MC Sun Collection 1979, fo. C-10, 11.
149 MC Knight Fieldnotes 1961, 22 Aug.
150 NA RG10, vol. 6755, file 420-10-4-1, pt. 3, 9 Aug. 1942.
151 S. Preston Collection 1984, 18 July.
152 HBCA A.74/43, fo. 9, 1929.
153 NA RG10, vol. 6755, file 420-10-4-1, pt. 3.
154 S. Preston Collection, 1984.
155 Francis and Morantz 1983:153.
156 HBCA DFTR/9, fo. 104, 1919.
157 Ibid., DFTR/15, fo. 160, 1922.
158 Ibid., A.74/42, fo. 21, 1929.
159 Ibid., A.93/46, fo. 3, 1925.
160 Long 1985.
161 NA RG10, vol. 6754, file 420-10-4-1, pt. 2, 8 Dec. 1939.
162 HBCA A.93/46, fo. 2, Notes on Coast Indian, 17 Aug. 1927.
163 Knight 1968:95.
164 MC Knight Fieldnotes 1961, June 20.
165 Ibid., July 3.
166 OMI Deschâtelets, LCB 3061 C43C; NA RG10, vol. 6752, file 420-10-2, 15 Dec. 1942.
167 NA RG10, vol. 6752, file 420-10-2, 3, 8 June 1946.
168 Ibid., vol. 10,289, file 43/3-3, 22 July, 1 July 1961.
169 HBCA B.135/a/196, 17 Oct. 1929.
170 AA St Peter's Mission Journal, 1902-1906, 9 July 1904.
171 HBCA B.133/a/74, 9 Aug. 1937; B.133/a/76, 2 Aug. 1939.
172 Long 1985:72; Flannery 1995.

CHAPTER FIVE

1 Grant 1988:17.
2 Buckley 1992.
3 Cumming and Mickenberg 1972:89.
4 Cited in Ornstein and Marchant 1973:III:71.
5 Dickason 1997:355.
6 Cumming and Mickenberg 1972:91-2.
7 NA RG10, vol. 3033, file 235, 225, pt. 1. Memo from Inspector of Indians Affairs and Reserves, 17 Aug. 1903.
8 Ibid., vol. 6754, file 420-10-4-1, pt. 1, 16 Mar. 1933.
9 Anderson 1961:131.
10 Paul-Emile 1952:182.
11 See Gaffen 1985:Appendix B.
12 HBCA B.77/a/57, 11 Nov. 1920.
13 Ibid., B.77/a/55, 12 Sept. 1914.
14 Ibid., DFTR/9, fo. 104, 1919.
15 Ibid., B.77/a/57, 29 July 1920.

16 MC Knight Fieldnotes 1961, 16 June.
17 HBCA B.227/a/57, 30 June 1925.
18 Cree Way 1975, Tommy Blackned.
19 Anonymous 1931:187.
20 Anderson 1961:156.
21 Scanlon 1975:10, HBCA B.135/a/196, 2 Nov. 1929.
22 Paul-Emile 1952:192.
23 Anderson 1961:215.
24 HBCA B. 372/a/22, 12 Aug. 1938.
25 Ibid., B.59/a/132, 30 Aug.–2 Sept. 1940; B.133/a/77, 20 Oct. 1940.
26 Ibid., B.372/a/23, 28 Oct. 1940.
27 Moccasin Telegraph 1942, December: 2.
28 HBCA B.409/a/1, 18 Sept. 1938.
29 Ibid., B.372/a/23, 1940.
30 Ibid., B.227/a/65, 8 Jan. 1936.
31 Ibid., B.147/a/40.
32 AA Rupert House Mission Journal, 26 Dec. 1944.
33 Preston, pers. comm., 28 Sept. 2000.
34 HBCA B.135/a/203.
35 Ibid., B.227/a/57, 5 July 1923.
36 Ray 1990b:189.
37 Keighley 1989:90.
38 MC Feit Collection 1982, 28 Aug.
39 HBCA B. 227/a/63, 24 Dec. 1934.
40 James 1985:88.
41 Robertson 1984:105.
42 MC Scott Collection 1981, 27 Oct., tape III–D–204T, Richard Blackned.
43 CRA Tanner Collection 1977, 18 July.
44 HBCA RG3/3B/1, 29 Mar. 1931.
45 MC Knight Fieldnotes 1961, 1 July.
46 MC Scott Collection 1981, 27 Oct., tape III–D–204T.
47 HBCA B.59/a/32, 18 July 1940; B.147/a/39, 2 Mar.1938; B.147a/40, 14 Oct. 1939.
48 Anderson 1961:173.
49 *The Canadian Encyclopedia* 1985:1542; Surtees 1992.
50 Anderson 1961:174.
51 Tanner, pers. comm., 10 Oct. 1999.
52 NA RG10, vol. 6750, file 420–10, 10 June 1924.
53 Linteau et al. 1989:502–3.
54 NA RG10, vol. 6750, file 420–10, 11 Aug. 1924.
55 Ibid., file 420–10A, 22 July 1926.
56 Ibid., 29 Oct. 1927.
57 Ibid., 23 Dec. 1927.
58 Ibid., file 420–10 5; 5 Feb. 1942.
59 HBCA RG 7 14–1–2(4), Special Joint Committee on the Indian Act, fo. 691, 25 July 1947.
60 NA RG10, file 420–10A, 8 Oct. 1929.
61 HBCA RG3/3B/3, 8 Jan. 1932.
62 Ibid., 29 Oct. 1931.
63 Ibid., B.135/a/197, 10 Nov. 1931; NA RG10, vol. 6750, file 420–10, 4 Dec. 1931.
64 NA RG10, vol. 6750, file 420–10A, 4 Oct. 1931.
65 HBCA RG3/3B/3, 6 Oct. 1931; 14 Mar. 1932.
66 Ibid., RG10, vol. 6750, file 420–10, 2 Mar. 1932.
67 Ibid., vol. 6755, file 420–10–4, 5 Feb. 1940.
68 Ibid., vol. 6750, file 420–10, 176318, July 1895.
69 Panasuk and Proulx 1979:206.
70 Dugal 1990:14.
71 Zaslow 1971:160.
72 See Morantz 1995:277.

73 NA RG10, vol. 6750, file 420–10, 8 Mar. 1895.
74 Ibid., 12 Nov. 1896; 12 Dec. 1896; 15 Dec. 1896.
75 Ibid., 23 Mar. 1897; 19 May 1897.
76 HBCA B.227/a/63.
77 NA RG10, vol. 6751, file 420–10X–5, 10 Dec. 1942.
78 Ibid., vol. 6750, file 420–10 5, 5 Feb. 1942.
79 Denmark 1948:43.
80 Borron 1890:89.
81 HBCA B.77/b/8, 4 Jan. 1909.
82 NA RG10, vol. 3708, file 19,502, pt. 2, 8 Jan. 1905.
83 Ibid., Relief Payments 1905; vol. 3174, file. 432, 659, Relief Payments, 1911–1913.
84 NA Diocese of Moosonee Records, 1–1, microfilm 81–4, reel 1, 12 Jan. 191.
85 NA RG10, vol. 3708, file 19, 502, pt. 2, 23 Feb. 1918.
86 Ray 1990b:210.
87 NA RG10, vol. 3708, file 19, 502, pt. 2, 21 Feb. 1925.
88 Ibid., file 486/23–17, locator X310, fo. 1, June-Oct. 1931.
89 Ibid., fo. 2, June-Oct. 1931.
90 Ibid., fos. 3–4, June-Oct. 1931.
91 Ibid., fo. 5, June-Oct. 1931.
92 Ray 1990b:205.
93 HBCA B.77/a/59, 6 June 1938.
94 MC Scott Collection 1981, 27 Oct., tape III-D-204T.
95 Ray 1990b:213.
96 Ibid., 212.
97 Keighley 1989:106.
98 HBCA B.147/a/40.
99 Ibid., B.147/a/41, 1 Oct. 1940.
100 Ibid., 7 Mar. 1941.
101 Harris 1976:146.
102 Diubaldo 1981:34–5.
103 Horn 1972a:178.
104 Ibid., 1972b.257.
105 Guinard 1951:6.
106 Honigmann 1981:218.
107 Paul-Emile 1952:179–82.
108 Harris 1976:161–2.
109 Paul-Emile 1952:182.
110 Harris 1976:164.
111 Paul-Emile 1952:185.
112 HBCA B.77/a/58, 14 Mar. 1925.
113 Paul-Emile 1952:185.
114 HBCA B.77/a/58, fo. 195.
115 Harris 1976:165.
116 HBCA B.77/a/58, 29 July 1925; Paul-Emile 1952:185.
117 Petersen 1974:45.
118 Zaslow 1979:105; Petersen 1976:137.
119 HBCA B.59/a/132, 24 June 1940; Petersen 1974:107.
120 HBCA B. 409/a/2, 15 Sept., 2 Oct. 1940.
121 Renison 1957:237.
122 HBCA B.59/a/131, fo. 32.
123 Ibid., B.142/a/12, 27 June, 6 July 1940.
124 MC Knight Fieldnotes 1961.
125 Scanlon 1975:9, 15.
126 Paul-Emile 1952:207, 212, 205.
127 Ibid., 1952:186.
128 Harris 1976:166.
129 Ibid., 167.
130 Paul-Emile 1952:186.
131 Petersen 1974:91.
132 John Long, pers. comm., 1 Mar. 2000.
133 Harris 1976:178.
134 Ibid., 187.
135 Paul-Emile 1952:188.
136 Petersen 1974:91.
137 Harris 1976:170–1.
138 Paul-Emile 1952:194, 196.

139 HBCA B.77/a/59, 8 July 1938.
140 Paul-Emile 1952:188.
141 NA Diocese of Moosonee Records, Correspondence 1–2A, 12, 23 Feb. 1929.
142 Preston 1975b:121.
143 OMI Deschâtelets LCB 3434 .R82W 2, 12 Apr. 1940.
144 Paul-Emile 1952:209.
145 OMI Deschâtelets LCB 3434 .R82W 3, 14 Jan. 1941.
146 Paul-Emile 1952:188, 254; W.A. Anderson 1961:174.
147 Ibid., 202–5.
148 HBCA B.59/a/132, 20 July 1940.
149 Paul-Emile 1952:209–10.
150 Ibid., 210–12.
151 OMI Deschâtelets LCB 3431 .R82H 13, fo. 1, "Rupert's House History" by Maud Watt, 30 Oct. 1941.
152 HBCA RG2/8/540, 27 Mar. 1936.
153 OA Watt Papers, MU 1385, 16 Aug. 1929.
154 Ibid., 17 Aug. 1929.
155 OA Watt Papers MU 1385, 17 Aug. 1929.
156 Moccasin Telegraph 1942, December:3.
157 Rogers 1967:2; Beare 1964:30.
158 OA Watt Papers MU 1385, 16, 17 Aug. 1929.
159 NA RG10, vol. 6750, file 420–10, n.d. (1932?) copy of a letter from Watt to District Manager, HBC.
160 Ibid., n.d. 1932[?].
161 Ibid., 17 Aug. 1932.
162 W.A. Anderson 1961:127–30.
163 Ibid., 133–7; NA RG10, vol. 6750, file 420–10, 17–18 Mar. 1932.
164 NA RG10, vol. 6750, file 420–10-4-1, pt. 1, 30 Mar., 18 Apr. 1933.
165 HBCA B.186/b/36, fo. 12, 1837.
166 Anderson 1961:184.
167 Marshall 1987:67.
168 Denmark 1948:40.
169 NA RG10, vol. 6750, file 420–10-4-1, pt. 1, 4 July 1933, 3 Aug. 1936.
170 Ibid., Report of Treaty Nine Annuity Payments, Rupert House, 1936.
171 Cree Way 1975.
172 CRA Denton Collection 1983, tape 6, side 2.
173 Cree Way, 1975, John Blackned.
174 Kerr 1950:70.
175 OA Watt Papers MU 1385, 5 July 1932.
176 Ibid., [1933?].
177 Ibid.
178 MC Scott Collection 1981, tape III-D-204T, Richard Blackned.
179 NA RG10, vol. 6754, file 420–10-4-1, pt. 1, 16 Sept. 1937.
180 OMI Deschâtelets LCB 3434 .R82W 2, 12 Apr. 1940.
181 Moccasin Telegraph 1942, December:3.
182 NA RG10, vol. 6755, file 420–10-4-1 pt. 3, 8 Aug. 1941.
183 HBCA RG3, series 67–68, Oct. 1952, "brief history of beaver preserves."
184 Cree Way 1975.
185 HBCA B.59/a/131, 18 Aug., 19 Dec. 1938.
186 NA RG10, vol. 6755, file 420–10-4-1, pt. 3, 16 Dec. 1941.
187 HBCA B.59/a/132, fo. 6; 1 Jul. 1940.

188 Ibid., B.59/a/131, 18 Mar. 1939.
189 Ibid., B.142/a/11, 11 Jan. 1939.
190 Ibid., RG3, series 67–68, Oct. 1952, "brief history of beaver preserves."
191 NA RG10, vol. 6754, file 420-10-4-1, pt. 2; 23 Dec. 1940.
192 HBCA RG3, series 67–68, Oct. 1952.
193 NA RG10, vol. 6755, file 420-10-4-1, pt. 3, 5 Sept. 1942.
194 Ibid.; pt. 4, 3 Feb. 1943.
195 Ibid., pt. 3, 16 June 1941.
196 Ibid., vol. 6752, file 420-10-1-1-3, sixth annual report.
197 Ibid., vol. 6755, file 420-10-4-1, pt. 3, 17 June, 18 July 1941.
198 HBCA RG2/7/157, 27 Oct., 26 June 1947.
199 NA RG10, vol. 6755, file 420-10-4-1, pt. 3, 2 Sept. 1942.
200 Ibid., vol. 6752, file 420-10-1-3, reports 1945, 1947.
201 Ibid., vol. 6751, file 420-10X 5, 10 Dec. 1942.
202 Ibid., vol. 6752, file 420-10-1-3, 1947 report.
203 Ibid., vol. 6749, file 420-8-4KE-1 1, 21 Apr. 1942.
204 Ibid., vol. 6755, file 420-10-4-1, pt. 3, 7 Aug. 1941.
205 OMI Deschâtelets LCB 3063 .H83C 16, 7 July 1937.
206 NA RG10, vol. 3708, file 19,502, pt. 2, RCMP Report, 30 July 1941.
207 Ibid., vol. 6755; file 420-10-4-1, pt. 3, report by Hugh R. Conn 1942.
208 HBCA RG7 NSD, correspondence file 6-9-9 (4), 17 Dec. 1957; file 6-9-3 (17), 27 July 1959.
209 Ibid., vol. 6755, file 420-10-4-1, pt. 1; 19, 31 Oct. 1942.
210 Ibid., vol. 6753, file 420-10-4AB-4-3, 7 Mar. 1950.
211 HBCA RG7 NSD correspondence file 6-9-9(4), 30 July 1958.
212 Ibid., RG7/1/1575, 1 Aug. 1951.
213 Ibid., RG3, series 67–68, Oct. 1952, "brief history."
214 NA RG10, vol. 6752, file 420-10-1-1, 8 July 1947.
215 Ibid., file 420-10-1-3, report by Hugh Conn, 1948.
216 HBCA RG3, series 67–68, fo. 2.
217 Ibid., report of 1952; Keighley 1989:197–8.
218 Harris 1976:145–6.
219 HBCA RG7, NSD correspondence file 6-9-2(10), 25 Nov. 1946.
220 Kerr 1950:162.
221 OMI Deschâtelets, LCB 3434 R82W, 21 Apr. 1947.
222 Kerr 1950:48; Preston, pers. comm., 28 Sept. 2000.
223 MC Knight Fieldnotes 1961, fo. 5, 20 June, David Salt; fo. 3, 4 July, Charlie Hester.
224 CUAA Cooper Papers, box 3; Sotrac 1978.
225 Tanner 1987:60–1.
226 MC Knight Fieldnotes 1961, fo. 2, 23 Aug.; fos. 8–9, 11–12 July.
227 Preston 1980a:40.
228 Tanner 1986:32.
229 MC Feit Collection 1979, fos. 3–4, 13 Dec.
230 HBCA B.133/a/75, 14 July 1938.
231 Flannery and Chambers 1985:3, 21.

CHAPTER SIX

1 HBCA B.147/a/40, 11 Oct. 1940.
2 Titley 1986:202; Zaslow 1988:161.
3 Buckley 1992:8–9.
4 Prins 1996:51.
5 Miller 1989:96.
6 NA RG10, vol. 3033, file 235, 225, pt. 1, 17 Aug. 1903.
7 Ornstein and Marchant 1973:III:88–9; 97–207.
8 Ibid., 127.
9 Richardson 1975:36.
10 Ornstein and Marchant 1973:III:207.
11 NA RG10, Mistassini, file 27074-3, 30 July 1945; file 36-1-19, 28 Aug. 1952.
12 Ibid., file 87/30-1, 3 July 1953.
13 Ibid., 21 Aug. 1953.
14 Ibid., file 27074, 10 Apr. 1947.
15 Ibid., 21 Aug. 1953.
16 Ibid., file 74/30-9, 28 Jan. 1959, 20 Jan. 1960, 19 July 1960.
17 Ornstein and Marchant 1973:III:158.
18 Dorais 1997:32; Linteau et al. 1989:2:244.
19 Elberg and Visitor 1976:58–9.
20 Ibid., 60.
21 Diamond 1988:155.
22 Zaslow 1979:111.
23 Petersen 1974:230.
24 Valpy and Barnes 1968:7.
25 Preston 1968:174.
26 Niezen 1998:32.
27 See also Marshall, Diamond and Blackned 1989.
28 MC Scott Collection 1981, tape III-D-197T, 30 Nov; MC Sun Collection 1979, B-3.
29 CRA Tanner Collection 1977, 6 July; David Denton, pers. comm. 30 July 2000.
30 MC Feit Collection 1982, 28 Aug. Joe Ottereyes.
31 Craik Collection 1977, tape III-D-85T, side 2, 20 July.
32 MC Feit Collection 1982, 31 Aug., Joe and Louise Ottereyes.
33 MC Turner Collection 1974, tape III-D-27T, fo. 12.
34 Moccasin Telegraph 1953, August:19.
35 S. Preston Collection 1984, June 14, Beatrice Fairies.
36 HBCA B.59/a/8, 7 Mar. 1744.
37 Ibid., B.133/a/67, 2 Nov. 1926.
38 Leiths 1912:162.
39 HBCA RG3/44A/1.
40 Ibid., B.496/a/1, 21 Jan., 14 Apr. 1939.
41 Ibid., B.496/a/2, 7 Jan. 1941.
42 Ibid., B.133/a/68, 18 Dec. 1928.
43 Anderson 1961:39.
44 Flannery 1995:42.
45 Borron 1890:91,83.
46 Walton 1921:7.
47 Scanlon 1976:26.
48 Petersen 1974:37.
49 Ibid., 107.
50 Flannery 1995:75.
51 Paul-Emile 1952:264.
52 Anonymous 1951:45; Petersen 1974:188.
53 Renison 1957:261.
54 NA RG10, file 486/23-17, locator X310. Report of James Bay Agency, June-Oct. 1931.
55 HBCA B.227/a/66, 18 Jan. 1938.
56 Ibid., B.133/a/73, 28 Aug. 1935.

57 Anonymous 1938:64.
58 Abel 1989:79.
59 Titley 1986:86–7.
60 Zaslow 1988:171.
61 Young 1984:260.
62 Ibid., 262; Zaslow 1988:173.
63 NA RG10, file 27074-3, Inspection Report of Abitibi Agency, 19 Nov.1945; Marshall 1987:83.
64 Wills 1984:9.
65 Young 1984:259.
66 Paul-Emile 1952:187.
67 Ibid., 187–8.
68 See Abel 1989:82–3.
69 Paul-Emile 1952:189, 260–2, 256.
70 Ibid., 261.
71 NA CMS Diocese of Moosonee, Correspondence of Bishops, 1–2A, 14 Nov. 1929.
72 Ibid., 30 July 1931.
73 Petersen 1974:91.
74 Paul-Emile 1952:191, 197.
75 Ibid., 198, 196.
76 Ibid., 200.
77 Crowe 1991:178.
78 Elberg and Visitor 1976:53.
79 Kerr 1950:62–3.
80 NA RG18, acc. 85–86/048, vol. 56, file TA-500-8-1-34, 31 Dec. 1956.
81 HBCA B.496/a/1, 20 Jan. 1938.
82 Knight Fieldnotes 1961.
83 HBCA B.135/a/197, 18 Aug. 1931.
84 NA RG18, Commissioner's Report 1930, fos. 42–3; RG10, file 486/23–17, vol. X310, Report of James Bay Agency, 1931.
85 Waldram et al 1995:163.

86 Wills 1984:16.
87 Knight Fieldnotes 1961.
88 Anonymous 1951:46.
89 HBCA B.59/a/132,15, 22 July 1940.
90 NA RG18, vol. 83–84/068, box 23, file 567–60, fo. 140. Aug. 1951; RG10, Mistassini Records, file 27074-3, Inspection of Abitibi Agency, 19 Nov. 1945.
91 Kerr 1950:66; Waldram et al. 1995:162.
92 MC Feit Collection 1979, 13 Dec. 1979, Joe Ottereyes.
93 HBCA B.133/a/76, 23 Aug.
94 Balikci Fieldnotes 1957, card #75.
95 NA RG18, vol. 83–84/068, box 23, file 567–60, 15 Apr. 1946; fo. 137, Aug. 1951.
96 Marshall 1987:97.
97 Anonymous 1949:43–5.
98 Ibid., 44.
99 Knight 1968:33.
100 Neilson 1948:151.
101 NA RG10, Mistassini, file 27074, Abitibi Agency Inspection Report, 19 Nov. 1945.
102 Ibid., RG18, vol. 85–86/048, box 56, file TA-500-8-1-34, fo. 54; 18 Sept. 1951.
103 Balikci Fieldnotes, 1957.
104 Ornstein and Marchant 1973:11:24.
105 Moccasin Telegraph 1953, Apr. 19.
106 Salisbury 1986:42–3, 49.
107 Neilson 1948:150.
108 Crowe 1996:180; Wills 1984:7.
109 Wills 1984:18; Moccasin Telegraph 1955, Breakup:29; HBCA unclassified fur conservation file, 12 Feb. 1958.

110 HBCA, unclassified fur conservation file, 4 July 1958.
111 Wills 1984:7–9, 81–3.
112 Ibid., 18.
113 Chance 1970:i.
114 Walker 1953:6.
115 Wills 1984:21–3, 33.
116 Honigmann 1962:18; Wills 1984:23.
117 Wills 1984:25.
118 Walker 1953:17; Preston, pers. comm. 23 Oct. 2000.
119 Wills 1984:28.
120 Ibid., 12.
121 Ibid., 10.
122 Buckley 1992:108.
123 Frenette 1985:16–19.
124 Marshall 1987:21, 38.
125 Linteau et al. 1989:25–6; Marshall 1987:54–5.
126 Frenette 1985:17.
127 HBCA B.227/a/61, 13 June 1932; B.227/a/65, 21 Sept. 1936.
128 See Cruikshank 1996.
129 HBCA B.227/a/64, 15 Sept. 1935.
130 Ibid., B.133/a/72, 25 May 1935.
131 Ibid., B.133/a/68, 17 June 1929, 14 June 1935.
132 Ibid., B.227/a/65, 13 June 1936.
133 Ibid., B.227/a/64, 17 June 1935.
134 Frenette 1985:32.
135 HBCA B.227/a/64, 11 June 1936, 13 July 1936, 7 Sept. 1935.
136 Ibid., B.227/a/61, 20, 30 June 1932.
137 Frenette 1985:27, 38.
138 Scanlon 1975:8; HBCA RG 3/35/3; 3/35/5.
139 Hand 1964:2; Rousseau 1949:35.
140 Frenette 1985:76, 80–1.
141 Roslin 1999:5.
142 *Montreal Gazette*, 30 Oct. 1999:A16.
143 Tanner, pers. comm., 10 Oct. 1999.
144 Ornstein and Marchant 1973:II:27.
145 Moccasin Telegraph 1964, Winter:22; Beare 1964:30.
146 Moccasin Telegraph 1954, December:13.
147 HBCA unclassified, Indian Affairs file, Aug. 1955.
148 Moccasin Telegraph 1959, Winter:30.
149 Ibid., 1965, Summer:21.
150 Chance 1970:17.
151 Bernier 1967:18, 23, 32–3.
152 Scanlon 1975:84.
153 LaRusic 1970:B–33.
154 Scanlon 1975:84.
155 LaRusic 1970:B–35–7; 1968:17.
156 Frenette 1985:55.
157 Scanlon 1975:87.
158 LaRusic n.d.:4.
159 Frenette 1985:54, 64.
160 Tanner 1968:52.
161 LaRusic 1970:B–54.
162 Ibid., B–16.
163 Tanner 1968:49–52.
164 Moccasin Telegraph 1967, Summer:41; 1966, Winter:25.
165 HBCA B.227/a/57, 1922; B.227/a/60, 6 June, 30 Sept., 18 Oct. 1931.
166 La Rusic 1970:B–41, 46; Tanner 1968:58.
167 Berkes 1972:179.
168 Beare 1964:30.
169 Frenette 1985:50.
170 LaRusic n.d.:5.
171 Marshall 1987:124.
172 See Ornstein and Marchant 1973:II:49.

173 LaRusic 1970:B–22, 25.
174 Ornstein and Marchant 1973 11:49.
175 Ibid., 73.
176 Preston, pers. comm., 23 Oct. 2000.
177 OA Watt Papers MU 1385, Jan 1923; Kerr 1950:147; MC Knight Fieldnotes 1961, Nellie Moar; Cree Way 1975.
178 Knight 1968:22.
179 OA Watt Papers, MU 1385, Jan. 1923; Kerr 1950:165.
180 Moccasin Telegraph 1959, Summer:2.
181 HBCA RG7, general correspondence 3–12–20, 1 Nov. 1967.
182 Kerr 1950:165–7.
183 MacLean 1950:38, 41.
184 NA RG10, vol. 10,815, file 44/20–4, pt. 1, 29 Dec. 1948.
185 Ibid., vol. 6962, file 44/20–2, 27 Nov. 1959; file 486/20–2, pt. 5, 2 May 1960.
186 Kerr 1950:234, 165–6.
187 Ibid., 71, OMI Deschâtelets LCB 3434 R82W, 21 Mar. 1945.
188 Kerr 1950:71–3.
189 Preston, pers. comm., 23 Oct. 2000.
190 Kerr 1950:72–3.
191 NA RG10, vol. 10,858, file 44/30–8, pt. 1, 5 Oct. 1955.
192 AA CMS Diocese of Moosonee Records, Bishops Records, 20 Sept. 1941.
193 NA RG10, vol. 10, 858, file 44/30–8, pt. 1, 14 Aug. 1957.
194 Ibid., 15 July 1958.
195 Ibid., file 44/30–1, 30 Dec. 1959.
196 Elberg, Hyman, Salisbury 1972:53.
197 HBCA B.142/a/11, 22 June 1938.
198 Rogers 1965:34; LaRusic 1968:13.
199 Preston 1982:39.
200 Salisbury 1986:20.
201 HBCA RG7/1/1763, 14–1–8, 1943; NA RG10, vol. 10,819, file 44/20–10–16, pt. 1, 23, Aug. 1951.
202 NA RG10, vol. 10, 815, file 44/20–4, pt. 1, 17, 30 Sept. 1957; 31 Oct. 1959.
203 Kerr 1950:128–30.
204 NA RG10, vol. 10,815, file 44/20–4, pt.1, 17 Sept. 1957.
205 Ibid., vol. 6752, file 420–10–2 3, 8 June 1946.
206 Salisbury 1986:44.
207 Kerr 1950:168–71.
208 MC Feit Collection, 1979, 13 Dec.; Milloy 1999:205.
209 Knight 1968:38.
210 MC Feit Collection 1979, 13 Dec.; 1982, 24 Aug., Joe Ottereyes; 1983, 29 Aug., Stewart Ottereyes.
211 Knight 1968:40.
212 Wills 1984:18.
213 MC Feit Collection 1982, 25 Aug.
214 HBCA B.142/a/11, 30, 10 Mar. 1939; 23 Jan. 1939.
215 Walker 1953:9.
216 HBCA B.59/a/32, 1 Jan. 1941; B.186/a/112, 8 Aug. 1938.
217 Knight 1968:41.
218 NA RG10, vol. 10,845, file 44/29–1, pt. 1, 10 Mar. 1958.
219 HBCA RG3/BB/4, weekly report, James Bay District, 23 Feb. 1940.
220 Ibid., RG7/6D/7, 14–1–1, 23 Oct. 1957.

221 LaRusic 1968:15.
222 Ornstein and Marchant 1973:II:137–8, 41–2; Désy 1968:135.
223 Ornstein and Marchant 1973:II:98.
224 Buckley 1992:8.
225 Paul-Emile 1952:221.
226 Abel 1989:82–3, 84 n.38.
227 Petersen 1974:107, 40.
228 Zaslow 1979:108; Dorais 1997:31.
229 Dickason 1997:311.
230 Petersen 1974:188; Moccasin Telegraph 1955, Freeze-up:11.
231 Diubaldo 1989:181, 185.
232 Richardson 1975:75.
233 HBCA B.227/a/67, 9 Aug. 1939, 11 June 1938.
234 Ibid., 227/a/63, 14 June 1934; B.227/a/65, 23 Aug 1936.
235 NA RG10, vol. 10,858, file 44/30–8, pt. 1; 14 Aug. 1952.
236 Kerr 1950:55; Neilson 1948:152; Marshall 1987:83.
237 Salisbury 1986:36.
238 MC Knight Fieldnotes 1961, 21 June; Preston 1975:4.
239 Rogers 1965:31.
240 Kerr 1950:54; HBCA B.409/a/1, 3 Sept. 1940.
241 Paul-Emile 1952:205.
242 Petersen 1974:189.
243 Zaslow 1979:108.
244 Barman, Hébert, McCaskill 1986:13.
245 Satzewich and Wotherspoon 1993:124.
246 Marshall 1987:83, 92; Wintrob and Sindell 1970:C–9; Salisbury 1986:36.
247 S. Preston Collection 1984.
248 Neilson 1948:152.
249 17 Sept. 1987.
250 Ornstein and Marchant 1973:II:181–3; Gauthier 1973:3.
251 Salisbury 1986:36.
252 Preston 1968.
253 Désy 1968:154–5.
254 Burnaby 1982.
255 Ornstein and Marchant 1973:II:162, 229.
256 Kerr 1950:54–8.
257 Knight 1968:4.
258 Wintrob and Sindell 1970:C–9; Sindell 1968:85.
259 Cree Way 1975, Anonymous, story of when girls first married.
260 MC Knight Fieldnotes 1961, 1 July, Josephine McLeod Diamond.
261 NA RG10, vol. 10,845, 44/29–1, pt. 1; 10 Mar. 1958.
262 Preston 1974:93; Salisbury 1986:37.
263 NA RG10, vol. 10,545, file 44/29–1, pt. 1, 24 Mar. 1958.
264 McGregor 1989:25, 29, 125.
265 Miller 1996:203.
266 NA RG10, vol. 3033, file 235,225, pt. 1, fo. 44.
267 Ibid., vol. 10,819, file 44/20–10–17–pt. 1, 27 Aug.1947.
268 MC Feit Collection 1979, 13 Dec.
269 NA RG10, vol. 3033, file 235,225, pt. 1, 17 Mar. 1932; HBCA B.59/a/132, 7 Dec. 1940.
270 Kerr 1950:66.
271 MC Feit Collection 1979, 13 Dec. 1979, Joe Ottereyes.
272 Scanlon 1975:70.
273 Kerr 1950:65–6.
274 Honigmann 1962:25.
275 Preston, pers. comm. 23 Oct. 2000.

276 Dunning 1959:119–22.
277 Ibid., 119.
278 NAA Honigmann Papers, box 26, misc.
279 HBCA B.147/a/40, 10 Oct. 1939.
280 Ray 1990:221.
281 Copy in author's possession.
282 Goodwill and Sluman 1984, 159, 161.
283 NA RG10 vol. 6750, file 420–10A, 14 Aug. 1907.
284 HBCA RG 7, vol. 14-1-2(6), general correspondence, 9 Aug. 1945.
285 Scanlon 1975:70–1.
286 Moccasin Telegraph 1949, Summer:23.
287 HBCA RG7, vol. 14-1-2(6), 9 Aug. 1945.
288 Satzewich 1997:250, 237.
289 Dickason 1977:293.
290 Kerr 1950:65.
291 Walker 1953:7.
292 Balikci Fieldnotes 1957, card 645.
293 HBCA B.227/a/69.
294 Dickason 1997:294.
295 Ornstein and Marchant 1973:III:26; Dickason 1997:259.
296 Rogers 1963:25.
297 HBCA B.227/a/63, 31 July 1934.
298 Ibid.
299 Ibid., 2 Aug. 1934.
300 Ibid., B.227/a/68, 17 June 1939.
301 MC Turner Collection 1974, tape III–19T, side B.
302 Honigmann 1962:60.
303 CRA Tanner Collection, 1978.
304 Dunning 1959:118.
305 Preston 1983.
306 Richardson 1975:76.

307 McGregor 1989:59–60.
308 HBCA B.227/a/66, 29 June 1937.
309 Moccasin Telegraph 1959, Summer:1; Preston, pers. comm., July 1999.
310 Honigmann 1962:61.
311 HBCA B/a/74, 16 June, 9 July 1937.
312 Ibid., B.59/a/131, 19 July 1938, 27 Oct. 1938.
313 Ibid., B.77/a/57, 18 Aug. 1920.
314 NA CMS Diocese of Moosonee, 1–2A, microfilm 81–4, reel 1, 18 Jan. 1932.
315 Ibid., file 486/23-17, locator x310, fo. 2.
316 CMS Diocese of Moosonee, 1–2A, microfilm 81–4, reel 1, 3 Feb. 1929, 18 Jan. 1932.
317 HBCA B.372/a/22-23, 1938-40; Honigmann 1962:60.
318 Kerr 1950:85.
319 Ibid., 85, 65; Knight 1968:94.
320 Flannery, pers. comm., 16 Mar. 1994.
321 Chance 1970:14.
322 Holden 1970:A74.
323 Frenette 1985:76–8.
324 Wills 1984:73.
325 Preston 1968; Valpy and Barnes 1968:7.
326 Désy 1968:8, 135.
327 Rogers 1967:9; Salisbury 1986:5.
328 Rogers 1965:276–7.
329 Salisbury 1986:29, 32–3.
330 Preston, pers. comm., 23 Oct. 2000.
331 Wills 1984:74–5.
332 Salisbury 1986:33–4.
333 Ibid., 16.
334 Ciaccia 1988:39.
335 LePage 1988:28.

336 Knight Fieldnotes 1961.
337 NA RG10, vol. 6755, file 420-10-4-1, pt. 3, 14 July, 4 Dec. 1941.
338 Richardson 1975:54.
339 HBCA B.77/b/8, 14 Sept. 1906.
340 MC Turner Collection 1974, tape III-D-20T, side B.
341 Crowe 1996:163.
342 Francis and Morantz 1983:158-60.
343 Cree Way Project 1975, Hannah Bay massacre story.
344 HBCA B.77/a/57, 28 Aug. 1920.
345 S.W. Horral, pers. comm., 30 July 1986; Long 1994a.
346 NA RG10, vol. 6750, file 420-10A, 4 Oct. 1931.
347 Ibid., RG18, vol. 83-84/068, box 23, file 567-60, fo. 169, 23 Mar. 1943.
348 Davies 1948:355.
349 Zaslow 1988:155.
350 NA RG10, vol. 6750, file 420-10A, RCMP report, 27 Sept. 1931, 5 Apr., 20 Oct. 1939.
351 Ornstein and Marchant 1973:III:4-5, re report: "Administration of Justice Beyond the 50th Parallel."
352 Dickason 1997:490, fn.13; Ornstein and Marchant 1973:III:28.
353 HBCA B.496/a/2, 12 Dec. 1940.
354 Ornstein and Marchant 1973:III:82.
355 NA RG 10, Mistassini Records, file 74/30-9, 15, 17, 22 July 1957.
356 Ibid., vol. 10, 817, file 44/20-9, pt. 2, 23 Oct. 1957; Denmark 1948:43.
357 Ornstein and Marchant 1973:III:85.
358 Knight 1968:38; Désy 1968:128.
359 HBCA B.77/a/59, 18 May 1939.
360 Ibid., B.227/a/67, 16 Dec. 1938.
361 Ibid., B.77/a/60, 17 July 1940.
362 Ibid.
363 NA RG10, vol. 6755, file 420-10-4-1, pt. 3, 5 July 1942.
364 HBCA B.147/a/41, 4 May 1941.
365 MC Knight Fieldnotes 1961, 21 Aug.
366 Chance 1968:3.
367 Ibid., 1970:17.
368 Wills 1984:5, 13.
369 Knight 1968:26.
370 Finnie 1944:57.
371 Désy 1968:175.
372 Wills 1984:13-14.
373 Balikci Fieldnotes 1957.

CHAPTER SEVEN

1 Davis 2001.
2 Dyck 1991:3.
3 Long 1985; 1994b.
4 Tough 1996:301.
5 See Goodwill and Sluman 1984.
6 Walker 1953:17.
7 Dickason 1997:309-14, 312.
8 Chance 1970:33.
9 Wadel 1969.
10 Ornstein and Marchant 1973:III:237.
11 Satzewich and Wotherspoon 1993:95.
12 Ibid., 245.
13 Preston 1986b:240-1.

CHAPTER EIGHT

1 Richardson 1975:18–19.
2 Ornstein and Marchant 1973:III:215.
3 O'Reilly 1988:33; Dickason 1997:383.
4 Awashish 1988:32.
5 O'Reilly 1988:33.
6 Awashish 1988:43.
7 Morantz notes, 22 Nov. 1973.
8 O'Reilly 1988:30.
9 Salisbury 1986:55.
10 Awashish 1988:44.
11 Salisbury 1986:55–6.
12 Ibid., 56–7.
13 Awashish 1988:45.
14 Ibid., 45; Dickason 1997:383.
15 Salisbury 1986:57.
16 Dickason 1997:250.
17 Hawthorn and Tremblay 1966:1:35.
18 Salisbury 1986:95.
19 Ibid., 98.
20 Chance 1970:20.
21 See Morantz 1997.
22 Grand Council of the Crees 1995:493.
23 Fogelson 1989:139

Bibliography

MANUSCRIPT SOURCES

Archéotec, Montreal (AR)
    Pierre Trudel. Great Whale River. 1978. Interviews
American Museum of Natural History, New York (AMNH)
    Alanson Skinner – Correspondence. Acc. 1908–48 and 1909–60
American Philosophical Association, Philadelphia (APA)
    Frank G. Speck Papers. Acc.#1429
Anglican Archives (AA)
    Diocese of Moosonee Records, Schumacher, Ontario
        St Barnabas (Waswanipi) Parish Registers
        St Peter (Rupert House) Mission Records
Catholic University of America Archives, Washington, DC (CUAA)
    John Cooper – Fieldnotes and articles
Cree Regional Authority, Nemaska, James Bay (CRA)
    David Denton. 1983. Rupert House. Interviews
    Adrian Tanner. 1976–8. Fort George. Interviews
Hudson's Bay Company Archives (Provincial Archives of Manitoba; National Archives of Canada (HBCA))
    A. Headquarters Records
        A.74 District Manager's Annual Reports
        A.93 Notes, Correspondence regarding fur trade in Canada
    B. Post Records
        B.59 Eastmain Post
        B.77 Fort George Post
        B.133 Mistassini Post
        B.135 Moose Post
        B.142 Nemiskau Post
        B.143 Neoskwskau Post
        B.147 Nichikun Post

B.186 Rupert House Post
B.227 Waswanipi Post
B.372 Great Whale River
B.409 Old Factory River Post
B.496 Kanaaupscow Post
DFTR Records
District Fur Trade Records
RG7 General Correspondence
Museum of Civilization, Hull, Que. (MC)
　Urgent Ethnology Program Reports
　　Harvey Feit. 1968–70 Waswanipi. Interviews/Life Histories
　　Rolf Knight. 1961 Rupert House. Fieldnotes
　　Colin Scott. 1977–82. Wemindji. Interviews/Life Histories
　　Frank Sun. 1979. Wemindji. Life Histories
　　Lucy Turner. 1974. Great Whale River. Transcribed Interviews
National Anthropological Archives, Smithsonian Institution, Washington, DC (NAA)
　John Honigmann. Great Whale River Acc.# boxes 26 & 27
　Truman Michelson. James Bay Coast.Acc. #3399
National Archives of Canada, Ottawa (NA)
　Church Missionary Society Records (CMS) Acc. MG 17 B2
　　Watkins Papers, Microfilm 78-13, reel 24 (A–97)
　　Peck Papers, Microfilm 78-13, reel 38–42
　　Diocese of Moosonee Records.Correspondence and Papers of Bishops of Moosonee, microfilm 81-4, reel 1
　Department of Indian Affairs, Acc. RG10
　　Black Series. Headquarters Files
　Royal Canadian Mounted Police Records (RG18)
　Methodist Missionary Society (MMS) Acc. MG 17 C1
　　Correspondence: Maritimes, 1840–5
　Walton, W.G. Letterbook Acc. MG30 D133
Oblats de Marie Immaculée (OMI)
　Archives Deschâtelets, Ottawa
　　Diocese of Moosonee, Office of the Bishop
　　Correspondence, 1944–48, Acc. LCB 3434
　　Registre des Missions Indiennes, 1851–1887, Témiscaminque
Ontario Public Archives (OA)
　James Watt Papers. Acc. MU 1385
Personal Collections
　Asen Balikci. Great Whale River. Fieldnotes
　Brian Craik. Rupert House. Audio Tapes
　Richard J. Preston. Rupert House. Fieldnotes
　Sarah Preston. Rupert House. Life Histories

SECONDARY SOURCES

Abel, Kerry 1989 Matters Are Growing Worse. Government and the Mackenzie Missions, 1870–1929. In *For Purposes of Dominion. Essays in Honour of Morris Zaslow*. Kenneth Coates and William Morrison, eds. North York, Ont.: Captus Press: 73–85.
- 1993 *Drum Songs. Glimpses of Dene History*. Montreal and Kingston: McGill-Queen's University Press.

Adams, Howard 1995 *A Tortured People. The Politics of Colonization*. Penticton, BC: Theytus Books.

Anderson, J.W. 1935 The Rupert House Brigade. *The Beaver*, December:13–20.
- 1957 The Kicker. *Moccasin Telegraph*: 2.
- 1961 *Fur Trader's Story*. Toronto.

Anderson, William A. 1961 *Angel of Hudson Bay. The True Story of Maud Watt*. Toronto: Clarke Irwin.

Anonymous 1931 Radio in the Far North. *The Beaver*, March:187–8.
- 1935 Notes. *The Beaver*, December:64.
- 1938 Ontario Hydro Dam on the Kenogami. *The Beaver*, Spring:64.
- 1949 The Nutrition and Health of the James Bay Indians. *Arctic Circular* 2(4).
- 1951 Tuberculosis Survey: James and Hudson Bays, 1950. *Arctic Circular* 4(3):45–7.

Appleby, Joyce, Lynn Hunt, and Margaret Jacob 1994 *Telling the Truth about History*. New York: W.W. Norton.

Armitage, Peter, and John C. Kennedy 1989 Redbaiting and Racism on Our Frontier: Military Expansion in Labrador and Quebec. *Canadian Review of Sociology and Anthropology* 26:798–817.

Asad, Talal 1986 The Concept of Cultural Translation in British Social Anthropology. In *Writing Culture: The Poetics and Politics of Ethnography*. James Clifford and George Marcus, eds. Berkeley: University of California Press:141–64.

Audet, René 1979 Histoire du caribou du Québec-Labrador et évolution des populations. In *Dossier Caribou*. F. Trudel and J. Huot, eds. *Recherches amérindiennes au Québec* 9(1–2):17–28.

Awashish, Philip 1988 The Stakes for the Cree of Quebec. In *Baie James et Nord Québécois. Dix Ans Après (James Bay and Northern Quebec. Ten Years After.)* Sylvie Vincent and Garry Bowers, eds. Montreal: *Recherches amérindiennes au Québec*:42–5.

Axtell, James 1985 *The Invasion Within. The Contest of Cultures in Colonial North America*. New York: Oxford University Press.

Barman, Jean, Yvonne Hébert, and Don McCaskill 1986 Introduction. In *Indian Education in Canada*. Vol. 1. *The Legacy*. Jean Barman, Yvonne

Hébert, and Don McCaskill, eds. Vancouver: University of British Columbia Press:1–22.

Bauer, George   1973   *Tales from the Cree*. Cobalt, Ont.: Highway Book Shop.

Beare, G.A.   1964   Quebec District. Report by District Manager. Moccasin Telegraph, Summer: 30–1.

Berkes, Fikret   1972   A Case Study in Northern Quebec. Indians and the Quévillon Mill-Multiple Use of Resources. In *Environmental Aspects of the Pulp and Paper Industry*. Fikret Berkes, B. Ott, M.J.A. Butler, and W.A. Ross, eds. Montreal: Terra Nova: 165–87.

– 1986   Chisasibi Cree Hunters as Missionaries: Humour as Evidence of Tension. In *Actes du Dix-Septième Congrès des Algonquinistes*. William Cowan, ed. Ottawa: University of Ottawa: 15–27.

Bernier, Bernard   1967   The Social Organization of the Waswanipi Cree Indians. *Anthropology of Development*. Montreal: McGill University.

Bhaba, Homi K.   1997   The Voice of the Dom. Retrieving the Experience of the Once-Colonized. *Times Literary Supplement*, 18 August:14–15.

Bider, J.R.   1976   The Distribution and Abundance of Terrestrial Vertebrates of the James and Hudson Bay Regions of Quebec. *Cahiers de Géographie de Québec* 20(50):393–408.

Bishop, Charles A.   1974   *The Northern Ojibwa and the Fur Trade: An Historical and Ecological Study*. Toronto: Holt, Rinehart and Winston.

Bishop, Charles and Toby Morantz, eds.   1986   Who Owns the Beaver? Northern Algonquian Land Tenure Reconsidered. *Anthropologica* 18 (1–2).

Borron, E.B.   1890   Report on the Basin of Moose River and Adjacent Country Belonging to the Province of Ontario. *Sessional Papers of Ontario*, No. 87. Toronto: Warwick & Sons.

Bouchard, Serge, ed.   1980   *Mémoires d'un Simple Missionnaire, le Père Joseph-Etienne Guinard, O.M.I. 1864–1965*. Québec: Ministère des affaires culturelles.

Bourassa, Robert   1973   *James Bay*. Montreal: Harvest House.

Bragdon, Kathleen   1993   Vernacular Literacy and Massachusett World View, 1650–1750. In *Algonkians of New England: Past and Present. Dublin Seminar for New England Folklife. Annual Proceedings 1991*. Peter Benes, ed. Boston: Boston University: 26–34.

Brightman, Robert   1988   The Windigo in the Material World. *Ethnohistory* 35(4):337–79.

Brown, Jennifer S.H.   1987   "I Wish to Be as I See You": An Ojibwa-Methodist Encounter in Fur Trade Country, Rainy Lake, 1854–1855. *Arctic Anthropology* 24(1):19–31.

– 1996   Reading Beyond the Missionaries, Dissecting Responses. *Ethnohistory* 43(4):713–19.

Buckley, Helen   1992   *From Wooden Ploughs to Welfare. Why Indian Policy Failed in the Prairie Provinces*. Montreal and Kingston: McGill-Queen's University Press.

Burgesse, J.A.   1942   Tribal Laws of the Woodlands. *The Beaver*, March:18–23.

Burnaby, Barbara 1982 On the Success of School Programmes Involving a Native Language. In *Papers of the Thirteenth Algonquian Conference*. William Cowan, ed. Ottawa: Carleton University: 251–60.

Carrière, Gaston 1957 *Les Missions Catholiques dans l'Est du Canada et l'Honorable Compagnie de la Baie d'Hudson, 1844–1900*. Ottawa: Université d'Ottawa.

– 1969 *Histoire Documentaire de la Congrégation des Missionnaires Oblats de Marie-Immaculée dans l'est du Canada, 1861–1900*, Vol. 8. Ottawa: Université d'Ottawa.

Carter, Sarah 1991 Two Acres and a Cow: Peasant Farming for the Indians of the Northwest 1889–1897. In *Sweet Promises: A Reader on Indian-White Relations in Canada*. J.R. Miller, ed. Toronto: University of Toronto Press: 353–80.

Chance, Norman 1968 *Conflict in Culture. Problems of Developmental Change Among the Cree*. Ottawa: Canadian Research Centre for Anthropology. St Paul University.

– 1970 *Developmental Change Among the Cree Indians of Quebec*. Montreal: McGill University Cree Project.

Ciaccia, John 1988 The Practical and Philosophical Stakes. In *Baie James et Nord Québécois. Dix Ans Après. (James Bay and Northern Quebec. Ten Years After)* Sylvie Vincent and Garry Bowers, eds. Montreal: Recherches amérindiennes au Québec: 39–41.

Coates, Kenneth 1988 Best Left as Indians: The Federal Government and the Indians of the Yukon, 1894–1950. In *Out of the Background. Readings on Canadian Native History*. Robin Fisher and Kenneth Coates, eds. Toronto: Copp Clark Pitman: 267–84.

– 1991 *Best Left as Indians. Native-White Relations in the Yukon Territory, 1840–1973*. Montreal and Kingston: McGill-Queen's University Press.

Cohen, David William 1989 The Undefining of Oral Tradition. *Ethnohistory* 36(1):9–18.

Comaroff, Jean, and John Comaroff 1991 *Of Revelation and Revolution. Christianity, Colonialism and Consciousness in South Africa*. Vol. 1. Chicago: University of Chicago Press.

Comaroff, John, and Jean Comaroff 1992 *Ethnography and the Historical Imagination*. Boulder, Co.: Westview.

Conn, Walter 1986 *Christian Conversion: A Developmental Interpretation of Autonomy and Surrender*. New York: Paulist Press.

Cooke, Alan 1964 The Exploration of New Quebec. In *Le Nouveau Québec. Contribution à l'étude de l'occupation humaine*. J. Malaurie and J. Rousseau, eds. Paris: Mouton & Co.: 137–80.

– 1976 A History of the Naskapis of Schefferville. Report to the Naskapi Band Council of Schefferville. Typescript. 87 pp.

– 1979 L'indépendance des Naskapis et le Caribou. *Recherches amérindiennes au Québec* 9(1–2):99–104.

Cooper, John M. 1933 The Cree Witiko Psychosis. *Primitive Man* 6(1):20–1.

– 1934 The Northern Algonquian Supreme Being. Catholic University of America. *Anthropological Series* 2:1–78.
– 1939 Is the Algonquian Family Hunting Ground System Pre-Columbian? *American Anthropologist* 41:66–90.
Copland, Dudley 1985 *Coplalook. Chief Trader Hudson's Bay Company, 1923–35*. Winnipeg: Watson Dwyer.
Cree Way Project 1975 Collection of Oral Accounts. Waskaganish, James Bay.
Crosby, Alfred W. 1986 *Ecological Imperialism. The Biological Expansion of Europe, 900–1900*. Cambridge: Cambridge University Press.
Crowe, Keith 1991 *The History of the Original Peoples of Northern Canada*. Montreal and Kingston: McGill-Queen's University Press.
Cruikshank, Julie 1990 *Life Lived Like a Story. Life Stories of Three Yukon Elders*. Vancouver: University of British Columbia Press.
– 1991 *Reading Voices. Dan Dhá Ts'edenintth.'é Oral and Written Interpretations of the Yukon Past*. Vancouver: Douglas & McIntyre.
– 1996 Discovery of Gold on the Klondike: Perspectives from Oral Tradition. In *Reading Beyond Words. Contexts for Native History*. Jennifer S.H. Brown and Elizabeth Vibert, eds. Peterborough, Ont.: Broadview Press: 433–59.
Cumming, Peter A., and Peter H. Mickenberg, eds. 1972 *Native Rights in Canada*. Toronto: General Publishing.
Curran, W. Tees, and H.A. Calkins 1917 *In Canada's Wonderful Northland*. New York: G.P. Putnam & sons.
Davies, Irene 1948 Sub-Arctic Odyssey. *RCMP Quarterly* 13(4):355–66.
Davies, K.G., ed. 1965 *Letters from Hudson Bay, 1703–40*. London: Hudson's Bay Record Society, no. 25.
Davis, Natalie Zemon 2001 Polarities, Hybridities: What Strategies for De-Centring? In *De-Centring the Renaissance: New Essays on Early Modern Canada*. Germaine Warkentin and Carolyn Podruchny, eds. Toronto: University of Toronto Press: 19–32.
Denmark, D.E. 1948 James Bay Beaver Conservation. *The Beaver* 279:38–43.
Denton, David 1981 Investigations archéologiques dans la région du futur réservoir Caniapiscau, Québec. In *Interventions archéologiques – 1. Direction générale du patrimoine*, ed. Québec: Ministère des affaires culturelles.
– 1989 La période préhistorique récente dans la région de Caniapiscau. *Recherches archéologiques au Québec* 19(2–3):59–75.
– 1998 From the Source to the Margins and Back. Notes on Mistassini Quartzite and Archaeology in the Area of the Colline Blanche. In *L'Eveilleur et l'Ambassadeur. Essais archéologiques et ethnohistoriques en hommage à Charles A. Martijn. Paleo-Québec* 27. Roland Tremblay, ed.. Montréal: Recherches Amérindiennes au Québec: 17–32.
Désy, Pierrette 1968 Fort George Ou "Tsesa-Tsippi." Contribution à une étude sur la désintégration culturelle d'une communauté Indienne de la Baie James. Ph.D. dissertation, Université de Paris.

Diamond, Billy 1988 A Debate on the Positive and Negative Aspects of the Implementation of the Agreement. In *Baie James et Nord Québécois: Dix Ans Après. (James Bay and Northern Quebec. Ten Years After)*. Sylvie Vincent and Gary Bowers, eds. Montréal: Recherches amérindiennes au Québec: 143–62.

Dickason, Olive 1997 *Canada's First Nations. A History of Founding Peoples from Earliest Times*. 2nd ed. Don Mills, Ont.: Oxford University Press.

Diubaldo, Richard J. 1981 The Absurd Little Mouse: When Eskimos Became Indians. *Journal of Canadian Studies* 16(2):35–40.

– 1989 You Can't Keep the Natives Native. In *For Purposes of Dominion. Essays in Honour of Morris Zaslow*. Kenneth Coates and William Morrison, eds. North York, Ont.: Captus Press: 171–85.

Dorais, Louis-Jacques 1997 *Quaqtaq. Modernity and Identity in an Inuit Community*. Toronto: University of Toronto Press.

Drapeau, Lynn 1996 Conjurors: The Use of Evidentials in Montagnais Secondhand Narratives. In *Nikotwâsik iskwâhtêm, pâskihtêpayih! Studies in Honour of H.C. Wolfart*. John Nichols, and Arden C.Ogg, eds. Algonquian and Iroquoian Linguistics, Memoir 13. Winnipeg: 171–94.

Ducruc, Jean-Pierre, Richard Zarnovican, Vincent Gerardin, and Michel Jurdant 1976 Les Régions écologiques du territoire de la Baie de James: Caracteristiques dominantes de leur couvert végétal. *Cahiers de Géographie du Québec* 20(50):365–92.

Dugal, Benoit 1900 *40 Ans d'evolution vers la conservation*. Chicoutimi, Que.: Association Chasse et Pêche.

Dunning, R.W. 1959 Ethnic Relations and the Marginal Man in Canada. *Human Organization* 18(3):117–22.

Dyck, Noel 1991 *What is the Indian "Problem." Tutelage and Resistance in Canadian Indian Administration*. St John's, Nfld.: ISER, Memorial University.

– 1997 Tutelage, Resistance and Co-Optation in Canadian Indian Administration. *Canadian Review of Sociology and Anthropology* 34 (3):333–48.

Eberstadt, Fernanda 1993 Northern Light. Review of Smilla's Sense of Snow by Peter Hoeg. *The New Yorker*, September 20: 118–19.

Elberg, Nathan, J and K Hyman, and R.F. Salisbury 1972 *Not By Bread Alone: The Use of Subsistence Resources Among James Bay Cree*. Montreal: Anthropology of Development. McGill University.

Elberg, Nathan, and Ronnie Visitor 1976 *The End of the Line: Communications in Paint Hills*. Montreal: Anthropology of Development, McGill University.

Elton, Charles 1942 *Voles, Mice and Lemmings*. Oxford: Clarendon Press.

Erickson, Vincent 1983 "The Mohawks Are Coming": Elijah Kellogg's Observations. In *Quatorizième congrès des Algonquianistes*. William Cowan, ed. Ottawa: Carleton University: 37–48.

Feit, Harvey 1978 Waswanipi Realities and Adaptations: Resource Management and Cognitive Structure. Ph.D. Dissertation, Montreal, Anthropology, McGill University.
- 1991 The Construction of Algonquian Hunting Territories. In *Colonial Situations. Essays on the Contextualization of Ethnographic Knowledge. History of Anthropology*. George Stocking, ed. Madison, Wisc.: University of Wisconsin Press: 109–34.
Finnie, Richard 1944 *Canada Moves North*. Toronto: Macmillan.
Firth, Raymond 1989 Fiction and Fact in Ethnography. In *History and Ethnicity*. ASA Monograph No. 27. Elizabeth Tonkin, Maryon McDonald and Malcolm Chapman, eds. London: Routledge.
Fisher, Robin 1979 *Contact and Conflict: Indian-European Relations in British Columbia, 1774–1890*. Vancouver: University of British Columbia Press.
- 1996 The Northwest from the Beginning of Trade with the Europeans to the 1880s. In *The Cambridge History of the Native Peoples of the Americas*. Vol. 1, Part 2. Bruce Trigger and Wilcomb Washburn, eds. New York: Cambridge University Press: 117–82.
Flannery, Regina 1935 The Position of Woman among the Eastern Cree. *Primitive Man* 8:81–6.
- 1995 *Ellen Smallboy. Glimpses of a Cree Woman's Life*. Montreal and Kingston: McGill-Queen's University Press.
Flannery, Regina, and M. Elizabeth Chambers 1985 Each Man Has His Own Friends: The Role of Dream Visitors in Traditional East Cree Belief and Practice. *Arctic Anthropology* 22(1):1–22.
- 1986 John M. Cooper's Investigations of James Bay Family Hunting Grounds, 1927–1934. In *Who Owns the Beaver? Northern Algonquian Land Tenure Reconsidered*. Charles Bishop and Toby Morantz, eds. *Anthropologica* 18 (1–2): 108–44.
Flannery, Regina, Mary Elizabeth Chambers, and Patricia Jehle 1982 Witiko Accounts from the James Bay Cree. *Arctic Anthropology* 18(1):57–77.
Fogelson, Raymond 1989 The Ethnohistory of Events and Nonevents. *Ethnohistory* 36(2):133–47.
Francis, Daniel, and Toby Morantz 1983 *Partners in Furs. A History of the Fur Trade in Eastern James Bay, 1600–1870*. Montreal and Kingston: McGill-Queen's University Press.
Frenette, Jacques 1985 *The History of the Chibougamau Crees. An Amerindian Band Reveals Its Identity*. Chibougamau: Cree Indian Centre of Chibougamau.
Gaffen, Fred 1985 *Forgotten Soldiers*. Penticton, BC: Theytus Books.
Gauthier, Gilles 1973 Étude sur la conduite et l'attitude des Indiens du diocèse de Moosonee dans le milieu du travail moderne, leur intégration économique. MA dissertation, Department of Sociology. University of Ottawa.

Given, Brian J. 1987 The Iroquois Wars and Native Arms. In *Native People, Native Lands. Canadian Indians, Inuit and Métis.* Bruce Cox, ed. Ottawa: Carelton University Press: 3–13

Godsell, Phillip 1932 *Arctic Trader: An Account of Twenty Years with the Hudson's Bay Company.* New York: G.P. Putnam.

Goodwill, Jean, and Norma Sluman 1984 *John Tootoosis. A Biography of a Cree Leader.* Winnipeg: Pemmican Publications.

Goody, Jack 1986 *The Logic of Writing and the Organization of Society.* New York: Cambridge University Press.

Grand Council of the Crees 1995 *Sovereign Injustice. Forcible Inclusion of the James Bay Crees and Cree Territory into a Sovereign Quebec.* Nemaska (Eeyou Astchee): Grand Council of the Crees.

Grant, John Webster 1984 *Moon of Wintertime. Missionaries and the Indians of Canada in Encounter since 1534.* Toronto: University of Toronto Press.

Grant, Shelagh D. 1988 *Sovereignty or Security? Government Policy in the Canadian North 1936–1950.* Vancouver: University of British Columbia Press.

Guinard, Joseph 1951 Mémoires du Révérend Père Joseph Guinard, O.M.I., missionnaire de 1892 à 1943. Typescript, Archives Déschâtelets, Ottawa.

Hand, Joan 1964 Quebec-Land of Development. Moccasin Telegraph, Summer: 1–3.

Harkin, Michael, and Sergei Kan 1996 Introduction. Special Issue. Native American Women's Responses to Christianity. *Ethnohistory* 43(4):563–72.

Harmon, Daniel 1957 *Sixteen Years in the Indian Country. The Journal of Daniel William Harmon, 1880–1816.* Kaye W. Lamb, ed. Toronto: Macmillan.

Harris, Lynda 1976 *Révillon Frères Trading Company Limited. Fur Traders of the North, 1901–1936.* Toronto: Ministry of Culture and Recreation.

Hastrup, Kirsten 1992 Introduction. In *Other Histories.* Kirsten Hastrup, ed. London: Routledge: 1–13.

Hawthorn, Harry B., and Marc-Adélard Tremblay 1966–67 *A Survey of the Contemporary Indians of Canada. Economic, Political, Educational Needs and Policies.* 2 vols. Ottawa: Department of Indian Affairs.

Hickerson, Harold 1973 Fur Trade Colonialism and the North American Indians. *Journal of Ethnic Studies* 1(2):15–44.

Hill, Jonathan 1988 Introduction. In *Rethinking History and Myth. Indigenous South American Perspectives on the Past.* Jonathan Hill, ed. Urbana, Ill.: University of Illinois Press: 1–17.

Holden, David E.W. 1968 Modernization among Town and Bush Cree. Appendix A. In *Developmental Change among the Cree Indians of Quebec.* Norman Chance, ed. Ottawa: Department of Regional Economic Expansion.

Honigmann, John J. 1962 *Social Networks in Great Whale River. Notes on Eskimo, Montagnais-Naskapi and Euro-Canadian Community.* Ottawa: National Museums of Canada.
– 1981 West Main Cree. In *Handbook of North American Indians. Subarctic,* Vol. 6. June Helm, ed. Washington, D.C.: Smithsonian Institution: 217–30.
Horn, Michiel 1972a Problems Old and Not So New. In *The Dirty Thirties. Canadians in the Great Depression.* Michiel Horn, ed. Toronto: Copp Clark: 177–85.
– 1972b The Morass of Relief. In *The Dirty Thirties. Canadians in the Great Depression.* Michiel Horn, ed. Toronto: Copp Clark: 251–260.
Hubbard, Mina 1908 *A Woman's Way Through Unknown Labrador. An Account of the Exploration of the Nascaupee and George Rivers.* London: John Murray.
Hugh-Jones, Stephen 1989 Waribi and White Man: History and Myth in Northwest Amazonia. In *History and Ethnicity.* ASA Monograph No. 27. Elizabeth Tonkin, Maryon McDonald, and Malcolm Chapman, eds. London: Routledge: 53–69.
Ignace, Marianne Boelscher 1991 Haida Public Discourse. *Canadian Journal of Native Studies* 11(1):113–35.
Iserhoff, S.R. 1925 The Good Old Days. *The Beaver*: 6.
James, William C. 1985 *A Fur Trader's Photographs. A.A. Chesterfield in the District of Ungava, 1901–4.* Montreal and Kingston: McGill-Queen's University Press.
Keighley, Sydney Augustus 1989 *Trader, Tripper, Trapper. The Life of a Bay Man.* Winnipeg: Watson & Dwyer.
Kerr, A.J. 1950 *Subsistence and Social Organization in a Fur Trade Community. Anthropological Report on the Rupert House Indians.* Ottawa: National Committee for Community Health Studies.
Kidwell, Clara Sue 1996 Comment: Native American Women's Responses to Christianity. *Ethnohistory* 43(4):721–5.
Klass, Morton 1995 *Ordered Universe. Approaches to the Anthropology of Religion.* Boulder, Co.: Westview.
Knight, Rolf 1965 A Re-Examination of Hunting, Trapping and Territoriality among the Northeastern Algonkian Indians. In *Man, Culture and Animals. The Role of Animals in Human Ecological Adjustments.* Publication No. 78. A. Leeds and A.P. Vayda, eds. Washington: American Association for the Advancement of Science.
– 1968 *Ecological Factors in Changing Economic and Social Organization among the Rupert House Cree.* Anthropology Papers No.15. Ottawa: National Museums of Canada.
Laliberté, Marcel 1978 La forêt boréale. In *Images de la préhistoire du Québec.* Claude Chapdelaine, ed. Recherches amérindiennes au Québec 7 (1–2):87–98.

- 1981 Rapport d'analyse des Sites GaGd-1, GaGd-8, GaGd-Ll et GaGd-16 du Lac Kanaaupscow, Baie James, Québec. In *Interventions archéologiques* No. 3. Directions générale du patrimoine, ed. Québec: Ministère des affaires culturelles.
LaRusic, Ignatius   1968   *The New Auchimau. A Study of Patron-Client Relations among the Waswanipi Cree*. Montreal: McGill Cree Project, McGill University.
- 1970 From Hunters to Proletarians. Appendix B. In *Developmental Change among the Cree Indians of Quebec*. Norman Chance, ed. Ottawa: Department of Regional and Economic Expansion.
- n.d. Managing Mishtuk: The Experience of Waswanipi Band in Developing and Managing a Forestry Company. Draft copy.
Leach, Edmund   1989   Tribal Ethnography. Past, Present, Future. In *History and Ethnicity*. ASA Monograph No. 27. Elizabeth Tonkin, Maryon McDonald, and Malcolm Chapman, eds. London: Routledge: 34–47.
Leacock, Eleanor   1954   *The Montagnais "Hunting Territory" and the Fur Trade*. American Anthropological Association. Memoir 78.
- 1958 Status among the Montagnais-Naskapi of Labrador. *Ethnohistory* 5(3):200–9.
- 1969 The Montagnais-Naskapi Band. In *Contributions to Anthropology: Band Societies*. Anthropological Series 84. Bulletin 228. David Damas, ed. Ottawa: National Museum of Canada.
- 1978 Woman's Status in Egalitarian Society: Implications for Social Evolution. *Current Anthropology* 19(2):247–75.
Leacock, Eleanor, and N. Rothschild, eds.   1994   *Labrador Winter. The Ethnographic Journals of William Duncan Strong, 1927–1928*. Washington: Smithsonian Institution.
Leith, Charles, and Arthur Leith   1912   *A Summer and Winter on Hudson Bay*. Madison, Wisconsin.
LePage, Pierre   1988   L'apprentissage difficile d'une coexistence harmonieuse. In *Baie James et Nord Québécois: Dix Ans Après. (James Bay and Northern Quebec. Ten Years After)*. Sylvie Vincent and Garry Bowers, eds. Montreal: *Recherches amérindiennes au Québec*: 25–9.
Linteau, Robert, R. Durocher, J-C Robert, and F. Ricard   1989   *Histoire du Québec contemporain. De la conféderation à la crise (1867–1929)*, Vol. 1. Québec: Boréale.
Long, John S.   1978   Education in the James Bay Region during the Horden Years. *Ontario History* 70(2):78–87.
- 1985 Treaty No. 9 and Fur Trade Company Families: Northeastern Ontario's Halfbreeds, Indians, Petitioners and Métis. In *The New Peoples: Being and Becoming Métis in North America*. Jacqueline Peterson and Jennifer S.H. Brown, eds. Winnipeg: University of Manitoba Press: 137–62.

- 1986 The Reverend George Barnley and the James Bay Cree. *Canadian Journal of Native Studies* 6(2):313–31.
- 1986 "Shaganash." Early Protestant Missionaries and the Adoption of Christianity of the Western James Bay Cree, 1840–63. Ph.D. dissertation, Toronto, Department of Education. University of Toronto.
- 1987 Manitu, Power, Books and Wiihtikow: Some Factors in the Adoption of Christianity by Nineteenth Century Western James Bay Cree. *Native Studies Review* 3(1):1–30.
- 1988 The Rev. G. Barnley, Wesleyan Methodism and the Fur Trade Company Families of James Bay. *Ontario History* 77(1):43–64.
- 1990 John Horden. In *Dictionary of Canadian Biography*. Vol. XII. Frances Halpenny, ed. Toronto: University of Toronto Press: 445–7.
- 1991 Budd's Native Contemporaries in James Bay: Men of "Refined Feelings," Representatives of "The Whiteman's Civilization" & "Real Bush Indians." *Journal of the Canadian Church Historical Society* 33(1):79–94.
- 1994 Thomas Vincent. *Dictionary of Canadian Biography*. Vol. XIII. Ramsay Cook, ed. Toronto: University of Toronto Press: 1060–1.
- 1994a "The Justice Which Ought to Come from Their Own Hands." The Imposition of Euro-Canadian Law & Order on the Western James Bay Cree, unpublished ms. 18pp.
- 1994b "The Government Is Asking for Your Land." The Treaty Made in 1905 at Fort Albany According to Oral Tradition, unpublished ms. 150 pp.

Loring, Stephen   1987 Arctic Profiles. William Brooks Cabot (1858–1949). *Arctic* 40(2):168–9.

Lowie, Robert   1925 Windigo, a Chipewyan Story. In *American Indian Life*. E.C. Parsons, ed. New York: Buesch & Co: 325–6.

Lytwyn, Victor   1993 The Hudson Bay Lowland Cree in the Fur Trade to 1821: A Study in Historical Geography. Ph.D. dissertation, Winnipeg, Man., Department of Geography. University of Manitoba.

MacGregor, Roy   1989 *Chief: The Fearless Vision of Billy Diamond*. Markham, Ont.: Penguin Books.

Mackenzie, Marguerite   1977 Montagnais Dialectology – One More Time. Presented at the Ninth Algonquian Conference, Worcester, Mass., 25 October.

MacLean, C.S.   1950 James Bay Cabin. Moccasin Telegraph, March: 38–42.

MacPherson, John T.   1930 *An Ethnological Study of the Abitibi Indians. Report*. Division of Anthropology. Ottawa: National Museums of Canada.

Marshall, Susan   1987 *Light on the Water. A Pictorial History of the People of Waswanipi*. Waswanipi: Waswanipi Band.

Marshall, Susan, Lizzie Diamond, and Sara Blackned   1989 *The Medicinal Use of Plants and Animals by the People of Waskaganish*. Nemaska: Cree Regional Authority.

Martijn, Charles A., and Edward Rogers   1969 *Mistassini-Albanel: Contributions to the Prehistory of Quebec*. Travaux divers No. 25. Québec: Centre d'études nordiques. Université Laval.

Mattox, W.G. 1964 *Fort Nascopie on Petitsikapau Lake*. McGill Sub-Arctic Research Paper No. 18. Montreal: McGill University.

McCardle, Bennett Ellen 1982 *Indian History and Claims. A Research Handbook*. Ottawa: Treaties and Historical Research, Indian and Northern Affairs.

McFeat, Tom 1974 *Small-Group Cultures*. New York: Pergamon Press.

Miller, J.R. 1989 *Skyscrapers Hide the Heavens. A History of Indian-White Relations in Canada*. Toronto: University of Toronto Press.

– 1991 Owen Glendower, Hotspur and Canadian Indian Policy. In *Sweet Promises. A Reader on Indian-White Relations in Canada*. J.R. Miller, ed. Toronto: University of Toronto Press: 323–52.

– 1996 *Shingwauk's Vision. A History of Native Residential Schools*. Toronto: University of Toronto Press.

Miller, Raymond 1914 A Canoe Trip from Lake Temiscaming to Lake Abitibi. *Rod and Gun* 16(2):114–20.

Milloy, John S. 1999 *A National Crime. The Canadian Government and the Residential School System, 1879–1986*. Winnipeg: University of Manitoba Press.

Moccasin Telegraph 1941–68 Fur Trade Staff Paper, Anonymously written articles.

Morantz, Toby 1980 The Fur Trade and the Cree of James Bay. In *Old Trails and New Directions*. Papers of the Third North American Fur Trade Conference. Carol Judd and Arthur Ray, eds. Toronto: University of Toronto Press: 38–58.

– 1982 Northern Algonquian Concepts of Status and Leadership Reviewed. A Case Study of the Eighteenth Century Trading Captain System. *Canadian Review of Sociology and Anthropology* 19(4):482–501.

– 1983a *An Ethnohistoric Study of Eastern James Bay Cree Social Organization, 1700–1850*. Ottawa: National Museum of Man.

– 1983b "Not Annuall Visitors." The Drawing in to Trade of Northern Algonquian Caribou Hunters. In *Actes du quatorizième congrès des Algonquinistes*. William Cowan, ed. Ottawa: Carleton University: 57–74.

– 1984 Oral and Recorded History in James Bay. In *Papers of the Fifteenth Algonquian Conference*. William Cowan, ed. Ottawa: Carleton University: 171–92.

– 1986a Historical Perspectives on Family Hunting Territories in Eastern James Bay. In *Who Owns the Beaver? Northern Algonquian Land Tenure Reconsidered*. Charles A. Bishop and Toby Morantz, eds. *Anthropologica* 18 (1–2):64–91.

– 1986b A Look at the Past – Inuit Life on the James Bay Coast Presented at the Fifth Inuit Studies Conference, Montreal, 18 November.

– 1987 Dwindling Animals and Diminished Lands. Early Twentieth Century Developments in Eastern James Bay. In *Papers of the Eighteenth Algonquian Conference*. William Cowan, ed. Ottawa: Carleton University: 209–28.

- 1988 "Gift Offerings to Their Own Importance and Superiority." Fur Trade Relations, 1700–1940. In *Papers of the Nineteenth Algonquian Conference*. William Cowan, ed. Ottawa: Carelton University: 133–46.
- 1990 "So Evil a Practice."A Look at the Debt System in the James Bay Fur Trade. In *Merchant Credit and Labour Strategies in Historical Perspective*. Rosemary Ommer, ed. Fredericton: Acadiensis Press: 203–22.
- 1992a Old Texts, Old Questions: Another Look at the Issue of Continuity and the Early Fur-Trade Period. *Canadian Historical Review* 73(2 June):166–93.
- 1992b Aboriginal Land Claims in Quebec. In *Aboriginal Land Claims in Canada. A Regional Perspective*. Kenneth Coates, ed. Toronto: Copp Clark Pitman: 101–30.
- 1995 Provincial Game Laws at the Turn of the Century: Protective or Punitive Measures for the Native Peoples of Quebec? In *Papers of the Twenty-Sixth Algonquian Conference*. David Pentland, ed. Winnipeg: University of Manitoba: 175–90.
- 1997 Cree Ethnopolitics. Paper presented at the Department of Anthropology, University of Tromso, Tromso, Norway, April.
- 1998 The Past and Future of Ethnohistory. *Acta Borealia* 1:67–79.
- 2001 Plunder or Harmony? On Merging European and Native Views of Early Contact. In *De-Centring the Renaissance: New Essays on Early Modern Canada*. Germaine Warkentin and Carolyn Podruchny, eds. Toronto: University of Toronto Press: 48–67.

Morantz, Toby, and Ira Chaikin 1985 Report of the Ontario Land Claims Project. Typescript, 100 pp. Grand Council of the Crees.

Nanuwan 1929 Solomon Voyageur. *The Beaver* 259(4):162–3.

Neilson, James M. 1948 The Mistassini Territory of Northern Quebec. *Canadian Geographical Journal* 37(42):144–157.

Nicholson, Alan 1924 Obituary for John Iserhoff. *The Beaver*, December: 49.

Niezen, Ronald 1997 Healing and Conversion. Medical Evangelism in James Bay Cree Society. *Ethnohistory* 44(3):463–89.

Nock, David A. 1988 *A Victorian Missionary and Canadian Indian Policy: Cultural Synthesis v. Replacement*. Waterloo, Ont.: Wilfrid Laurier University Press.

Ohnuki-Tierney, Emiko, ed. 1990 *Culture Through Time. Anthropological Approaches*. Stanford: Stanford University Press.

Ommer, Rosemary 1990 Introduction. In *Merchant Credit and Labour Strategies in Historical Perspective*. Rosemary Ommer, ed. Fredericton: Acadiensis Press: 9–15.

Ornstein, Toby and Valerie Marchant 1973 *The First Peoples in Quebec. A Reference Work on the History, Environment, Economic and Legal Position of the Indians and Inuit of Quebec*, vols. 1–3. La Macaza, Que.: Manitou College.

O'Reilly, James   1988 The Role of the Courts in the Evolution of the James Bay Hydroelectric Project. In *Baie James et Nord Québécois. Dix Ans Après. (James Bay and Northern Quebec. Ten Years After).* Sylvie Vincent and Garry Bowers, eds. Montreal: *Recherches amérindiennes au Québec*: 30–8.

Paine, Robert   1977 The Path to Welfare Colonialism. In *The White Arctic. Anthropological Essays on Tutelage and Ethnicity.* Newfoundland Social and Economic Paper No. 7. Robert Paine, ed. St. John's, Nfld.: ISER, Memorial University: 7–28.

Panasuk, Anne-Marie, and Jean-René Proulx   1979 Les Rivières à Saumon de la Côte-Nord ou "Défense de Pêcher – Cette rivière est la propriété de..." *Recherches amérindiennes au Québec* 9(3):203–18.

Patterson, Palmer   1971 The Colonial Parallel: A View of Indian History. *Ethnohistory* 18 (1):1–17.

Paul-Emile, Sister   1952 *Amiskwashi: La Baie James. Trois Cents Ans.* Ottawa: Editions de l'Université d'Ottawa.

Pentland, David   1978 An Historical Overview of Cree Dialects. In *Papers of the Ninth Algonquian Conference.* William Cowan, ed. Ottawa: Carleton University: 104–26.

Petersen, Olive Mackay   1974 *The Land of Moosoneek.* Bryant Press.

Ponting, J. Rick   1986 Relations Between Bands and the Department of Indian Affairs. A Case of Internal Colonialism? In *Arduous Journey. Canadian Indians and Decolonization.* J. Rick Ponting, ed. Toronto: McClelland and Stewart: 84–111.

– 1997 *First Nations in Canada. Perspectives on Opportunity, Empowerment, and Self-Determination.* Toronto: McGraw-Hill, Ryerson Ltd.

Preston, Richard J.   1968 Functional Politics in a Northern Indian Community. In *Proceedings of the 38th International Congress of Americanists* 3:169–78.

– 1974 The Means to Academic Success for Eastern Cree Students. In *Proceedings of the First Congress, Canadian Ethnology Society.* Jerome Barkow, ed. Ottawa: National Museum of Man. Papers in Ethnology No. 17:87–96.

– 1975a *Cree Narratives: Expressing the Personal Meaning of Events.* Ethnology Service Paper No. 30. Ottawa: National Museum of Man. Mercury Series.

– 1975b Eastern Cree Community in Relation to Fur Trade Post in the 1830s: The Background of the "Posting" Process. In *Proceedings of the Sixth Algonquian Conference.* William Cowan, ed. Ottawa: Carleton University: 324–35.

– 1975c A Survey of Ethnographic Approaches to the Eastern Cree-Montagnais-Naskapi. *Canadian Review of Sociology and Anthropology* 12(3):267–77.

– 1980a Eastern Cree Notions of Social Grouping. In *Papers of the Eleventh Algonquian Conference.* William Cowan, ed. Ottawa: Carleton University: 40–8.

- 1980b The Witiko: Algonkian Knowledge and Whiteman Knowledge. In *Manlike Monsters on Trial. Early Records and Modern Evidence*. Marjorie Halpin and Michael Ames, eds. Vancouver: University of British Columbia Press: 111–31.
- 1983 Some Continuities in Algonquian Leadership. Presented at the Fifteenth Conference of Algonquianists, Cambridge, Mass., October.
- 1986a Notions of History Implicit in East Cree Narratives of the Past. Report prepared for the Cree Regional Authority.
- 1986b Twenty Century Transformations of the West Coast Cree. In *Actes du dix-septième congrès des Algonquinistes*. William Cowan, ed. Ottawa: University of Ottawa: 239–52.
- 1987 Catholicism at Attawapiskat: A Case of Culture Change. In *Papers of the Eighteenth Algonquian Conference*. William Cowan, ed. Ottawa: Carleton University: 271–86.
- 1988 James Bay Cree Syncretism. In *Papers of the Nineteenth Algonquian Conference*. William Cowan, ed. Ottawa: Carleton University: 147–55.
- 1999 Reflections on Culture, History and Authenticity. In *Theorizing the Americanist Tradition*. Lisa Philips Valentine and Regna Darnell, eds. Toronto: University of Toronto Press: 150–62.

Preston, Sarah 1986 *Let the Past Go. A Life History Narrated by Alice Jacob*. Canadian Ethnology Service Paper No. 104. Ottawa: National Museums of Canada.
- 1987 Is Your Cree Uniform the Same as Mine? Cultural and Ethnographic Variations on a Theme. In *Papers of the Eighteenth Algonquian Conference*. William Cowan, ed. Ottawa: Carleton University: 287–98.

Price, Richard 1983 *First-Time. The Historical Vision of an Afro-American People*. Baltimore: John Hopkins University.

Prins, Harald E.L. 1996 Tribal Networks and Migrant Labor: Mi'kmaq Indians as Seasonal Workers in Aroostook's Potato Fields, 1870–1980. In *Native Americans and Wage Labor*. Alice Littlefield and Martha Knack, eds. Norman, Okla.: University of Oklahoma Press: 45–65.

Ray, Arthur J. 1974 *Indians in the Fur Trade. Their Role as Hunters, Trappers and Middlemen in the Lands Southwest of Hudson Bay 1660–1870*. Toronto: University of Toronto Press.
- 1980 Indians as Consumers in the Eighteenth Century. In *Old Trails and New Directions. Papers of the Third North American Fur Trade Conference*. Carol Judd and Arthur Ray, eds. Toronto: University of Toronto Press: 255–71.
- 1990a The Decline of Paternalism in the Hudson's Bay Company Fur Trade, 1870–1945. In *Merchant Credit and Labour Strategies in Historical Perspective*. Rosemary Ommer, ed. Fredericton, NB: Acadiensis Press: 188–202.
- 1990b *The Canadian Fur Trade in the Industrial Age*. Toronto: University of Toronto Press.

Renison, Robert J. 1957 *One Day at a Time. The Autobiography of Robert John Renison*. Toronto: Kingswood House.

Rhodes, Richard, and Evelyn Todd 1981 Subarctic Algonquian Languages. In *Handbook of North American Indians. Subarctic*. Vol. 6. June Helm, ed. Washington, DC: Smithsonian Institution: 52–66.

Rich, E.E. 1967 *The Fur Trade and the Northwest to 1857*. Toronto: McClelland and Stewart.

Richardson, Boyce 1975 *Strangers Devour the Land: A Chronicle of the Assault upon the Last Coherent Hunting Culture in North America, the Cree Indians of North America and Their Vast Primeval Homelands*. New York: Knopf.

Ridington, Robin 1988 *Trail to Heaven. Knowledge and Narrative in a Northern Native Community*. Iowa City: University of Iowa Press.

Robertson, Heather 1984 *A Gentleman Adventurer. The Arctic Diaries of R.H.G. Bonnycastle*. Toronto: Lester & Orpen Dennys.

Rogers, Edward S. 1963 *The Hunting Group-Hunting Territory Complex among the Mistassini Indians*. Bulletin 195. Ottawa: National Museum of Man.

– 1965 Nemiscau Indians. *The Beaver*, Summer: 30–5.

– 1969 Band Organization Among the Indians of Eastern Subarctic. In *Contributions to Anthropology: Band Societies*. Anthropological Series 84. Bulletin 228. David Damas, ed. Ottawa: National Museums of Canada: 21–50.

Rogers, Mary Black 1987 "Starving" and Survival in the Subarctic Fur Trade: A Case for Contextual Semantics. In *Le Castor Fait Tout. Selected Papers of the Fifth North American Fur Trade Conference, 1985*. Bruce Trigger, Toby Morantz, and Louise Dechêne, eds. Montreal: Lake St Louis Historical Society: 618–49.

Roslin, Alex 1999 The Nation 6 (13):5.

Rousseau, Jacques 1949 Mistassini Calendar. *The Beaver*, September: 33–7.

– 1952 Persistence aiennes chez les Amérindiens de la forêt boréale. *Cahiers des dix* 17:183–208.

Salisbury, Richard F. 1986 *A Homeland for the Cree. Regional Development in James Bay, 1971–1981*. Montreal and Kingston: McGill-Queen's University Press.

Satzewich, Victor 1997 Indian Agent and the "Indian Problem" in Canada in 1946: Reconsidering the Theory of Coercive Tutelage. *Canadian Journal of Native Studies* 17(2):227–57.

Satzewich, Vic, and Terry Wotherspoon 1993 *First Nations: Race, Class and Gender Relations*. Scarborough, Ont.: Nelson Canada.

Scanlon, James 1975 *The Inlanders. Some Algonquians and Indians in Nouveau Quebec*. Cobalt, Ont.: Highway Bookshop.

Scanlon, James, ed. 1976 *Letters from James Bay*. Cobalt: Highway Bookshop.

Scott, Colin 1983 The Semiotics of Material Life among the Wemindji Cree Hunters. Ph.D. dissertation, Montreal, Department of Anthropology. McGill University.
- 1992 La rencontre avec les Blancs. *Recherches amérindiennes au Québec* 22(2–3):47–62.
Sexé, Marcel 1923 *Histoire d'une famille et d'une industrie pendant deux siècles, 1723–1923*. Paris: Plon.
Sindell, Peter 1968 Some Discontinuities in the Enculturation of Mistassini Cree Children. In *Conflict in Culture: Problems in Developmental Change among the Cree*. Norman Chance, ed. Ottawa: Canadian Research Centre for Anthropology. St Paul University.
Sivuaq, Paulussi 1988 The Extinguishment Clause in the Agreement. In *Baie James et Nord Québécois. Dix Ans Après. (James Bay and Northern Quebec. Ten Years After)*. Sylvie Vincent and Garry Bowers, eds. Montreal: *Recherches amérindiennes au Québec*: 291
Skinner, Alanson 1911 *Notes on the Eastern Cree and Northern Saulteaux*. Anthropological Papers of the American Museum of Natural History 9(1). New York.
Smith, Donald B. 1990 *From the Land of the Shadows. The Making of Grey Owl*. Saskatoon, Sask.: Western Producer Prairie Books.
Smith, James G.E. 1976 Notes on Witiko. In *Papers of the Seventh Algonquian Conference*. William Cowan, ed. Ottawa: Carleton University: 18–38.
Sotrac 1978 *Cree Traplines (1977). James Bay Territory*. Quebec: Sotrac.
Speck, Frank G. 1923 Mistassini Hunting Territories. *American Anthropologist* 35:289–308.
- 1977 *Naskapi. The Savage Hunters of the Labrador Peninsula* (first published in 1935). Norman, Okla.: University of Oklahoma Press.
Spielmann, Roger 1998 *"You're So Fat!" Exploring Ojibwe Discourse*. Toronto: University of Toronto Press.
Sun, Frank 1980 *Aspects of Syncretism Between Traditional Cree and Christian Religious Beliefs*. Ottawa: National Museums of Canada. Typescript, 84 pp.
Surtees, Robert J. 1992 *The Northern Connection. Ontario Northland since 1902*. North York, Ont.: Catpus Press.
Tanner, Adrian 1968 Occupation and Life Stories in Two Minority Communities. In *Conflict in Culture. Problems of Developmental Change among the Cree*. Norman Chance, ed. Ottawa: Canadian Research Centre for Anthropology. St. Paul University: 47–67.
- 1971 Existe-t-il des territoires de chasse? *Recherches amérindiennes au Québec* 1(4–5):69–83.
- 1979 *Bringing Home Animals: Religious Ideology and Modes of Production of the Mistassini Cree Hunters*. New York: St Martin's Press.
- 1983 Introduction: Canadian Indians and the Politics of Dependency. In *The Politics of Indianness. Case Studies of Native Ethnopolitics in Canada*. Social

and Economic Papers, No.12. Adrian Tanner, ed. St John's, Nfld.: ISER, Memorial University: 1–35.

– 1986 The New Hunting Territory Debate: An Introduction to Some Unresolved Issues. In *Who Owns the Beaver? Northern Algonquian Land Tenure Reconsidered*. Charles Bishop and Toby Morantz, eds. *Anthropologica* 18 (1–2):19–36.

– 1987 The Significance of Hunting Territories Today. In *Native People, Native Lands*. Bruce Cox, ed. Ottawa: Carleton University Press: 60–74.

Taylor, J. Garth 1994 Northern Algonquians on the Frontiers of "New Ontario," 1890–1945. In *Aboriginal Ontario*. Edward S. Rogers and Donald B. Smith, eds. Toronto: Dundurn Press: 344–76.

Tester, Frank, and Peter Kulchyski 1994 *Tammarniit (Mistakes) Inuit Relocation in the Eastern Arctic, 1939–63*. Vancouver: University of British Columbia Press.

Thomas, Nicholas 1994 *Colonialism's Culture. Anthropology, Travel and Government*. Princeton, NJ: Princeton University Press.

Thwaites, Rueben Gold, ed. 1896–1901 *The Jesuit Relations and Allied Documents*. Cleveland.

Titley, Brian E. 1986 *A Narrow Vision: Duncan Campbell Scott and the Administration of Indian Affairs in Canada*. Vancouver: University of British Columbia Press.

Tonkin, Elizabeth 1992 *Narrating Our Pasts. The Social Construction of Oral History*. Cambridge: Cambridge University Press.

Tough, Frank 1996 *"As Their Natural Resources Fail." Native Peoples and the Economic History of Northern Manitoba, 1870–1950*. Vancouver: University of British Columbia Press.

Townsend, Joan 1983 Firearms against Native Arms. A Study in Comparative Efficiencies with an Alaskan Example. *Arctic Anthropology* 20(1):1–33.

Traversy, Normand 1976 Étude du castor à la Baie James. Environnement Baie James. *Symposium 1976*. Compte rendu. Montreal: Société de developpement de la Baie James.

Trudel, Pierre 1992 On découvre toujours d'Amérique. *Recherches amérindiennes au Québec* 22(2–3):63–72.

Turner, Lucien 1979 *Indians and Eskimos in the Quebec-Labrador Peninsula. Ethnology of the Ungava District* (first published in 1894). Quebec: Coméditex.

Turner, Terence 1988 Ethno-Ethnohistory: Myths and History in Native South American Representations of Contact with Western Society. In *Rethinking History and Myth. Indigenous South American Perspectives on the Past*. Jonathan Hill, ed. Urbana: University of Illinois Press: 235–81.

Vaillancourt, Louis-Philippe 1984 À propos d'orthographe. In *Papers of the Fifteenth Algonquian Conference*. William Cowan, ed Ottawa: Carleton University: 21–32.

Valentine, Lisa Phillips 1995 *Making It Their Own. Severn Ojibwe Communicative Practices*. Toronto: University of Toronto Press.

Valpy, Michael, and Michael Barnes 1968 The Politics of Educating Fort-Rupert Indians. *Globe and Mail*, 22 January: 7.

Van Kirk, Sylvia 1980 *"Many Tender Ties." Women in Fur Trade Society, 1670–1870.* Winnipeg: Watson & Dwyer.

Vansina, Jan 1985 *Oral Tradition as History.* Madison, Wisc.: University of Wisconsin Press.

Vincent, Sylvie 1982 La tradition orale montagnaise. Comment l'interroger? *Cahiers de Clio* 70:5–26.

– 1992 L'arrivé des chercheurs de terres. Récits et dires des Montagnais de la moyenne et de la Basse Côte-Nord. *Recherches amérindiennes au Québec* 22(2–3):19–29.

– 1996 Compatibilité apparente, incompatibilité réelle des versions autochtones et des versions occidentales de l'histoire. L'exemple Innu. Presented at Les obstacles ontologiques dans les relations Interculturelles, Université Laval, October 7–10.

Wadel, Cato 1969 *Marginal Adaptations and Modernization in Newfoundland.* St. John's, Nfld.: ISER Memorial University.

Waldram, James B., D.A. Herring, and T.K. Young 1995 *Aboriginal Health in Canada. Historical, Cultural and Epidemiological Perspectives.* Toronto: University of Toronto Press.

Walker, Willard 1953 Acculturation of the Great Whale River Cree. MA dissertation., Tempe, Az., Department of Anthropology, University of Arizona.

Wallerstein, Immanuel 1974 *The Modern World-System: Capitalist Agriculture and the Origins of the European World-Economy in the Sixteenth Century.* New York: Academic Press.

Walton, W.G. 1920 Game in the Hudson Bay Country. *American Wildlife* 9(3):18–19.

– 1921 Life Conditions of the Native Races on the East Coast of Hudson's Bay. Told in *Memoranda and Correspondence between W.G. Walton of Fort George and the Dominion Government Spectator.* Ottawa.

Warren, Kay B. 1989 *The Symbolism of Subordination. Indian Identity in a Guatemalan Town.* Austin, Tx.: University of Texas Press.

White, Geoffrey 1991 *Identity Through History. Living Stories in a Solomon Islands.* Cambridge: Cambridge University Press.

Willis, Jane 1973 *Geneish: An Indian Girlhood.* Toronto: New Press.

Wills, Richard H. 1984 *Conflicting Perceptions. Western Economics and the Great Whale River Cree.* Chicago: Tutorial Press.

Wintrob, Ronald M., and Peter Sindell 1970 Education and Identity Conflict Among Cree Youth. Appendix C. In *Developmental Change among the Cree Indians of Quebec.* Norman Chance, ed. Ottawa: Department of Regional and Economic Expansion.

Wolf, Eric R. 1982 *Europe and the People without History.* Berkeley, Ca.: University of California Press.

Young, T. Kue 1984 Indian Health Services in Canada: A Sociohistorical Perspective. *Social Science and Medicine* 18(3):257–64.

Zaslow, Morris 1971 *The Opening of the Canadian North, 1870–1914*. Toronto: McClelland and Stewart.

- 1975 *Reading the Rocks. The Story of the Geological Survey of Canada, 1842–1972*. Toronto: Macmillan.
- 1979 The Dilemmas of the Northern Missionary Diocese. The Case of the Anglican See of Moosonee. *Laurentian University Review* 11(2):101–16.
- 1988 *The Northward Expansion of Canada, 1914–1967*. Toronto: McClelland and Stewart.

Index

airplane travel: advent of, 138–9; chartered by Crees, 139; flying doctor service, 185, 190; helicopters, 309 nXIII; negative effects on Crees, 140; sea planes, 193, 303 nXII
alcohol, 234; whisky pedlars, 298 nXXXIII
Anderson, J.W., 282 nV, 292 nI; death of daughter, 280 nIX; on debt, 25; on radio, 136; using Catholic mission, 168; wife, 288 nXLVII
Anderson, John, 78, 152
Atkinson, Sam (Atkins), 101, 152

Barnley, George, 63, 74
bear: chin 285 nXXI; feast, 57, 111; importance of, 58, 250
beaver: ban on killing (non-Indian), 143; changes re hunting, 123; closed season, 144; importance of, in trade, 32; scarcity of, 158; stocking of, 161, 167; white trappers, 141, 158. *See also* beaver preserves; Quebec, game legislation
beaver preserves, 131, 166; Catholic mission role, 168; conditions, 160–1; control by HBC, 172, 307 nXXXVIII; endorsed by Crees, 161; Great Whale River, 169; and HBC criticism of 170; marketing of furs, 170; Mistassini, 169, 199; mode of operation, 162; Nottoway, 165–6, 172; Old Factory, 167–9; organized by hunting territory, 168, 307 nXL; RCMP re infractions, 236; registered traplines, 166–7; role of Crees, 163, 171; Rupert House, 160; success of 162, 164, 171; tallymen, 168–9
Bishop Horden Memorial Residential School, 213
Blackned, Charlie, 105, 117, 121
Blackned, John, 51, 285 nXXVI; re beaver preserve, 162–3; re surveyors, 284 nXV; on times of scarcity, 111, 122; re trespass, 233
Blackned, Richard, 139, 148
Bonnycastle, R.H.G., 139
Borron, E.B., 37, 237; recommended hospital, 184, 237

Canada: competition with Quebec, 180, 239; established provincial boundaries, 40, 134; family allowance, 208–9; fiduciary trust, refusal, 252; health budget inadequate, 308–9 nVII; and department, 185, 186; Indian right to vote, 237; indifference to Crees, 250; justice system imposed, 233–4, 236; meagre funding of Fort George Catholic hospital, 186–7; and obligations, 130; old age pensions, 209; relief, first program, 146, 304 nXIX; subsidies to north, 131; transfer of lands to provinces, 40, 132–4; no treaties, no protection, 145, 185; Waswanipi reserve, 202
canoes: canvas, 294 nXIII; motorized, 135–6, 303 nVI. *See also* Hudson's Bay Company, canoe factory
caribou, 283 nVII; decline of 50–1; as food, 33; George River herd, 285 nXXIV; preference for, 33
Cartlidge, Harry, 77, 136, 141; on Christianity, 291

nXVIII; re relief payments, 147
Charles Fort, 17. See also Rupert House
Charlton Island, 140; Inuit residence, 287 nXL; beaver preserve in nineteenth century, 161, 293 nIX; stocked with beaver, 161
Chesterfield, A.A., 86, 98, 292 nIV
Chibougamau: band chief Jimmy Mianscum, 233; fur trade post, 198; lake, 197–8; town, 201. See also Ouje-Bougoumou band
clothing, 55
Coasters: change of posts, 125; lifestyle, 113; material culture, 56–7; moved inland, 24, 114, 125, 128, 244; and railroad towns, 125; reliance on imported foods, 35; rhythm of life at post, 56; self-reliance 300 nLI
colonialism: bureaucratic, 8–9, 134, 201, 248, 309–10 nXIV; challenges to, 246; discrimination in government transfer payments, 208–9, 201; disparity in wages for same work, 200; enclave economy, 195, 200–1; general discussion, 5–8, 132, 241–2; justice system, alien and difficult, 236; and imposed 234–5; leadership emasculated, 229; mentality, differences in, 247; and in Indian Affairs, 314 nXLIII; outside agents, 222–3, 224, 246–7; welfare v. economic development, 208–9. See also Canada; Indian Affairs
communication: mode, presyllabics, 82; radiophones, 193; telephones, 177, 308 nII. See also radio
Conn, Hugh, 142, 166, 169, 221, 314 nXL
Coon Come, Matthew, 255
Cooter, David, 37, 149, 288 nXLVI
Couchees, William, 197
Cowboy, Matthew, 36, 114, 299 nXLI; re freighting, 100; re hunting territories, 173
credit (debt): amount determined treatment, 288 nXLIV; beginnings, 31; controls, 116, 123; Cree v. Inuit, 65; defence of its use, 149, 164; description of system, 31, 112, 114–15, 244; hip-pocket ledger, 149; as status, 31–2; as wards of the state, 299 nXLIV
cycles, animal, 122, 298 nXXXIX

Diamond, Billy, 180, 219, 228, 231, 255, 316 nIII
Diamond, Eddie, 217–18
Diamond, Malcolm, 307 nXXXIX; hunting territory, 165; petition re schools, 181; traditional leader, 228
diseases: Cree medicines, 44; death toll at Rupert House, 45; epidemics, 187, 190, 286 nXXX; late 1800s, 43–5; medicines at post, 44; smallpox at Moose Factory, 189; tuberculosis, 184–5, 189, 190–1, 309 nXII. See also health
Doré Lake, 198–9, 234
Dunne-za. See oral tradition

Eastmain Post (and band), 38; Catholic mission, 157; Chief Walter Tammatuk, 228; constituted a reserve, 178; housing situation, 211; post manager, Alec Louttit, 301 nLXII; reduced number on relief, 148; welfare, 210
employment: canoe factory, 203; commercial fishery, 201–2; construction work, Rupert House, 204; greater opportunities in south, 201; guiding, 197, 202; Indian Affairs' conflicting policies, 207, 314 nXLIX; mining jobs closed to Crees, 200; oscillate between trapping and wage labour, 202; payment in kind, 35; at post, 35, 112, 117, 119, 125–6, 129; prospecting work, 197, 200; wage work, 193, 298 nXXXIV. See also Hudson's Bay Company, employment at post
Esquinamow, Matthew, 293 nIX; brother of Richard Matthew, 101; influence of 101

Fairies, Beatrice, 63, 125, 215, 301 nLX
food: country, 109–10; disparity by region, 111; goose hunting, 208; hares, 285 nXXV; imported, 33–4, 112, 301 nLVII; sharing, 37–8, 285 nXXXIII; whales, 286 nXXXI
Fort Albany, Treaty No. 9, 61
Fort Chimo, 38; airfield, 310 nXV; diseases at, 45; Indians from, 92; travel to, 296–7 nXXVII
Fort George Post (and band), 38; arrival of Catholic priests, 151; Chief John Chishka-

mush, 314 nXLVII; Chief Robert Kanatewat, 228, 231; Chiefs Peter Waskigan and John Naposh, 228; Coaster-Inlander division, 230; competition, Anglicans and Catholics, 151; Cree-Inuit relations, 63, 310 nXVI; distressed state, 297 nXXXII; encroachment of white trappers, 142; housing, 211; hospitals, 186, 187, 188; leave reserve, 315 nIV; Nouveau-Québec, 180; nursing station, 186; provincial school, 181, 313 nXXXV; residential schools, 156–7, 187–8; social life, 137
Fort Mackenzie, 118, 298–9 nXL
Fort Nascopie, 39
foxes, cycles, 298 nXXXIX; importance of, 293 nVI; ranched, 298 nXXXVI; silver, prices of, 112, 294 nXII, 298 nXXXVI.

Geological Survey of Canada, 41, 197; R. Bell, 41; F.H. Bignell, 41, 284 nXV; A.P. Low, 41, 113; at Waswanipi 198
George, Rupert, 84
Georgekish, George, 118
Gillam, Zachariah, 17–18
Gillies, Donald, 98–9, 101, 234
Great Whale River Post (and band), 38; Chief Sam Masty, 227, 229; community meeting, 232; Cree-Inuit relations, 63, 310 nXVI; deaths from starvation, 110; employment, 203; handicraft program, 196, 310 nXVII; Indian agent, 222, 225; Inuit v. Cree housing, 195; leadership, 228; measles epidemic, 190; mid-Canada line, 195–6; Nouveau-Québec, regional headquarters, 180; radar stations, 194; radio broadcasts, 137; school, 195
Griffin, Mrs, 154
Griffiths, Owen, 58, 100, 103, 105, 135
Guinard, Joseph-Etienne, 76–8

Hannah Bay, 14, 235
health: care by Catholics, 183, 186; deterioration of, 185; doctors, annual visits, 189; hospitals at Fort George, 184, 186–7, 188, 192; malnutrition, 190; medical ships, annual visit, 190, 309 nXI; merits of country food, 191; nursing stations, 186, 188, 192, 202; population increase, 192; sanatoriums, 189, 191; surveys, 189, 190. *See also* diseases
Herodier, Gaston, 99, 293 nV
Hester, Charlie, 114
Hester, Matthew, 302 nLXV
Horden, John, 74, 81, 213, 290 nX
Hudson's Bay Company: air transport, 138; beaver preserves, 163; and inspection, 164; business practices, 36–7, 115–16, 223, 283 nXI, 299 nXLVI, 300 nLXIX; canoe factory, 203–4, 311 nXXI; charter of, 17; competition, benefits to the Crees, 99, 101–6, 108, 170; control ended of village life, 208; Crees' views of, 71; difficulties for foreign-born personnel, 70, 294, nXVI; employment at posts, 112, 117, 119, 127, 129, 194, 283 nVIII; employment, reduction of, 117, 127, 140, 298 nXXXVII, 299–300 nXLVII; image of 67–8; managers' treatment of Crees, 66, 68–9, 223; and lease of Nottoway, 161, 166; Native employees, obligations, 127; radio department, 137; S&D rations questioned, 211; supply system restructured, 140; wages of managers cut, 299 nXLIII
hunting territory, 112, 244; beaver preserves, based on, 166–7; coastal resources, 114; confusion re, 173; continuity and change, 172–3; J. Cooper report, 304 nXV; family hunting territory system, 20, 158–9, 200–1, 306 nXXXII–III; encroachment by whites, 142; form of beaver conservation, 158; R. Knight's description, 128; location of M. Diamond's, 165; poaching, 166; size of, 159; trespass, 233

Indian: defined by lifestyle, 60–1; Indian Affairs classification, 62; marriage ban, 62; as separate group, 61
Indian Affairs Branch (department): assimilation policy, 246; bureaucracy, 232; conflicting policies, 207, 212, 246; consultative process, 311–12 nXXIV; control of Indian bands, 228, 229–30, 311–12 nXXIV; district offices, 201, 221, 231–2; doctors' annual visits, 189; elections, band

council, 225–6; financing of beaver preserves, 163; handicraft program, Great Whale River, 196; Indian agents, 129, 189, 190, 200, 221–5, 229; Indian status, 134, 207–8, 210, 249; registration of Indians, 129, 243, 287 nXXVII; relief re Quebec game laws, 145; S&D rations, 110; sales tax position, 237; subsidy of commercial fishery, 202–4; supervision of beaver preserves, 221, 225; takeover of Fort George Catholic hospital, 188; welfare payments, 209; welfare *v.* economic opportunities, 212, 249. *See also* Canada; colonialism
Inlanders: attitude towards permanent employment, 114; beadwork, 286 nXXVIII; Coasters joining, 114; departure ceremony, 59; fear of starvation, 113; hunting strategies, 54, 123–4
Inuit: Belcher Island *v.* mainland, 38; at Charlton, 42, 284 nXVI, 287 nXL; family allowance, 312 nXXXVII; former independence, 240; jurisdiction over, 150, 305 nXXI; at Little Whale River, 38; living conditions at Great Whale River, 195; and at Old Factory, 65; RCMP overseeing, 235; radio broadcasts, 137; relations with Crees, 63; soapstone carving, 196; trading sealskin boots, 55–6, 63, 64; treatment at Moose Factory hospital, 192; work at post, 64–5
Iserhoff, Charles, 83, 92, 153, 284–5 nXXIX, 288 nIII, 291 nXIX

Iserhoff, John, 118, 288 nIII
Iserhoff, Samuel, 83, 288 nIII; criticism by Catholics, 153; opening prayer, 226

Jacob, Willie, 105, 117, 121
James Bay and Northern Quebec Agreement, 199, 202; agreement in principle, 253, classification of members, 301 nLXIII; Cree-Naskapi Act, 316 nII; features of, 253–4; re Inuit, 316 nII
James Bay hydroelectric project, 232, 251; challenge in court, 252; Great Whale River project, 255, 316 nIV; opposition to, 248
James Bay territory: differences within, re game, 33, 53; geographic and ecological description, 28–30; industrial activity, 141; and isolation from, 132; jurisdiction over, 28; little infrastructure, 177; military use considered, 310–11 nXVIII; size, 28; summer travellers, 41–3, 44
Jolly, Billy, 81, 125

Kakabat, George, 291 nXV
Kanaaupscow Post, 103–4, 105, 113, 223; families at, 295 nXX; medical treatment, 183, 189; sales tax, 236–7; social life, 295 nXIX; winter freighting, 120
Kawapit, Andrew, 53–4
Kawapit, John, 45; assistant chief, 229; on caribou, 50–1; on competition, 106, 296–7 nXXVII; on hunting strategies, 121; on stoves, 286 nXXIX

Lake Nemiscau, 39
Lake St Jean region, 39
land tenure. *See* hunting territories
language (Cree): code switching, 292 nXXI; divisions, 46–7; liturgical 93–4; nicknames, 295 nXX; *wemstukshiokan*, 287 nXXXVI
Larivière, Hervé, 179, 200, 221, 223–4, 314 nXLIV
Leacock, Eleanor: on gender equality, 10; on hunting territories, 19–20; on social organization, 19
leadership (Cree): chiefs, function of, 229; and growing assertiveness, 230, 232; and Cree Regional Authority, 253; and distinctions between traditional and Indian Affairs, 228; discussion of, 18, 19, 227–30, 233, 281 nXIX–XX; elections to band council, 225, 226, 227–8; formation of government bands, 231; Grand Council of the Crees, 253; via Indians of Quebec Association, 232, 253; on national and international scene, 255–6; politics of embarrassment, 316 nV; referendum on Quebec independence, 256; regional structure, 231; status, 229; trading captains, 19, 281 nXVI; undermined, 224, 249
Little Whale River Post, 37; first resident minister, 75

McTavish, D.C., 32, 59–60, 66, 123
Mark, Fred, 152–4, 305 nXXV
Masty, Sam: on alcohol, 234; chief, 229; leader,

characteristics of, 227; re W.G. Walton, 84, 90
Matagami, 201, 202
Matthew, Richard, 99; assisted Rev. Mark, 152; brother of Matthew Esquinamow, 101; discharged, 294 nXVIII; manager at Kanaaupscow, 103-4
Mayappo, Samuel, 109-10
mining activity 111, 145, 197; and Cree employment, 200; at Great Whale River, 203. *See also* William Couchees
mistabeo (*mistaapew*): spirit helper, 91
Mistassini Post (and band): Anglican church, 78; beaver preserve, 169, 199; bureaucratic complications re tax, 237; Catholic priests, 78; Chief Smally Petewabano, 227, 231; description of Crees, 80, 170; food, 111; guiding, 203; hunting, main occupation, 202; marriages, 130; mining activity, 197; nursing station, 179, 186; reserve, 178-80; school, 179, 201, 214; statuses, 229-30; supplied from Rupert House, 38; transport, 120; vote for women, 226; welfare, 313 nXXX
mixed ancestry (country born): hunting rights, 129; as HBC employees, 127-8; marriages, 63, 83, 129-30, 154; origins of, 126-7; post servants, 36, 127; preferential treatment, 36, 59-60
Moar, Frank, 129, 136, 229
Montagnais (Innu), 40, 46
moose: feast, 111; northern limits, 285 nXXVII; return of, 53

Moose Factory: company families, 128; diseases, 45; employment for Crees from east coast, 126; hospitals, 184-5; men in First World War, 134; Treaty No. 9, 61
Moosonee, 140, 184
Moses, Ted, 219, 255

Naskapis, 46; Cree-Naskapi Act, 316 nII; material culture, 47; traders' views, 22
Neacappo, Samson, 122, 294 nXIV
Nemiskau Post (and band), 39; air travel, 138; attitude of manager, 69, 100, 210; band division, 206; canoe transport to 1941, 120; closed, 314 XLVIII; employment, non-post, 206; facilities, 206; food scarcity, 210; state of buildings, 68
Neoskweskau Post (and band), 39; closed, 198; deaths from starvation, 110; employment, non-post, 206; forest fires, effects of, 113; fused with Mistassini band, 231; winter outpost, 311 nXIX
Nichikun Post (and band), 39; attitude of manager, 69, 223; closed, 198; food shortages, 110; fused with Mistassini band, 231; employment, non-post, 206; necessity of, 113; reopened, 107, 311 nXIX; starvation, 149; supplying, difficulty of, 149
Nicholson, Alan, 66, 67, 119
North West Company, 97-8
Nottoway preserve, 161, 165, 166

Old Factory Post (and band), 65, 105, 109; Anglican mission, 153; Catholic 157, 306 nXXVIII; Chief John Georgekish, 228; construction boom, 206; development of settlement, 206; French-language school, 181; preserve, 167; radio broadcast, 137; relations with government, 311-12 nXXIV; relations with Inuit, 65; scarlet fever, 190; school, 214, 218
Ontario, government of: game laws, 143, 145, 205; recognition of mixed ancestry Indians, 61. *See also* Treaty No. 9
oral tradition, 11-17; *atiukan* and *tipachimun* stories, 11-13; concept of time, 12-13; Cree epistemology, 12-16; and Dunne-Za epistemology, 12; narrative forms, 14, 16
Orford, T.J., 126, 221
Oskelaneo, 120, 140
Ottereyes, Joe: re bows and arrows, 54; disability, 210; on family allowances, 209; on government, 174, 221; on moose, 53; on welfare, 209
Ouje-Bougoumou band, 199; outfitted in Mistassini, 199; village, 199. *See also* Chibougamou

Paint Hills. *See* Old Factory Post
Papp, George, 104-5
Peck, James, 75
powatakan (dream spirits), 91, 175

Quebec, government of: beaver preserves, 160, 165, 166, 308 nXLIV;

boundary extensions, 40, 133, 220; competition with Canada, 180, 215, 239; game legislation, 28, 143–4, 145, 207–8, 233; and exemption of Indians, 144; game wardens, 143, 221, 313 nXXXIX; hunting rights to Natives, 143, 233, 314 nXLIX; hospital, in Fort George, 188; re Indian title, 134; interest in James Bay, 221; legislation re crown lands, 144; Nouveau-Québec, 145, 180, 308 nIII; reserves and settlements, 178–9; sales tax, 236–7; schools, 215, 313 nXXXV–VI

radio: beginnings in James Bay, 136–7, 303 nIX; effects on fur prices, 137; at Fort George, 136; two-way radio at Catholic missions, 137; use for medical advice, 192

railways: Canadian National Railway, 140, 197; Canadian Pacific Railway, 40, 139; Grand Trunk Railway, 53; North Railway Company, 140; Quebec–Lake St Jean Railway, 39; Temiskaming and Northern Ontario Railroad (Ontario Northland Railway), 140, 186, 304 nXIV

Ray, George, 68, 101, 104, 114–15, 117, 127, 295 nXXI

registered traplines. See beaver preserves

relief (and transfer) payments: attempts to control, 147–8; attitude to, 147, 304–5 nXX; and beaver preserves, 163; family allowance, 208–9;

old age pensions, 209; "rationers," 210; S&D rations, 110, 146, 147–8, 210–11, 221; welfare, 209–10, 211, 212, 218; widow's rations, 148

religion (Cree, Anglican, Catholic): after life, 89–90; Anglican mission, 79–80, 204, 205; Catholic missions, 75–6, 96, 150–1, 156–7, 186, 288 nXVII; changes due to decline in animals, 124; Christmas observances, 60, 238; church attendance, 91; Church Missionary Society, 75, 152, 305 nXXIV; commitment to Christianity, 81; competition, Anglicans and Catholics, 75–6, 96, 150–2, 154–5, 229, 239, 288, nI; conjuring, 81; conversions 74, 79, 87, 88–92, 96, 292 nXXIV; Cree beliefs and practices, 79, 80, 87–8, 91, 175, 238, 280 nX; and loyalty to Anglicanism, 156, 305 nXXVI; Native clergy, 83, 152–3, 290 nXIII, 305 nXXVI; Pentecostalism, 156; prayer books, 82, 93; role of catechists, 92–3, 96; and role of literacy, 93–5; and role of missionaries, 92–3; sin 89, 290 nXIV; singing, 92; syncretism 88, 95–6; teaching tools, 60, 158

Renouf, Ernest, 101, 108, 135, 293 nX; anti-Catholic stand, 152, 154

Revillon Frères Company, 99, 112; aid to Catholic mission at Fort George, 151; arrival in James Bay, 98–9; changed conduct of trade, 25; Cree employees, 100, 108, 109, 296 nXXIV; criticism of

Catholic trade, 154–5; extent of operations, 108; merger with HBC, 109; stores, location in 1921, 98, 100, 293 nVIII 103, 294 nXV, 297 nXXX; working arrangement with HBC, 108

Richard, L.A., 53, 145; "Chief White Beaver," 145; established Rupert House beaver preserve, 160; "pay off debt to Indians," 166

roads, 177; Chibougamou to Amos, 200; and to Mistassini, 199; and to St Felicien, 199; winter, 120

Romanet, Louis, 135, 302 nV

Rousseau, Jacques, 41, 74, 284, nXIV, 285 nXXVII

Royal Canadian Mounted Police: beaver preserve infractions, 236; Constable Covell, 143, 189, 235, 314 nLI; and Kupkee, 236; Moose Factory detachment, 143, 235, 314 nLII; oversee Inuit communities, 235; restrictions in Quebec, 143, 235; vaccinations, 189

Rupert House Post (and band), 38; beaver preserve, 159–62; canoe factory, 203–4, 311 nXXI; community hall, 205–6; construction boom, 204; elections, 229; debt, 116; freezer plant, 208, 311 nXXII; MacLean's camp, 204; marriages, 129; nursing station, 188; schools, 181, 214, 230, 313 nXXXIII; supply post, 38–9, 116, 120

Rupert's Land, 40

Salt, David, 100, 128–9
schools, 212–3; Anglican, 187; Catholic, 126, 156,

157, 213, 215; criticism of, 217; control by outsiders, 218, curriculum, 214–15, 216; effects of, 216, 217, 218; and French language, 181; government subsidies, 212–13; legacy of, 247; promoted by government, 218; provincial, 216; residential schools and Cree leaders, 219–20; rivalry between Anglicans and Catholics, 213–14; supervision by churches, 214; teachers, 214; and winter hunting, 125, 201, 218

Senneterre, 119, 140, 141, 197

servants, company. *See* mixed ancestry

Shecapio, Isaac, 227

Shecapio, Matthew, 228

Simpson, George, 63

Skinner, Alanson, 284–5 nXIX

Smallboy, Ellen, 47–50

social life: with Catholics, 155; class/racial distinction, 59; dances, 58–9; departures, 59; feasts, 57, 59; at Fort George, 137; magic lantern shows, 60; marriages, 57, 58, at post, 286 nXXXIV, 297 nXXXVIII; target shooting, 59; at Waswanipi, 198; wheel of fortune, 158

social organization, 19; according to hunting strategies, 32, 281 nXVIII; changes by end of 1960s, 230–1, 244; family, 301 nLVI; forms of social control, 233–4; HBC as arbitrator, 235; hunting groups, 121–3; influences on, 130; precontact, 29, in times of scarcity, 122–3, 285

nXXIII. *See also* leadership

Spencer, Miles, 41, 63

starvation, 109–10, 122, 149, 176; deaths due to, 110, 122, 149, 164, 304 nXIX; end of 1800s, 52–3, 122; fear of, 113; malnutrition, 190; at Nichikun, 149; stories of, 121

Stephens, Robert, 160

survival: boom of 1920s, 124; scarcity of food, 5, 27, 121, 122, 149, 210

syllabics, literacy, 94–5, 215; in schools, 214, 289 nIX

Tadoussac, 17

technology: electricity, 138; guns *v.* bows and arrows, 54; muskets, 55; post-First World War, 123; tractors, 120; windcharger, 138, 158, 303 nX

telegraph, 41; effect on fur prices, 36, 112

trade, conduct of: competition, 24, 32, 101–6, 111, 292 nI, 154–5; consumer demands, 32; cooperation between companies, 107; of country food, 33; Crees creating inter-post competition, 106; Cree dependence on, 23–4, 296 nXXV; international dependence on, 23; marten and mink over beaver, 32; payment, 35; price differences, 294 nXII, 298 nXXXV; stores of ex-Revillon Frères men, 107

trade goods: examples of kind, 33–4, 149; imported foods, 33–4, 123; prices of, 36, 203; sealskin boots, 55

traders, independent: Belcher Fur Company, 296 nXXXVI; Olav Briere, 107–8, 228, 297 nXXIX; Gabriel Fleury, 111, 298 nXXXIII; Sandy Lorimer, 107–8; Emmet McLeod, 107–8; 170; Jack Palmquist, 104–5, 296 nXXII, 307 nXLI; George Papp, 104, 296 nXXII

transport: boat, 119; canoe brigades, 117–19; combined modes, 120; horse teams, 119, 121, 301 nLV; Inuit teamsters, 64; mode in late 1800s, 56; tractors, 120. *See also* airplane travel; canoes; railways; roads

trappers, white: effects of, 142; use of poisoned bait, 142–3

Treaty No. 9, 61, 133–4, 283–4 nXIII

Udgarten Harold, 64, 287 nXXXIX

Vincent, Thomas, 61, 67, 76, 83, 290 nXI

Voyageur, Samuel, 111, 118, 183; characteristics of, 300 nLII; chief, 300 nLIII; views on Christianity, 291 nXVIII

Wall, J.J., 143, 186

Walton, W.G., 44, 50, 84, 130; business as anti-Christian, 313, nXXXII; on Crees, 85, 86; denunciation of Catholic priests, 151; destroyed drums, 91; helped by wife, 85; influence of, 84–5; reindeer herding, 50; role as doctor, 86, 184; writing of books, 93–4

Wapachee, William, 76, 81, 289 nIV, nVIII

Wars: First World War, effects of, 108, 134, 135, 302 nIII; Second World War, effects of, 177, 207, 213, 309 nXIV, 314 nLII
Waswanipi Post (and band): beaver preserves requested, 161; Catholicism, 75–7, 78, 289 nV–VI; chiefs in 1927, 32, 314 nXLV; closing of post, 200; constituted a reserve, 178–9; elections, 226; employment, guiding, 203; encroachment of white trappers, 141–2; food resources greater, 111; Indian agent, visit, 225; influx of outsiders, 198; living conditions in 1960s, 211; mining activity, 197; nursing station, 186; proposal to relocate, 200; prospectors hunting, 145; Protestant v. Catholic conflict, 76–8; provincial school, 313 nXXXVI; reserve status, 202; residential school, Chapleau, 213; schools, 213–14; supplied from Rupert House, 38; transport, 119–20; use of air travel, 138; welfare payments, 211

Watt, James S.C., 110; attitude to debt, 115–16; canoe factory, 203; re Coasters return to hunting, 128; development of beaver conservation schemes, 159–60, 162, 245

Watt, Maud, 67, 110, 158, 287 nXXXVIII, nXLIII; bakery, 171, 308 nXLV; community hall, 205–6; emissary to Quebec, 160; owner of beaver preserve lease, 160; parents of, 307 nXXXVII; pressing for Catholic school, 156; radio communications with priests, 156

welfare. *See* relief (and transfer) payments

Whiskeychan, Andrew, 160
Whiskeychan, Harriet, 114
Wiestchee, Charlie, 114
witiko, 52, 74
women: demand to vote at Mistassini, 226; division of labour, 49–50, 282 nXXII; employment at post, 35, 301 nLXI; English, 63, 75; fishing methods, 285 nXXII; 10; marriage, ban on, 62, 63, 114, 125, 129; move to Moose Factory, 126; seating in church, 292 nXXIII; travel with canoe brigade, 300–1 nLIV; wives of company servants, 36